D1000500

Existential America

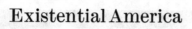

GEORGE COTKIN

Existential

America

The Johns Hopkins University Press

Baltimore and London

© 2003 The Johns Hopkins University Press
All rights reserved. Published 2003
Printed in the United States of America on acid-free paper
9 8 7 6 5 4 3 2 1

The Johns Hopkins University Press
2715 North Charles Street
Baltimore, Maryland 21218-4363
www.press.jhu.edu

LIBRARY OF CONGRESS CATALOGING IN PUBLICATION DATA

Cotkin, George, 1950–
    Existential America / George Cotkin.
        p.   cm.
Includes bibliographical references and index.
    ISBN 0-8018-7037-2 (acid-free paper)
    1. Existentialism—United States—History—20th century.   2. Philosophy,
American—20th century.   I. Title.
    B944.E94 C68 2003
    142'.78'0973—DC21

2001007186

A catalog record for this book is available from the British Library.

For Marta, again and again

Contents

1960–1993

Postwar Student and Women's Movements

Illustrations follow page 88

Acknowledgments

EXISTENTIALISM posits that at each moment we exist within a situation. The situation of the writer working on a long-term project can be full of anguish and despair. But this situation can be transcended somewhat with the help of friends and colleagues only an e-mail message away. James Hoopes, Nelson Lichtenstein, Robert W. Rydell, Ann Schofield, Craig Harlan, and Sarah Elbert have always been ready to offer comments on chapters and large amounts of support. Helpful in a variety of ways have been Harry Hellenbrand, Andreas Hess, Larry Inchausti, Steven Marx, Leila Rupp, and Dick Simon. I am deeply indebted to Hazel E. Barnes for her support of the project, her answers to my questions, and her generous reading of the entire manuscript. Arthur M. Schlesinger, Jr., kindly responded to some of my questions. Respondents to my Author's Query in the *New York Times* helped me comprehend the deep inroads paved by existentialism in America. Many have shown, through kind words, suggestions, and admonitions, that there is some exit from the loneliness of the long-distance writer: Robert Abzug, Thomas Bender, Casey Nelson Blake, Howard Brick, Paul Croce, Tom Dalton, Roxanne Dunbar-Ortiz, Cristina Giorcelli, David A. Hollinger, Ralph Leck, Diane Michelfelder, Lewis and Elisabeth Perry, Giovanna Pompcle, Joan Rubin, David Settino Scott, Richard Shaffer (whose heated encouragement proved useful during a difficult time), Carolyn Stefanco, Tyler Stovall, Leslie Sutcliffe, and Quintard Taylor.

Thank you to Jean Schoenthaler for pleasantly guiding me through the Will Herberg Papers at Drew University in Madison, New Jersey. Thanks as well to the staffs of the following institutions, for their invaluable assistance and their permission to use materials in their collections: Princeton University, the Walter Lowrie Papers; the University Archives at the University of Minnesota, the David Swenson Papers; the State Historical Society of Wisconsin, materials in the S.D.S. Collection; and the Schlesinger Library at Radcliffe College, the Betty Friedan Papers. Cal Poly Interlibrary Loan, under the superb direction of Janice Stone, has been of critical assistance to me in writing this book, as has the rest of the Kennedy Library staff.

Parts of some chapters first appeared in article form in *American Studies, The Historian,* and *Letterature d'America.* I also thank the Humanities Center audience at Oregon State University for allowing me to share some of my ideas with them. Robert J. Brugger, my editor at the Johns Hopkins University Press, has been supportive and informed. Melody Herr, acquisitions assistant at Hopkins, has dealt expertly with a host of publishing matters and in the process become an e-mail friend. Mary V. Yates has skillfully edited my manuscript.

Finally, two personal notes. My father has enriched my life by his proximity in the last few years. And my wife, Marta Peluso, has stood by me through some serious existential crises. As Beauvoir understood, the individual exists with and for other individuals.

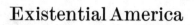

Existential America

Chapter One

Introduction

1 NEARLY EVERYONE, it seemed, coming of age in 1950s and 1960s America danced to the song of French existentialism. "I'd put on long black gloves . . . smoke Camel cigarettes and read Sartre," remembered Anne Rice, best-selling author of vampire tales. "It felt terrific."[1] As a senior at the University of Michigan in 1956, poet and novelist Marge Piercy embraced existentialism to distance herself from bourgeois culture. Remembering photographs she had seen of Juliette Gréco—dark chanteuse, friend of Sartre and Beauvoir, girlfriend of Miles Davis—Piercy adopted Gréco's existential style of dress: "black jeans, a black turtleneck, my hair down and a lot of dark red lipstick and eye make-up."[2] Existentialism extended into Piercy's politics, as she followed the leftist commitments of Sartre and Beauvoir. She was not alone. Civil rights activist Robert Moses, while jailed in Mississippi, reread Camus's *The Rebel* and *The Plague*. Moses stated, "The main essence of what he says is what I feel real close to—closest to."[3]

The meaning, excitement, and fashion of existentialism transformed the lives of many people. Hardly a college student in the 1960s could be found without a dog-eared copy of Walter Kaufmann's collection *Existentialism: From Dostoevsky to Sartre* (1956). As one such former student recalled, "The quaint notions of my childhood religious experience crumbled in the face of this onslaught of new ideas."[4] Alice Kaplan recalled that in the mid-1960s, the very word "existentialism" summoned up a world of "hard talk and intellect" to which she wanted to belong.[5] Roxanne Dunbar-Ortiz, later a leader of the radical feminist collective Cell-16 in Cambridge, Massachusetts, vividly recalled her initial confrontation with existentialism in Sartre's *Being and Nothingness:* "The words exploded in my head. I read that huge turgid tome, retaining words that defined my feelings—*ennui,* alienation, nausea."[6]

Existentialism changed my life as well. After my initial introduction to existentialism in a college French-language course in the late 1960s, I tried to make sense of the elegantly simple prose of Albert Camus's *L'Etranger.* Like Kaplan, I was excited by the roll of the word "existential," especially as pronounced by my teacher, with perfect French inflection. It distanced me from the Coney Island scene and transported me into French café life, into a rich intellectual world full of serious ideas about the depths of the human condition. Later, reading Germaine Brée's *Camus and Sartre* (1972), I confirmed my allegiance to Camus over Sartre. Camus's notion of the rebel, in contrast to the increasingly shrill Marxism of Sartre (which seemed to me at the time to be in conflict with his existentialism), struck me as the proper response to our absurd condition. It helped shape my political engagement. From Camus, Sartre, and Beauvoir I learned that no matter how difficult it might be to lead an authentic existence, the very attempt to act in good faith was valuable. And from them I also began to comprehend the necessity to endure.

2   "IN GENERAL, evil is not an American concept," remarked French existentialist Jean-Paul Sartre in 1950. "There is no pessimism in America regarding human nature and social organization." Existentialist fellow travelers Simone de Beauvoir and Albert Camus, with a certain hauteur, agreed with Sartre. Americans, they felt, lacked a sense of anguish about the problems of existence, authenticity, and alienation; instead, American character swaggered with confidence and naive optimism. In Beauvoir's phrasing, Americans had no "feeling for sin and for remorse." Even the more generous Camus derided American materialism and optimism.[7] America, home of the brave, land of the free, was nonexistential, according to these French visitors.

But the French missed certain darker and deeper elements in the history of the American mind and spirit. For one thing, at the precise historical moment in the mid–twentieth century when Sartre and company registered their comments, they and their dark vision enjoyed widespread popularity among Americans. No less than Europeans, Americans participated in the conversation of existentialism. In fact, existential modes of thinking had long before sunk deep roots in American thought and culture. The very notion of America as bereft of anguish is absurd. Death and despair appear as much in the American collective consciousness as does the luck-and-pluck optimism of Horatio Alger's heroes. How could anyone taking a glance at the despairing visages of nineteenth-century villagers collected in the volume *Wisconsin Death Trip* doubt the haunting presence of what Hawthorne famously referred to as "the power of blackness"?[8] And how could anyone ignore the existential anguish at the heart of the African-American experience? Philosopher Lewis Gordon asks whether slaves "did not wonder about freedom; suffer anguish; notice paradoxes of responsibility; have concerns of agency, tremors of broken sociality, or a burning desire for liberation"?[9]

How could it be otherwise? After all, existentialism begins with Sartre's maxim that men and women everywhere, as part of the human condition, are "condemned to be free," forced to confront the dilemma of existence, to seek infinitude in the face of limits.[10] To be existential is to have those dark nights of the soul when the loneliness of existence becomes transparent and the structure of our confidence lies shattered around us. To be existential is to encounter those moments when vainglorious systems of logic totter and polite evocations of Sunday preachers fail to touch the core of being. To be existential is to wrestle most fully with the jagged awareness of one's own finitude, with the thunderbolt fact that I will die and that my death will be my own, experienced by no one else. At such moments, the abstract is rendered concrete. As novelist Carson McCullers put it, "Death is always the same, but each man dies in his own way."[11] To be existential is to recognize, in the face of all these somber truths clutched close to our own sense of being, that we must act. Despite the dread and anguish that accompany the shocking recognition of our freedom, that threaten to stall us in our tracks, we must take responsibility for our lives; we must create the world anew. To be existential is, ultimately, to join with Camus's Sisyphus in a tragic acceptance of the limitations of existence while exulting in each affirmative breath of life, in each push of the stone up the mountain.

Existential moments, then, are common. Sometimes, as in those individuals described by American philosopher William James as having a once-born, skin-deep religious faith, such encounters are fleeting, unable to penetrate the core of self. While once-born individuals may have a cheery disposition and seem untroubled by the existential darkness, they all too often lack the depth to deal with the calamities that everyone must encounter in life, and with the aforethought of death. In other individuals, existential moments mount up and shake the very foundations upon which they stand. Thus in those biblical passages in which Job protests his fate, we find the essence of an existential cry of anguish and rebellion: "I am ready to argue with God" (Job 13:3).

That existential ways of thinking are both historically specific and an inherent part of the human condition follows logically, as well as paradoxically, from Heidegger's and Sartre's insight that the individual always exists within a "situation." Situations are a universal fact of human existence, even though the particulars of any one situation are, of course, specific and constrained. Everyone confronts the ultimate situation, the "limit" situation of finitude. Yet existentialism, as a way of thinking about and depicting the world, emerged most strongly out of the tremors that shook modern Europe beginning in the nineteenth century. The inhuman, alienating implications of modern capitalist production and warfare, the unfulfilled promise of science, the decline of religious certitude, the challenges issued by Darwin, Freud, and modern physics—all contributed to existentialism's claim to pertinence. Sartre and Heidegger expressed, in philosophical and literary terms, the essentials of existentialism. In so doing, they attempted to characterize aspects of the timeless nature of the human condition and to respond to the quickening pace of alienation and despair in their own era.

Yet existentialism resists easy definition; literary evocations often strike closest to the heart of the matter. Even Sartre, the person most associated with existentialist philosophy, wavered about its precise meaning. On the one hand, Sartre remarked in 1960, "I do not like to talk about existentialism. It is the nature of an intellectual quest to be undefined. To name it and to define it is to wrap it up and tie the knot."[12] On the other hand, in the late 1940s he had jauntily attempted to tie the knot by announcing that existentialism begins with the recognition that "existence precedes essence." All individuals, ultimately, were responsible for what they made of themselves. For the existentialist, "every truth and action implies a human setting and a human subjectivity." Critical terms for this "human setting," or human condition, were "anguish, forlornness, despair." In sum, "it's all quite simple."[13]

Ah, if only it were so simple. Theologian Paul Tillich usefully distinguishes between the existential and existentialism. Existential, for Tillich, "refers to a human attitude," while existentialism is "a philosophical school" dedicated to "analysis of the human predicament."[14] Other attempts to pin down the meaning of existentialism have relied upon a genealogical definition that discovers existential aspects in the doctrines of Kierkegaard, Nietzsche, Heidegger, and other precursors. But these philosophical excursions into the creation of a tradition confuse as much as elucidate because the members of the existential circle are often as notable for their differences as for their similarities. Invariably, definition depends upon who is doing the defining, and what philosophical axes they have to grind. In fact, the name "existentialism" was imposed upon Sartre. Unexistentially, he had little choice but to be an existentialist. Conversely, Camus, because of his differences with Sartre over political issues, declared himself not an existentialist even though he and Sartre shared many philosophical and literary premises.

Faced with problems of definition, philosophers and literary critics have sought to squirm free of precise definitions, preferring wisely to circle around the term. Thus Walter Kaufmann acknowledged that "existentialism is not a school of thought nor reducible to any set of tenets." What, then, might be this entity called existentialism? Kaufmann appeared to be as befuddled as anyone else. He initially proposed that existentialists shared a "perfervid individualism."[15] Yet, thankfully, he felt uncomfortable with this almost useless proposition. He returned again and again to the problem of definition—almost in the manner of the historian who declared the practice of intellectual history akin to trying to nail jelly to the wall—categorizing existentialism as "a timeless sensibility" fashioned out of an emphasis on "failure, dread, and death." Kaufmann still found existentialists preoccupied "with extreme states of mind generally."[16] But such asides hardly cleared up the definitional problems of existentialism, only serving to plunge the quest for analysis into the realm of psychology more than philosophy.

Kaufmann later proclaimed existentialism "not a philosophy but several different revolts against traditional philosophy." He alliteratively captured the drift of "so-called" existentialism by associating it with a heightened awareness of "dread, despair, death, and dauntlessness."[17] His four D's of thought and literature in many ways capture the essential outlines of an existentialist perspective. And they also suggest the importance of movement. All existentialists begin with dread and despair, anguish and doubt, with recognition of the boundary situation imposed upon us by death. To dwell on such insights, to rub salt into those wounds, is nihilistic, a genuine but ultimately impotent cry of despair and rage, a paradoxically comforting pose in the face of the abyss. In its more strenuous forms, existentialism posits that there are paths through nothingness—religious transcendence for some, secular projects for others. Existentialism, then, is not concerned solely with the nature of Being but with the possibility of Becoming. The motive power of existentialist thought is found in its recognition that Becoming occurs not in an orgy of ease or self-realization therapeutics but at the cost of constant struggle with the nothingness and absurdity inherent in the human condition.

Many have attempted to pierce the heart of the definition of existentialism. Anthony Mansard suggested, in *Dictionary of the History of Ideas*, that existentialism pivoted around "themes of authenticity and moral choice, of the individual as isolated in a hostile world."[18] Mansard avoided much of what is implicit in his definition: notions of dread, despair, and death, which were central to Kaufmann. Both failed to deal with the anguished religious aspects of existential choice in Kierkegaard; indeed, Kaufmann seemed most concerned to divorce existentialism from religious themes and to appropriate it as a weapon against various analytic modes of philosophizing. But existentialism is a capacious mansion, capable of housing both secular and religious figures.

Maurice Natanson, a phenomenologist teaching at the University of California at Santa Cruz, hit the nail half on the head when he noted that

> existential thought is characterized, first, by a profound concern for
> the everlasting categories of man's being, his fear, dread, suffering,

aloneness, anguish, and death; second, by the fact that it takes man as the object of its inquiry, but man as an "unhappy consciousness," as a fragmentary and fragmented creature who locates his existence in a cosmos that is at once overpowering, threatening, and demanding; third, by its internal un-neutrality toward God—the existentialist's dialogue takes place in an empty cathedral, and the protagonists debate the terminology of the mass and, more important, for whom the mass is to be said; and fourth, by a decisive concern with man's authenticity in existence, his gift of freedom which is his anguish, his total responsibility which is his dread.[19]

In this otherwise bravura summation of existentialism Natanson failed to drive home the upside of existential freedom: the freeing from the shackles of tradition, the possibility of a more authentic existence, and the headiness that comes with the freedom to create and to be creative. As Hazel E. Barnes, Sartre's American champion and translator of his *Being and Nothingness,* recognized, existentialism presented itself bravely as "the literature of possibility."[20]

3 THE POSSIBILITY—nay, the reality—of an existential awareness at the center of the American experience defines *Existential America.* The history of existential thinking in America began before Sartre first uttered the word "existential." Existential concerns have long colored the American intellectual temper. Dread, despair, death, and dauntlessness helped frame the existential imperatives of figures as diverse as Jonathan Edwards, Herman Melville, Emily Dickinson, William James, Edward Hopper, and Walter Lippmann. These Americans belong in the pantheon of thinkers and artists who are labeled existentialist precursors. Americans initially confronted existentialism as a somewhat developed philosophical system in the late 1920s with minister Walter Lowrie's popularization and analysis of Danish religious existentialist Søren Kierkegaard. Within a decade, American Neo-Orthodox theologians were using Kierkegaardian language and categories to promote a tragic religious sensibility in contrast to the polite pieties that they damned in mainstream Protestantism. By the late 1940s and early 1950s, Americans as diverse as former communist Whittaker Chambers, novelist Thornton Wilder, and painter Mark Rothko had become entranced by Kierkegaardian anguish and inwardness. The implications of this rush to Kierkegaard proved, in general, to be politically conservative. Kierkegaardian inwardness and religious anxiety did not bode well for political radicalism or reform; it supported for some intellectuals a retreat from leftist commitments of the 1930s.

Not surprisingly, the conversation of existentialism reached a fevered peak with the post–Second World War arrival of Sartre and French existentialism. For many intellectuals, Sartrean existentialism perfectly captured the human condition in general, and more specifically the reality of an existence lived under the shadow of totalitarian butcheries and potential atomic annihilation. But these same intellectuals often distanced themselves from French existentialism because they viewed the Cold War and literary politics of Sartre and Beauvoir as naive and retrograde. Nonetheless, New York intellectuals, no less than the popular press, played a significant role in making the ideas of French existentialism part of the intellectual coin of the realm in the postwar years. Intriguingly, some intellectuals and writers associated with the New York crowd proved to be existentialists in all but name. Art critic Harold Rosenberg and novelists Ralph Ellison and Norman Mailer made existentialism central to their work while at the same time attempting mightily to avoid being reduced to mere followers of French fashion. The influence of French existentialism on American culture proved to be immense, even when underacknowledged. Thanks to important analyses and anthologies tumbling from presses in the mid-1950s on, a generation of students coming of age in the 1960s were thoroughly acquainted with the writings of Sartre, Camus, and Beauvoir. Indeed, the intellectual history of civil rights and New Left leaders Robert Moses and Tom Hayden cannot be understood apart from their engagement with the thought of Camus. Betty Friedan's clarion call for feminism, *The Feminine Mystique* (1963), developed out of her early confrontation with existential modes of thought, and specifically in tandem with her reading of Beauvoir's *The Second Sex* (1952). The achievements of the sixties generation, then, emerged in large part out of their grappling with existentialist issues and writers.

One question remains to be considered: Is it fair to speak of a particularly American expression or style of the existential, and if yes, how might this affect our understanding of America's intellectual and cultural history? William Dean Howells once told Edith Wharton that "what the American public always wants is a tragedy with a happy ending."[21] While American existentialists did not put a happy face on the pessimism and despair of European existentialism, neither did they contentedly wallow in such despair. They refused to make a fetish out of nihilism. In the hands of most of the Americans examined in this volume, the existential grounds of anguish and despair functioned not as benumbing forces but as goads to action and commitment. As writer and music critic Albert Murray realized, existentialism plays itself out as an extended blues refrain. From the bump and grind of painful experiences, etched into consciousness daily, transcendence may occur. As Ralph Ellison once put it, "There *is* an existential tradition within

American Negro life and, of course, that comes out of the blues and spirituals."[22]

Existentialism, American style, also jibes well with American antinomianism, that willingness of the lonely individual to rebel against entrenched authority in the name of his or her most intense beliefs. Antinomianism, like existentialism, challenges easy certitude, entrenched religion, and moribund political assumptions. Not all antinomians need be existentialists, but most American existentialists are antinomians. Camus's ideal of the rebel, the individual in favor of life and commitment, would have been familiar to precursors in the American antinomian tradition. In contrast to in France and Germany, in America there have been few serious attempts to develop a sustained existentialist system, to erect precisely the type of philosophical edifice that Kierkegaard railed against. Critic Cal Bedient finds American poetry dominated by "an extreme fluidity of form—loose or complex, meandering or braided—[that] is peculiarly, if not solely, American. . . . It is haunted by the limit at which the universal is deaf to everything."[23] In a similar fashion, American existentialism, marked by fluidity of form, by the quick but biting use of concepts, may seem to feed into presumptions about the ephemeral nature of American thought. This book, however, hopes to demonstrate that the American confrontation with an existential perspective has been creatively valuable and culturally significant.

Much of the best in American thought and culture for the last two hundred years has come from thinking existentially, from a willingness to confront death and finitude with a spirit of critique and rebellion. Many intellectuals and artists of influence found their voice through existentialism. It led them, even when they retreated from politics, to at least understand the despair that leads to totalitarianism. Many of them were able to create art, the ultimate existential testament to overcoming the despair inherent in the human condition. To every Starbuck in American culture who comes to hunt whales only for material gain, there is the existential thrust of an Ahab who berates Starbuck's refusal to contemplate "a little lower level" of existence. Ahab must punch through the "pasteboard masks" of the inauthentic and the mundane.[24] His staring into the abyss of nothingness ends tragically, in madness and in the drowning of his crew. But a later-day Ahab, Ellison's Invisible Man, emerges from his underground existence desirous of human community. Chastened by his experiences, he announces, "There's a possibility that even an invisible man has a socially responsible role to play. . . . Who knows but that on the lower frequencies, I speak for you?"[25]

4   *Existential America* is a cultural and intellectual history, rather than a history of philosophy.[26] Thus Kierkegaard and Sartre, Beauvoir and

Camus, loom larger on its pages than Heidegger, Husserl, or Merleau-Ponty. While critical to the philosophical expression of existentialism, Heidegger and Husserl, for example, failed to quicken the pulse of large numbers of American thinkers and artists. Heidegger achieved his greatest influence only in the 1980s, when academics rushed through the gates of decon- struction. But American existentialism should be seen as more than a case study in the diffusion of European ideas. African-American writer Richard Wright delighted in showing off his collection of books by Kierkegaard, and he also bragged, "Everything that he [Kierkegaard] writes in those books I knew before I had them."[27] *Existential America* attempts to trace expres- sions of existential thinking both as received from European sources and as growing from American minds. I hope that other scholars will pursue themes and individuals lightly touched upon in this volume, for American existentialism, like experience in the words of William James, "has ways of *boiling over*," of escaping from the pages of any volume.[28]

1741–1949

*American Existentialists
before the Fact*

Chapter Two

The "Drizzly November"
of the American Soul

1 THE EXISTENTIAL shading in American thought arises from both the country's Calvinist heritage and the vicissitudes of everyday life. No American, from the seventeenth century until the present, no matter how tenaciously he might cling to ideals of progress, has managed to avoid the fact of his own mortality and that of his loved ones. Puritan parents worried that their dying child might end up in hell, uncomforted by the assurance that the infant would reside in a nicer room in hell than an older sinner.[1] Material dreams as well often turn into dust. Speculators have been devastated by the financial panics and depressions that have formed the roller-coaster ride of the American economy. Americans from all walks of life have confronted existence as dark and forbidding, no less often than as light and cheery.

These dark thoughts and realities help explain the bloody battlefields of the Civil War, the annihilation of the Native Americans, and the horrors of slavery and class struggle. The optimism and crass materialism of Americans, so remarked upon by foreign analysts, may only serve to hide the darker underpinnings of the American soul. Think here of Emerson, once thought of as a sage of cheeriness, now more rightly seen in somber colors. His sainted aunt, Mary Moody Emerson, slept in a coffin-shaped bed and wore her burial shroud when traveling. Emerson needed to gaze upon death, and hence he opened the coffin of his wife Ellen a year after her burial.[2] This coffin-consciousness did not figure only in the morbid minds of the Emerson family. Melville begins *Moby-Dick* with Ishmael ruminating on "coffin warehouses."[3] The image reappears in the name of the proprietor of the Spouter-Inn, Peter Coffin, and in the coffin built aboard the *Pequod* for Queequeg that will later save the life of Ishmael. As demonstrated by historians Lewis O. Saum and Michael Lesy, Americans in the nineteenth century could not keep death at arm's length. The reality of death permeated their lives and endowed them with a pessimistic and constrained sensibility.[4]

This common reckoning with the presence of death did not necessarily issue forth as resignation or even as rage against God, as in Herman Melville's fiction. Instead it deepened religious sensibility with the weight of responsibility; it combined comprehension of the chaos of the world with undiminished faith in God's divine plans. Few expressed this better than Abraham Lincoln. In his great Second Inaugural Address, Lincoln spoke as a chastened but vibrant moralist of the two sides in the Civil War: "Both read the same Bible, and pray to the same God; and each invokes His aid against the other. It may seem strange that any man should dare to ask a just God's assistance in wringing their bread from the sweat of other men's faces; but let us judge not that we be not judged. The prayers of both sides could not be answered; that of neither has been answered fully. The Almighty has His own purposes."[5]

The same sense of depth, of courage despite anguish and despair, arising out of the experiences of the Civil War affected Oliver Wendell Holmes, Jr., later to become a justice of the United States Supreme Court. Holmes had entered the war as a young man without vocational direction. Wounded in the war, he felt that he had been "touched with fire." In a famous address, "A Soldier's Faith" (1895), a chastened Holmes stared at the "vicissitudes of terror and triumph."[6] He came to base his philosophy and judicial practice upon the premise that power, pure and simple, ruled the world. "The life of the law has not been logic," he announced in his famous treatise *The Common Law* (1881), "it has been experience."[7] And the experiences of life refuted images of a polite sitting room strewn with tea and crumpets. "The law of the grub and the hen is the law also for men. We all have cosmic destinies of which we cannot divine the end, if the unknown has ends." In the face of a universe without values, Holmes, in his better moments, upheld a "noble nihilism."[8] The Civil War had been what existentialists commonly refer to as a "boundary situation," from which he emerged with a sense of the absurd in life and a hard realism about power. His hardihood and toughness in the face of the nothingness of the universe, his refusal to flinch from the recognition of the utter meaninglessness of human existence, these aspects marked his existential sensibility. Lincoln and Holmes, their sensibilities forged in the crucible of war, understood the existential essentials of death, dread, despair, *and* dauntlessness.[9]

2 IN HIS PASSIONATE embrace of religious paradox and in his insistence that "an idea is the fashion in which the heart apprehends an idea and so acts toward the object," Puritan theologian Jonathan Edwards, according to Perry Miller, figures as a kindred spirit to Kierkegaard.[10] Calvinism was erected, as George Santayana stated, upon an "agonised con-

science," for the Calvinist was "divided between tragic concern at his own miserable condition, and tragic exultation about the universe at large." This tension meant that the Calvinist must "feel a fierce pleasure in the existence of misery, especially of one's own, in that this misery seems to manifest the fact that the Absolute is irresponsible or infinite or holy."[11] Here too one finds hints of Kierkegaardian paradox. This is not to proclaim any exact correspondence between American Calvinism and European existentialism, Kierkegaardian or otherwise. But there is in American Calvinism, as John Patrick Diggins has indicated, a sense of moral anguish and rebellion against the "conscience" of American liberal optimism.[12] This chastened sensibility, which Diggins finds stretching from the founding fathers to Reinhold Niebuhr, can be viewed as existential in its general contours.

Jonathan Edwards dominates the American Puritan intellectual experience. Born in 1703, he attended Yale College; by 1722 he had begun his long ministerial career. Although he lived most comfortably in his own mind, Edwards had prodigious powers of concentration and energy. He could spend thirteen hours at his desk, exercise by chopping wood, think aloud during walks in the woods, and still minister to his congregation. He confronted the enormous mystery of creation, the distance between God and man. Despair and awe commingled in his theology, as did empiricism and idealism in his philosophy. He rejected the free-will doctrines of the Arminians in part because they failed to give sufficient weight to the calamities of life. Pain and suffering were real for Edwards; no rose-tinted glasses for him. The sweat of his labor, the uncertainties of everyday existence, and the mystery of it all deepened rather than diminished his faith.

The Puritan emphasis on predestination and the favoring of essence preceding existence, as encapsulated in the doctrine of original sin, suggests a distance from the freedom and possibility associated with existentialism as it became known in the years after the Second World War. Yet when the veil of Puritanism is lifted, affinities become recognizable. Dread, despair, and death are the Puritan holy trinity—defining the realities of the human experience after the fall from grace. Although Puritans upheld the communitarian ideal of Winthrop's "City upon a Hill," their realities were often structured by a syntax of radical loneliness and alienation, of longing for salvation and dread of damnation. There were, to be sure, no Nietzschean proclamations of the demise of God, but there were anxieties associated with a belief in a God so powerful, so distant, and so daunting. Even within the deterministic assumptions of predestination dogma, Puritan theologians such as Edwards found space for choice, for monumental decisions to accept personal responsibility: "I trust it will be allowed by all, that in every act of *will* there is an act of *choice;* and that in every *volition* there is a *preference,* or a prevailing inclination of the soul, whereby, at that instant, it is out of a state of perfect indifference, with respect to the direct object of the volition."[13]

Edwards rebelled against the aridity and domination of abstract systems through his emphasis on experience and action. Although he took second place to none in the colonies as a man of science, in the view of Perry Miller he "always exalted experience over reason."[14] Puritan religion bursts at the seams with passion. Yet passion does not replace logic, experience does not dethrone reason. All elements combine in the Puritan conversion experience when the individual, stripped of pretense before God, acknowledges his or her sins. Yet he or she may still magically receive irresistible grace. Puritans studied this mysterious process of conversion with a trained and careful eye, so much so that one might speak of a Puritan phenomenology of the conversion experience.[15]

But salvation, no matter how minutely surveyed or deeply felt, danced on rocky cliffs of doubt. Puritanism never claimed to be an easy religion. Satan could be encountered anywhere, even in the hearts of those presumably saved. Dread of damnation, anxiety and despair over salvation, all became essentials of the Puritan religious experience in the American wilderness of the mind and heart. However exemplary the life that had been led, in the face of deceiving appearances one could not rest confident in matters concerning one's immortal soul. At the "boundary situation" of death, the reality of man's utter distance from God became crushingly apparent. Given the hardness of existence, the dark shadows of original sin, the Puritan could hardly welcome death as surcease. In a religion powered by dread, despair, and death, the realities of hell loomed large. Edwards evoked harsh visions of the "great furnace of wrath, a wide and bottomless pit, full of the fire of wrath, that you are held over in the hand of that God, whose wrath is provoked and incensed as much against you, as against many of the damned in hell. You hang by a slender thread."[16]

Let us not forget, however, that even though one might "hang by a slender thread," the Puritan existential awareness never descended into the pit of passivity (however philosophically logical such a conclusion might appear). The last piece of Walter Kaufmann's puzzle of existentialism—"dauntlessness"—powered the entire intellectual and experiential machinery of Puritanism. In the face of demons, the chaos of impressions, the seductions of sin, and the temptations of the flesh, there raged within the best of the Puritans, and certainly within the life and work of Edwards, a dauntless quality, a heroism in the proud flag of their faith. In his "Farewell Sermon" to his congregation at Northampton, from whose pulpit he had been dismissed in 1750, Edwards announced that "although I have often been troubled on every side, yet I have not been distressed; perplexed, but not in despair; cast down, but not destroyed."[17]

3   THE "POWERS OF blackness" outlived Puritanism. They survived the softer light of human progress associated with the theology of Charles Chauncey and the birth of the Enlightenment. Dread, despair, death, and dauntlessness may not always have figured centrally in the popular imagination caught up in visions of Manifest Destiny, quick wealth, and eternal progress. But existential thoughts continued to flourish in some of the minds that dominated America at midcentury, in the dark tales of morality and original sin that haunted Nathaniel Hawthorne's imagination, in the somber shading of Edgar Allan Poe's mysteries, in the observations of Lincoln and Walt Whitman during the Civil War, and, most important, in the prose of Herman Melville, perhaps the Dostoevsky of American existentialism.

The despair that permeates much of Melville's fiction mirrored that of his own life. Born in 1819 to a well-connected but economically strapped family, Melville saw his genteel world crumble when his father's business failed. He worked in a bank and taught for a time before escaping to the sea. His journeys around the world supplied the settings for his South Sea novels, and for his metaphysical quest in his greatest work, *Moby-Dick* (1851). Throughout his life Melville struggled to confront his own demons, his despair about the nature of God and His creation. As his friend Hawthorne phrased it, "He can neither believe, nor be comfortable in his unbelief; and he is too honest and courageous not to try to do one or the other."[18] Fame and financial security eluded Melville. His masterpiece, *Moby-Dick,* flopped. He retreated into long periods of silence, supporting his family by working as a customs inspector in New York City.

Melville presents the spectacle of a world of dread and anguish, of radical alienation and aloneness. Novelist Walker Percy remarks that Melville "believed in the depravity of man and blamed God for it," in contrast to Dostoevsky, "who believed in the depravity of man and looked to God to save him from it."[19] Most famously in *Moby-Dick,* but no less so in the novella "Bartleby" (1853), Melville confronted the existential abyss, the sense of the absurd, the longing for meaning in a world abandoned by God, or a world in which God's ways rarely seemed benign. In Melville, Camus recognized a kindred spirit: "If a painter of the Absurd has played a role in my idea of literary art, it is the author of the admirable *Moby Dick,* the American, Melville."[20] Despair and dauntlessness battle in Melville's pages, not to define truth but to glimpse some inkling of possibility. But failure litters Melville's literary landscape quite as often as success.

Consider the Kafkaesque story of Bartleby. His employer is a lawyer, full of Christian goodwill and capitalist common sense, who attempts to comprehend the action, or rather inaction, of his scribe Bartleby. With each passing day Bartleby withdraws more and more into himself, to the point of refusing to perform any tasks whatsoever, declining them with the polite but firm refrain, "I would prefer not to." As the lawyer ruminates about Bartleby, he is filled with Christian solicitude and concern (when not being irked by his employee's passivity), recognizing that "his poverty is great, but his solitude, how horrible!"[21] Bartleby's affliction, in the prognosis of his self-anointed savior, tragically resists traditional interpretation or intervention: "I might give alms to his body," the lawyer states, "but his body did not pain him—it was his soul that suffered, and his soul I could not reach."[22]

Bartleby remains ineffable and radically alone. Resolute in his choice, or his preference of will, he rebels against whatever afflicts him by withdrawal. The mystery of his choice to withdraw and of the withering away of his body remains unsolved, despite the concluding revelation that Bartleby's previous employment had been in the "dead letters" section of the post office—sorting through, one imagines, the ultimate silences, the poignancy of letters undeliverable, of lines written but never to be read. So too Bartleby's life, as the lawyer painfully comes to realize, is inexplicable by either science or sentiment. Thus Bartleby, perhaps like Kafka's hunger artist, or Melville himself, stands as the sad apotheosis of the radically alienated individual, untouchable by charity, impregnable by design, dauntless only in his inexplicable rage to defy the world in the most confounding manner: by choosing not to live.

If Bartleby is a character of resolute passivity, then Captain Ahab explodes as dauntless obsession. At once determined to gain revenge against the white whale that has maimed him and stolen his innocence, Ahab constantly attempts to decipher the signs of the world, to strike through the "pasteboard masks" of reality. With every change of wind direction, Ahab appears more and more conscious of a world abandoned by God, a world into which human beings are (in Heideggerean terms) thrown, without any reasonable hope of comprehension or salvation. Perhaps in this absurd world the only possibility of salvation, or sanity, lies in raging against fate, in harpooning the mystery, in the pain of the human condition. In his mania for meaning, even in his apocalyptic obsession with revenge, this modern existential hero Ahab personifies man as both tragic and absurd, seething with despair and dread. He stares at the face of death yet remains dauntless, charging forward against the darkness.

Moby-Dick captures, as Richard Brodhead observes, a terrifying anxiety about the cosmos, a deep worry about the nature and possibility of meaning.[23] "I wonder," Stubbs remarks, "whether the world is anchored any-

where?"[24] Aloneness and suicide walk the dark streets of this anxious, uncertain world. Thus Ishmael, aptly named after the wandering, exiled son of
Abraham, explains at the outset of the novel his reasons for taking to the sea
from time to time:

> Whenever I find myself growing grim about the mouth; whenever it
> is a damp, drizzly November in my soul; whenever I find myself in-
> voluntarily pausing before coffin warehouses, and bringing up the rear
> of every funeral I meet; and especially whenever my hypos get such
> an upper hand of me, that it requires a strong moral principle to pre-
> vent me from deliberately stepping into the street, and methodically
> knocking people's hats off—then, I account it high time to get to sea
> as soon as I can. This is my substitute for pistol and ball. With a philo-
> sophical flourish Cato throws himself upon his sword; I quietly take to
> the ship. (795)

But there is no quiet, no rest to be found. That is, of course, the ironic commentary on Ishmael's logic. The coffins of the street that he seeks to avoid
are exemplified in the coffinlike ship. The sign of death hangs always above
one's head.

The vestments of Calvinism remain in Melville's closet, as indicated early
in the novel during Father Mapple's sermon. Mapple preaches from a raised
pulpit resembling a ship's masthead. Once he has ascended to the top, the
pulpit is closed off to all others. Mapple's well-stitched cloth of faith con-
ceals a world without meaning and, more horrifying, without salvation. In
this shock of recognition, man retains only an existential striving to define
himself, to create meaning. Like Ahab, he must create his own compass; out
of a common needle he "can make one of his own, that will point as true as
any" (1346). Such hubris and such hope comprise Ahab's "fatal pride"
(1347), representing for Melville perhaps the heavy burden of modern, existential man.

4   AT FIRST GLANCE William James's pragmatic philosophy appears
    distant from Melville's despairing theology of absence.[25] Jamesian odes
to strenuosity, to struggle, to religious faith, all have a strong hint of the Salvation Army street-corner rally. But in every breath of optimism, in each invocation of faith, James desperately struggles to keep the devil at bay. His
entire public philosophy may be seen as an existential cry in the wilderness,
an attempt to create some order in a chaotic universe, a plea not to paint
over the hustle and bustle of experience with weak-tea abstractions, and,
most important, a recognition that out of dread and despair may arise the

wisdom that makes it possible to live a meaningful and energetic life. "Forget the low in yourself, then," writes James, "think only of the high. Identify
your life therewith; then, through angers, losses, ignorance, ennui, whatever
you thus make yourself, whatever you thus most deeply are, picks its way."[26]

The emotional turmoil and family romance of James's early years hardened his outlook on life; he endured a continuing struggle to overcome
neurasthenia, to break free from "the nightmare or suicidal view of life."[27]
The son of a brilliant but eccentric father, William James feared that life was
passing him by. His friends, and two of his younger brothers, fought in the
Civil War while he remained safe at home. He became a physician but never
practiced medicine. Crises of vocation, philosophy, and faith defined much
of his existence. Depression and despair, so deep as to be disabling, stalked
him throughout his young manhood. Thus when he cried out earnestly,
pleadingly, in his popular essays for a life of strenuous engagement and responsibility, he was enunciating his own heartfelt needs. He managed to rally
himself, to convince himself that life was worth living. Long before Camus
announced suicide to be the essential philosophical question, James grappled with the issue at point-blank range, through personal experience and
psychological reflection.

No less than New England Puritans, or his own existentialist grandchildren, James confronted the abyss of contingency and absurdity. To be sure,
in his radical empiricism he attempted to present a phenomenological description of the objects and experiences of the world in a nondualist fashion by positing a logic of relations. But within this universe of relations much
remained to confound, to elude our grasp, to plunge us into a sea of despair.
A world so deeply anarchic struck James as horrific, but no less so than its
counterweight, the world constructed by philosophers and soothsayers as
ultimately rational, progressive, and boringly benign. In vituperative language that Kierkegaard would have applauded, James railed against the
falseness, the illusory security that Hegel, much like an amiable dry-goods
salesman, had attempted to market as the Absolute. Grand theories, comforting to the weak of heart and unnecessary for the strong of temper, only
got in the way of the Jamesian plunge into the welter of the world.[28]

James painfully realized that this world could quickly overwhelm the individual. His most repellant image came to him in a dream of his own fate:
an epileptic cowering in the corner, the apotheosis of humanity stripped of
its fortitude. The resources of the individual, while substantial, constantly
needed to be marshaled for the struggles of everyday life. In a Kierkegaardian leap of faith, or certainly in a logic riddled with philosophical pot-
holes, James enunciated his doctrine of "The Will to Believe" and his phenomenology of the religious experience. He offered a deepening of

possibility to himself and his fellows as they struggled against the forces of darkness and evil, both internal and external to themselves. In opting to have God and faith on his side, James sought to avoid the God-bereft world of Melville, or of his own contemporary, Friedrich Nietzsche. The Jamesian notions of God and faith, however, were essentially existential, less a means of escape from the clutches of dread than impassioned pushes through regions of darkness.

James believed in God as an ally against the emptiness of the *tedium vitae.* He wanted everyone, including himself, to be dauntless, without being reckless. In order to achieve this end, one needed to make a choice, to direct, by an act of will, one's energies toward the realization of worthy goals. Determinist systems of thought died in the steady lava-flow of history and necessity, in the scientific method, which in the hands of scientists such as John Tyndall and Thomas Huxley seemed to celebrate an attitude of watchful waiting for sufficient facts to accumulate before a decision could be launched. This struck James as an excuse for inaction, for death in life. Even if he did not employ Sartrean terms to discuss this passivity as inauthentic or as an act of choice in itself, he carefully delineated its tight boundaries and attempted to invoke a God to whom our actions actually did make a difference. The Jamesian imperative to act translated into the heroic, existential ideal that defined his philosophy and colored his life.

Within this context of heroic struggle, the Jamesian God approved of the individual's attempts to seize the devil by the throat. James occasionally came perilously close to valorizing pain and heroic struggle in the name of God and faith. No less than Edwards and Melville, he understood pain and struggle as central to the human condition, avoided only by pure luck or pure fantasy, both of which were illusions sooner rather than later to be shattered by the push of experience or the unavoidable reality of one's mortality. Indeed, James perfectly captured this type of consciousness in his famous figure of the healthy-minded, or once-born, soul. This essentially "inauthentic" individual has, or affects to have, a complacently upbeat attitude toward the universe, a "feeling that Nature, if you will only trust her sufficiently, is absolutely good."[29] Once-born faith, without anguish or dread, misses the monumental in the Protestant conception of the radical aloneness of the sinner in the shadows of original sin, lightened only by occasional, inexplicably kind glints of salvation. Without depths of despair, and a steely soul to match them, the once-born individual cannot confront and overcome adversity.

In contrast, James proffered his own ideal of the twice-born sick soul. This religious personality—exemplified typically in the lives of saints, mystics, and religious revolutionaries, and in the devotions of many less celebrated individuals—faced the chaos of a world marked by contingency and the absurd. The twice-born individual ruminated on doubt yet acted firmly and decisively. Out of despair the individual chose to act with the chastened realization that life is without guarantees, that history leads us nowhere in particular, and that God's presence, albeit welcome, does not guarantee any immediate victory of good over evil. From such a stance, the individual partakes of "a genuine portion of reality," and thus engages with "the deepest levels of truth."[30]

5 AN EXISTENTIAL sensibility helped define other American thinkers besides Melville and James. Glimpses of it, for instance, are found in the writings of Emily Dickinson and Stephen Crane. Although their styles were radically different, each of them worried over the existential question of what it meant to exist in a world in which God seemed to be uninvolved or indifferent. Surrounded by professing Christians at school, Dickinson could only remark in 1848 that "there is a great deal of religious interest . . . many are flocking to the ark of safety."[31] She remained existential in her stance: "I am standing alone in rebellion."[32] Unlike Ahab, she refused to search for the logic of God's universe. She powerfully envisioned the universe as existing under the sign of death. But in this vision, death does not shade out all lightness and joy. Rather, it grants meaning and value to life: "Death sets a Thing significant."[33] Dickinson's view is as existential as the death-saturated theology of Karl Barth or certain sections of Kierkegaard. Under the shadow of death, she discovers meaning in experience, in her careful empirical observations, and in her intense pleasure in simple being:

> Endow the Living—with the Tears—
> You squander on the Dead,
> And They were Men and Women—now,
> Around Your Fireside—
>
> Instead of Passive Creatures,
> Denied the Cherishing
> Till They—the Cherishing deny—
> With Death's Ethereal Scorn—[34]

Death's scorn appears in much of Stephen Crane's poetry and fiction. Crane, the son of a Methodist minister, rejected bourgeois comfort, opting instead for experience and adventure. All of his writing is directed against the loss of faith. Henry Fleming, the protagonist of *The Red Badge of Courage* (1895), confronts the life-defining and life-denying "boundary situation" of war. He flees at first from the conflict but later becomes a participant. Lofty ideals are demonstrated to be banal; all that matters is acceptance of the nature of the world: "He himself felt the daring spirit of a savage, religion-mad. He was capable of profound sacrifices, a tremendous death."[35] Crane's magnificent short story "The Open Boat" (1898) employs a shipwreck to denote that we are all adrift, longing for God but cast back upon our own resources for survival. Even then survival is as much a matter of happenstance as of skill. Meaning eludes the survivors: "None of them knew the color of the sky." Death lurks around every corner, waiting to strike. Even when death is swift, of those "crushed . . . all to blood," "some had the opportunity to squeal."[36]

The sketches in this chapter can only begin to hint at the existential motherlode in American intellectual and cultural life, for existential themes are, of necessity, present in all art and thought that aspires to greatness and depth.[37] Eugene O'Neill's plays are existential because they tap the core of human loneliness and alienation. His *Long Day's Journey into Night* (1941) anticipates, in many ways, themes that inform Sartre's play *No Exit* (1944). In O'Neill, characters are locked into their histories, unwilling or unable to push their freedom and responsibility, with horrible consequences. Only when he is at sea, away from his family, can Edmund, one of the sons in O'Neill's play, experience even temporary transcendence: "For a moment I lost myself—actually lost my life. I was set free! I dissolved in the sea, became white sails and flying spray, became beauty and rhythm . . . I belonged, without past or future, within peace and unity and a wild joy, within something greater than my own life, or the life of Man, to Life itself!" In O'Neill, epiphanies such as this are gained only in drunken, temporary revery; they are absent from the inauthentic and unfulfilled lives of his characters.[38]

Painter Edward Hopper's canvases also survey, in their own manner, the loneliness of modern urban existence. Hopper is particularly unsettling and central to the American consciousness because he challenges, or at least brings to the fore, this alienation. While nostalgia informs some of his canvases, especially his paintings of Victorian mansions, his works dealing with urban America record a different feeling. This new America is not the land of optimism or boosterism, teeming with projects for growth. The world he depicts is furtive, without connections. Or the connections made are fleeting, a look frozen onto the canvas. The voyeuristic eye sympathetically evokes the fundamental loneliness of the human condition. Whether the subject of his painting is viewed through a window or is looking out a window, a gnawing sense of despair rules.

In Hopper's *Room in New York* (1932), the viewer espies a couple in a room. The man reads a newspaper, engrossed in the news rather than in the presence of the woman sharing the room. The languid woman taps at the piano without enthusiasm. Both are adrift in time, alone with their thoughts but violated by our gaze. In his paintings from the 1920s, Hopper delved into this loneliness of existence in both private and public spaces. *Automat* (1927) shows a young woman at night in a diner drinking a cup of coffee. Surrounded by the objects of existence—chair, table, radiator—she is cold to the world, huddled into herself. In *Sunday* (1926) we encounter a shop owner, perhaps a bartender, sitting alone on a sidewalk. No customers; perhaps they are all at church. He plays a waiting game. Life passes him by, or at least exists elsewhere. There is no sense of Thoreauvian exultation in being alone, just the bleak reality of radical loneliness.[39]

6   CULTURAL CRITICS Joseph Wood Krutch and Walter Lippmann in the late 1920s brought an existential awareness to the tensions of modernity in America. Each in his own fashion gazed into the existential abyss and suggested how to live after doing so. At the historical moment when Kierkegaard was poised to become well known in America for his impassioned leap into faith, Lippmann and Krutch had already stepped into the fray. While they too began from the starting point of doubt, unlike Kierkegaard and religious existentialists, they remained anchored in the churning waters of uncertainty.

An existential crisis of the spirit threatened not only religion but the moral standards and the ethical energy of American society at large in the years around the First World War. This should hardly be surprising. Before the First World War, many had recognized the banality inherent in Victorian views of progress, efficiency, and culture. In contrast, the Lost Generation of the 1920s had declared, in the words of F. Scott Fitzgerald, that they had "grown up to find all Gods dead, all wars fought, all faiths in man shaken."[40] Ernest Hemingway, armed with these assumptions, depicted a generation often stunted by boredom and impotency, captured most fully in the characters of Jake Barnes and his drifting friends in *The Sun Also Rises* (1926). At its best, the work of the Lost Generation enunciated a metaphysical condition of despair and alienation. But all too often there is more than a hint of ennui in such renderings, a feeling that the important questions have been decided once and for all. As Jake announces, "I only wished I felt religious."[41] But he doesn't, and that is that. Thus Lost Generation writers and intellectuals embraced an essentially existential perspective. And the problems they confronted were the stuff that defined much of the existential style of thinking in Krutch and Lippmann.

Few thinkers of the 1920s confronted the existential problem of meaning, questions about God and man, in a more sustained, anguished manner than Joseph Wood Krutch. Born in Tennessee in 1893, Krutch earned a

Ph.D. at Columbia University. Known as a drama critic and author of a host of books on subjects ranging from Restoration-era comedy to Edgar Allan Poe, Krutch contemplated long and hard the implications of the decline of religious certitude and the failure of technological progress to address the fundamental problem of the meaning of human existence. While Krutch later came to regret the "aesthetical Existentialism" that flavored his *The Modern Temper* (1929), theologian Reinhold Niebuhr at the time found the work vitally important for its realization "that the problem of religion is the problem of life."[42] While Krutch and Niebuhr agreed on the problem, they parted over the vitality and validity of religious sentiments in the modern age.

The Modern Temper addresses in a rambling and personal manner the professional, intellectual class, individuals like Krutch himself who were unable "to achieve either religious belief on the one hand or exultant atheism on the other." This constituted the spiritual crisis confronting Western civilization. His generation were "victims" who could "never expect to believe in God" and who had "begun to doubt that rationality and knowledge have any promised land into which they may be led."[43] Krutch marveled at the edifices of science and technology, but he knew that they did not contain wisdom, nor did the Baconian method of science promote salvation. Each new step in modern knowledge, from Freud to Nietzsche, undermined exalted conceptions of the human being. Increased knowledge and modern skepticism had shattered once commonly held beliefs in myth and the Christian God. Krutch lamented the disappearance of illusions that had at least allowed their adherents to experience "a cheerful certitude . . . [a] sense of the essential rightness of life" (18). With the devolution of such myths, in a universe that was reckless and without ethical direction (14), modern men and women were adrift. Radically free, they were overwhelmed, unable to act to impose their will on the world. As historian Peter Gregg Slater remarks, *The Modern Temper* "was more concerned, in both its description and emotional motifs, with the loss of faith in man than with the loss of faith in divinity."[44]

Yet some continued, as Krutch recognized, to act with faith and energy to uphold ideals of social engineering or pure revolutionary zeal. Krutch marveled at the primitivism of "new barbarians" such as the Russian Bolsheviks. These individuals believed with a furious certainty, which imparted to them "an optimism so simple and so terrible" (240). In contrast, for Americans such as Krutch, "skepticism" had "entered too deeply into our souls ever to be replaced by faith" in God or utopias. All that remained for Krutch and his compatriots was to live with a "wisdom" that "must consist, not in searching for a means of escape which does not exist, but in making such peace with it [the world] as we may" (247).

These sentiments echoed the ennui expressed in the fictional works of the Lost Generation. Such a modern temper was deeply existential in confronting the abyss of meaning, in recognizing that man was alone, shorn of meaning and certitude. Krutch's "aesthetical Existentialism" lacked both the faith of a Camus in man and the Sartrean imperative to create; thus it was as barren and impotent as the world inhabited by many of Hemingway's characters. Krutch later viewed his existential feelings as having been mistaken because complacency more than dread had pervaded the text of *The Modern Temper*. But the complacency belonged more to Krutch in the 1920s than to any essence of existentialism. Krutch chose to be an aesthete and an observer rather than a participant.

Walter Lippmann shared much of Krutch's view and vocabulary. But he was less the bystander than the engaged intellectual seeking an escape from the despairing cul-de-sac of modern existence. Their analyses of the problems of modernity proved meaningful for a host of religious thinkers proclaiming, within the sinews of a tragic religion, the value of a return to the centrality of sin, a perspective that allowed them to engage the world and to understand it. Lippmann and Krutch could not go this far. Both respected the power of a passionate inwardness, especially when it was exerted outward into the world, but they were often incapable of mustering it for themselves. Thus despite respect for a religious framework, Lippmann's religion of disinterestedness proved to be uninspiring.

Lippmann began as a man of the world. As a Harvard undergraduate he was an intimate of William James; he later served in the socialist administration in Schenectady, New York. Marvelously gifted as a stylist and a cultural critic, Lippmann kept his finger on the pulse of American culture's directions and problems. His *A Preface to Morals* (1929) is more an impressionistic painting than a work of sustained analysis; it creates an existential mood.[45] The work follows in the tradition of Henry Adams and others of the nineteenth century who confronted a world in which religion had ceded its power. Faced with a need to believe, unable to embrace modern religion or to accept a religion of science, thinkers such as Adams retreated into a vision of medievalism, in which unity and belief were organically intertwined, quite a contrast to the chaos and skepticism of the present historical moment. In similar fashion, Lippmann praised the organic unity of medieval religion: "A medieval cathedral, like the medieval philosophy, was built slowly over generations and was to last forever; it is decorated inside and out, where it can be seen and where it cannot be seen, from the crypt to the roof."[46] But the First World War and the skeptical disposition of science had rendered traditional beliefs untenable. The "acids of modernity" had, alas, done little to diminish the need for belief.

Beginning with the assumption that modern, cosmopolitan men and women required belief and craved religion, Lippmann attempted in *A Preface to Morals* to construct a viable sensibility out of the shards of older religion. The central problem of modern religion, in his analysis, was "how mankind, deprived of the great fictions, is to come to terms with the needs which created those fictions" (144). Lippmann proposed a religious humanism, an "imaginative construction," borrowed in part from some of Freud's concepts on the maturation of the individual from infancy to adulthood. He wanted this "modern fable," through its symbolism, to allow modern men and women to respond reasonably to an often confusing, dangerous, and difficult world. Lippmann presented to his readers what he had come to adopt for himself—a "philosophy of life" intended to help lift the individual "from helpless infancy to self-governing maturity" (175).

Lippmann maintained the practical value of his humanistic religion. This confidence required an immense imaginative leap in America of the 1920s, when the opposing powers of fundamentalism and skepticism raged. He was deeply concerned with the cult of personality, the boosterism, and the Red Scare of his era. The march of the Ku Klux Klan had allowed emotionalism to defeat science, prejudice to overcome open debate. Lippmann recognized and even respected aspects of fundamentalism, since it supplied its believers with a species of truth. But fundamentalism remained the religion of the isolated, small-town mentality. It could not, in Lippmann's analysis, gain the assent of "the best brains and the good sense of a modern community" (30–31).

The principles of Lippmann's high religion were varied, though he emphasized most fully the quality of disinterestedness. Disinterestedness seemed to transform Lippmann's earlier ideal of the technical intellectual—someone who calmly, objectively, and with sober reflection addressed a specific problem—into a moral or religious ideal. Thus the "virtue" of disinterestedness was "to transcend the immediacy of desire and to live for ends which are transpersonal. Virtuous action is conduct which responds to situations that are more extensive, more complicated, and take longer to reach their fulfillment, than the situations to which we instinctively respond" (224).

Lippmann developed an ethics marked by reflection and commitment. His keywords were "courage, honor, faithfulness, veracity, justice, temperance, magnanimity, and love" (221). The enthusiasms of the prophets of progress of the nineteenth century, the certitudes of the emotionally charged fundamentalists of the 1920s, and the horrors of the jingoists of the First World War, Lippmann argued, must be jettisoned. Desires must be controlled. The world did not exist to satisfy the individual; adherence to such a belief only brought disappointment. Lippmann's stoic comprehension of the relationship between the individual and the environment represented for him maturity—the ability to see the world for what it is, not for what the individual wanted. The moralist, in Lippmann's view, worked to reform and to redirect men's wants. The effective statesman no longer pandered to the unrestrained desires of the masses; he courageously instructed the people to "learn to want" what is best for them in the long term (283).

Lippmann's modern individual leader, blessed by the high religion of disinterestedness, faced pain with fortitude and without vain expectations: "And so the mature man would take the world as it comes, and within himself remain quite unperturbed." This mature individual acted as a scientist did when testing an hypothesis. If the experiment failed, it only represented a mistake that might be corrected by continued rational consideration and hypothesis formation. This new man, this stoical individual, would "move easily through life"; whether it be "comedy, or high tragedy, or plain farce, he would affirm that it is what it is, and that the wise man can enjoy it" (329–30). So ended Lippmann's act of moral contrition and persuasion in *A Preface to Morals*.

Various problems afflict Lippmann's religion of disinterestedness. There is, for example, its undeniable elitism. "Disinterested" leaders molded public opinion; they decided the values to be imparted to the masses. In his disdain for the needs of the concrete individual, Lippmann missed the existential imperative to begin with the individual unit. Moreover, while Lippmann maintained that the masses could be instructed and led, this increasingly sounded like a formula for passive acceptance of political realities. Disinterestedness overran engagement and commitment. Without them, it lacked spirit. Lippmann well comprehended the corrosive effects of the "acids of modernity" on his generation of intellectuals. Sobriety, distance, maturity, all recommended themselves as valuable dispositions. But in the face of an abyss of meaning, the tragedy of the First World War, in the midst of the depression, Lippmann's nostrums rang hollow, irrelevant to an energetic, individually centered engagement with the world and with the problem of the self. While Lippmann never forgot the existential dark night of the human soul, he erred in imagining that he, and other leaders of opinion, could wish it away with their Realpolitik.

7 AMERICAN CULTURE as expressed in the hard-boiled detective novels of the 1930s and in the film noir of the 1940s faced existential realities of despair, absurdity, and contingency. It did so without any influence from European philosophy. Indeed, popular American film and fictional noir spread its magic toward Europe. The style of James M. Cain's classic noir novel *The Postman Always Rings Twice* (1934), for example, in-

fluenced Camus to write his own novel, *The Stranger*, in a similar style. Sartre's magnum opus, *Being and Nothingness* (1943), may in some senses be seen as positing a noir universe, a sensibility that paralleled the American noir and tragic view of life.

Dashiell Hammett's classic detective novel *The Maltese Falcon* (1930) pivots around a cast of disreputable characters' lust for a fabulously rare and valuable sculpture of a falcon.[47] This object of their desire may or may not actually exist. Thus their frenetic hunt may be in vain, a mere grasping after an illusion. In the middle of the novel Hammett breaks for some philosophical reflection by having his detective hero Sam Spade tell the story of a man named Flitcraft. In so doing, Hammett offers an existential parable worthy of Kierkegaard or Sartre.

Flitcraft, a well-to-do and apparently contented family man, without any known vices or longings, suddenly disappears, "like a fist when you open your hand."[48] Years later Spade tracks him down, finding Flitcraft living comfortably with a new wife and family—an existence not dissimilar to the one from which he had escaped. Flitcraft explains to Spade that one day his life changed irrevocably in the flash of an existential instant. As he strolled past a construction site, a beam hurtled down just in front of him, chipping off a piece of the sidewalk, which flew up and hit him in the face. The event caused only minor physical cuts but left a deep mental scar that touched Flitcraft's very being. The experience frightened him, shaking him out of his normal existence, throwing his universe of values and certitude into chaos. He has confronted, quite by chance, an absurd situation that brings him face to face with his own mortality: "He felt like somebody had taken the lid off life and let him look at the works" (71).

The "works" reveal a conventional man, someone who had attempted to be "in step with his surroundings" (71). His life had been "a clean orderly sane responsible affair," shattered, it seemed, by the falling beam. Now Flitcraft is shocked by the fact that his habits had covered up the disorder and contingency of existence. Death—no longer an abstraction, something that happens to others—defines the limits of the situation of life while paradoxically opening up the possibilities of freedom. "Life could be ended for him at random by a falling beam: he would change his life at random by simply going away" (71). After a couple of years of aimless drifting, Flitcraft settles down, marries anew (a woman similar to his previous wife), and returns "naturally into the same groove he had jumped out of" before. The spin that Sam Spade puts on this story is tough and cynical: Flitcraft "adjusted himself to beams falling, and then no more of them fell, and he adjusted himself to them not falling" (72).

Here we have Hammett's take on the human condition. Men and women

sleepwalk through existence, clutching at illusions of comfort and complacency. When the natural order cracks in an existential moment, the potential for freedom, for a new birth, opens up. We admire Flitcraft for taking
the leap at the opportunity. But in the end his existence remains untrans-
formed; he is unable to live fully in the hurricane of his own potential death.
Instead he opts to sneak back into the shelter of the inauthentic. He plays
the role, once again, of the good husband and citizen.

Extreme situations and moral choices color the world of American film
noir. Despite the French sound of the designation, film noir was a staple of
Hollywood, and it predated Sartrean existentialism. The action in film noir
almost always takes place at night. The "children of darkness," to use a
noirish biblical phrase of Reinhold Niebuhr's, are encountered in the dim
light of the city. In this liminal space, the veneer of respectable moral propriety is sandpapered away. Truth is complex and elusive, lost in the shadows. At every corner of the labyrinth of the city, the hero confronts an extreme situation, a reality that explodes ideals of progress, optimism, and
morality. This is the "dangerous and sad city of the imagination," in the
words of film critic Robert Warshow, where "we are afraid [of what] we may
become."[49] This is the existential terrain of the noir thriller that dominated
American film and literary culture from the 1930s into the 1950s.

In nearly all noir films, certitude is defunct and human relationships are
strained. Self-will and self-interest define the powerful and damn the naive.
Against these powers stands the stoic individualist with his own code of
honor. The politics of the noir film, with its valorization of the heroic male,
remain problematic. After all, human relationships in noir are questionable
at best; human solidarity is absent. The interiors of noir are as bleak as in
any painting by Hopper, human relations as strained as in any play by
O'Neill.

The hard-boiled hero of noir fiction and film is deeply suspicious of
human nature, or at least of the motivations of others. Aware of man's ra-
pacity and capacity for sin, the hard-boiled hero seeks to escape illusion. He
remains, however, in danger of surrendering to its allure—especially when
it takes the form, as it invariably does in noir, of the mysterious woman. The
noir hero is then perplexed, often left without a moral compass. He is in
search of meaning, of a reason for existence—his own and that of others.[50]

In the classic noir thriller *D.O.A.* (1949), Frank Bigelow, a small-town ac-
countant, wants to get away from the smothering love of his secretary,
Paula.[51] He flees to San Francisco, where every time he comes across an
attractive woman, he hears bells of guilt ringing. In the interim, he learns
that a Mr. Phillips has urgently been trying to contact him about a life-and-
death matter. Bigelow does not return the calls. Instead, he goes to a hip

nightspot where a group of jive jazz musicians are wowing the audience, although he is most moved by the blonde at the bar. He procures her phone number for a later rendezvous, only to return to the hotel and find that the ever-faithful Paula has sent him flowers. He throws the phone number away.

The next morning Bigelow awakens with stomach problems. Doctors give him the crushing diagnosis that he has luminous poisoning and will live anywhere from a day to a week; no reprieve or antidote is possible. After a second opinion confirms his death verdict, Bigelow rushes out onto Market Street. Alone, overwrought by the fate that has intruded upon his mundane, comfortable existence, Bigelow suddenly experiences a sense of calm. His life, at last, has achieved purpose. He determines to find out why he has been poisoned and by whom.

This leads Bigelow on a rather convoluted chase, full of intrigue and mystery, all related to a simple bill of sale that he had notarized six months earlier. If he had only returned the earlier phone call, instead of choosing not to interrupt his vacation, perhaps someone would not have been murdered, Bigelow included. Such are the odd turns of life.

The remainder of the film chronicles Bigelow's increasingly desperate attempts to punch through the pasteboard mask of the cause of his impending death. He faces the threats of a psychopathic killer without fear, since the sentence of death is already upon him. He resolves the mystery and even manages to save another person's life. Most significantly for the existential content of the film, Bigelow's knowledge of his impending mortality forces a quick reevaluation of his life: he decides that he does love Paula, but that there is no chance to right previous slights. There are no second chances; choices are made. His last words at the police station, after he explains the entire story, are for Paula who is waiting for him at the Allison Hotel in Los Angeles. She awaits a life of security and happiness that is absent from the hand that life has dealt Bigelow.

THUS WE HAVE in American writers, philosophers, cultural critics, and noir stylists, without any influence from European existentialism, indications of a deeply held existential attitude. Such an attitude was, to be sure, only part of American culture; it coexisted with a sense of progress, empowerment, and optimism. One can dwell full time in the prison-house of despair only at the cost of becoming self-indulgent and passive, just as a lifetime "moral holiday," in James's terms, can lead to the self-indulgence and passivity of a naive optimism. Indeed, as we shall see in the work of Hazel E. Barnes, Ralph Ellison, and Norman Mailer, American existentials combine elements of noir pessimism with a Jamesian heartiness, a dauntlessness that is bathed in a sense of the tragic.

In any case, through the work of James, Melville (who underwent a revival of interest in the 1920s), and noir novelists, the ground in America had been prepared for the arrival of Kierkegaardian existentialism in the early 1930s. America, no less than Europe, boasted its core of serious existential thinkers. This existential tradition, firmly held if not developed into a systematic world view, helps to explain, in part, why European existentialism struck such a resonant chord once it arrived on American shores.

1928–1955

Kierkegaardian Moments

Chapter Three

Kierkegaard Comes to America

1 DURING A WINTER of world war in 1944, the work of nineteenth-century Danish religious thinker Søren Kierkegaard surfaced as a topic of conversation at an informal White House dinner. After hearing President Roosevelt praise mystery writer Dorothy Sayers, a young minister named Howard A. Johnson remarked that Kierkegaard had deeply influenced Sayers. Not surprisingly, Roosevelt admitted that he knew nothing of Kierkegaard. Johnson, a disciple of Kierkegaard's biographer and translator Walter Lowrie, patiently outlined the essentials of Kierkegaard for the president. Roosevelt jotted down some ideas and citations. A few weeks later he told Frances Perkins, his secretary of labor, "You ought to read him [Kierkegaard]. It will teach you something." And what was that "something," according to the president of the United States? "Kierkegaard gives you an understanding of what it is in man that makes it possible for these Germans to be so evil."[1]

Alas, no record exists of Roosevelt's developing this particular insight. Nor did he, as far as is known, return to the work of the founder of modern existentialism. But for such an un–philosophically oriented individual as Roosevelt, even the whisper of interest in Kierkegaard fascinates and indicates the speed with which Kierkegaard had entered into the conversation of American intellectual and cultural life.

Before 1932, few English speakers knew the existential thought of Kierkegaard, although he may have attained some influence among Scandinavians living in the United States. Ignorance about Kierkegaard ended in the 1930s, thanks to the efforts of Episcopal clergyman Walter Lowrie. Lowrie's importance comes from his yeoman efforts to bring Kierkegaard to America; he figures as an impresario of ideas. Although not a particularly original thinker himself, Lowrie engaged the theological debates of his era. And his success at popularizing Kierkegaard helped define American cultural and political discourse after the Second World War.

Lowrie initially encountered Kierkegaard in the 1920s, when in his fifties. Not content to read Kierkegaard in translation, he resolved to translate

Kierkegaard into English. In 1932, at age sixty-four, Lowrie began to study Danish. Within a few years he had flooded the presses with translations of Kierkegaard, had contacted others to translate some of Kierkegaard's work, and had himself undertaken to write a biography of Kierkegaard, which he published in two volumes in 1938. Lowrie's almost manic championing of Kierkegaard continued unabated until his death in 1954. By that time he had published a one-volume condensation of his longer biography and had translated fifteen works by Kierkegaard as well.

Driven by the force of ideas and religious tensions, Lowrie admitted that "whatever provokes in me a crisis of faith is a matter of life or death to me, a vivid religious experience." "Dangerous" authors such as Kierkegaard, Karl Barth, or Albert Schweitzer provoked him, bringing him to a crisis of thought more than of faith (his never wavered).[2] The energy of crisis, the excitement of encountering religious thinkers who were in a white heat of anguished faith, appealed to Lowrie's sensibility. Out of such encounters he constructed his own views, or at least found support for his own intellectual and spiritual inclinations.

Resolutely rejecting the label of theologian, Lowrie instead saw himself as a preacher who published on a wide variety of religious topics. But existential imperatives occupied the center of his theology: the singular nature of belief, the pressing implications of death, and the otherness of God. These imperatives easily aligned with the life and work of Kierkegaard.

Lowrie came to Kierkegaard late in a remarkably active life. Born in Philadelphia in 1868 to a clergyman father, Lowrie attended Princeton as an undergraduate in the 1880s, during its days as a hotbed of devout Presbyterianism. After graduation he gained, in 1893, a master's degree from Princeton Theological Seminary, followed by study in Germany and travel throughout Europe. By 1894 Lowrie had returned to the United States, soon to become an Episcopal minister. Although Lowrie worked in an urban mission during the 1890s, social reformism was not his métier. He spent a year in the mid-1890s doing scholarly research at the American School for Classical Studies in Rome. A few years later he published *Monuments of the Early Church* (1901), a work that analyzed early Christian art, with emphasis on spirit over body in the art. In 1907, after serving various churches in the United States, Lowrie assumed the duties of rector of St. Paul's American Church in Rome, where he remained until his retirement in 1930. During these years Lowrie embraced European culture, perfected his German- and Italian-language skills, and devoured the latest theological and religious writing in Europe.[3]

Lowrie saw in himself many of the same qualities that made Kierkegaard such a singular personality and striking thinker. Even before he learned of

Kierkegaard, Lowrie's religious views had a distinctly antinomian air about them. He was, as one of his admirers put it, often out of step with religious trends, just as Kierkegaard had been.[4] Also in common with Kierkegaard, Lowrie preferred an ironic, paradoxical mode of analysis rather than a simple expository one.

While devoted to the gospels as the revelation of the divine command-ments, Lowrie rejected religious fundamentalism as naive: "I was driven from the denomination [Presbyterian] in which I was born because I did not believe in the inerrancy of the Scriptures."[5] Liberal theology's easy beliefs in progress and in the divinity of man left him cold. "We with our modern Humanism have lost all sense for the fact that for God it was a profound hu-miliation to become man" (25). While Lowrie identified with much of reli-gious modernism, he felt especially uncomfortable with its social activism and optimism. He craved a religious sensibility that thundered, that con-fronted the existential abyss, that transformed the self like a dagger in the brain. Like others in the American antinomian tradition, such as Anne Hutchinson, he longed to be considered by other ministers "as a danger-ous person. In the company of theologians of any sect or of any school I feel like a lion in a den of Daniels" (13).

Beginning in the 1890s, a Neo-Orthodox revolt against religious liberal-ism rumbled through America.[6] Neo-Orthodox theologians maintained that an overly optimistic view of human nature and progress dominated the lib-eral theology of thinkers such as Henry Ward Beecher, Henry Churchill King, and others. In their view, liberals were too darned assured of their own salvation, too unacquainted with spiritual anguish. Even if the Kingdom of God was not to be realized on this earth, liberal ministers rested too com-fortably in their belief that God smiled down upon middle-class America, and that all was, by and large, right with the world. Such a one-story-deep religion, in William James's opinion, could not surmount the obstacles tossed in front of it by life.

In his rejection of liberal theology, Lowrie found a mentor in Albert Schweitzer. A cousin of Jean-Paul Sartre's, Schweitzer was a man of great talent and passion—a skilled organist, expert on Bach, theologian and pas-tor. Schweitzer's *The Mystery of the Kingdom of God: The Secret of Jesus' Messiahship and Passion* so impressed Lowrie when he read it in 1901 that he undertook to translate the volume into English. Lowrie was particularly attracted by Schweitzer's concept of a "thoroughgoing eschatology," an over-riding concern with religion in the face of death as a means for compre-hending Jesus. "You made me a critical eschatologist," Lowrie wrote later to Schweitzer, "and the logic of the situation has compelled me to become a believing one."[7]

Schweitzer and his "thoroughgoing eschatology" criticized the liberal ideal of Jesus as a moralist, confined in many ways to the age in which he lived. In the hands of Schweitzer, with the approval of Lowrie, a heroic, living, and messianic Jesus replaced the historical and distant Jesus. The new Jesus sharply preached the transitory nature of the world and "the expectation of a better world to come, 'beyond good and evil.'" Jesus acted in the nearness of death. Lowrie found this existential notion quite valuable, and it would later inform own his work on Kierkegaard. Such an eschatological sense, with the presence of death hovering nearby, defined the vivid, lived religious consciousness of Schweitzer and Lowrie.[8]

"We need a new cosmology!" declared Lowrie, one that will help us in "directing our hope and orienting our life towards the beyond, as did Jesus in his way, and as the Church did in its way."[9] For Schweitzer and Lowrie, this meant a powerful "God-consciousness" to counterbalance the worldly consciousness of liberal religion based upon an optimistic, evolutionary model of progress (40). Both men cried out for a quickening of the will, inspired by the figure of Jesus. Out of this "intensity" and "clarity" modern men and women would be able to experience Jesus, the fullness of religion, the centrality of death, and the sudden, awesome closeness of God (50). They would have an existential religious life.

Hard on the heels of Lowrie's engagement with Schweitzer came the First World War. The war had a powerful effect on thinkers such as Lowrie, at least in retrospect. Disgusted with the "easy optimism" that he associated with mainstream Christianity, Lowrie surveyed the ruins of his beloved European civilization after "the shock of the Great War." The "Kingdom of God seemed ruthlessly unmasked, nothing more than a new Tower of Babel."[10] The "shock of the Great War," along with the increased strains in the outlook of genteel Victorianism, became common cultural stigmata in the 1920s as intellectuals, both religious and secular, attempted to deal with essentially existential questions: What does it mean to be human in the face of an absent or radically different God? How are new values and morals to be constructed? How does one live under the sign of death?

2 IN CONTRAST TO secular thinkers of the 1920s such as Joseph Wood Krutch and Walter Lippmann, Lowrie argued that American faith could be reinvigorated. But the God that Lowrie desired lay buried in the weak pieties of genteel religion. Instead of liberal theology, or even fundamentalism, Lowrie sought a religious perspective that sweated with anguish and celebrated ultimate salvation. He craved a religion based on faith and paradox more than doctrinal logic or placid ritual. Unlike Krutch, he did not need to marvel at any perceived primitive energy on the part of Soviet work-

ers. Instead, he discovered a theology of fevered anguish in the work of Barth. And since Barth spoke to Lowrie, Lowrie decided to explicate, as he had earlier done with Schweitzer, the main lines of Barthian theology in a book, *Our Concern with the Theology of Crisis* (1932). Here Lowrie sought to transform American religious practice by a "return to the theology of the Reformation" as enunciated by Barth.[11]

Lowrie joined others in the turn to Barth largely out of frustration with the meek posture of liberal Protestantism and the progressivist nature of secular culture. By the mid-1920s, articles about Barth were pouring forth from the American religious press—hardly surprising during a period that witnessed the rediscovery of Jonathan Edwards's theology. In 1928 Douglas Horton translated some of Barth's sermons under the title *The Word of God and the Word of Man.*[12] Barth's crisis theology emphasized the majestic, mysterious, and distanced nature of God. Men and women depended on God for salvation. Faith was deemed absurd, marked by paradox and contradiction. In the midst of this tough religion, men and women faced their deaths with fear and trembling.

But not everyone swallowed Barth whole. Reinhold Niebuhr, one of America's leading religious thinkers, disliked what he perceived as the antipolitical implications of Barth's theology.[13] Yet he welcomed Barth's "note of tragedy," which he called "a wholesome antidote to the superficial optimism of most current theology."[14] Although some commentators, such as Wilhelm Pauck, considered Barth a quietist on social reform, Niebuhr used Barth's theology as a goad to action and responsibility in the political realm.[15] Anticipating Sartre and Camus, Niebuhr declared that we "have to depend for emancipation upon the morally sensitive souls who have no assurance of God to save them from despair but who develop what moral energy they can while walking always on the narrow ledge at the side of the abyss of despair."[16]

Lowrie agreed with Barthians that in this world the individual needed to be active rather than withdrawn from the daily affairs of life. But activity and social reform must never be confused with achieving the Kingdom of God, for God, that distanced and immense power, required no help in erecting His Kingdom. Men who claimed to act on God's behalf in the task of building the Kingdom were by definition burdened with an unrecognized, and hence dangerous, hubris (*Our Concern,* 33). But this recognition failed to decide what role the individual and the church should play in social reform. For Niebuhr, individual and church must act to reform, albeit in a chastened manner. In contrast, Lowrie took his Barthian theology away from politics toward faith alone. Lowrie's religious and social views would in turn resonate only for those who were frustrated with the political realm, those who were searching for a theology and philosophy that absolved them of a reformist political responsibility.

Our Concern with the Theology of Crisis registers Lowrie's initial encounter with Kierkegaard. In fact, Lowrie seems to have undertaken his analysis of Barth primarily as a means of getting at Kierkegaard. Barth based a good deal of his theology of crisis on Kierkegaardian foundations. As Lowrie read Barth, he announced that "the most acclaimed and the most detested article of theology that Barth borrowed from S[øren] K[ierkegaard] was the assertion of the endless qualitative difference between God and man."[17]

While Lowrie admired the bluster and bark of Barth's theology, he rejected as perverse its overemphasis on original sin. To be sure, Lowrie took a back seat to no one in finding that men commonly sinned. He refused, however, to chain theology to any doctrine that offered no escape route. To do so would be to undermine the point of faith and the potential for salvation. In the mode of existential theology, Lowrie examined the centrality of death and the offer of salvation through anguish and despair. These themes dominated his work. "Death and resurrection are two themes which are always prominent in Barth's thought," Lowrie wrote (*Our Concern,* 144), and he identified most with these themes when they constituted Barth's "existential moment": that horrifying instant when man confronted his aloneness, recognized his distance from God, and realized that "the fact of the limitation of our life is what gives life movement. We carry our death about with us" (177). Throughout his book, Lowrie applauded the death-saturated insights of Barth. "Death is significant . . . with reference to this present life of which it is the end. It is not, as we like to think, merely an event which some day we shall encounter; but because it is the only event we can certainly count on, it defines what we *are* in every moment" (35). This existential insight defined much of existentialist thought in that century. But Lowrie, and Barth, nurtured their death-centered vision not as an end but as an opening into eternity. For both of them, out of this existential moment comes anguish aplenty, but also the possibility of resurrection by "watching, waiting, expecting, living as on the brink" (69).

Lowrie invoked Kierkegaard and Barth as battering rams against liberal theology's confusion of the here-and-now with the eternal Kingdom of God. Liberal theology stood condemned by Lowrie for many reasons: it struck him as relativistic and vapid, overemphasizing the power of man, underestimating the power of God, reducing Jesus to a moral exemplar, supporting the illusion of social reform as an end in itself, and downplaying the horrible centrality of death. In contrast to this easy Christianity that afflicted Americans, Lowrie proposed a religion that questioned the very meaning and purpose of existence.

Lowrie wanted his presentation of Kierkegaard and Barth to "wrench" readers out of their "superior and secure position as spectator." Jazz-age Americans consumed religion as a product, a set of comforting rituals or sentimental slogans that exalted man and his earthly accomplishments. Barth's "theology of crisis," in contrast, commanded the individual to experience the existential dread of damnation and the possibility of divine salvation. For this individual, life was now defined—using terms that Nietzsche had uttered—as "living dangerously," through a return to the "thoroughgoing eschatology" that Schweitzer had recommended (*Our Concern*, 45–46). In the fighting language that Niebuhr would make famous in *Moral Man and Immoral Society* (1932) and *The Nature and Destiny of Man* (1941), Lowrie railed against utopian reform and praised a "chastened spirit," paradox, irony, and a tragic sensibility (96–98).

Borrowing a central motif from Kierkegaard, "the object of faith is the absurd,"[18] Lowrie argued that faith had nothing to do with certitude, knowledge, or empirical evidence. If it did, then there would be little point in talking of faith or belief. Faced with paradoxical notions and patently absurd possibilities in the central categories of Christianity, the believer thrived under such contradictions through the act of faith, faith in the absurd. With Kierkegaard and Jonathan Edwards before him, Lowrie proclaimed salvation an incomplete movement in time. Salvation produced a feeling of "comforted despair" (*Our Concern*, 109), a constant, anguished test for the Christian. In essence, Lowrie accepted the Kierkegaardian analysis of faith as "sickness unto death" (109). Finally, Lowrie, Barth, and Kierkegaard transformed the image of God as a sentimental protector or an anthropomorphic deity into a God that could never be reduced to an object for human contemplation. From Barth, Lowrie learned that God is always the subject, never the object: "No one can speak *about* God (as an object), unless it be God himself" (140). When Lowrie attempted to capture the presence of God in this world, he revealed a vision of God as threat and chaos: God could be encountered indirectly, "in the thunderstorm, in leviathan, and in behemoth" (125). Lowrie demanded a new vision of God and the religious life for Americans. In order to save Americans from a weak-kneed religious liberalism, Lowrie determined to bring Kierkegaard into the conversation of American theology and the hearts of Christians.

3   LOWRIE OBSESSED about his mission to popularize Kierkegaard for an English-speaking audience.[19] At first glance, the marriage of Lowrie and Kierkegaard was an unlikely one. Robust and active, Lowrie enjoyed a rich social life. Kierkegaard, in contrast, was melancholic and withdrawn from the affairs of the world. Yet each in his own way sought to think deeply

about the primacy of faith over religion. And each showed no hesitation in building a religious perspective that was at once nonsystematic and nonacademic. Indeed, both Lowrie and Kierkegaard shared an animus against professional philosophers and theologians.

Even more important, Lowrie agreed with Kierkegaard in recognizing the dialectical intertwining of the stages of human existence. In *Either/Or* (1843) Kierkegaard set these stages out as the aesthetic, the ethical, and the religious. Although often seen as progressive, they were in Kierkegaard coexistent. In the aesthetic stage, the individual confronts the dread of constantly flitting about from one ideal to another. Each object of attention is grasped with intensity and initial satisfaction, as Don Juan is drawn into each new romantic interlude. But without a firm mooring or set of values, one object of affection quickly replaces another, ultimately leading to a state of moral emptiness. For this individual, "time stands still, and so do I. All the plans I project fly straight back at me; when I want to spit, I spit in my own face."[20] Ironically, despite his pressing religious concerns, Lowrie resembled the Kierkegaardian aesthete, moving from one Continental thinker to another, translating peripatetically, and working in the history of art, theology, and biography. At the same time, Lowrie valorized Kierkegaard's ethical stage for its sense of propriety and necessity. He agreed with Kierkegaard's character Judge William's advice to his aesthetic friend: "What I have said so often to you I say once again, or, more exactly, I shout it to you: Either/Or."[21] Stand at the crossroad and choose, shouts Judge William. Lowrie too maintained that one must choose belief in a momentous leap of faith that alone lifted one from the worst pain of despair into salvation. Much like Kierkegaard, Lowrie exulted most in the ideal of the Knight of Faith, the passionate religious figure for whom the demands of the universal in ethics were transfigured by the absurd faith demanded by belief in God. This was an ideal rather than a realization for each man. In recognizing this, Kierkegaard appeared to Lowrie as the brilliant psychologist of the multilayered religious personality. And in Kierkegaard, Lowrie found someone who, in language at once poetic and religious, grappled with the concerns that defined his own existence.

In his quest to make Kierkegaard a household name in America, Lowrie acted on a host of fronts. Soon after his initial encounter with Kierkegaard via Barth in the mid-1920s, Lowrie began to read Kierkegaard in German translation. But reading another's translations proved unsatisfying, akin to experiencing religion secondhand. "Even at my advanced and tottering age," wrote Lowrie (he was then in his sixties), "I had the courage to learn Danish—well enough to read it."[22] Already fluent in German, Lowrie began, logically enough, with German translations of Kierkegaard: "The first translations I made from Kierkegaard were made from Schrempf's translation. I translated Schrempf rather freely, and what I wrote sounded pretty good to me." But as he learned Danish, Lowrie revised his opinion of his own translations, finding them "far removed . . . from the style of Kierkegaard." He then began translating Kierkegaard from the Danish originals, a task made easier by Danish being cognate with German. Thus Lowrie learned Danish as he translated Kierkegaard. "I have fallen in love with Kierkegaard's style," he wrote, "and it seems to me (perhaps I delude myself) that the most literal reading is also the most effective."[23]

Lowrie did more than undertake to translate Kierkegaard. He became enmeshed in a transatlantic network to make Kierkegaard a household name. He quickly established cordial working relationships with others who were laboring to translate Kierkegaard into English, such as American philosopher David Swenson and English Catholic Alexander Dru. As Lowrie humorously wrote to Dru, "My slogan is: 'To put the name of Soren Kierkegaard in the mouth of every American!'"[24]

Lowrie's chief collaborator David Swenson had, in the 1890s, at the age of twenty, happened upon a Danish-language copy of Kierkegaard's *Concluding Unscientific Postscript* in the stacks of a local library. The experience transformed him. Swenson spent the night and the next day taking in the lengthy book "at a single gulp."[25] In 1916, Swenson, a professor of philosophy at the University of Minnesota, published the first scholarly analysis of Kierkegaard to appear in America, "The Anti-Intellectualism of Kierkegaard," in the *Philosophical Review*. In this introduction to Kierkegaard, Swenson discussed the philosopher's style and substance, remarking on similarities between Kierkegaard and William James, finding that both expressed their personal spirit in their philosophical writings. Kierkegaard always functioned for Swenson as an exemplar of style, "wrapped up in a covering of humor, wit, pathos, and imagination" with "lyric expressions of doubt, despair, and faith." Like Lowrie, Swenson revered Kierkegaard as "a thinking personality who exists in his thought."[26]

Swenson's Danish-language skills (he was a Danish-reading Swede) and philosophical background eclipsed Lowrie's. Yet from the beginning Lowrie dominated the relationship. The two discussed at length the proper English counterparts for Kierkegaard's Danish. Would *"angst"* work better than "dread" or "anxiety"? They spent two years worrying about how to translate the Danish *"Smuler"*: should it be "scraps," or "tidbits," or the term that Swenson appropriated, "fragments"? In the end they disagreed about which term worked best.[27] Lowrie did appreciate and learn from the more careful, scrupulous Swenson, a point that he acknowledged when he dedicated his biography of Kierkegaard to Swenson as "the Nestor of Kierkegaardian

Study in America."[28] But without Lowrie's intercession, Swenson would never have managed the immense feat of making Kierkegaard a familiar name among American religious thinkers and intellectuals.

Lowrie emerged as a Kierkegaardian entrepreneur, getting Oxford University Press to agree to publish translations of Kierkegaard that he, Dru, and Swenson had labored on. Since Oxford fretted about the lack of an audience for Kierkegaard, Lowrie used some of his considerable personal fortune to underwrite the publications: "I prefer to take the risk rather than leave it to another."[29] When a paper shortage occurred in Britain during the early days of the Second World War, Lowrie transferred publication to the Princeton University Press, under the same arrangements. His initial investment, in both time and money, soon paid immense dividends, as sales of Kierkegaard climbed and his name became well known. Although Lowrie desperately believed in making Kierkegaard famous in America, he was at times proprietary in his concern. After learning in 1936 about John Wild's teaching a very popular philosophy class on Kierkegaard at Harvard, and that a student at Harvard, Marjorie Glicksman (later Grene), had just completed a dissertation on Kierkegaard, Lowrie wrote to Swenson, "We are in danger of falling behind in the procession."[30]

A major step in the popularization of Kierkegaard was the publication of Lowrie's two-volume biography in 1938, followed in 1942 by his *A Short Life of Kierkegaard.* In both these works, directed to a general audience, Lowrie placed himself in the background. As Swenson remarked to Lowrie at the time of publication, "You have subordinated yourself to your subject, and without slavish subjection have made of yourself an instrument for the revelation of your hero."[31] By Lowrie's own estimate, quotations from Kierkegaard constituted nearly 40 percent of the two-volume biography, which was designed to let the Danish poet of religion speak in his own voice and draw readers into the original texts, which were then in the process of being translated.[32] Lowrie succeeded in this effort, although his narrative overwhelmed his interpretation. A most unlikely reviewer in the *New Republic,* avant-garde novelist Henry Miller, pronounced the work a "remarkable phosphorescent condensation of difficult material."[33] The "difficult material" that Lowrie had wrapped his hands around was the entirety of Kierkegaard's life and thought. He had presented Americans with an explosive gift.

4 IN SPEAKING OF the miracle of the resurrection of Christ and the forgiveness of sin, the apostle Paul stated, "It was through one man that sin entered the world, and through sin death, and thus death pervaded the whole human race, inasmuch as all have sinned" (Rom. 5:12). A pas-

sionate recognition of the certitude of sin and death and of the unbelievable possibility of salvation defines the essential constituents of a Christian tradition that stretches from Paul to Augustine, from Kierkegaard to Lowrie and Niebuhr. Call this tradition the Augustinian strain of piety, or the paradoxical anguish of Kierkegaard; it serves as the beating heart of an existential Christianity.

Lowrie emphasized how Kierkegaard placed himself squarely against that complacent form of Christianity wherein good works and outward acts of churchgoing and good manners equaled faith. While Kierkegaard respected outward forms of piety, he believed that they should not substitute for a strenuous faith that touched the inward soul of man. Kierkegaard also rebelled against theological and philosophical systems such as Hegel's whereby the nature of the dialectic magically led to a progressively higher state in which contradictions and apparent paradoxes were logically transcended. The true Knight of Faith, in Kierkegaard's view, lived within contradiction and paradox; out of the anguish of unresolved confrontations with paradox came the power of faith, the responsibility of the momentous choice to believe. For Kierkegaard, religion was not, as the Hegelians seemed to suggest, a matter of adhering to an abstract philosophical or theological system. Instead, his views paralleled those of William James as expressed in *The Varieties of Religious Experience* (1902), with its emphasis on the power of concrete faith.

Kierkegaard characterized his *Concluding Unscientific Postscript* (1846) as an "existential contribution" by which he intended to move away from Hegelian abstract systems toward the concrete individual who lives passionately within his own experiences. The individual experiences the great pain of living in the recognition that he must die—that he will die his own death, not some abstract death. And yet "it is the path we must all take— over the Bridge of Sighs into eternity."[34] Mining this vein in all of his books, Kierkegaard trembled at the pain and despair that defined existence. He recognized the essential paradox of man's finiteness and desire for transcendence: "Faith has hopes, therefore, for this life, but note well, on the strength of the absurd, not on the strength of human understanding, otherwise it is only good sense, not faith."[35]

Faith, for Kierkegaard and Lowrie, began and ended with passion: "If passion is eliminated, faith no longer exists, and certainty and passion do not go together."[36] This constituted the radical nature of Kierkegaard's assertion, especially in the light of nineteenth-century attempts to rationalize religious belief or to place the workings of faith in a quasi-scientific or psychological framework. Instead, Kierkegaard enthusiastically accepted the paradox of faith as the only key to unlock the door of religious belief. He placed the believer in what would seem to an outside observer, at least, to be a difficult position. If certainty and passion were separate entities, then what did it mean to consider oneself saved? Rather than finalities, objects to be possessed, life and faith were processes for Kierkegaard, states of becoming within the finiteness of time that would only be transcended in the realm of the infinite. For Lowrie, Kierkegaard's work helped one in the process of "becoming a Christian." This process of becoming, for both Lowrie and Kierkegaard, pivoted on the struggle toward God in the "endless effort to become a Christian."[37]

Belief, then, existed wholeheartedly within the pain of doubt, rendering the search for meaning more powerfully compelling and absolute. The parable of Abraham's unwavering faith in God demonstrated for Kierkegaard the paradox of belief and the suspension of the ethical. Wracked by anguish at the apparent absurdity of God's commandment that he sacrifice his son Isaac, Abraham, the Knight of Faith, holds on to his faith. Paradoxically, out of that belief and anguish comes salvation. God rescinds His command. Abraham knew that he had to suspend his ethical views for a more universal faith. While the tragic hero wins the admiration of his fellows by clinging to ethical standards, the Knight of Faith's suspension of the ethical is harder, for his actions may result in social derision. Moreover, Abraham believes in the absurd: he believes that in sacrificing Isaac he will be rewarded by the return of Isaac. Thus Abraham "believed on the strength of the absurd, for there could be no question of human calculation, and it was indeed absurd that God who demanded this of him should in the next instant withdraw the demand."[38]

Kierkegaard's existential religion began with the individual looking inward, experiencing first dread, then despair as he or she realizes that salvation can come only through divine intervention. At all times the individual clings to belief, ever aware of the absurdity of that belief. The comprehension of God, no less than of faith, sits securely in the seat of the absurd. All is paradox, but no less powerful for that fact. As Kierkegaard put it in *Fear and Trembling,* "How monstrous a paradox faith is, a paradox capable of making a murder into a holy act well pleasing to God, a paradox which gives Isaac back to Abraham, which no thought can grasp because faith begins precisely where thinking leaves off."[39]

5 LOWRIE ADORED Kierkegaardian imperatives. He proudly proclaimed himself a preacher of the gospel, a "Protestant Catholic," challenging the religious divisions in Christendom. In a Kierkegaardian manner, Lowrie carefully discussed the distinction between religion and faith. The former was mere ephemera, a matter of tradition more than choice. Faith,

in contrast, represented the absolute conviction that Christ had died for our sins and that our only hope of salvation lay in faith in this fact. As Lowrie wrote in his two-volume biography of Kierkegaard, Christianity is more properly viewed as a faith than as a religion: "It is the only religion which bases the hope of an eternal blessedness upon something historical, which moreover by its very nature cannot be historical, and so must become so by virtue of the absurd."[40]

Kierkegaard's religious views helped Lowrie distance himself from the common religious institutions of his era. Kierkegaard became the exemplar of the passionate believer for whom the established churches held little allure. Lowrie found Kierkegaard's critique of established religion to be especially relevant within the American context. American Protestantism in its early days had had passion, but by the 1930s it had become "established" and "respectable." At present, Lowrie remarked, "the notion is . . . generally repudiated that men ought to fear God."[41] In his introduction to Kierkegaard's highly polemical *Attack upon "Christendom,"* Lowrie acknowledged the oddity of a clergyman like himself translating such a deeply anticlerical work. But he found Kierkegaard's immanent critique "positive and positively edifying," viewing it as coming from a man of steely faith.[42] He considered Kierkegaard's attack upon established religion relevant to his own age, even though the priests were no longer, by and large, well-paid retainers of the church. Lowrie rebelled against the huge amounts of money being spent on churches and cathedrals. He derided monuments to the comfort and confidence of the middle class while he exalted the "sickness unto death" that composed the true and permanent crisis of Christendom.[43]

Yet Lowrie was discomforted by the rebirth of certain strains of a conservative theology in America that talked excessively of sin and the fear of God. As noted earlier, the rise of Neo-Orthodoxy, which Lowrie had supported by his popularization of Barth, and as expressed in the work of Reinhold Niebuhr and Joseph Haroutunian, had become stalled on the doctrine of original sin and the degree of evil in the world. Thus in *Wisdom and Folly in Religion: A Study in Chastened Protestantism* (1940), Haroutunian resurrected Jonathan Edwards as a model of Christian thought concerning damnation and sin. For Haroutunian, the Protestantism of his own day failed to question the sovereignty of man. It only supported a doctrine of "justification by works of love" and an ideal of divine love (in place of election and predestination): "Such Protestantism has lost its soul."[44] The solution: a return to the Protestantism of the Reformation. In a highly supportive introduction to Haroutunian's work, Reinhold Niebuhr championed the doctrine of sin as a valuable corrective to an easy belief in justification through love. Haroutunian's work, in the words of Niebuhr, spoke to all who have been unable to escape the tragic sense of life, to all who contemplate with fear and pity the lot of suffering, sinful man on the torn earth, to all wrestlers with God. It speaks to and it confirms our doubt in the efficacy of religion to save us from disaster. . . . It honors the honesty of those who do not want to fool themselves with wishful thinking about beneficent deities who speak nothing but human happiness. It makes no effort to justify the ways of God to man.[45]

Or as Lowrie phrased it in an autobiographical fragment, "I do not object to the doctrine of total depravity but to the way Calvinists have of living up to it."[46]

In fact, Niebuhr eventually accepted Lowrie's opinion, finding in 1956 that in his own earlier works, such as *The Nature and Destiny of Man* (1941), he had overemphasized the doctrine of original sin and the "corruption of human nature"; more attention should have been paid to the possibility of grace.[47] An existential crisis of faith, a sense of anguish, brought man to despair, to the brink. Yes, sin enveloped man. But the leap into faith and the fullness of salvation did not entail any final accounting, at least in the finite world, or any sense of complacency. In Kierkegaard's terms, man vainly thought of grace as a given, *"as a matter of course."* In Kierkegaard's words, no doubt seconded by Lowrie, "Christianity is just as lenient as it is austere, that is to say infinitely lenient. When the infinite requirement is heard and upheld, heard and upheld in all its infinitude, then *grace* is offered."[48] Salvation becomes possible.

Lowrie rejected original sin as an unfathomable burden. Salvation punctured original sin, arriving as a mysterious "matter of course." When taking on the foibles of liberal theology, Lowrie, like Haroutunian, felt comfortable returning to aspects of the Protestant Reformation. If pushed, he agreed with Niebuhr on many points about how man's freedom of choice brought forth sin. In a world often rife with sinful actions, Lowrie shared Kierkegaard's conviction that religion without fervent belief was empty. Lowrie engaged in a difficult balancing act. His existentialism demanded human freedom, hence he rejected original sin, other than as a metaphorical construct. Yet he resisted joining the camp of liberal theology. His religious view was, as he often stated, one of "comforted despair," an inner despair that could never be banished from the earthly journey toward "becoming a Christian."

Thus the lines between Neo-Orthodoxy and religious liberalism blur. Historian Richard Wightman Fox notes that Niebuhr's vision, despite all of his attacks on Christian liberalism, "remained firmly liberal: human experience over divine revelation, social reform over individual salvation, ethics over theology."[49] While Lowrie's impassioned faith and Kierkegaardian stance were unrelentingly opposed to liberal ideals, they nevertheless shared with liberalism certain presuppositions regarding the possibility of salvation and human freedom. To be sure, with Barth and Niebuhr, Lowrie emphasized human sin and the immeasurable distance between man and God. But through the gospels and faith, expressed in a "thoroughgoing eschatology" of love, salvation emerged.

To bring this complex question of sin and salvation to a close, let me quote from an essay Lowrie composed only a few years before he died in 1954. In "Does Anybody Love God?" Lowrie suggested that salvation exceeded the bounds of faith and obedience:

> It would be tragic indeed if men were to suppose that the God who has made himself known to us as Father could be satisfied by obedience without love, or that Jesus Christ, who for us men and for our salvation came down from heaven and was made man and died for us, can be content merely with faith and worship. Kierkegaard affirmed in his journal, "God has only one passion—to love and to be loved." Suppose that in the whole of Christendom, where many, many millions of men profess to believe in God, nobody could be found who really loves him! This dreadful suspicion, far as it may be from the truth, might, I should think, prompt every man to interrogate anxiously his own heart.[50]

In Kierkegaard, then, Lowrie discovered license to express his own deepest belief that faith and love of God might lead to salvation when the individual began to "interrogate anxiously his own heart." Such interrogation, for Lowrie and Kierkegaard, protected the individual from complacency, driving him into an existential relationship with God, a relationship predicated on despair and hope, faith and absurdity. Lowrie had found these lessons confirmed in Kierkegaard, the father of existentialism.

6   LOWRIE HAD strong political views, but he generally had the good sense to keep them private. The inwardness of Kierkegaard well suited Lowrie's personal needs as he entered into the ninth decade of his life. In his ivy-covered home in Princeton, Lowrie increasingly felt frustrated by the events that shook the world in the 1930s and 1940s. He had initially been supportive of Franklin Roosevelt and the New Deal. But Roosevelt, "our Duce," had failed miserably in comparison with the Italian fascist leader Benito Mussolini. The New Deal had made no "permanent reforms." It had only "improved capitalism without erecting a different system." There is a radical perspective in these views, a type of either/or-ism that has Kierke-

gaardian intonations. Lowrie's political views, however, were colored most fully by his lifelong identification with German and Italian culture. Lowrie adored Mussolini, increasingly in contrast to Roosevelt, because he had succeeded in his efforts to lower prices, work with labor, and run things in a practical manner.[51] In 1939, after the Munich Conference, Lowrie penned a revealing acrostic that captured his political sympathies, and antipathies.

> Mussolini, Hitler, Chamberlain, Daladier—which wins?
>   MuSsolini
>   HiTler
>   ChAmberlain
>   DeLadier
>   whIch
>   wiNs?[52]

Lowrie came to believe that Roosevelt had "instigated Japan's attack on Pearl Harbor." In the causes of the Second World War, which pitted his beloved Germany and Italy against the Allies, he unearthed a cabal of Jews and British jingoists.[53] Once America had been drawn into the war, Lowrie worried mostly about the fate of religious belief. Perhaps during the war it would be best "to declare a moratorium of religion." Only after the war might it be possible to "slump back to the old position of regarding religion as a consolation."[54] Lowrie maintained that in politics, "Might Makes Right," nothing more, nothing less. In such a world, "God, Religion, Christianity, have nothing to do with this dispute." Neither the United States nor Great Britain had God on its side any more than did Germany and Italy. Here Lowrie made a point similar to Lincoln in his Second Inaugural Address, except for its different effects. Lincoln recognized that both sides believed that they fought under the sign of God, but he was willing to make judgments on the justness of one cause over another. Yet Lincoln acted with chastened fortitude and devotion to his ideal of union. Lowrie, in contrast, preferred to sit on the sidelines, despairing over the renewed destruction of European culture, failing to comprehend the historical and political context for the rise of Hitler and fascism to power.

Lowrie's political analyses did not come directly from Kierkegaard, although the latter's style of antithetical thinking, without movement toward the middle, may have had some effect. Kierkegaard no doubt granted to Lowrie a sense of inwardness in matters of the world and the flesh. One gained a strangely comfortable distance in the realization that the world was chaotic, and that the individual could not discern any logic or plan to it. Only in faith, only in the inner life, might sustenance be found. These views must have helped sustain Lowrie in the dark days of the Second World War, even if they failed to help him understand the ethical issues and moral imperatives involved in the conflict.

But for some of Lowrie's contemporaries Kierkegaardian inwardness did not necessarily lead to political quiescence, even in the face of Nazism. In 1942 H. A. Reinhold, a Catholic priest at St. Paul's Church in Yakima, Washington, related to Lowrie his own story of Kierkegaard and the challenge of fascism. Since 1923, while living in his native Germany, Reinhold had been "a fierce addict of Soren Kierkegaard." His equally fierce disdain for Hitler had forced Reinhold to flee Germany and to fight against Hitler. For Reinhold, Kierkegaard's was a "voice arguing outside the house which should make us bustle to clean our house and stir about." To "stir about" meant, for Reinhold, to be an antifascist, a voice in the German wilderness protesting the denigration of true Christian values.[55] Alas, Lowrie failed to "stir" on a critical issue of his time.

7   BY THE END of the Second World War, Lowrie had largely accomplished his task of making Kierkegaard famous in America, a thinker discussed at White House dinner parties. But with the late 1940s a new species of existentialism emerged, associated with Jean-Paul Sartre. In his late eighties Lowrie had to respond to the existential challenge of Sartre and address the relation between him and Kierkegaard. Not surprisingly, given his attachment to Kierkegaard and religion, Lowrie dismissed Sartrean, atheistic existentialism.

Lowrie had become aware of Sartre by 1947, through an article by his student Howard A. Johnson. Johnson much preferred Kierkegaard to Sartre, although he found in both thinkers a "mood" of angst appropriate to the present historical period. Sartre "knows the problem as Kierkegaard knows it, but he does not know Kierkegaard's solution. He shares Kierkegaard's *dread*. In a word, Sartre is Kierkegaard without God."[56] Or as Johnson put it in a letter to Lowrie, referencing Kierkegaard's well-known statement about the comfort that a Christian feels when adrift in an immense sea, "The difference is that Kierkegaard floats over the 70,000 fathom. Sartre sinks."[57]

Lowrie disdained Sartre and the French school of existentialism even more than his disciple did. To him, Sartre represented a false claimant to the throne of existentialism. Over a decade earlier, in his biography of Kierkegaard, Lowrie had addressed the question of existentialism in its German formulations by Friedrich Nietzsche, Martin Heidegger, and Karl Jaspers. While these thinkers did have certain affinities with Kierkegaard, Lowrie believed that such connections were often stretched beyond the breaking point. In terms of their styles of thinking, for instance, Nietzsche and Kierkegaard were joined; each "followed 'infinite reflection' beyond the farthest horizons." But Kierkegaard's denunciations of Christendom were not equivalent to Nietzsche's announcement that God is dead. The search for affinities between Nietzsche and Kierkegaard, as undertaken in Jaspers's book *Man in the Modern Age* (1931), was in Lowrie's opinion overblown. Certainly each thinker bravely encountered the "irrational" and the "absurd." In Lowrie's gloss, "This seems to me reasonable—but I cannot see why the 'Existential Philosophy,' which sets out to rescue the irrational from being ignored or devoured by reason, *must* reject the opposite irrational positions of both of the great thinkers it appeals to."[58] Lowrie uncovered deep existential meaning only in the productive paradox of the rational and irrational. Yet finding existential meaning failed to move the antinomian Lowrie to be part of any school that called itself "existentialist," unless it followed Kierkegaard's brand of Christian existentialism.

In response to Johnson's article on Sartre and Kierkegaard, Lowrie wrote, "The Kierkegaard/Sartre article might have mentioned the remark of some French critic, 'After the first W.W. [World War] Da-da was the fashion; after the Second W.W. Sartre introduced the vogue of Ca-ca.'"[59] Within a year Lowrie would present his own critique of Sartre: "From reading Sartre's plays and novels one may get the impression that Existentialism means chiefly the expression of crude and disgusting thoughts in vulgar words."[60]

"I protest indignantly against the common association of Kierkegaard *and* Sartre," proclaimed Lowrie in his essay "'Existence' as Understood by Kierkegaard and/or Sartre," published in the *Sewanee Review* in 1950. It hardly seemed fair for an "elderly clergyman" such as Lowrie to be forced to read Sartre's works.[61] But Lowrie entered the fray, defending the religious Kierkegaard against associations with the atheistic Sartre.

Sartre failed on a host of fronts, according to Lowrie's slight article: he is little more than a borrower from Heidegger; he is drawn to obscure metaphysics; he wallows in despair. Although Lowrie found Sartre's emphasis on death a useful tonic for an age that too often avoided the issue, he believed that Sartre's "preoccupation with death" was "macabre" because death was viewed simply as a *terminus* for the individual (390). For Kierkegaard (and Lowrie), in contrast, death opened up the individual to eternity. While Sartre's existentialism might share certain terms and emphases with Kierkegaard's views, it ran aground on the crucial issue of salvation. Sartre remained stuck, according to Lowrie, in the Kierkegaardian stage of the aesthetic, never making it to the stages of the ethical or the religious. For Kierkegaard, dread and anxiety, the "sickness unto death," existed within the experience of the individual's *"striving,"* of a "passionate tension which involves *suffering*" as this singular individual "cries out for reconciliation" and thus "exists in the highest sense only when he is 'grounded transparently in God'" (388–89).

According to Lowrie, Sartre failed to appreciate Kierkegaard's concept of dread. Sartre cannot overcome anxiety *(angoisse)* because he lacks a sense of the eternal (392). True, of course. But Lowrie failed to comprehend the importance of Sartrean authenticity and transcendence. Both become ways of overcoming the "nausea" of existence. Yet Lowrie correctly stated the logic of Sartre's position, which associated anxiety with freedom. Since man constantly confronts choices, he will constantly confront anxiety. In making his distinction between Sartrean anguish and Kierkegaardian despair, how-ever, Lowrie slighted the logic of "comforted despair" that had originally drawn him to Kierkegaard. While Kierkegaard presented a view of salvation, he also forced the individual in this world into confinement in anguish and despair, into a particular type of religious melancholy. Thus in a manner of speaking both Sartre and Kierkegaard condemned individuals to be anxious and to suffer.

FOR MANY THINKERS in the period from the publication of Lowrie's Kierkegaard biography in 1938 to the mid-1950s, dread and anxiety, espe-cially as formulated by Kierkegaard, came to function as powerful metaphors for their age and for human experience. Lowrie erred in his view that most Americans lacked a sense of death. In the shadow of the Second World War, the bombing of Hiroshima and Nagasaki, and the Cold War, a sense of death had become pervasive, part of the anxiety that confronted the culture. In-deed, as the poet W. H. Auden understood, these years composed an "age of anxiety." It remained to be seen, however, exactly what implications this anxiety at the heart of experience would have for American thought and culture.

Chapter Four

A Kierkegaardian Age of Anxiety

1   By THE MID-1940S, everyone, from soldier to statesman, seemed to be reading and talking about Søren Kierkegaard. "I feel that if people could instill in their lives the principles and thoughts by which Søren Kierkegaard wrote and lived, perhaps the world might be a better place," recorded Lt. E. MacFerguson, a U.S. Naval Reserve officer stationed in Florida in 1945. Yet MacFerguson's hope was mingled with anxiety: "I am beginning to wonder very sincerely whether we have gained anything by fighting a war, for the age seems replete with distrust, doubt and unfaithfulness. . . . [We] found more real brotherhood and honesty while under fire than I have seen since returning to the States."[1]

Around the same time, a minister at Davidson College Presbyterian Church noted with relief his waning enthusiasm for Kierkegaard: "I scarcely see how a man could live long under the strain of such tremendous existential Christian thought."[2] Philosopher Otto Kraushaar had anticipated such concerns as early as 1942, when he predicted that Kierkegaard would soon be "taken up by spiritually footloose intellectuals and made the darling of a literary coterie." Such a romance would be short-lived because "the path of salvation which he [Kierkegaard] maps out is pitched so steeply that few will have either the desire or the courage to go all the way."[3]

By the close of the 1940s, fascination with the "strain" of Kierkegaard's existential thought had spread throughout American culture. "A great deal of Kierkegaard's work," wrote poet W. H. Auden, in a volume he edited of Kierkegaard's writings, "is addressed to the man who has already become uneasy about himself"; it is designed to make him anxiously aware "that his condition is more serious than he thought."[4] For many intellectuals, Auden included, Marxist faith in dialectical materialism had once allayed anxiety. But the God of communism had failed. Forsaking his boyish faith in Marxism, Auden, relocated to the United States since the 1930s, found "mature" inspiration in Kierkegaard. Yet he did not see himself as trading one simple set of beliefs for another. In contrast to Marxism, wherein the laws of historical determinism trumped forces of contingency, Kierkegaardian religious thought remained tense, anxious, chastened, and problematic. This made Kierkegaard, in Auden's estimation, a "dangerous author." The Kierkegaardian bravely confronted paradox, irony, and tragedy—ingredients that struck a resonant chord in Auden and many of his fellow intellectuals in the postwar years. Auden described Kierkegaard as "a prophet calling the talented to repentance."[5] Even with choice, man "can neither guarantee nor undo the consequence of any choice he makes." Religious faith tiptoed around the brink of despair.[6]

Auden, in effect, helped create an identity for the postwar years when he published his 1946 Pulitzer Prize–winning poem with the title *The Age of Anxiety*. The poem's characters are debilitated by existential anxiety:

> Violent winds
> Tear us apart. Terror scatters us
> To the four coigns. Faintly our sounds
> Echo each other, unrelated
> Groans of grief at a great distance[7]

The poem captures the loneliness of individuals as "things thrown into being" (81).[8] Liberal pieties vanish with the destruction of the Temple of Faith and Reason. "I've lost the key to / The garden gate" (50), bewails one character. Humans exist in a world of deceit, chasing utopian dreams such as fascism and communism: "does your self like mine / Taste of untruth?" (7). After the death of communism, only religious truth mattered for Auden. Consumed with issues of faith and redemption, he feared that his fellow intellectuals and artists "would rather be ruined than changed, . . . rather die in our dread / Than climb the cross of the moment / And let our illusions die" (134).

Taken with the pathos of Auden's poem, young composer and symphony conductor Leonard Bernstein created his Symphony No. 2 for Piano and Orchestra, "The Age of Anxiety" (1949). Discordant rhythms and clashing cymbals captured the anxiety at the heart of the modern experience in "a kind of scherzo . . . in which a kind of fantastic piano-jazz is employed, by turns nervous, sentimental, self-satisfied, vociferous."[9] Like Auden's poem, it is an attempt to find courage and transcendence in the face of God's "appalling promise" (137).

A discourse of anxiety exploded into the vocabulary of everyday life in the postwar years. To be sure, this happened in no small part because of the legacy of the Second World War, the birth of the atomic age, and the emerging Cold War. The immediate postwar years also witnessed intense battles between labor and capital, the onset of the modern civil rights movement, and the rise of a culture based on consumption. Kierkegaardian categories of anxiety helped fashion much of the rhetoric of postwar American intellectuals. A flood of translations of Kierkegaard's writings from Princeton University Press made this intellectual expression possible. In addition, in 1946 Princeton published *A Kierkegaard Anthology,* whose editor, Robert Bretall, announced that "Kierkegaard's 'time' has come."[10] In 1950 *The Meaning of Anxiety* by Rollo May told Americans how to transform anxiety from a negative into a positive aspect of life.[11] As the character in William March's best-selling novel *The Bad Seed* (1954) remarked, "I was reading the other day . . . that the age we live in is an age of anxiety. You know what? I thought that was pretty good—a pretty fair judgment."[12] If so, then what, intellectuals wondered, were we to do in the dark light of such Kierkegaardian, existential knowledge? How might anxiety serve to induce courage rather than to freeze conviction?

2 THE POSTWAR YEARS in America exist as both an age of grand expectations and an age of doubt, couched in a revival of religion.[13] A 1950 symposium in *Partisan Review* indicated that "the mid-century years may go down in history as the years of conversion and return" on the part of intellectuals to religion.[14] While few *Partisan Review* intellectuals testified to deep religious faith (Auden being a strong exception), the symposium recognized that a religious revival was afoot in America. Even if most intellectuals remained nonbelievers, they now adopted the language of religion in their own work and thinking, presenting themselves as chastened and savvy thinkers. They contended that they had abandoned the false gods of communism or faith in the ability of science and technology to liberate humanity. In place of such belief systems, many intellectuals proposed a world view based on irony, paradox, and complexity that appealed especially to an upcoming generation of academic literary critics.

But this perspective also produced anxiety. Showered with academic appointments, entering into the solid domain of genteel luxury, this generation of intellectuals grew anxious about their status in the face of the democratization of the mind associated with mass culture. As intellectuals, they expected to stand as an adversarial culture. As influential proponents of anticommunism and literary standards, they found themselves increasingly endowed with cultural prestige. At the same time, they imagined that they felt on their necks the hot breath of Senator Joseph McCarthy's populist hordes. Intellectuals of the postwar years felt a mixture of confidence and insecurity. Such gyrations of the mind and soul brought them to consider Kierkegaard a kindred spirit.

For many of these thinkers, Kierkegaard promised a curious escape from chaos. Escape from anxiety, it appeared, only plopped one into new forms of anxiety: a religion more of "dread" than of "redemption." Rather than a religion of pious progress, Kierkegaard's religious supporters Walter Lowrie, Reinhold Niebuhr, and Will Herberg celebrated a sense of the tragic; they reveled in a vision of an incomprehensible God drawn from the Old Testament. Communist apostate Whittaker Chambers expressed this Kierkegaardian view in his testimony during the libel trial of former State Department official Alger Hiss: "Between man's purpose in time and God's purpose in eternity, there is an infinite difference in quality."[15]

Kierkegaard's mode of thinking paralleled that of many intellectuals of the Cold War era. During this period American political thought focused on the challenge of totalitarianism in general and the containment of the Soviet Union in particular. The very notion of a totalitarian enemy became, in the words of historian Abbott Gleason, "the great mobilizing and unifying concept of the Cold War."[16] The Soviet system became synonymous with totalitarian, godless enterprise. Many American intellectuals urged that an absolute difference existed between the United States and the Soviet Union. In this battle Americans had to make a choice to contain the Soviet Union. Sitting on the sidelines, refusing to act, irresponsibly allowed a totalitarian regime to prosper.[17] The choice, as Whittaker Chambers made clear, was between faith in God and faith in communism. Kierkegaard's mode of argument, positing two opposites, seemed to fit comfortably into this perspective. As he wrote, "Either/or is the word before which the folding doors fly open and the ideals appear—O blissful sight! . . . Yea, either/or is the key to heaven!"[18] Kierkegaard, unlike Sartre, was dead, and thus he could not utter a peep of protest against appropriations of his existential philosophy in the cause of the Cold War.

Leftist intellectuals generally dismissed Kierkegaardian perspectives and the turn toward the tragic and religious sense of life. Poet Archibald MacLeish announced in 1955 that the "Age of Anxiety" would soon become an "Age of Despondency," with an "Age of Desperation just around the corner."[19] Independent leftist critics C. Wright Mills and Irving Howe had warned, in the 1940s, about the cunning influence of Kierkegaard on intellectuals. Both Mills and Howe worried that an existential, Kierkegaardian emphasis on anxiety, inwardness, and religious transcendence presaged a shift from a pragmatic concern with changing the world to an almost neurotic interest in "personal tragedy." A tragic sense of life prioritized, for Mills, "personal malady" over politics: "Alienation must be used in the pursuit of truths, but there is no reason to make a political fetish out of it."[20] Howe concurred, finding Kierkegaardian intellectuals "so immersed . . . in *man's* cosmic suffering that they maintain their silence about the here-and-now sufferings of *men;* so fascinated are they by their private problems that they are indifferent to the social catastrophe which tortures all humanity." Perhaps they were not quite indifferent, Howe admitted, but helpless—less willing, in Marx's phrase, to change the world than simply "to mourn for it."[21]

In 1943, in the pages of *Partisan Review,* Norbert Guterman launched a political broadside against Kierkegaard's concept of the absurd and his religious passion. Echoing the resolutely atheist philosopher Sidney Hook's condemnation of the religious turn of intellectuals, Guterman maintained that "one can be a Kierkegaardian without trying to change either oneself or the world"[22]—an odd charge, since the notion of a transformation in one's being, through the leap into despair, defined Kierkegaard's thought. Apparently Guterman meant that Kierkegaard's emphasis on pure thought led to "a kind of theoretical existence" (138), at least in comparison with the materialist underpinnings of Guterman's Marxism. Guterman claimed that Kierkegaard's religious intensity combined empty individuality with deceptive autonomy achieved through social isolation. Kierkegaard's "religious radicalism was always accompanied by complete political quietism. The content of his demand for individual freedom is revealed to be absolute obedience" (139).

3 WHILE GUTERMAN excoriated Kierkegaard in the pages of *Partisan Review,* Otto Kraushaar, a professor of philosophy at Smith College, offered in the *Journal of Philosophy* the fullest early analysis of the political implications of Kierkegaard's thought.[23] In this article, entitled "Kierkegaard in English," Kraushaar wrote, "I labored hard to understand him, and myself," yet Kraushaar realized that he would "remain on the outside looking in on Søren Kierkegaard's storm-tossed soul."[24]

Although Kraushaar hesitated to call Kierkegaard a poet, as Lowrie had done, he viewed him as a religious writer wanting, as he put it in his article, "to *evoke* reflection rather than to transmit concepts or information" (565). One theme predominated in Kierkegaard: "the problem of the individual human existence, how it can transcend superficiality, chance, unreflected immediacy, nihilism—in short, how the individual can avoid becoming a complete cipher" (566). Thus Kraushaar raised the issue of his age: How to maintain individualism in the face of totalitarianism and mass culture? The totalitarianism concept allowed Nazi Germany and the Soviet Union to be understood as comparable political states, each growing out of the shift from tradition to modernity, and as comparable psychological responses to the problem of modern anxiety. Cold Warriors used the term "totalitarian" as a shorthand condemnation of the Soviet Union. American leftists employed it to condemn either the Soviet Union or Nazi Germany while continuing to be wary of aspects of American society that expressed a totalitarian temper. The European tradition of existentialism—as exemplified by Kierkegaard, Karl Jaspers, and Erich Fromm—with its emphasis on the individual in a "boundary situation" easily lent itself to a critique of totalitarianism.[25]

Surprising, then, that Kraushaar equated Kierkegaard's subjectivist thinking with "spiritual totalitarianism." The fact that Kierkegaardian man lived by faith and followed God absolutely, like Abraham, indicated for Kraushaar that the affairs of the day-to-day world were inconsequential compared with the infinite: "Just as long as the individual passionately embraces God's supreme authority, all else will take care of itself" (602). Thus Kierkegaard's God-saturated philosophy "is not inconsistent with any form of political tyranny, social injustice, and inhumanitarianism. He proposes no positive criterion whatever for deciding the moral superiority of one political or social system over another, while at the same time [in *The Present Age*] he vents his spleen on the democratic tendencies then current in his native Denmark" (602).

Kraushaar mixed up issues. Did the absolute word of God necessarily translate into political quietism? Abolitionist John Brown heard God's voice and acted in the temporal world. But as Kraushaar implied, absolute religious convictions did have political implications. Otherwise why make the argument that Kierkegaard's lack of criteria beyond faith could be used to support any political system? Although Kierkegaardian religion was not necessarily quietist, its political implications were unclear. Kierkegaard's hierarchy of values placed greatest emphasis on the passion of the individual and the exercise of the will. Such vitalism had a potential romance with fascism structured into it.

Much of Kierkegaard's venom in *The Present Age* (English translation 1940) was directed against the standardization and leveling of belief, both spiritual and political, in the nineteenth century. Kierkegaard opposed tendencies in mass culture to reduce the individual to a cipher of conformity and deference to the dominant opinion. He viewed the problem of his age as "understanding and reflection, without passion. . . . Nowadays not even a suicide kills himself in desperation."[26] Modernity bred overrationalization, which led to "indolence" (4). Kierkegaard contended that "unless the individual learns in the reality of religion and before God to be content with himself, and learns instead of dominating others, to dominate himself, content as priest to be his own audience, and as author his own reader, if he will not learn to be satisfied with that as the highest . . . then he will not escape from reflection" (35).

Kraushaar acknowledged the intrepidity of the Kierkegaardian individual as a force toxic to totalitarianism. After all, as Kierkegaard wrote in *The Pres-*

ent Age, "by leaping into the depths [of one's individuality before God], one learns to help oneself, learns to love others as much as oneself" (36). Nonetheless, Kraushaar found that the political implications of Kierkegaard's theology had "a greater kinship with totalitarianism than with democratic humanism" ("Kierkegaard in English," 603). Kierkegaard invested all authority in God, rather than in man. Thus he avoided the quasi-mystical associations between the absolute and the state that characterized Hegel's philosophical system: "Admirers of Kierkegaard, were too ready to welcome 'discipline' and 'stern authority' without inquiring too carefully into its forms and objectives." Kierkegaard's passionate individualism, while in some ways a corrective to the communal fascism of totalitarian systems, lacked an "unambiguous criterion for deciding between the right and wrong of political ideas and practices" (603).

Julius Seelye Bixler, a professor at the Harvard Divinity School, disagreed with the image of the proto-totalitarian Kierkegaard. To him, Kierkegaard, the rebel against conformity, offered a "sane and healthy relativism." While Kierkegaard promotes only a partial answer to our "social ferment," Bixler found that his productive paradox concerning the power of man and the ultimate power of God led to a humbling sensitivity that undermined the "spiritual authoritarianism" Kraushaar had warned against. Kierkegaard, Bixler wrote, "makes us keenly aware of the problem the individual confronts in his own soul in all its mystery, its unclassifiability and its moral urgency." Rather than presenting us with the radically subjective individual, Kierkegaard sees the individual as sharing problems, and solutions, with other men: "The decisions are the individual's own but he is not alone in making them. Each life is isolated but it is capable of being redeemed."[27]

Sociologist and management theorist Peter F. Drucker found Kierkegaard's devout faith "meaningful for the modern world in its agony."[28] Drucker maintained that Kierkegaard's intense inwardness and fervent God-centeredness battled against any totalitarian temper. A single question drove Kierkegaard: "How is human existence possible?" (586). Drucker found Kierkegaard's answer to be: Only in "tension" between the individual's existence "in the spirit and as a citizen in society" (589). "Human existence," wrote Drucker, "is not possible in time, only society is possible in time" (590). The social or temporal realm took a back seat to the spirit: "But existence in the spirit, 'in the sight of God,' requires that man regard all social values and beliefs as pure deception, as vanity, as untrue, invalid, and unreal" (591–92). Man exists absurdly, through "simultaneous existence in time and eternity . . . as one crushed between two irreconcilable ethical absolutes." Human existence is tragedy and despair: "It is existence in fear and trembling; in dread and anxiety; and, above all, in despair" (592).

How, then, to endure human existence? Drucker revised downward expectations for human existence. Tragedy worked against the naive optimism and utopianism of social organizations that had dominated the first half of the century. Totalitarian movements arose out of "the affirmation of the meaninglessness of life and the non-existence of the person." Totalitarian ideology confronted the problem of death by suggesting not how to live but how to die, through "the Nazi glorification of self-immolation" (597).

The meaning of despair for the individual became confused in Drucker's formulation. On the one hand, Drucker seemed to recommend despair over naive optimism. On the other hand, the Nazis seemed to transcend despair through death. Valid transcendence of despair and anxiety came for Drucker only with "existence in faith" to "overcome the awful loneliness, the isolation and dissonance of human existence" (598, 602). Faith offered the individual a sense of possibility that made life bearable, thanks to the promise of salvation and eternal life. Yet Drucker painted a tepid, un-Kierkegaardian existence, a life of rules and regulations, a holding pattern maintained until death lifted the individual into the realm of the infinite.

4 REINHOLD NIEBUHR also engaged the problem of totalitarianism and the despair of modern existence. Less a theologian than a prophet, less a philosopher than a moralist, Niebuhr dominated the American political and moral landscape of the 1940s and 1950s. Although he began as a radical socialist, he moved steadily toward a position of "moral realism," most famously in his Gifford Lectures, published in 1941 as *The Nature and Destiny of Man*. Niebuhr's vision of the world mirrored much in Kierkegaard: an emphasis on sin, a recognition of the infinite distance between man and God, and an acute sense of anxiety. Yet Niebuhr was also the Christian as advocate and activist, fighting to reform the world in a practical rather than a utopian spirit. Niebuhr benefited from Lowrie's translation of Kierkegaard, as did many others. Indeed, as Niebuhr's biographer Richard Wightman Fox puts it, "Kierkegaard's notion of anxiety—the existential dread of the human being face to face with his own finitude and moral inadequacy— was the key addition to Niebuhr's conceptual armor" in *The Nature and Destiny of Man*.[29] Moreover, Niebuhr's overall perspective was existential because it stressed man's freedom and ultimate responsibility.[30] Sin exists, and it dominates. But man remains responsible to act, within limits. And the limits that Niebuhr had put upon political action by the 1940s were clearly predicated upon firm anticommunism, New Deal reformism, and slow progress on the question of race.[31]

Niebuhr's *The Nature and Destiny of Man* served as the foundational text for a generation of liberals, led by Arthur M. Schlesinger, Jr., who upheld liberal democracy and battled totalitarianism. At first Schlesinger, like most liberals, dismissed any claims for the sinful nature of man: "We had been brought up to believe in human innocence and virtue." That changed because "nothing in the system of human perfectability had prepared us for Hitler and Stalin. The concentration camps and the gulags were proving human nature capable of infinite depravity."[32] Conservatives, such as Walter Lowrie and Whittaker Chambers, joined with liberals in championing this chastened perspective based on notions of sin and tragedy.[33]

Niebuhr had long labored to return a sense of existential sin to the conversation of American intellectuals. In looking back on the publication of *The Nature and Destiny of Man* in 1941, Niebuhr admitted that he may have overemphasized sin and the "corruption of human nature" and consequently downplayed the possibility of grace.[34] In Niebuhr's general outlook, Kierkegaardian anxiety and freedom coexisted. The human condition is marked by limitation and infinitude. Anxiety from "self-determinism" is a "precondition of sin."[35] Yet the anxiety of choice also makes creativity possible: "Man is anxious not only because his life is limited and dependent and yet not so limited that he does not know of his limitations. He is also anxious because he does not know the limits of his possibilities" (*Nature and Destiny*, 183). As Kierkegaard phrased it in *The Concept of Dread*, "If the object of dread is a something, then there is no leap, but a quantitative transition."[36] When man posits himself apart from God, or as a god, then he enters into the sins of pride and sensuality.

Niebuhr promulgated a view of Christian man that intended to steer between the twin evils of unrestrained human freedom and power, on the one hand, and the equally dangerous nihilism and anarchy that arose out of a lack of meaning, on the other. As an answer to this either/or, he proposed the "prophetic religion" of Christianity, so that "individuality can be maintained. This faith would do justice to both the natural and the spiritual bases of individuality." Niebuhr's Christian religion

> takes history seriously, it affirms the significance of the distinctive character achieved by each individual within the tensions of historical existence, tensions which have their root in natural, geographic, economic, racial, national, and sexual conditions. But since it interprets history from the standpoint of the eternal (i.e. since it sees the source and end of history beyond history) it gives the individual a place to stand within a world of meaning, even when and if the particular historical movement into which he is integrated should fail completely. (*Nature and Destiny*, 69)

Niebuhrian man acted freely within the paradoxical and ironic confines of history and his own limitations. The Christian conception of history compelled man to a chastened but energetic understanding of existence: "Christianity is not a flight into eternity from the tasks and decisions of history. It is rather the power and the wisdom of God which makes decisions in history possible and which points to proximate goals in history which are usually obscured either by optimistic illusions or by the despair which followed upon the dissipation of these illusions."[37]

While Niebuhr appreciated Kierkegaard as a "profound" analyst of anxiety (*Nature and Destiny*, 44), he backed away from Kierkegaard's overflow of passion. In *Fear and Trembling*, most famously, Kierkegaard had presented Abraham, in his acceptance of God's command that he kill his son, as acting against the ethical or universal. Such "absolute" action lacked ethical sanction and in fact could not be explained to one's fellows; it existed mysteriously as an act of devotion and faith. For Niebuhr this "passionate subjectivity" could just as easily involve false as true worship. What standards, Niebuhr asked, distinguished "the true God . . . from a false one? In other words, a passionate Nazi could meet Kierkegaard's test. There are standards of judgment in Renaissance and liberal universalism which make their ethic preferable to this kind of hazardous subjectivity."[38]

Here Niebuhr addressed a problem that other critics and followers of Kierkegaard recognized: Kierkegaard seemed to prioritize passion over reason, at least when discussing moral choices. The subjective interests of the individual, if passionately felt and believed, were valid, if presumed to be in accord with the absolute will of God. Abraham's decision to kill his son might appear to be murder or madness according to conventional ethics. For Abraham and Kierkegaard, it accorded with the absolute and the demands of faith. The chief Kierkegaardian control for subjectivity, Niebuhr found, lay in Kierkegaard's counsel that "Christian love is universal love, expressed as a sense of duty." This, Niebuhr concluded, sounded much like Kant's ethical imperative. But such Kantian universalism revealed "the sweat of a plodding righteousness, and it hides the fact of the self's continued finiteness." Niebuhr cooly respected Kierkegaard's passion and comprehension of the power of guilt and sin, but he preferred "a genuine commerce of repentance and faith between finite and sinful man and the grace of God."[39]

5   NIEBUHR STRESSED anxiety as a precondition to freedom, fully in keeping with the Kierkegaardian temper of the times. The psychological aspects of anxiety, the gnawing sense of despair and guilt, needed to

be overcome so that democracy might flourish and individuals might spurn totalitarianism. Such concerns about the tensions of life, the demands of the finite and the infinite, connected intellectuals in the postwar years to the discourses of anxiety and totalitarianism. They framed these worries along existential lines. The essential question of totalitarianism had less to do with the political economy of fascism or communism than with the personality structure and lived experiences of modern men and women. Fascism and communism became cultural and psychological problems rooted in the alienation of modern man.

Rollo May's *The Meaning of Anxiety* (1950) presented Kierkegaard as a secular psychologist and therapist for an "age of anxiety." May's work disappointed those, like Lowrie and Drucker, with a deep interest in spreading the religious imperatives of Kierkegaard. Prior to publication of *The Meaning of Anxiety*, May had contacted Lowrie. Might he, May asked, translate *"Angst"* as "anxiety" rather than as "dread," as Lowrie had done? Grudgingly, Lowrie gave May permission to shift the translations, despite the efforts of Lowrie's disciple Howard A. Johnson to persuade May to be consistent with the term "dread." At least Johnson took heart in assuring Lowrie that May was "1) a devout Christian, 2) an eminent psychiatrist, and 3) devoted to S.K. I expect him to make a real contribution with his book."[40] Johnson was only partly right. Although May was devoted to Kierkegaard and was a first-rate psychologist, his personal beliefs in Christianity did not prevent him from stripping Kierkegaard of religious intonations.

May attempted three things in his book. First, he sought to summarize the relevant literature on anxiety—philosophical (Spinoza, Pascal, Kierkegaard, Heidegger), psychological (Kurt Goldstein and Freud), and sociopsychological (Erich Fromm). Second, he wanted to explore the connection between modern anxiety and the totalitarian temper. Third, and most important, he intended to transform anxiety into an opportunity for courage and growth. He understood anxiety as an individual problem with vast social implications. Indeed, he hewed closely to interpretations offered in Erich Fromm's *Escape from Freedom* (1941).[41] Fromm had argued that modern men and women were torn by a state of anxiety. Totalitarianism redirected and harnessed such anxiety for its own nefarious purposes. How, asked Fromm and May, might individuals beset with anxiety function without succumbing to the siren song of the totalitarian state?

May began his book by attempting to distinguish anxiety from fear. Fear was something specific, a response to a particular threat: a poisonous snake, a rain-slicked road. Anxiety, in contrast, presented itself as a more generalized feeling, divorced from any particular cause. Anxious, subjective feelings threatened the core values of the individual. Since anxiety was nonspecific, and since it came at the individual from all sides, escape was impossible. Borrowing his overall structure from Heidegger's ontology, May considered anxiety to be part of the human condition. As Heidegger had phrased it, "That which anxiety is anxious about is Being-in-the-world itself."[42]

Though part of the existential human condition, anxiety manifested itself historically. Following the analysis of Albert Camus (the "mortgage of fear and anguish" that besets modern man) and the poetry of Auden, May described the present as an "age of anxiety."[43] The pitch of anxiety had increased in recent years, for familiar reasons: the depression, the Second World War, the atomic bomb, the Cold War. But these causes were specific and hence fit into the category of fear as much as anxiety. Indeed, May suggested a genesis of modern anxiety that reached back to the Renaissance. And by the end of the nineteenth century, May argued, alienated man had emerged, burdened by "insecurity, powerlessness, doubt, aloneness and anxiety."[44] Thus May's work refused to confine anxiety to the causal context of the Cold War era. He admitted that the Cold War played a role, but he preferred to confront anxiety as an ontological state. Since anxiety issued from the human condition, May's particular existential vision focused on the therapeutic self-realization and personal transformation that Mills and Howe had warned against.

May favored Kierkegaard's existentialist perspective as a way of comprehending modern anxiety and, most important, as a way of working his way to a solution. At first glance this seems an odd choice, given that Kierkegaard's key work on anxiety, *The Concept of Dread* (from which May borrowed copiously), begins with an attempt to demonstrate the collective nature of original sin. But May secularized Kierkegaard's analysis of dread and his emphasis on the critical leap toward God arising out of the either/or choice. Kierkegaard's *The Concept of Dread*, like any great work of depth and difficulty, can be read on a number of levels. It is a subtle study of the individual in dread, caught in the tension between the temporal and the infinite; it is also a critique of Hegelian abstraction. Yet it is saturated with the dialectic of religious despair and faith that empowers all of Kierkegaard's writings. "Dread is the possibility of freedom," writes Kierkegaard. But freedom is weighted with difficulty, absurdity, and is resolved only through faith.[45]

May argued that fascism was a psychological response to despair and anxiety. In times of anxiety, "people grasp at political authoritarianism in the desperate need to be relieved of anxiety" (*Meaning of Anxiety*, 10). Yet he made this anxiety largely ahistorical. He framed it in the language of Heidegger and Tillich as fear of nonbeing, of ceasing to exist or of existing with the horrendous recognition of the meaninglessness of existence. Fascism served, in May's analysis, to abolish the fear of nonbeing by sweeping the individual up into a collective purpose. Fascism took neurotic concerns and redirected them toward the mass hysterics of anti-Semitism or warfare.

Analysis soon gave way to therapy. May wanted his readers to acknowledge the problem of anxiety ("Innocence is ignorance," wrote Kierkegaard),[46] and then to transform problem into possibility. Kierkegaard, according to May, worried about how an individual might "will himself to be himself" (35). Kierkegaard maintained that only the individual, as individual, could experience salvation. Salvation would not come from conventional acts of piety. Rather, it came through religious conversion, in the dark night of the soul, when the individual realizes that he is damned, recognizes his inability to effect his own salvation, and, miraculously, transforms himself and receives redemption through God's love. May, like Tillich, replaced Kierkegaard's religious imperatives with standard existential terminology about the need for the individual to realize authentic selfhood.[47] Like Kierkegaard's process of "becoming a Christian," the road to authentic selfhood remained a difficult act of becoming, undermined by conventional modes of being (fitting into prearranged roles), social pressures, and a desire to escape into either self-defeating despair and guilt or a happy unconsciousness of one's own inauthenticity (35).

True freedom, authenticity, or self-actualization comes "only at the price of moving ahead despite" the pounding "shocks" of anxiety (56). May distanced himself from discussion of the social aspects of anxiety, away from political and even cultural analysis, toward a generalized discussion of how to overcome it. Anxiety proved to be valuable when it led an individual to greater effort and commitment. May noted that soldiers in the Second World War, by admitting their anxiety, became able to act with great courage under fire (228). Here again he seemingly confused the specifics of fear (fear of being killed in battle) with the more generalized aspects of anxiety (as part of the modern condition).

May also attempted to link Kierkegaard and Freud as twin exemplars of the triumph of courage over anxiety. But he failed to comprehend the depth of Freud's despair and the limits of his therapeutic consciousness. This contrasted with the more somber vision enunciated in Philip Rieff's celebration of Freud's chastened sensibility and "ethic of honesty" in facing the detritus of the modern age.[48] But with Freud, and existentialists, May concluded that "freedom involves responsibility," self-honesty, and human solidarity (233–34). "To venture causes anxiety. . . . Availing oneself of possibilities, confronting the anxiety, and accepting the responsibility and guilt feeling involved result in increased self-awareness and freedom and enlarged spheres of creativity." Selfhood comes when the individual "confronts, moves through, and overcomes anxiety-creating experiences" (233).

By the time he concluded his book, May had forgotten the particulars of modern existence, social context, and the role of corporate capitalism in shaping the modern anxiety-based personality structure. This failure constituted the core of his emerging therapeutic consciousness. In May's hands, Kierkegaardian anxiety had miraculously become apolitical and nonreligious, something that a proper attitude, desire for change and growth, and courage to create or love might overcome.

6   IN DECEMBER 1947 social philosopher Will Herberg worried that his friend, Rabbi Herschel Matt, was suffering from "a disease far worse than any neurosis . . . *the human condition*. All men are subject to it but most people escape its ravages by sinking below the level of self-awareness." For thinking men such as themselves, the anguish of self-awareness demanded a regimen of courage and, most important, *"faith* in the ultimate significance of things beyond our shortrange vision."[49]

Herberg developed a heartfelt theological response to the problem of the human condition. He borrowed eclectically from the work of religious existentialists as varied as Franz Rosenzweig, Nicholas Berdyaev, Karl Barth, Martin Buber, Emil Brunner, and, especially, Reinhold Niebuhr.[50] His central conviction of the power of anxiety as the means toward the leap of faith came from Kierkegaard. The final product of Herberg's pastiche might best be referred to as "born-again Judaism."[51]

Herberg's sincere struggle with the chaos of the postwar world, and with Marxism as the God that had failed, informed his acute rendering of the pain of modern anxiety in his book *Judaism and Modern Man* (1951). Herberg sensed that "the prevailing mood of our time is frustration, bewilderment, despair."[52] But, in the same vein being mined by May, Fromm, and Niebuhr, Herberg's existential engagement with religion and politics slipped when he confronted the question, What is to be done? Alas, as Herberg made clear in his next book, *Protestant-Catholic-Jew* (1956), most of his fellow citizens had chosen a tepid spiritual path. Herberg railed like a prophet for a self-awareness of anxiety as a Kierkegaardian prelude to the leap into true salvation.[53]

Like many in his generation of intellectuals, men such as Max Eastman, James Burnham, and John Dos Passos, Herberg began as a Marxist and ended as a conservative. Historian John Patrick Diggins demonstrates that Herberg smoothly shifted from the absolutes of the Marxist theory of history to a dedication to Judaism. Yet Herberg remained enough of a psychologist of belief to realize that both Marxism and religion bequeathed to the individual hope for salvation. "Until nine or ten years ago," he wrote in a 1947 article entitled "From Marxism to Judaism,"

> I was a thoroughgoing Marxist. . . . Marxism was to me, and to others like me, a religion, an ethic, and a theology: a vast, all-embracing doctrine of man and the universe, a passionate faith endowing life with meaning, vindicating the aims of the movement, idealizing its activities, and guaranteeing its ultimate triumph . . . a faith that staked everything on the dogma of Progress, that is, on the unlimited redemptive power of history . . . leading mankind through terrific struggles to a final perfection of uncoerced harmony amidst peace, plenty, and untroubled happiness.[54]

Of course, history had played cunning tricks on Herberg. Marxism "could not meet the challenge of totalitarianism because it was itself infected with the same disease" (26). Although Herberg recognized the role of economic and social histories in explaining both Nazi and Soviet totalitarianism, his analysis, like May's, focused on the emotional or religious appeal of such regimes: "Totalitarianism is not a political system; it is a spiritual regime, a way of life."[55]

Along with Niebuhr and other theorists of the tragic sense of life, Herberg believed that the true path to either religious salvation or secular wisdom began with anxiety and doubt. By 1950, as historian Richard Wightman Fox argues, a long tradition (both religious and secular) of tragic thinking had come to define American thought.[56] In his revolt against the absolutism and certitude that defined totalitarian faith, Herberg's born-again Judaism promoted an anxious faith. With Kierkegaard, Herberg felt that each individual trembled before God. The notion of such an anguished conscience appealed to those in revolt against the complacency of Marxists and of mainstream American religion. It did not, however, translate into an easy religion.

Herberg's existential theology closely followed that of Niebuhr and Kierkegaard. Paradox, irony, and the incommensurate nature of the God/human relationship were the defining features: "Evil is rooted in man's spiritual freedom and consists in the wrong use of that freedom, in sinful disobedience to God" ("From Marxism to Judaism," 28). Thus man is neither innately good nor fully depraved. All that matters is "the eminent dignity of the human personality . . . the infinite value of the individual human soul" (29). In any case, Herberg's Niebuhrian language indicated that freedom of will allowed for both good and evil, and it warned against doctrines satiated with optimism or benumbed with pessimism. Herberg's prophetic Judaism became "not a refuge from reality but a challenge to realistic thinking. It means an endless grappling with problems that are never fully solved" (31).

Herberg confronted with undeniable power the wasteland of modern existence in *Judaism and Modern Man.* Writing in the wake of the Holocaust, in the age of totalitarianism and the atomic bomb, Herberg discovered that "today, the all-absorbing problem is life itself, bare survival" (3). These "primitive" and existential problems were to be encountered by a "postmodern generation." "Man is the problem," warned Herberg: "The horrors of the hell within, the chaos and evil in the heart of man. It is this glimpse of hell within that so frightens us. . . . Whatever it is that has gone wrong . . . it is something within the soul of man" (6).

Herberg desired to penetrate into the absent soul of man: "Modern man . . . stands lost, bewildered, unable to understand himself or to master the forces of his inner and outer life. Despairingly, he confronts a universe that is bleak, empty and hostile" (25). Herberg began with the "ultimate questions of existence," with the "metaphysical dread" (14–15) of our finitude. In existential terms, he found that "human existence is nothing if it is not personal—concrete, individual, irreplaceable" (11). As he later noted in his introduction to a popular reader, *Four Existentialist Theologians* (1958), existentialism powerfully comprehended "experiential concreteness, personal concern and commitment, the uniqueness of the existing individual, the primacy of enacted being (existence) over the mere concept of being."[57]

Herberg's Kierkegaardian Judaism promised both realism and transcendence. He searched for "existential commitment to some system of values which, despite an inescapable element of relativity, is felt to be somehow anchored in ultimate reality" (*Judaism and Modern Man,* 16–17). He praised Kierkegaard as "that strange melancholy Dane, whose influence we feel on every side of contemporary thought . . . who says something about our world and ourselves."[58] Herberg's Kierkegaardian leap into faith, no less than his politics, involved a hard core of moral realism.[59] Because significant choices were invariably morally ambiguous, the individual faced existential situations with "fear and trembling."[60] Meaningful and compelling faith must be more than mere affirmation or rational decision to believe. For Herberg, faith was "*total* commitment" (*Judaism and Modern Man,* 38), a decisive break with the past. Following Jewish theologian Martin Buber and Kierkegaard, Herberg laid his existential cards on the table:

> The "leap of faith" that springs out of the decision for God—is not a leap of despair but rather a leap in triumph over despair . . . it is a leap that is made because—wonderfully enough—God has *already* been found. Faith is risk, venture, decision: so it is for us while we are still

on this side of the abyss. We must dare the leap if the gulf is ever to be crossed; but once the decision of faith has been made, it is seen that the leap was possible only because the gulf had already been bridged for us from the other side. The reality of the decision remains, but we now see that what we had to decide was whether or not to accept the outstretched hand offered us over the abyss as we stood bewildered, anxious and despairing at the brink. (39)

Lack of absolute security becomes not a liability but a positive good. If straining after meaning in the political arena is an antidote to totalitarian certitude, in the religious realm it helps the individual resist "self-absolutization and idolatry" (40).

Herberg argued that modern men and women craved tradition and community, and he uncovered the best grounding available to the born-again Jew in historical Judaism. Thus he made a controversial, but perhaps necessary, leap from the existential crisis of modern men and women into the welcoming arms of Judaic tradition.[61] Jewish theologian Milton Steinberg regarded *Judaism and Modern Man* as "more representative of Will Herberg than of the Jewish tradition."[62] Herberg considered the Jewish tradition to be living and breathing best when it responded to the existential needs of the individual. Judaism promoted salvation as much as a body of laws. In fact, his Jewish tradition resembled Niebuhr's Christian tradition: "Salvation is thus not the denial of personality but its enhancement through the power of personal communion in which all barriers of alienation are removed" (*Judaism and Modern Man*, 51). And historical Judaism bequeathed to its followers an institutional and law-entrenched mooring to protect against the despair that afflicted the individual.

Unfortunately, Herberg found the ship of Judaism, and of religion in general, adrift in modern America. A vague faith in faith and social camaraderie in the churches had replaced Kierkegaard's anguish. In *Protestant-Catholic-Jew* Herberg argued that the third-generation children of European immigrants in the United States had dropped all aspects of their inherited culture, save one: religious affiliation. Through religion, by and large, the third-generation children maintain their sense of individuality while also managing to "sustain their Americanness and yet confirm the tie that bound them to their forebears." The "spiritual values" of the three predominant religions in 1950s America all presumed the importance of democracy, which in turn stood for "the fatherhood of God and brotherhood of man, the dignity of the individual human being, etc."[63]

Herberg thus discovered an emerging American consensus in religious fellowship. But he worried that American religion had become confused with the "American Way of Life," defined as belief in the Constitution, free enterprise, social egalitarianism, and mobility (*Protestant-Catholic-Jew,* 92). Herberg had little against these values as such; over the years they would become the essence of his conservatism. Yet like Lowrie before him, he found much of American religion empty, marked by rote optimism and belief in progress. Such easy certitude led, in Herberg's view, to an American form of the totalitarian temper. Issues were reduced to "plain and simple, black and white" moral "crusades" (92). He remained confident, however, that the pluralistic nature of American institutions and countervailing powers would offset the dangers of zealous moralism.[64]

In the end, American faith struck Herberg as shallow, an "inner, personal religion . . . based on . . . *faith in faith*" (*Protestant-Catholic-Jew,* 103). He failed to find existential angst in the revivalism of Billy Graham that swept across 1950s America. Religion in America "becomes a kind of protection the self throws up against the radical demand of faith" (276). Borrowing from sociologist David Riesman's influential model of the other-directed personality, Herberg argued that American religion had become a form of social adjustment and therapy: "the conquest of insecurity and anxiety, the overcoming of inner conflict, the shedding of guilt and fear, the translation of the self to the painless paradise of 'normality' and 'adjustment.' Religion, in short, is a spiritual anodyne designed to allay the pains and vexations of existence" (283–84).[65]

Herberg attempted to maintain the anguish that constituted Kierkegaardian faith, but he failed to find an appreciative audience for his message. After a lecture in a Chicago synagogue, he admitted that his condemnation of "peace of mind" and "adjustment" theologies had "upset the audience."[66] Most Americans were not intellectuals with a tragic sensibility; anxiety did not appeal to his fellow citizens.[67] Instead, the common run of Americans were flesh-and-blood human beings looking for pat answers and easy sociability in their religious sentiments.

Herberg hoped that an emerging generation of Americans would engage in a more energetic, existential search after God, one that combined anxiety with courage.[68] But as things developed, the baby-boomer generation's search for God and authenticity took it in existential directions that Herberg found distasteful, both religiously and politically. With each passing year his critique of American religion became more muted as his disdain for liberalism and the emerging counterculture became more shrill.[69]

7 KIERKEGAARDIAN anxiety shadowed the anticommunist politics of both liberal Arthur M. Schlesinger, Jr., and conservative Whittaker Chambers. Both men were pivotal figures in postwar American anticom-

munism. Schlesinger exemplified urbane liberalism and helped found the organization Americans for Democratic Action. A man of extreme temperament, Chambers had progressed from an undercover communist agent to a born-again Christian. His fingering of Alger Hiss as a former colleague in the Communist Party spy apparatus catapulted Chambers to the center of the emerging postwar Red Scare. He explained his personal journey, and the contemporary fight against communism, in terms of sin and redemption. Schlesinger and Chambers both employed existential language, culled from Niebuhr and Kierkegaard, to stiffen the American resolve to combat communism abroad and at home. Critic Harold Bloom has remarked that "temperament, and not theology, determines the self's stance in religion."[70] If so, then both Schlesinger and Chambers developed a politics and a theology of anticommunism that fit each one's temperamental need for a tragic faith: faith in democracy for Schlesinger, faith in God for Chambers.[71]

Schlesinger knew about Kierkegaard and existentialism before he composed *The Vital Center* (1949), his call for a renewal of liberal vigor. Existentialism served as "fashionable confirmation" for ideas he already held. He learned of Kierkegaard probably from conversations with his friend Reinhold Niebuhr. In addition, Schlesinger no doubt read articles on existentialism in the pages of *Partisan Review*. He remembered that he may have first begun his "existentialist fellow-traveling" while a student of literary historian Perry Miller at Harvard. In any case, the brief notes to *The Vital Center* reveal Schlesinger's awareness of Albert Camus's recently translated novel *The Plague* and of Kierkegaard's key concepts. Whatever the origins and depth of Schlesinger's existential fellow traveling, his work fits into the period's discourse of anxiety and search for courage.[72]

In *The Vital Center* Schlesinger summoned Kierkegaard, as well as Camus, to reinvigorate liberalism. Liberalism had erred in the 1930s and 1940s in its sentimental belief in human perfectability. Such beliefs had often allowed liberals to be seduced by communism or by the excitement of the Popular Front period. Disabused of their faith in communism in the postwar years, liberals needed to pledge themselves to an aggressive anticommunist foreign policy. Liberalism also needed to dedicate itself to social reform at home by continuing the New Deal agenda. Schlesinger sought to protect his reform politics from both communist fellow travelers and rabid right-wing anticommunists.

A crucial political testament, *The Vital Center* stands in effect as an intellectual and cultural history of the anxiety of the era, and as a call to courageous action. In the initial chapter, "Politics in an Age of Anxiety," Schlesinger, like Herberg and May, described a new and pervasive sense of anxiety arising from modern "industrial organization and the post-industrial state, whatever the system of ownership."[73] In addition, America faced a difficult and long-term conflict between capitalism and communism, "a choice that we cannot escape" (8). Borrowing from Erich Fromm, Schlesinger promoted a psychological more than a political or economic reading of totalitarianism. Because of his training as a historian, Schlesinger avoided reducing totalitarianism's appeal to psychology. Yet anxiety ate at the heart of modern industrial experience and the Cold War. In the now dominant discourse, anxiety obliterated utopian memories of a time when "the sun of optimism was still high in the sky." A handful of thinkers—Dostoevsky, Kierkegaard, Nietzsche, Sorel, Freud, those "charting possibilities of depravity" (39)—had broken down the naiveté of the nineteenth century. In time, astute politicians of depravity such as Hitler and Stalin learned how to manipulate anxiety in order to build their totalitarian systems.

Schlesinger presents totalitarianism as a political faith that allows the totalitarian state, through mechanisms of terror, to allay the anxiety of the modern world. Totalitarianism promises certainty and truth, power and progress, in contrast to the "alienation and fallibility" of free societies (57). Yet there is a contradiction in Schlesinger's analysis of the relationship between totalitarianism and anxiety. Totalitarianism relieves anxiety by organizing the "social energy" of the masses by instilling "loyalty, emotion, and faith," which is then "focused upon a single object, and this concentration requires the maintenance of a high pitch of tension throughout society" (77). Totalitarian states replace anxiety with manufactured tensions. By focusing on fear, or by promoting tensions—hatred of the Jew in the case of fascist Germany, hatred of the "vestiges of capitalism" in the case of the Soviet Union—the state directs the attention of the mass, and the bureaucracy, toward a particular "problem" or fear (77). The totalitarian state is organized less against anxiety—a generalized emotion—than against specific tensions and fears, which are "resolved" by orchestrated hysteria and concentrated action. The health of the state thus depends on a form of perpetual tension (anticipating the concept of continuous revolution).

Whatever the difficulties present in Schlesinger's model, the problem of anxiety vexed Western democracies. Schlesinger resolved the problem in Kierkegaardian terms by moving from and through anxiety to courage. He replaced Kierkegaardian or Niebuhrian religious salvation with the courage and community of American pluralistic democracy. But he retained existential imperatives. In *The Vital Center* he quoted a well-known line from Kierkegaard about the "dizziness of freedom" in an age when "anxiety is the official religion." Existentialism confronted anxiety and alienation, and it held man (here Schlesinger paraphrases Jean-Paul Sartre) "absolutely responsible for the use he makes of his freedom." Alas, "such a philosophy imposes an unendurable burden on most men. The eternal awareness of choice can drive the weak to the point where the simplest decision becomes a nightmare. Most men prefer to flee choice, to flee anxiety, to flee freedom" (52).

As pragmatist John Dewey had promoted more democracy to cure the problems of democracy in the 1920s, Schlesinger proposed more liberalism to cure the problems of liberalism in the 1940s. Liberalism must be reinvigorated as a "fighting faith." First, liberals needed to be adamant about the value of democracy and its institutions. Second, and more important, emotion needed to be pumped into the liberal creed. Schlesinger began with a chastened and Niebuhrian sense of the human condition. Liberals too often forgot the sinful nature of man. A new, vital liberalism better understood the world when armed with "moderate pessimism about man" (165).

While recognizing sin and tragedy, democracies needed to instill passion (the passion of the Kierkegaardian Knight of Faith) into liberalism—a difficult endeavor because democracy naturally diminished absolute truths, softened zealotry, and encouraged compromise. These values constituted for Schlesinger the powerful and compelling articles of liberal faith: "Free society will survive, in the last resort, only if enough people believe in it deeply enough to die for it" (245).

An additional problem, one emerging as a nagging concern to theorists of mass culture, further undermined Schlesinger's call for an existential commitment to democratic ideals. In postwar American society, "standardization . . . has reduced life to an anonymity of abundance. . . . We have made culture available to all at the expense of making much of it the expression of a common fantasy rather than of a common experience. We desperately need rich emotional life, reflecting actual relations between the individual and the community" (252).

In the face of these problems, Schlesinger issued heartfelt jeremiads to evoke passion in the individual. As a good anticommunist liberal, he refused to turn a blind eye toward the problems that confronted America, especially the avaricious nature of capitalism, the blight of racism, and the need for national health insurance. He pleaded for an existential awareness that would move democratic man from anxiety to dauntless courage. Liberals must develop a "new radicalism [that] derives its power from an acceptance of conflict . . . combined with a determination to create a social framework where conflict issues, not in excessive anxiety, but in creativity. The center is vital; the center must hold" (255). Thus "out of the effort, out of the struggle alone, can come the high courage and faith which will preserve freedom" against the forces of totalitarianism (256). Although the economic boom of postwar America brought real benefits to many, it failed to address the structural problems of the underclass. McCarthyism, moreover, helped whitewash Schlesinger's distinctions between security risks and acceptable dissenters.

8 WHITTAKER CHAMBERS'S book *Witness* (1952) overflows with Kierkegaardian conservatism and Kierkegaardian language. Here the either/or choice between faith in communism versus faith in God is explicit, as is the necessity to choose to act rather than to choose to be passive. Chambers used Kierkegaard to frame his own theological stance. On one level, *Witness* recounts Chambers's life in the Communist Party and his decision to leave the party and work as an informer against party members—most famously, Alger Hiss, a high-ranking official in the State Department, whom he accused of having been an agent of the Communist Party. On another level, *Witness* is a religious parable, with Chambers presenting himself as a despised Knight of Faith, sustained only by his anxious faith. He becomes "an involuntary witness to God's grace and to the fortifying power of faith."[74]

On most theological issues, Chambers seconded Niebuhr's emphasis on sin, the paradoxical nature of man, and the possibility of redemption.[75] He initially found solace in the absolutism of communism, which seemed to allay his anxiety about the meaning of existence: "Communists are that part of mankind which has recovered the simple power to live or die—to bear witness—for its faith. And it is a simple, rational faith that inspires men to live or die for it" (*Witness*, 9). Chambers—"slowly, reluctantly, in agony" (15)—realizes that communism is "the focus of the concentrated evil of our time" (8). Communism is a false faith.

Thus, "in despair," Chambers breaks with the party, thanks to a religious conversion that grips his "whole being." He enters into a covenant with God that would be "decisive for the rest of my life, and incomparable in that I never knew it again" (84). But Kierkegaardian religious faith is never easy or secure. In the depths, Chambers swims with a sense of "peace and a strength that nothing could shake," but at the surface levels he remains "an erring, inadequate man, capable of folly, sin, and fear" (85). No longer a communist, he becomes a religious man, opposed to the orthodoxy he once championed.

After agonizing about how his revelations concerning the communist spy network will damage the lives of former comrades, Chambers explicitly invokes Kierkegaard to sum up many of his own thoughts. In fact, one passage appears four times in *Witness:* "Between man's purpose in time and God's purpose in eternity, there is an infinite difference in quality."[76] The passage is significant for two reasons. First, through it Chambers tries to explain the power of his faith and the depth of his conviction. Second, it places Chambers in the tragic, chastened religious camp, within the discourse of anxiety common among intellectuals of this period.[77]

Chambers wavers about what drove him to become an anticommunist apostle. Perhaps God chose him.[78] Chambers admits that he never did regard himself "as an instrument of God. I only sought prayerfully to know and to do God's purpose with me. . . . I only knew that I had promised God my life, even, if it were His will, to death" (*Witness*, 85). How could he, since he "did not suppose that anyone could know God's will" (85)? With resolve forged by a belief that he acts with God's approval, Chambers decides to bear witness. He confronts either/or, the fullest existential choice that an individual can make: "a choice against death and for life. I asked only the privilege of serving humbly and selflessly that force which from death could evoke life" (196).

Chambers came up against the problem that had vexed Herberg and others: on what basis could one justify a passionate choice of a faith in God over faith in communism? On this score, Chambers had no ready answer. Nor did he have a response to an allied question raised by Schlesinger and others in their reviews of *Witness*. Schlesinger had distanced himself from Chambers's explicitly religious slant. Why, asked Schlesinger, could not liberal anticommunist rationalists (atheists and agnostics) stand up to the threat of communism? This imperative defined Schlesinger's *Vital Center* and the anticommunist polemics of philosopher Sidney Hook. As Schlesinger noted, "Many Fascists and Communists have found a belief in their own infallibility entirely compatible with a belief in God; while many people who have not believed in God have had a profound sense of humility and contrition."[79]

In part, Chambers's either/or pointed to a mind more deeply divided than Schlesinger's. Schlesinger respected modern science and technology. Chambers, in contrast, divorced himself from the technological and scientific frame of mind. Only a belief in God, he contended, might contain the dangerous faith in the power of science and technology and in the utopian idealism of communism.[80] Only with God on his side could Chambers fight on the two connected fronts of anticommunism and antitechnological faith. Much of *Witness* celebrates the pleasures of rural life, the value of milking a cow or of self-sufficiency. Yet Chambers, no less than Schlesinger, organized his book around competing faiths, each of which speaks to the human need for a sense of direction and completeness in the chaos of the modern world. While acknowledging that communism is evil, Chambers refused to ignore the evil also done under the sign of God's grace. Hence his invocation of Kierkegaard's existential anguish, the sense of distance between man and God. Choices must be made, actions carried out, all with a chastened sense of self.

In many ways Chambers deeply identified with Kierkegaard's presentation of Abraham, the Knight of Faith in *Fear and Trembling*. After all, Abraham too makes the ultimate sacrifice in the name of absolute values. The typical tragic hero, according to Kierkegaard, acts in accord with universal values. Even in failure, that individual is understood and respected because he or she has acted with high idealism. But the Knight of Faith answers to a higher authority, to a voice that beckons him or her to act without any comprehension from others. Chambers may have allies standing with him against his former comrades, but he places himself in the position of the loner, the man of faith waging a "dark, continuous struggle, that is by his soul, and his soul alone" (*Witness*, 798). As Kierkegaard phrases it, "The knight of faith . . . is kept sleepless, for he is constantly tired, and every instant there is the possibility of being able to return repentantly to the universal, and this possibility can just as well be a temptation as the truth. He can derive evidence from no man which it is, for with that query he is outside the paradox."[81] The Knight exists beyond civil society.

According to Kierkegaard, Abraham's faith is, as it must be, absurd: he believes that in sacrificing his only son, he will have that son returned to him. The structure of *Witness* hints at this theme. It opens with Chambers explaining his actions in a letter addressed to his children, and it ends with him trying to communicate to his son the power of God.[82] Chambers may envy certitude, but he does possess a sense of mission. At times he believes that God may be against him (769). This occurs at a critical moment in the narrative. Incriminating microfilm that Chambers claimed to have passed on to Hiss in the 1930s is identified by a technician at Eastman Kodak as having been produced after 1945. Such a "fact" would crush Chambers's credibility and exonerate Hiss. Thus he thinks again of Kierkegaard and the absolute difference between man's purposes and God's. It shakes him to the "frozen core" of his being:

> I had sought to bow to God's purpose with me to the point of my own destruction. By my acts in the world of time, I had succeeded only in transgressing God's purpose. By informing against conspirators, I had misunderstood God's purpose, and God was making that clear to me in the one way that reduced my error to the limit of absurdity. He was doing so by a simple mistake on the part of the one authority that the modern mind held infallible—science. It was an irony too great for me. I felt it to be neither cruel nor unmerciful. For the quality of God's mercy in that juncture must be sensed as a function of His purposes, and, like them, could not be measured by the human mind. I knew absolute defeat. (769)

The anguish of "spiritual exhaustion" (773) leads Chambers to a botched suicide attempt. He learns that "no one who has been through such an experience can be expected to be quite the same man again" (776). The experience renews Chambers's perception of himself as a Knight of Faith battling the communists. As a chastened individual, aware of the Kierkegaardian distance between man's purposes and God's, Chambers concludes that the "God of Love is also the God of a world that includes the atom bomb and virus, the minds that contrived and use or those that suffer them; that the problem of good and evil is not more simple than the immensity of worlds." In the temporal world, "evil can only be fought" (797–98). Through a dauntless, existential engagement with evil, Chambers encounters his sin and gains redemption; anxiety transforms itself into courage.

However, the Knight's courage of commitment wanes over the years. In 1954 Chambers read Albert Camus's *The Rebel,* a resolutely antitotalitarian and radical tome. In a letter to William F. Buckley, Jr., he said that he found Camus to be "stunting in an intellectual glider, rising above the currents of the tricky, upper air. I admire his skill in the qualified way with which we admire a skill we shall never be capable of, which seems to have little relevance to us, and which (perhaps because of our limitations) seems to have little to do with reality." His Kierkegaardian inwardness standing in contrast to Camus's resolute willingness to fight, Chambers admits that he has become distanced from the nitty-gritty of politics: "I no longer believe that political solutions are possible for us."[83] He has been chastened by his own allies; the crude excesses of McCarthyism have taken their toll on him. For the inward, chastened individual, distance becomes more important than passion. Ironically, as Howe, Mills, and others had prophesied, Kierkegaardian inwardness has transformed a passionate anticommunist into a passive spectator of events. The Knight of Faith has become the Knight of Resignation:

> The enemy—he is ourselves. That is why it is idle to talk about preventing the wreck of Western Civilization. It is already a wreck from within. That is why we can hope to do little more now than snatch a fingernail of a saint from the rack or a handful of ashes from the faggots, and bury them secretly in a flowerpot against the day, ages hence, when a few men begin again to dare to believe that there was once something else, that something else is thinkable, and need some evidence of what it was, and the fortifying knowledge that there were those who, at the great nightfall, took loving thought to preserve the tokens of hope and truth.[84]

9 FOLLOWERS OF Kierkegaard often stumbled into resignation through sentimentalism. For such individuals, the vicissitudes of human existence, anguish, and suffering received attention, but they failed to penetrate the core of being. "Tokens of hope and truth" to ease human existence appeared more appealing than the "comforted despair" that Kierkegaard preached. Nowhere are such sentiments more fully expressed than in the writings of Thornton Wilder, a novelist and dramatist of astounding range and erudition.

"Following some meditations of Soren Kierkegaard," Wilder (with Lowrie, Chambers, and Niebuhr) recognized "the extreme difficulty of any dialogue between heaven and earth . . . about the misunderstandings that result from the 'incommensurability of things human and divine.'"[85] Yet Wilder creatively misunderstood Kierkegaard's rendition of Abraham's silence in the face of the absurd and the infinite. Wilder intellectually acknowledged that distance, and he strongly believed in God. As a writer, however, he sought both to capture the distance and to diminish it.[86] He felt compelled to comprehend the language and actions of God: "I always see . . . the urge that strives toward justifying life, harmonizing it—the source of energy on which life must draw in order to better itself."[87] He subtitled his Kierkegaardian-inspired play *The Alcestiad* (1955) "A Play of Questions." The existential questions he asked in that play, and throughout his life, were, What makes a life worth living? How can people cope with their despair and finitude? and What does it mean to live under the cloak of death?

Such concerns animate Wilder's Pulitzer Prize–winning novel *The Bridge of San Luis Rey* (1927), a gently ironic story about a random event: the breaking of the bridge that spanned a deep chasm on the road from Lima to Cuzco. Five people perish when the bridge collapses. Franciscan Brother Juniper asks himself how he, a man of faith, can explain what "lawyers call 'acts of God,'" or the jarring contingency of existence.[88] Brother Juniper seeks to uncover the logic behind this event. While his faith is deep, it demands a scientific rationale, and on this score he will be vexed in two ways. First, scientific evidence cannot explain the random nature of life and death. Second, church authorities misread his act of devotion to God as a challenge to faith, and he is burned at the stake as a heretic. Along with Brother Juniper's quest for knowledge, Wilder recounts the concrete details of the five individuals who died on the bridge. A brilliant rendering of each life fails to resolve the mystery of life. The ways of God remain mysterious to man, a perfect Kierkegaardian coda for Wilder's story.

The conflict between faith and doubt, as well as between regret and renewal, defines this novel. Wilder attempts to clarify the contingent nature of existence, and in the process to convey some wisdom about life to his audience. Such didacticism typifies his writing, despite his struggles to overcome it.[89] Thus one character, Dona Maria, announces, "Tomorrow I begin a new life. . . . Let me live now. . . . Let me begin again" (48–49). But the opportunity for a new life is cut short on the bridge. The brevity of existence marks the book: "We do what we can. We push on . . . as best we can. It isn't for long, you know. Time keeps going by. You'll be surprised at the way time passes" (85).

What conclusions, besides these obvious ones, can we draw from this novel? Certainly, as Brother Juniper comes to realize, and as Kierkegaard would emphasize with greater passion than Wilder can summon in this early novel, "the discrepancy between faith and the facts is greater than is generally assumed" (136). Faith thrives on this very discrepancy. To be sure, "we ourselves shall be loved for a while and forgotten" (148), admits the Abbess, a woman of great charity and wisdom. She also exclaims, in words that one presumes echo Wilder's view, "But the love will have been enough; all those impulses of love return to the love that made them. Even memory is not necessary for love. There is a land of the living and a land of the dead and the bridge is love, the only survival, the only meaning" (148).

A certain comfort comes with this thought, but does it engage with conviction and passion the nature of existence? It lacks the full-blown fury of Melville, the complexity of James's universe, and the deep sorrow of Dickinson's poetry. Wilder wants to present tragedy without diminishing it. But sentimental desire for an essential order of things, his deep-grained optimism, his quest for a solution that is more rhetorical than anything else, undermines the existential depth of his novel. In a 1953 interview Wilder admitted, "Despite everything, I am still an optimist."[90]

A sneaky sentimentality, despite Wilder's best existential intentions, invades his most famous plays, *Our Town* (1938) and *The Skin of Our Teeth* (1942), as well as many of his novels. Like *The Bridge of San Luis Rey,* these plays seek to render in concrete fashion the reality of everyday existence. "Each individual's assertion," Wilder later wrote in Kierkegaardian terms, "to an absolute reality can only be inner, very inner."[91] At the same time, Wilder reasserts points he had made earlier: that life is short, death is inevitable, and we must enjoy life while we can. And we can do so, despite anxiety, with courage gained by our sense of being part of a larger, continuous human project.

In engaging, tragicomic style, *Our Town* presents Grover's Corners, New Hampshire, over a period of about fourteen years. Each act in the play reflects one of the three stages of life: daily life, love and marriage, and, finally, death (*Three Plays,* 24). Wilder paints each character vividly, allowing us to gain a sense of how his or her life will unfold. In act III, the dead speak. Wilder's stage notes announce that "when they [the dead] speak their tone is matter-of-fact, without sentimentality and, above all, without lugubriousness" (57). All well and good. But in the first two acts the audience has come to identify with the characters, to feel that the rhythms and realities of their lives are not all that different from ours. Wilder fails to avoid sentimentality. That the dead are repositories of wisdom alleviates some of the anguish that the audience might feel about life without redemption.[92]

The presence of the dead props up the Stage Manager's comment, "We all know that *something* is eternal . . . and that something has to do with human beings. . . . There's something way down deep that's eternal about every human being" (59). One recently deceased character decides to return to Grover's Corners to reexperience life, albeit vicariously. The weight of knowledge about how things will turn out proves to be a form of anguish. The dead "think only of what's ahead" (66). But what can be ahead for the dead? In answer to the question, "Do any human beings ever realize life while they live it?—every, every minute?" the Stage Manager responds, "No. . . . The saints and poets, maybe—they do some" (72). In the end, few understand the contingent nature of existence; few confront the immensity of the universe. Rather than bringing his readers to Kierkegaardian despair, to a boundary situation in which the anguished individual either leaps to faith or accepts existential responsibility, Wilder creates an overall mood of gentle regret for opportunities lost. Perhaps the audience, on their way out for a snack after the play, will experience a muffled and soon to be forgotten promise, "I will make more out of my existence."

The Skin of Our Teeth captures the eternal interplay between finite and infinite, with survival through the turmoil of existence. In this clever parody of the Adam and Eve story, the Antrobus family, their children, Henry (Cain) and Gladys, and their maid, Sabina, exist eternally. Strife and calamity coexist with calm and hope in a world that seems to be at odds with the Kierkegaardian ideas that so fascinated Wilder. Optimism defies anguish, but the triumph seems sentimental at worst, and unearned at best. As George Antrobus confidently puffs, "Oh, I've never forgotten for long at a time that living is struggle. I know that every good and excellent thing in the world stands moment by moment on the razor-edge of danger and must be fought for. . . . All I ask is the chance to build new worlds and God has always given us that. And has given us voices to guide us; and the memory of our mistakes to warn us." Who would want to argue with that? A few lines later Wilder lays the optimism on a bit too thick: "We've learned. We're learning. And the steps of our journey are marked for us here" (161), in books and in the events of existence. As Sabina states, without the anguished, tragicomic conviction of Samuel Beckett's characters in *Waiting for Godot,* "We have to go on for ages and ages yet. . . . The end of the play isn't written yet" (163).[93]

Wilder, as much as any intellectual discussed in this chapter, struggled to incorporate Kierkegaardian existentialism into his writing. He failed, despite a lifetime of trying, to reproduce Kierkegaard's passion and anguish in his work. He probably first encountered Kierkegaard, perhaps through Barth, during his stay at the American Academy in Rome in 1920, where he went after graduating from Yale and serving in the First World War. There Wilder met Walter Lowrie, then connected with the academy. Both shared capacious interests and deep religious feelings. At that time, Lowrie was reading Schweitzer and Barth and through them was beginning to get a sense of Kierkegaard. However, Wilder's fullest investigations into Kierkegaard occurred in two bursts, one in the 1930s and another in the late 1940s and early 1950s.

From Wilder's journals we can glean a sense of his impassioned engagement with Kierkegaard. He read Lowrie's biography of Kierkegaard in 1939 with "enthusiasm" and later read most of Kierkegaard's writings, either in English translation or in French. The postwar turn to Kierkegaard common among intellectuals proved especially appealing to Wilder, given his professed desire to engage in his plays and fiction the themes of dread, evil, and the human condition.[94] Indeed, he came to see in Kierkegaard's writing a brilliant exposition of the comedic and tragic approaches to literature that defined his own work as a dramatist and novelist. Thus in 1950, borrowing from Kierkegaard, Wilder stated, "The novelist cannot write a novel which is felt to be an absolutely comic novel or an absolutely tragic novel. From his vast vista, human experience can only be regarded as presenting a synthesis of both."[95] Such a synthesis defined Wilder's project in the plays and novels already discussed.[96] But the competing strains of tragedy and comedy in his work resulted in a standoff, raising uncertainties about the nature of Wilder's views on existential issues.

Wilder takes the reader to the edge of an existential abyss but then retreats, showing the audience a nicely lit exit sign that offers an alternative to Kierkegaard's anguished leap of faith. In Wilder's work, the tragedy of existence is eased instead by a belly laugh, a polite shock of recognition, or a chuckle at the foibles of humankind. Is it a mark of inspired vision or of divine failure, for example, that Wilder's most famous play dealing with existential themes, *Our Town,* is routinely performed without apparent controversy in high schools around the country? Perhaps it all came down, for Wilder, to the following advice, given by the character of the Watchman in the self-consciously existential play *The Alcestiad:* "Don't meditate upon the issues of life at three in the morning. At that hour no warmth reaches your heart and mind. . . . Wait until the sun rises. The facts are the same—the facts of a human life are the same—but the sunlight gives them a meaning."[97] There are worse messages, but also deeper ones.

In the end, Wilder's creative work retreats into sentimentality. He presents tragedy with a happy ending. His George Antrobus is no existential hero or Kierkegaardian Knight of Faith confronting despair. He evokes only George Babbitt, the arch American individualist of the can-do spirit. Part parody, to be sure, Antrobus expresses the other-directed, therapeutic consciousness; he adapts and gets along with everyone. He is a character who is cheerful to the end, which he knows will never come. His faith is in the progress of the human race. There is no sense of a chastened spirit in Antrobus, although the events that swirl around him should have bludgeoned him into one. Wilder's Americanization of Kierkegaardian issues softens the hard edges of despair.

10 KIERKEGAARD'S wide influence on American thought of the late 1940s and early 1950s extended to postwar painters as well as religious thinkers and literary figures. While some of these figures found in Kierkegaardian despair a call to creativity, many ultimately succumbed to despair and resignation. Mark Rothko and Barnett Newman, both leaders of the New York School of painting, were two who fell under the spell of Kierkegaard. Both came of age in the period of the Popular Front, when art was presumed to serve the purposes of social change. But by the late 1940s they had rejected representational painting and its political intent in favor of abstraction. It would be too simple to equate their retreat from leftist political engagement with a Kierkegaardian turn. Kierkegaardian thinking coexisted with radical politics in the case of socialist and Catholic worker Michael Harrington[98] and, as we shall see in chapter 8, of writer Richard Wright. But as Mills and Howe pointed out, it was thinkers and artists in retreat from radicalism who embraced Kierkegaard most readily. In a sense, then, Kierkegaard did help move individuals away from the radical politics of the 1930s to the conservative, inward cultural politics in the 1950s.

Between 1948 and 1950, Barnett Newman produced a series of works that made a conscious nod toward Kierkegaard: *Covenant, Abraham,* and *The Promise.* In these paintings, and most famously in the canvas *Onement I* (1948), Newman perfected his signature style of the "zip," a line of color dividing fields of paint on the canvas. The zip in part suggested, according to art historian April Kingsley, the flashing light of a nuclear explosion and the Old Testament Pillar of Fire. Destruction and transcendence thus coexist within Newman's work, pointing in the direction of the paradox of the romantic sublime, wherein terror and ecstacy mingle. At the same time, the zip may be interpreted as holding fields of color together in an almost Kierkegaardian state of tension, akin to the fragile balance between doubt and faith.

Inwardness and an emphasis on the absolute freedom of the individual define Newman's artistic and philosophical credo. With characteristic bravado and naiveté, he once exclaimed about one of his paintings, "You know, that painting means the end of the capitalist system."[99] And in a sense, it did, from Newman's perspective, because his fevered search for the sublime annihilated the logic of capitalism and replaced it with an ethos of total freedom. Rather than the false choices of capitalist consumerism, Newman's existential freedom remained rooted in the responsibility of the artist to choose freedom over despair and conformity. Modern existence, in Newman's view, demanded that human beings become artists, learning "to live the life of a creator" as a way to overcome "the meaning of the fall of man."[100] Art and creativity represented for Newman a mythological and heroic "act of defiance," which opened the path to transcendence through engagement with the canvas and the unconscious (160). In the end, the artist needed to listen as carefully to his or her own inner voice as Abraham had listened to the voice of God. "Painting, like passion," Newman wrote, "is a living voice, which, when I hear it, I must let it speak, unfettered" (179).

Mark Rothko, more than any other postwar American artist, confronted the abyss of despair and struggled to find the courage to create. Like most artists, Rothko struggled with his own inner demons. According to Newman, at one point in 1950 Rothko felt that "he could not look at his work because it reminded him of death" (201). Kierkegaard and Nietzsche helped Rothko find a language with which to express himself both on and off the canvas.[101] Like Kierkegaard, Rothko desperately attempted to overcome despair. As his friend composer Morton Feldman put it, "You have only to look at a Rothko [painting] to know that he wanted to save himself."[102]

Rothko was drawn to Kierkegaard's themes of faith, sacrifice, and creativity, especially as expressed in *Fear and Trembling*. Indeed, the story of Abraham and Isaac served Rothko as a parable of the act of painting itself.[103] Rothko told his friend Alfred Jensen in 1956, "Last year when I read Kierkegaard, I found that he was writing almost exclusively about that artist who is beyond all others. And as I read him more and more I got so involved with his ideas that I identified completely with the artist that he was writing about. I was that artist."[104]

Rothko's biographer James Breslin has summed up Rothko's fascination with Kierkegaard's narrative of Abraham: "It is easy to see why Rothko read Kierkegaard's Abraham—single-minded and silent, admirable and appalling, renouncing the world, confronting 'dread,' devoted to a vision he cannot explain."[105] Thus Abraham became Rothko, the modern artist beset with anxiety, attempting to muster the courage to overcome it through creation. Rothko came to see himself as following his own divine commandments, pursuing his own inner vision, no matter the cost. He placed upon himself impossible burdens of creativity and depth. He wanted, through his art, nothing less than transcendence. His paintings, with their fields of color, their refusal to be figurative, and their inherent mystery, intend to capture the silence that is the essence of faith, and of art. Alas, while Rothko could identify with the Kierkegaardian Knight of Faith, like Chambers he faltered in the end. The ineffable eluded him, and in his later paintings the colors become increasingly dark and somber, the weight of the work more anxious and depressing. The dark canvases of his art and life became merged, and in his final act he orchestrated his own destruction by suicide in 1970. From politics and engagement to inwardness and suicide, Rothko crept along with the burden of Kierkegaardian dread.

11 DESPAIR JOINED with courage defined the theology of Paul Tillich. Throughout much of his life, Tillich had been politically engaged, a fierce opponent of totalitarianism and a powerful, if ambivalent, proponent of existential theology. Tillich's notion of the "boundary situation" presented human beings with choices in an apparently meaningless, anxious, finite world. He urged, with Kierkegaard and May (his onetime student at Union Theological Seminary), that individuals in such anxious situations act with courage.[106] This became especially pressing for the postwar generation: "We have looked more deeply into the mystery of evil than most generations before us; we have seen the unconditional devotion of millions to a satanic image; we feel our period's sickness unto death."[107]

Courage to survive and grow came to Tillich through religious faith. He discerned two forms of courage arising out of modern anxiety: the courage to be a part of something and the courage to be oneself. Each had its good and bad aspects, the former dangerous for its group-think, the latter for its narrowness. Secular existentialists often lost sight of how personality realizes itself only within a community of other individuals and in communion with God. "Is there a courage to be," asked Tillich, "which unites both forms by transcending them?"[108]

Tillich's answer, in *The Courage to Be* (1952), delivered as the Terry Lectures at Yale University, represented his movement from politics "to the psychology of the therapy-minded age," in the words of religious historian Martin Marty.[109] In this work Tillich spoke of the "courage to accept acceptance" (155), whereby individuals open themselves up, without losing their individuality, to a mystical "power of being." Like Wilder, he urged seekers to go "beyond" the helter-skelter of existence to experience a larger purpose. By movement through the anxiety of "boundary situations" (situations such as the reality of recognizing one's finitude), the individual reaches an "absolute faith which says Yes to being without seeing anything concrete which could conquer the nonbeing in fate and death" (189).

Tillich may have used the tough language of Kierkegaardian existentialism, but he airbrushed away the despair. *The Courage to Be* lacks the heft of his earlier work. He papers over paradox with a sweet reasonableness much like Wilder's sentimental Kierkegaardianism. Tillich began his lectures with a paradox befitting Kierkegaard: The individual appears unable to conquer guilt, or to cast aside the recognition of the meaninglessness of existence. Yet in the "beyond," which is nonbeing, the individual will discover that "all forms of courage are re-established in the power of God above the God of theism." Tillich concludes, "The courage to be is rooted in the God who appears when God has disappeared in the anxiety of doubt" (190). Through doubt, God enters—a Kierkegaardian scenario. Discovery of a meaning beyond the self erases anxiety: "Every act of courage is a manifestation of the ground of being, however questionable the content of the act may be. The content may hide or distort true being, the courage in it reveals true being" (181). In the very language that he employed to reinstate a God for an age of anxiety and meaninglessness, Tillich paradoxically proposed a God who places the meaninglessness of existence in abeyance. Mystical effusions promised "acceptance of that which we do not know the power of" (181). This therapeutic vision verges on vitalism. Values and politics are left out of the discussion; all that remains is growth and self-actualization. In the summation of historian Richard Wightman Fox, Tillich's vision of responsibility and courage meant "responsibility to one's own self: adjust, develop, reach for fulfillment."[110]

12 WHILE AUTHOR Walker Percy never became an apostle of therapeutic culture, his engagement with Kierkegaard, like Tillich's, also ended in adjustment, with courage defined as acceptance of things.[111] Anxiety and courage are central themes for Percy. In an essay on existentialism he suggested that the possibility of the atomic bomb being dropped need not be a cause of anxiety: "The real anxiety question, the question no one asks because no one wants to, is . . . What if the Bomb should *not* fall. What then?"[112] Then man would come face to face with the permanency of his state of alienation.

Percy's characters are alienated; they suffer a quiet anguish. Their inward, religiously oriented despair opens them to salvation through acts of Kierkegaardian repetition (rotation is an associated concept frequently employed by Percy in his novels and essays). In the case of Binx Bolling, the protagonist of *The Moviegoer* (1959), salvation comes from a leap into the rhythms of life, a settling into a kind of chastened responsibility.[113] Existential angst powers Percy's Kierkegaardian universe, but as with Herberg, Chambers, and Wilder, it degenerates into a force of passivity and conservatism, as a courage to exist quietly, apart from the battles of society. It is a philosophical retreat from politics into the larger, more enduring questions of existence and the nature of truth.[114]

AT THE VERY MOMENT in the late 1940s and early 1950s when Wilder, Tillich, Percy, and others were embracing Kierkegaard, another form of existentialist philosophy was capturing the attention of Americans. French existentialism, associated with Jean-Paul Sartre, Simone de Beauvoir, and Albert Camus—more atheistic, hard-edged, and bleak, yet tinged with responsibility and commitment in the face of the absurd—began to push Kierkegaard into the background. The torch of existentialism passed from Kierkegaard to Sartre, with great implications for the history of American existentialism and culture.

William James, who looked deep into the abyss in both his philosophy and his personal life, finally forged a philosophy to overcome his dread. (Photograph by Alice Broughton. By permission of the Houghton Library, Harvard University. Shelf mark pfMS AM 1092.)

Edward Hopper, *Automat* (1927). In his urban paintings Hopper captured the loneliness of the modern world, the existential ache of alienation.
(Oil on canvas, 28⅛ × 36 inches. Des Moines Art Center Permanent Collections.)

Edmond O'Brien, playing Frank Bigelow in the noir classic *D.O.A.*, experiences life most fully only after he learns that he has but days to live. (Wisconsin Center for Film and Theater Research)

Arthur M. Schlesinger, Jr., and Whittaker Chambers. Although they disagreed on politics in general, they shared an anticommunist animus. Each was convinced that he could harness existential terms, borrowed from Kierkegaard, to rouse the American public. (Library of Congress)

This *New Yorker* cartoon from 1948 captures the cultural, and financial, allure of things French. Existentialism profited in some ways from such associations. (*The New Yorker* 24 [11 Sept. 1948]: 66)

In the film *Funny Face*, Audrey Hepburn is attracted by the charms of a French philosopher (modeled on Sartre), but she ends up with an American fashion photographer, played by Fred Astaire. (Wisconsin Center for Film and Theater Research)

Simone de Beauvoir found few things in America to her liking, other than Chicago novelist Nelson Algren. They are pictured here together in France. (Ohio State University Libraries)

In addition to popularizing existentialism through books and translations, Hazel E. Barnes discussed the doctrine on the television series *Self-Encounter* in 1961. (Courtesy of Hazel E. Barnes)

Richard Wright displays a copy of his underappreciated existential novel *The Outsider.* (Yale Collection of American Literature, Beinecke Rare Book and Manuscript Library)

Although Ralph Ellison disliked being reduced to any particular school of writing or thought, his work fits comfortably within the canon of American existentialism. (Library of Congress)

Robert Frank, "St. Petersburg, Florida" (*above*). Here Frank juxtaposes the immobility of the aged with the movement of the streaking car. "Covered Car—Long Beach, California" (*below*). In this classic image Frank presents his death-saturated vision of America, complete with palm trees, cryptlike building, and shrouded car. (Copyright *The Americans*, Robert Frank, courtesy Pace/MacGill Gallery, New York)

Robert Frank, "Bar—Las Vegas, Nevada" (*above*). The liveliness of the jukebox is juxtaposed with the languor of the man. "New Orleans Trolley" (*below*). Taken during the Jim Crow era, this photograph captures the pain of segregation and the confinement of African Americans. (Copyright *The Americans,* Robert Frank, courtesy Pace/MacGill Gallery, New York)

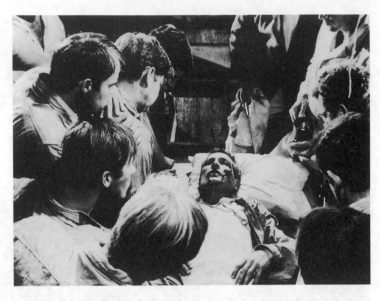

Paul Newman, playing Lucas Jackson in the film *Cool Hand Luke,* may be beaten to a pulp by the prison authorities, but he refuses to surrender his authenticity. (Wisconsin Center for Film and Theater Research)

Like many other student radicals in the 1960s, Tom Hayden acknowledged his debt to Albert Camus, although he was often unable to adhere to Camus's strictures on not confusing rebellion with repression. (Courtesy of Tom Hayden)

Betty Friedan disagreed with Simone de Beauvoir on a host of issues concerning feminism and aging, but she considered herself a true proponent of the existential perspective. (Library of Congress)

1944–1960

The Era of
French Existentialism

Chapter Five

The Vogue of French Existentialism

1 FASHION, "LIKE A thief in the night," sociologist René König writes, "intrudes everywhere, ultimately casting its spell even over those that had never the slightest intention of yielding to it."[1] All aspects of modern society, from furniture to clothing to ideas, according to Gilles Lipovetsky, "have been won over by the fashion process, with its fads and its rapid shifts of direction."[2] Certainly a degree of fashion and faddism had attached itself to the initial reception of Kierkegaard. By the mid-1940s, many were commenting upon the "vogue" of Kierkegaard in America.[3] However, Kierkegaard's popularity remained confined largely to intellectuals, theologians, and writers. The popular and middlebrow press ignored him, at least until the late 1940s, when he became recognized as a precursor of Sartrean existentialism.

In contrast, the dissemination of French existentialism in the United States between 1945 and 1948 occurred simultaneously at the levels of both popular and elite culture. In both cases, American ambivalence about French fashion and the cultural power of ideas determined the initial reception of French existentialism. Whether greeted with respect and awe or with disdain and dismissal, it was always a subject of intense fascination. This fact led some to maintain that French existentialist ideas were nothing more than ephemeral imports from Europe without particular relevance to America or even to that thing known as "the human condition." By using the terms of vogue and fad to characterize French existentialism, popular magazines reduced it to a passing philosophical fancy, an object for consumption and disposal. Yet existentialism escaped consignment to the garbage heap of fashion; it proved to have a hardier existence, a deeper resonance, than its initial popularizers ever imagined possible.

During this period, "fashion, chatter, and journalism" relating to existentialism occurred simultaneously with serious considerations of it by American intellectuals.[4] Both sets of interchanges—between popular culture and existentialism, and between intellectuals and existentialism—revolved around essentially the same set of concerns and cultural context. Ideas are encountered with an aura already surrounding them. Context as well as content accounts for the reception of and interaction with ideas. Thus the American fascination with French cultural capital, to employ the concept of sociologist Pierre Bourdieu, structured the reception of French existentialism in popular culture no less than in elite culture.[5] This meant that French ideas, art, and fashion arrived in America with a ready-made "horizon of expectations," the automatic prestige of their French label.[6]

Two cartoons that ran in the late 1940s in the *New Yorker,* a magazine that apotheosized a certain middlebrow style in America, capture this perception.[7] In one, a rather disheveled street vendor selling ties at twenty-five cents each looks askance at his nattily dressed competitor easily selling the same items, elegantly labeled cravats, at one dollar apiece. Another cartoon depicts a doughty group of women gathered in a living room, with one exclaiming, "I know what! Let's have an Old-Fashioned before we start talking French." The continuing allure of France, of things French, in American culture must not be underestimated as a factor in the popularity of French existentialism. Well into the 1960s and 1970s, the attraction of French intellectual fashions remained unchallenged. As Alice Kaplan recalled in her memoir *French Lessons,* "In 1966 I first heard the word 'existentialism.' . . . It was the longest word I had ever heard. French was this, too, always—even in beginning French classes you heard there was a France beyond the everyday, a France of hard talk and intellect, where God was dead and you were on your own, totally responsible."[8] There is a difference in attitude between the cartoons of the 1940s and Kaplan's later account. The cartoons recognized both the cultural power of French fashion and the inflated nature of that power. Fun is being poked at the pretentiousness of both the French and their American acolytes. In contrast, Kaplan's account expresses a high degree of seriousness and respect. For this fledgling French scholar, the power of French language and culture is no laughing matter.

2 BETWEEN 1946 AND 1948, American audiences were introduced to French existentialism in the pages of *Life,* the *New York Times Magazine, Time, Newsweek,* and fashion magazines such as *Vogue* and *Harper's Bazaar.* These popular discussions stressed Simone de Beauvoir's lifestyle and Jean-Paul Sartre's attachment to the bohemian café scene more than their ideas. A cult of personality developed whereby the general renown of existentialism became intimately connected to the personal life of the philosopher and even to the circumstances of the nation he or she represented.

By granting that connection between philosophy and philosopher, ideas and national circumstances, the American popular press depicted existentialism as something that would be nothing more than a vogue in what Henry Luce, owner of *Time* magazine, called the "American Century." The middlebrow publications of this period trumpeted a vision of America as a land bathed in the bright light of growth and contentment. The nation's productivity and economic growth were assured; Americans' great expectations of material and personal success were certain to be realized.[9] Against this vision, magazine articles on Sartre and Beauvoir regularly presented existential doctrines as pessimistic effusions arising largely out of the exigencies of the Second World War, contingent upon the hardships and scarcity of postwar Europe. Yet despite the philosophical and literary pessimism of French existentialism—perhaps the bleakest in the history of thought—the popular magazines pointed out that Sartre, Beauvoir, and Albert Camus themselves demonstrated a remarkably cheerful outlook on life. Existentialist pessimism was thus depicted as largely a pose, soon to give way to the natural happiness of these philosophers. The dismal pessimism of existentialism would vanish once, thanks to American largess, the postwar European economic recovery began; and soon, the press predicted, Sartre and Beauvoir would leave behind their quaint bohemianism to bask in the international renown and royalties they would receive from their massive flow of cultural productions. In sum, the triumph of postwar America would write a new design for French intellectual fashion.

It would be a mistake, however, to view the dissemination of existentialist ideas and personalities in the popular press as a story narrated over the inert intellectual bodies of Sartre, Beauvoir, and Camus. As Anna Boschetti has made clear, Sartre and his followers carefully orchestrated their reception in France in order to capture the intellectual field, thus assuring, albeit briefly, that existentialism would dominate.[10] Sartre and Beauvoir attempted to impose their philosophical perspective on the American intellectual field (or at least to influence its reception) as well. The early articles that they published, as well as their personal interventions in American intellectual life, were wedded to a model of the philosopher as personality. If a focus on the concrete life of the individual formed a philosophical and literary base for existentialism, then this mode of presentation should not appear outlandish.

The intellectual situation in the United States differed markedly from that in France. Sartre dominated the French intellectual scene as the Sorbonne genius who had transformed the fields of philosophy and literature at a stroke and established his influence by the founding of the journal *Les Temps modernes*. In the less intellectually rigid and more decentralized United States, Sartre found himself and his ideas quickly appropriated by the popular press; he did not receive the full hearing by intellectuals that he thought he deserved.[11] In part the failure of some American intellectuals to engage fully with existentialism in the period immediately following the Second World War testified both to the flux of American intellectual life and to the need for American intellectuals to distance themselves from popular, ephemeral culture. In America, Sartre ultimately had little control over the reception and dissemination of existentialism. And, as we shall see in the next chapter, various factors beyond the left-wing politics of Sartre and Beauvoir diminished the scope of their influence, at least in the late 1940s and early 1950s.

3   JUST BEFORE the Second World War ended in Europe, before the atomic bomb forever scarred the physical and mental landscape of modern men and women, the existential figure and ideas of Jean-Paul Sartre alighted on American shores. Sartre's first article for an American audience, "Paris Alive," translated by Lincoln Kirstein, appeared in the December 1944 issue of the *Atlantic Monthly*.[12] In that article Sartre related how the German occupation of France had elevated every situation to one of life and death in which every gesture "took on the nature of an engagement." At every step the individual confronted choices, decisions about how to respond to an "untenable situation," which Sartre referred to in existential language as "the state of man" *(la condition humaine)* (39). He quickly, without so naming it, sketched the essentials of existentialism. During the occupation, he said, "we lived in the fullest sense of that trite tag, 'Man is mortal'" (39). (Beauvoir in 1946 would publish a novel, *Tous les hommes sont mortels,* translated as *All Men Are Mortal.*) This shocking recognition of one's mortality, according to Sartre, liberated: "Never were we freer than under the German occupation" (39).

In this essay of less than one thousand words, Sartre vividly captured, in nonphilosophical language, the key existential themes of authenticity, choice, the "presence of death," loneliness, responsibility, and the notion that "in his freedom in choosing himself, . . . [man] chose the freedom of all" (39, 40). Placing existentialism within the life-and-death context of the occupation would have paradoxical consequences for the popular reception of existentialism. To be sure, it granted to Sartre and Camus the romantic cachet of Resistance fighters. Yet it also suggested that existentialism, despite the reference to the human condition, might be historically specific to the Second World War and the immediate postwar period. The popular press proved unable to handle the tension between existentialism as part of the human condition and existentialism as historically concrete.

While many existential terms had entered American intellectual life a few years earlier through Kierkegaard, they received renewed attention with

Sartre. Most important, they now escaped their earlier religious context, thanks to the resolute atheism of Sartrean existentialism. While French religious existentialists, such as Gabriel Marcel or Jacques Maritain, received a hearing among Catholic intellectuals, they were ignored, by and large, in the popular press.

The stylization of French existentialism and its leading apostles, Sartre, Beauvoir, and Camus, for American consumption during the 1940s was in large part the work of American fashion magazines. In 1945 Sartre was granted a forum for his ideas in *Vogue,* in an essay entitled "The New Writing in France." Idea and intellectual strolled hand in hand down the boulevard of fashion: the magazine's editors described Sartre as looking "like the men on the barricades in pictures of the Paris Insurrection. Just forty, he is small, intent . . . [with] his worn trench coat, his pipe, his heavy-rimmed glasses . . . indeed, a man of the Resistance."[13]

In this essay Sartre emphasized the readiness of young writers, tortured both literally and figuratively by the war, to burst forth with a new, hardier French fiction. He showcased Camus, placing him squarely in the camp of existentialism. Camus demonstrated a "profound pessimism" that arose out of the confrontation during the Second World War with knowledge of the "reality of Evil" (84). Whereas Americans, Sartre explained, had felt this evil only at a distance, through depictions of the "tortured corpses of Buchenwald," the French had experienced it firsthand for years. Camus understood this suffering: "In war death strikes by chance, but in the Resistance death *chose.*" Camus emerged from the war a chastened individual, "profoundly sombre" (85). His "pure austerity" offered "the promise of a classic literature, without illusions, but full of confidence in the grandeur of humanity . . . passionate yet restrained . . . a literature which strives to paint the metaphysical condition of man while fully participating in the movements of society" (85).

A year later *Vogue* returned to Paris to present "Portraits of Paris," a textual and visual rendering of the city's cultural life and times.[14] This time Sartre did not write the text of the article; a staff writer recounted the postwar shortages of food and coal. A "general feeling that life is precarious and nothing is certain but uncertainty" hung over the suffering city of Paris. "To the young this is particularly depressing for pessimism leads them to believe that there is no point in long years of studying for the professions" (156). Yet in the midst of scarcity and pessimism, fashion and opera are beginning to flourish anew. A haunting full-page photograph of Camus, taken by Cecil Beaton, graced the pages of the article. The caption noted that while Camus's book *The Stranger* "stresses the absurdity of man's predicament, in his philosophical lectures, Camus is far from despair, saying in effect that in the present crisis of man fear is the great enemy" (157). A less impressive portrait of Sartre also accompanied the piece. He stands in front of a modern painting, surrounded by open folio-sized art books. Here the doctrine of existentialism is explicitly named, with the caption reporting that Sartre, "a former Resistance writer," is the "leading exponent of the controversial French philosophy of Existentialism" (162).

Images of Sartre as the quintessential French intellectual continued to grace fashion magazines as often as the ideas of existentialism appeared in intellectual journals. In an important piece in *Harper's Bazaar,* Simone de Beauvoir presented Sartre's ideas and personality side by side.[15] Titled "Strictly Personal," as if the personality of Sartre could somehow be separated from his philosophy, this essay helped feed the American desire to see Sartre as a fashion, a representative type, the existentialist as intellectual personality. Responsibility for this pandering, however, lay with Sartre and Beauvoir themselves. They deliberately cultivated such images of themselves as a means of gaining the attention of Americans fascinated by French cultural fashion.

Beauvoir quickly dispensed with the essentials of existentialist philosophy that Sartre had detailed in his novels and plays and in his "big philosophical work, *L'Etre et le néant*" (did the untranslated title have more allure, more authority?). In a brief paragraph she noted, without directly referencing it, Sartre's distinction in *L'Etre* between the *pour soi* (the thing-for-itself, marked by consciousness) and the *en soi* (the thing-of-itself, marked by what it is rather than by what it does). On the one hand, there are "*things* that always remain exactly what they are, in the 'given' world of contingencies and circumstances," such as in "the sleep of trees or stones" (no doubt a reference to Sartre's famous discussion in his novel *Nausea* of the unchangingly inert quality of a chestnut tree). On the other hand, Sartre does not "exist in the mood of things, and tries to affirm himself as consciousness and pure liberty" (113).

But after this brief philosophical prelude comes the essence of Beauvoir's presentation: a glimpse of Sartre the man. Sartre, apostle of "consciousness and liberty," readers learn from Beauvoir, "hates the country . . . he feels at home only in cities, in the heart of an artificial universe filled with man-made objects" (113). In shotgun fashion Beauvoir reveals Sartre's tastes: "violent antipathy for persons swollen with self-importance" (113), disdain for "any possessions" (158). We learn that the philosopher "doesn't own so much as a bed or a table . . . not even a copy of his latest work." Despite his stingy disregard for things, we are told, Sartre is a generous fellow who "has always spent his money as fast as he earned it, sometimes a little faster" (158). He "eats and drinks copiously, he smokes to excess, but he doesn't find it difficult to undergo privations" (158).

The personal and philosophical coexist merrily in this essay. Beauvoir now informs her American readers that Sartre urges man, as an independent consciousness, "to project himself into the future." In another aside to existential doctrine, she contends that humans must free themselves from the inert, inauthentic life: "If a man chooses his own ends, if he pursues them with passion, but, at the same time, without forgetting that they are ends merely because he has chosen them, he thereby achieves an absolute existence that carries its own justification" (158). In conclusion, Beauvoir states that Sartre "feels no qualms about being happy." Yet he confronts his own boundary situation of death with rare equanimity: "He isn't disturbed by the ultimate prospect of death; he thinks about it seldom, and then with a great deal of tranquility. His death, so it seems to him, is a future event that will still be part of his life; it is the final and necessary limitation by which his life can be defined" (160).[16]

From lowbrow to highbrow, magazines and journals pushed the notion of existentialism as a vogue, an onslaught of Parisian fashion in the form of ideas. Janet Flanner, writing as Genêt in 1945 for the *New Yorker*, noted in her "Paris Journal" column that "Sartre is automatically fashionable now among those who once found Surrealism automatically fashionable."[17] In January 1946 *Time* characterized existentialism as yet "another faddist version of Materialism."[18] A few months later *Time* again referred to existentialism, in a review of Camus's *The Stranger*, calling it "the latest highbrow buzz-fuzz."[19] In the *Nation*, art critic Clement Greenberg pronounced existentialism an important vogue that captured a "historical mood" of pessimism that might be "aesthetically appropriate to our age."[20] In the same journal, editor for foreign affairs J. Alvarez del Vayo dismissed existentialism as a retrograde individualist philosophy and the latest European vogue, superseding the earlier vogues of Bergson and Nietzsche.[21] As late as 1949, in *The Vital Center*, Arthur M. Schlesinger, Jr., positively recommended the "vogue of existentialism" for its "willingness . . . to grapple with the implications" of the "anxiety," "frustration," and "isolation" associated with freedom.[22]

Journals of serious opinion rose to the challenge to provide their readers with the works of French existentialism in translation, and with articles and review essays on the subject. In this rush to publish, to be part of the zeitgeist of fashion, a journal like *Partisan Review* resembled *Vogue*. In 1946 the *Partisan Review* came close, for a brief moment, to establishing itself as an organ for French existentialism. In that year alone it published, in translation, two selections from Sartre's first novel, *Nausea*, as well as "Portrait of an Anti-Semite," a piece from his book that would be published in America three years later, *Anti-Semite and Jew*; brief excerpts from Camus's *The Myth of Sisyphus*; and translations of works by Beauvoir and Jean

Genet. *Partisan Review* also published review essays and articles from the pens of New York intellectuals William Barrett ("Talent and Career of Jean-Paul Sartre"), William Phillips ("Dostoevsky's Underground Man"), and Delmore Schwartz ("The Meaningfulness of Absurdity").

Other journals worked overtime to popularize the work of French existentialists in translation. In addition to the pieces already mentioned, Sartre's essay "Forgers of Myth: The Young Playwrights of France" appeared in *Theatre Arts* and his "American Novelists in French Eyes" in the *Atlantic;* Beauvoir's "Eye for Eye" was translated for *politics,* a radical journal edited by Dwight Macdonald.[23] Along with Schocken's publication of the full text of Sartre's *Anti-Semite and Jew,* the Philosophical Library made available Sartre's *Existentialism* (1947) and *What Is Literature?* (1949). The Philosophical Library also brought out a slim volume by Jean Wahl, *A Short History of Existentialism* (1949), to help satisfy the hunger for words by and about the existentialists.

4 DESPITE ITS CENTRAL presence by 1946 in serious journals, French existentialism remained a hot topic in the popular press. Here the image of the French existentialists as bohemians and café radicals predominated. Bernard Frechtman, one of Sartre's chief translators, bemoaned "the vogue in America of Jean-Paul Sartre and his philosophy," finding that the popular press in America had focused too much on Sartre's personality. His ideas had been reduced to "a journalistic conception of an erratic left-bank bohemianism," even though undiluted Sartrean existentialism was, Frechtman maintained, of particular relevance to Americans: "Sartre is occupied with a philosophy that is immediately involved in the peculiar confusions that beset this generation in all aspects of its civilization, the private as well as the public."[24]

While Frechtman and the *Partisan Review* crowd attempted to make Sartre's ideas available through translation and commentary, the popular press continued to busy itself with propagating an image and a set of associations for Sartre and his existentialist companions. The grubby, garret aspects of the philosophy appeared to replicate its pessimism and despair. Ideas and images became sewn into the very fabric of existentialism in the popular mind. This popular representation of existentialism, the deep association of it with fashion and bohemianism, served to marginalize it and to drive away some American intellectuals, who at this historical moment were cultivating a new image for themselves and for the intellectual in America.

Well into the 1950s, American popular culture unsteadily balanced two representations of the intellectual: a negative view of the intellectual as a dangerous alien or ineffective "egghead," and a more positive view of the intellectual as an expert, a dynamo of constructive ideas. To be sure, as critic Andrew Ross argues, resentment against the figure of the intellectual was widespread in American popular culture. As the Cold War deepened and anticommunist sentiment mounted, culminating in the Alger Hiss affair and the Rosenberg case, the vision of the intellectual as communist ideologue, as a dangerous figure to be contained, became common.[25] In the presidential election of 1952, conservative pundits damned Democratic candidate Adlai E. Stevenson for being too intellectual. In the same year, Louis Bromfield, a well-known rabidly anticommunist writer, defined "egghead" as follows: "A person of spurious intellectual pretensions, often a professor or the protégé of a professor. Fundamentally superficial. Over-emotional and feminine in reactions to any problem. Supercilious and surfeited with conceit and contempt for the experience of more sound and able men. . . . A self-conscious prig, so given to examining all sides of a question that he becomes thoroughly addled while remaining always in the same spot. An anemic bleeding heart." Such "eggheads," Bromfield further proclaimed, had supported traitors like Alger Hiss, allowed Stalinism to thrive in America, and appeased communism abroad.[26]

The other popular image of intellectuals suggested that they need be neither "eggheads" nor weak on communism. In this view, the thinker was depicted as vital, patriotic, and middle-class. In 1954 *Time* placed sociologist and intellectual David Riesman on its cover. The accompanying article briefly highlighted Riesman's seminal ideas as he had expressed them in *The Lonely Crowd* (1950) and in his recently published *Individualism Reconsidered* (1954). Riesman had posited a shift in the personality structure of Americans from the Victorian-style "inner-directed" individual, who followed his own moral and ethical gyroscope, to the emerging "other-directed" personality, who wanted to fit in, to get along with others. *Time* also offered, in an information box entitled "An Autonomous Man," biographical data that stressed the breadth of Riesman's knowledge, his avoidance of specialized lingo, and his refusal to rise in the hot-air balloon of pure theory. Riesman emerged as the intellectual as Everyman, comfortable with his large and active family, living most of the year in Chicago with two servants and summering on a Vermont dairy farm. He was a "vigorous, competent" tennis player, a man interested in clothing, food, and good wine, and a fan of movies ("but not 'message' movies, because movies' proper message is the 'enrichment of fantasy'").[27] Indeed, the Riesman of the *Time* profile had less in common with the alienated intellectual of the 1950s than with the emerging ideal of the *Playboy* male (although the article took care to present him as a family man and good father, to enhance his middle-class appeal).[28]

This new view of the intellectual as solid citizen seemed threatened by the image of the French existentialist as developed in the popular press, yet it also framed the popular depiction of the personal and intellectual trajectory of the existentialists. The depiction of Riesman in a sense represented the coming of age of the existentialist, his growing up into a responsible citizen. Issues of alienation and autonomy in an age of increasing conformity concerned both Riesman and the existentialists, but Riesman addressed these concerns without angst. Their opposing lifestyles, the café habitué versus the family man, defined their differences and in the eyes of the popular press indicated the superiority of Riesman both as a serious and relevant thinker and as a role model. As bohemians, cultists of fashionable ideas, the existentialists posed no real challenge to American social and cultural hegemony. They were objects of fashion, to be ogled and wondered at rather than to be taken seriously.

5 FROM THE BEGINNING, the popular representations of French existentialists had emphasized their bohemian café lifestyle and their distance from the respectable middle-class rhythms of America. In one of the first notices of Sartre and existentialism, *Time* magazine reported that Sartre's "temple . . . [is] the respectfully bohemian Café de Flore on the Left Bank. There he spends most of his writing and preaching day."[29] More detail on the bohemian café lifestyle was offered in a long essay in *Life* with the rather daunting subtitle "Amid Left-Bank Revels, Postwar France Enthrones a Bleak Philosophy of Pessimism Derived by a French Atheist from a Danish Mystic." We learn that Sartre rises early and spends much of his time at the Café de Flore, "writing in longhand, holding business conferences, receiving visitors and newspapermen and seeing friends."[30] The emphasis is on the sheer oddity of a philosopher and writer of such prodigious output working in a public café—the existentialist philosopher as curiosity. The early accounts of Sartre and Beauvoir often focused on their working and living accommodations. The *New York Times Magazine* presented Sartre in his café habitat, drink in hand, "appearing undisturbed by the buzzing about him." According to the article, Sartre's "life has been that of the unattached intellectual of the Left Bank, a life divided between the hotel room where he sleeps and the café table where he reads, writes, drinks, receives his friends."[31]

The popular press maintained that these bohemian habits would soon be cast off as success spoiled the leaders of existentialism and pushed them into respectability. Thus the *New York Times Magazine* found Sartre and Beauvoir's "early period of Bohemianism," when "no compromise with convention was permitted," to have become a thing of the past now that "Sartre is a pontiff, de Beauvoir a well-groomed literary lady who has abandoned hand-knitted hose for the sheerest of nylons." "Now that they are respectable and well heeled, the old defiance and desperation are going out of them. Steam heat and modern plumbing have lured them away from the cold and not very clean [hotel] Louisiana. The age of scandal is over, they are making their peace with society, and who knows but that Sartre may end up in the French academy and Simone de Beauvoir in the College de France."[32]

This perception of respectability clashed with the existentialists' popular reputation for pessimism. Nearly all the early commentators emphasized this element of French existentialism. The first notice of existentialism, Janet Flanner's 1945 "Paris Journal" column in the *New Yorker*, had characterized it as based upon a "disgust for humanity."[33] Since Sartre's magnum opus, *Being and Nothingness*, remained untranslated into English until 1956, such characterizations of existentialism generally relied on Sartre's literary representations of the doctrine, such as *Nausea* and his play *No Exit*, as well as on Camus's *The Myth of Sisyphus* and *The Stranger*. The premise of *No Exit*, which had a rather short run on Broadway in 1946, revolved around a set of damned souls forced to endure the "crushing weight of eternity," according to one reviewer, proving the Sartrean point that hell is other people.[34] *Time* magazine remarked weakly that out of such existential despair came the responsibility to act, to make something of one's life.[35] The popular press, while aware that Camus had sought to distance himself from existentialism, nevertheless linked him with an existentialist style of despair and pessimism. In a review of *The Stranger* in *Time*, bleakly titled "Man in a Vacuum," the writer argued that "existential pessimism underlines every cold, gross, irrational detail of the story."[36]

Yet most observers described the leading existentialists as happy in their personal lives. Just as Sartre had been described as a merry philosopher during his visit to New York City in the early spring of 1946, Camus was perceived as "unduly cheerful" in light of the *"absurdiste"* aspect of his writing. When asked about the apparent contradiction between his personal optimism and his philosophical pessimism, Camus replied, "Just because you have pessimistic thoughts, you don't have to *act* pessimistic."[37] In similar fashion, the essay in *Life* had described Sartre as a hard worker who was nevertheless able to enjoy himself. Sartre and Beauvoir would "fortify their pessimism with succulent dinners topped by excellent vintages and rounded out by age-ripened liquors," then head for the nightclubs to dance into the wee hours of the morning.[38] In these popular accounts, the emphasis on the personal happiness of the subjects seemed to reduce their philosophical pessimism to a pose.

The popular accounts of existential pessimism linked it to the specifics of the war and the postwar European experience. Once scarcity and suffering ended in Europe, the relevance of existentialism too would vanish. The present dark period in French history, remarked a writer for *Life*, had helped the existentialists develop a bleak philosophy. "France was literally crushed in 1940 and the subsequent occupation. Many, particularly the intellectuals, feel lost, abandoned and hopeless." Thus "the intellectuals of the Left Bank, facing the uncertainties of postwar European life, think they have found in this new philosophy at least a partial answer to their problem."[39] In the strange existentialist juxtaposition of "degradation and dignity," reported *Time*, "Sartre's philosophy undoubtedly responds to the desperate need among modern pagans in Europe and elsewhere to find some rational justification for individual life and effort."[40]

The personal journey into luxury and success being experienced by Sartre and Beauvoir served as an analogue for the recovery of Europe. With economic recovery, the philosophical despair of existentialism would become a distant memory. Uncompromised bohemianism and a culture of scarcity, connected to a philosophy of despair, were in the process of being left behind as Sartre and Beauvoir embraced a "respectable and well heeled" lifestyle. *Time* satirically captured this scenario when it "reported" that the existentialists were now being referred to in Paris as the "excrementalists," and that such once "true-blue bohemians" as Sartre had been corrupted; they were now "bourgeois," they were "making money." Pascal, a waiter at the Café de Flore, once the bustling headquarters of existentialism, lamented the drop in patronage now that existentialism, its reputation "tarnished," was being challenged by the faddish ism's such as "Lettrism" and "Sensoralism" that "menace us today. We must combat them if we wish things to remain as they were in the good old days" of two years ago. Such was the cash value of existentialism from the perspective of a Parisian waiter.[41]

The centrality of existentialism in popular culture is attested to by the increasing number of satires directed against it. To succeed, satire must focus on an object sufficiently familiar for people to get the joke. By 1948, existentialism was firmly lodged in the popular mind as a French philosophy of bleak despair, marked by abstract concepts and big words: phenomenology, ontology, metaphysics. In a satirical *New York Times Magazine* article, "Thingness of Things," Paul F. Jennings described the hottest new fashion in French thought, the doctrine of "resistentialism." Founded by one Pierre-Marie Ventre, author of the play *Puits clos*, resistentialism "is a philosophy of tragic grandeur" that reverses humanity's long-term epistemological quest to fix the nature of things. In contrast to traditional philosophy, counter-phenomenological resistentialism "is the philosophy of what Things think about us.'"[42] So conditioned had Americans become to the presumed out-rageousness of French philosophical fashion that one person, not realizing that it was a takeoff on existentialism and Sartre's play *Huis clos*, was re-ported to have found resistentialism to be a "wonderful theory" and hoped that Ventre's *Puits clos* "would hit Broadway soon."[43]

Similarly, in the more highbrow journal of opinion *Partisan Review*, poet Delmore Schwartz launched satirical barbs at the pretentious quality of ex-istentialist thought. He worried that while the fad of existentialism might be in decline, the philosophy continued to be "taken more and more for granted, like cynicism, optimism, surrealism, alcoholism, and practically all the other well-known topics of conversation." Schwartz thus proposed a "re-vival of interest in the meaning of existentialism." He recommended that the essential meaning of existentialism could "be reduced to the following formulation: *Existentialism means that no one else can take a bath for you.*"

> This example is suggested by Heidegger, who points out that no one else can die for you. You must die your own death. But the same is true of taking a bath. And I prefer the bath as an example to death because, as Heidegger further observes, no one likes to think very much about death, except indigent undertakers perhaps. Death is for most a dis-tant event, however unpleasant and inevitable.
>
> A bath, however, is a daily affair, at least in America. Thus it is some-thing that you have to think about somewhat everyday, and while you are thinking about it, and while, perforce, you are taking a bath, you might just as well be thinking about what existentialism means. Oth-erwise you will probably just be thinking about yourself, which is nar-cissism; or about other human beings, which is likely to be malicious, unless you are feeling very good; or worst of all, you may not be think-ing at all, which is senseless and a waste of time.[44]

Perhaps the ultimate satire of existentialism, one that revealingly juxta-posed the falsity of intellectual fashion with the presumably real values of the *haute couture* world, appeared in the film *Funny Face* (1956). In this movie, bohemian book-clerk Jo Stockton, played by Audrey Hepburn, adores a French philosophy called empathicalism, the brainchild of one Pro-fessor Flauster. To make a long, absurd story short, Jo stumbles into the world of high fashion. She meets fashion photographer Dick Avery, played by Fred Astaire, and winds up going to Paris for a fashion shoot. This has been her dream all along: to see the Paris described in the song "Bonjour, Paris" as populated by a "den of thinking men, like Jean-Paul Sartre." While there, she enters a bohemian café and attempts to discuss philosophy with the esteemed Professor Flauster (clearly a spoof on Sartre). Flauster is, of course, a lecherous phony, more interested in seducing Jo than in thinking deeply. She punches him in the face, telling him, "You are supposed to talk like a philosopher, not a man." Dick Avery (the Astaire character) is a phony too, but a self-aware phony, and his self-awareness is his saving grace, granting him authenticity in the ephemeral world of fashion. In the end, Jo Stockton and Dick Avery fall in love, the fashion industry survives, and even the doctrine of empathicalism, stripped of its jargon and chief proponent, is found to have a bit of value, since the exercise of empathy is shown to be valuable.

IT WOULD BE a mistake to think that during the postwar years American interpreters simply reduced existentialism to fashion, caricature, and satire—to what Schwartz might have considered to be "senseless and a waste of time." Certainly the popular press had presented existentialism as a fashion. But as fashion sociologist René König realized, fashions take on a life of their own; they extrude beyond the boundaries of the ridiculous and insinuate themselves into all the nooks and crannies of culture. The very fashion of existentialism, in even its narrowest sense—a black sweater, short cropped hair in the style of Juliette Gréco—became a way for young women to identify themselves, through their dress, with something outside the middle-class consensus of Cold War America. Dress does, to a degree, make the man and the woman. And to dress in the style of the Parisian existentialist culture was to make a larger statement of protest through assertion of a counteridentity.

At the same time, existentialism, while being dismissed by the popular press, became part of the conversation of culture. It proved especially appealing to the young and to those outside the consensus. Intellectuals could only at their own risk ignore existentialism. In some cases the popular reception of existentialist ideas and the popular representation of the intellectual prevented the acceptance of existentialism among some intellectuals, such as those associated with the *Partisan Review*. But as the popularity and fashion of existentialism increased in the 1950s, other intellectuals responded to the clamor and rose to the challenge of existentialism. They slowly moved away from the popular view of existentialism as specific to the postwar European situation and demonstrated its relevance to American culture.

Chapter Six

New York Intellectuals and French Existentialists

1 SPEAKING ON behalf of the group known as the New York intellectuals, Mary McCarthy recalled that "[we] were all taken, more or less, with the existentialists."[1] That simple phrase "more or less" reveals much. "More" in the sense that between 1946 and 1948, New York intellectuals centered around the influential high modernist *Partisan Review* worked to popularize central texts in existentialism, to evaluate its strengths and weaknesses, and to judge how well it responded to the spirit and needs of the age. Thus in the vein of "more or less," art critic Clement Greenberg, hardly a fan of existentialism, admitted, "Whatever the affectations and philosophical sketchiness of Existentialism, it is aesthetically appropriate to our age."[2] In the end, the "less" would predominate among most New York thinkers. They rejected existentialism and its French apostles Jean-Paul Sartre and Simone de Beauvoir, despite existentialism's apparent affinities with the spirit of their age and with their own mode of thinking.

What happened? Certainly the fashionableness of existentialism made the New York intellectuals wary; they worried constantly about what they perceived as the horrific effects of popular and middlebrow culture. Given its popularity, existentialism fell victim to this early divide between high and popular culture. Even more significant in accounting for the lack of enthusiasm for French existentialism among the New York crowd were shifts in politics and cultural power. First, Sartre's radical "third way" position between Soviet communism and American capitalism in the postwar years tainted his existentialism for the New York thinkers who were by this time fully committed to their own anticommunist views. Second, although devotees of European high modernism, the New Yorkers stood increasingly confident about their own literary judgments and place in the cultural pantheon. They rejoiced when the center of postwar culture shifted from Paris to New York. While the New York intellectuals applauded European modernists of an earlier generation, they were in general less enthusiastic in championing the work of contemporary, politically independent Europeans such as Sartre and Beauvoir. In addition, the French existentialists demonstrated little interest in the thought of the New Yorkers. All of these facts made it unlikely that the New York intellectuals would celebrate French existentialists and their doctrines. New York intellectuals met the existentialists' boat at the dock and showed them around town but wanted them to leave quickly. Yet in their own manner some New York intellectuals worked in a thoroughly existential mode, albeit without designating it as such.

2 By the end of the 1940s, New York City dominated as the cultural and intellectual hub of the United States, if not of the world, in many areas: dance, theater, painting, publishing, and music.[3] The city became an ever more powerful magnet attracting aspiring intellectuals and artists; it became the place to be, the center of intellectual life in America. In New York City, as Anatole Broyard, coming from New Orleans recalled, "there was a sense of coming back to life, a terrific energy and curiosity. . . . [It] was like Paris in the twenties."[4] Dan Wakefield, a young novelist from Indiana, remembered that going to New York's Greenwich Village in the 1950s "was like walking into a dream" of energy and intellectual excitement.[5]

In this period New York defined the life of the mind and culture in America. Young soldiers just returned from the Second World War and armed with the G.I. Bill flocked to New York for education, both formal and informal. The polyglot city was also very much part of a worldwide conversation of culture. One of the unanticipated benefits of the horrors of the Second World War for New York City had been the migration of many of Europe's leading intellectuals and artists. New York became, in effect, a brave outpost for Dada, surrealism, and Frankfurt School theory.

The influx of European thinkers and the concentration of wealth and resources in New York City contributed to the idea that Europe had been eclipsed. Given the wartime destruction and the threat of Soviet communism, most American analysts of cultural power believed that New York had entered a golden age. In terms of painting, the New York School of artists, abstract expressionists and color field painters, confidently stepped forward. Barnett Newman spoke for many when he proclaimed in 1945, "New York artists have begun to feel themselves the leaders and bearers of the artistic tradition of Europe instead of, as heretofore, only its reflection."[6]

Excitement burst out all over the city, reflected in the group of thinkers known as the New York intellectuals. Although largely Jewish by birth and native to the city, or to Jewish ghettoes in places like Chicago, the New York intellectuals coalesced in the 1930s around their faith in Marxism and modernism. For them, serious thinking meant resistance to the dangerous allure of proletarianization, as well as to pure aestheticism. By the late 1940s the romance between the New York intellectuals and Marxism had withered.

Fascination with modernism and the desire to be *au courant* with European trends in thought and culture remained. Yet the New York intellectuals felt more comfortable with dead modernist masters such as Henry James and Franz Kafka than with living, politically engaged figures such as Jean-Paul Sartre. The former could be appropriated more easily, and they could not take a firm stance on issues of particular moment, such as the Cold War, the nature of Stalinism, the Marshall Plan, or nuclear proliferation.

In the postwar years, New York intellectuals focused their energies on undermining the Soviet Union, both at home and abroad. Many of them, though opposed to Stalinism in the 1930s, had accepted the program of Leon Trotsky. Such distinctions between different forms of communism lost their appeal in the aftermath of the Second World War. New York intellectuals demonstrated no interest in reclaiming what might be valuable in Marxist thought from its co-optation by Lenin and Stalin. In their view, America now reigned as the arsenal of democracy, and they viewed Stalin's bloody stain as the logical result of all communist, totalitarian systems. Moreover, thanks to the influence exerted by Hannah Arendt's *The Origins of Totalitarianism* (1951), New York intellectuals considered it a truism to equate totalitarianism with communism and fascism. Thus New York intellectuals, despite their own nagging sense of the contradictions and problems of capitalism, came to celebrate American democracy. The age of ideology, Daniel Bell confidently asserted in 1960, had passed; the Soviet Union and other communist states maintained control only through totalitarian measures. In contrast, the pluralistic United States was progressive and democratic. New York intellectuals marshaled support to fight communist totalitarianism and pledged allegiance to a vital liberalism. In the words of Arthur M. Schlesinger, Jr., the dangerous allure of totalitarianism in the "age of anxiety" required of liberals a "continuous and exacting commitment" to democratic principles, and demanded "recharging the faith in democracy with some of its old passion and principle."[7] This oppositional stance, in the minds of the New York thinkers, marked a new sensibility or maturity, a newly chastened liberalism or tragic sense of life.[8] With each passing year, New York thinkers became less able to appreciate how any sane person could reject their perspective. By the mid-1950s, some of them had grown deeply conservative, their names gracing the masthead of William F. Buckley's conservative journal *National Review*. Many, such as Schlesinger, Lionel Trilling, and Richard Hofstadter, inhabited the liberal camp, while Daniel Bell and Irving Howe continued to refer to themselves as social democrats. Others, like Dwight Macdonald and Paul Goodman, appeared to be quasi anarchists. In essence, the political posture of the New York intellectuals, while varied, reached consensus around anti-Stalinism.

Whether democratic socialists, new conservatives, liberals, or even anarchists, the New York intellectuals also feared the power of popular and middlebrow culture. A culture of conformity, these chastened intellectuals maintained, diminished cultural standards and undermined independent political activity. Mass cultural forms, such as kitsch art, imposed conformity wherever they appeared. Stalinism and postwar American capitalism, they argued, produced a cultural apparatus that led to the standardization of culture and the end of critical distance. With this narrow appreciation for the power of popular culture and the importance of cultural mongrelization at the core of modernism, New York intellectuals disdained the cultural celebrity enjoyed by the French existentialists. The notoriety of the French in the popular press, and their fame in Europe, forced the New Yorkers to confront existentialism— to make sense of the new movement and to assess its implications for their own ideology. Such interrogation pivoted around politics, both the politics of Cold War anticommunism and that of literary reputations.

3   AT THE MOMENT when French existentialism arrived in New York, American intellectuals were confronting existential themes through the work of novelists Franz Kafka and Fyodor Dostoevsky. These writers, with their emphasis on the absurd and tragic nature of the human condition, appeared both timely and enduring to the New York intellectuals. The New Yorkers especially identified with Kafka.[9] As Leslie Fiedler put it, "Only Kafka belongs particularly to us, and behind him the witty anguish of Kierkegaard, but Kafka is especial, polysemous, obsessive, fragmentary, a Jew."[10] The author of parables such as *The Trial* and *The Castle,* Kafka captured in his taut, symbol-laden prose the anguish of modernity, the alienation of modern men and women in a world where God's presence, or role, appeared mysterious or ambiguous, at best. Kafka became for the New York intellectuals the writer who captured "exactly and literally the human condition."[11] His allegories addressed anxiety and alienation in a spare language while confronting the faceless bureaucratic horror of modern existence. Although Philip Rahv, an editor of *Partisan Review,* hesitated to judge Kafka's worth as writer too quickly, he admitted, "It is clear that if Kafka so compellingly arouses in us a sense of immediate relatedness, of strong even if uneasy identification, it is because of the profound quality of his feeling for the experience of human loss, estrangement, guilt, and anxiety—an experience increasingly dominant in the modern age."[12]

Rahv also appreciated existential themes in Dostoevsky. Although Dostoevsky's most important novels focused on religious concerns with sin and redemption, they also confronted the existential possibility of total freedom.

What if, for example, one could get away with murder? Rahv identified with Dostoevsky's framing of these questions and with his stark insights into the problematic nature of absolute freedom and the necessity for responsibility in the face of that freedom. While nihilism, a world without values, stalked the pages of Kafka and Dostoevsky, these authors also detailed the absurdity of man's existence in the world. Their images of alienation, of the crushing power of a faceless bureaucracy in a world marked by that absurdity, became part of existentialism. Expression of this vision through art constituted the protest and the solution—the upholding of humanity's creative capacities in the face of such horrendous realities. Dostoevsky, no less than Kafka, according to Rahv, spoke to the horrors of totalitarianism and the choices incumbent upon intellectuals in the postwar years. Both writers' confrontation with death, the ever-present reality, granted special significance to their work in an age of mass destruction and inhumanity. Some, like poet Randall Jarrell, found this appeal nothing more than a conceit of overwrought metaphysics, a position that forced Rahv to bellow in protest, "If there's anything that's real, it's death!"[13]

The definitive efficacy of thinking through death, despair, anxiety, and alienation as guides to modern existence might have received a full hearing when the New York intellectuals confronted French existentialism between 1946 and 1948. Rahv well comprehended the existential challenge, the "loneliness and exclusion" of modern man in conflict with society: "Even his hope for salvation is ambiguous. He fears it as the final betrayal, the ironic confirmation of his despair."[14] New York intellectuals wondered whether despair could coexist with hope. But while they often addressed these themes in their own work, in the end they did so largely without coming fully to grips with the work of French existentialists. Two trains of despair and responsibility either passed in the night or derailed on the broken tracks of cultural politics.

4   AT FIRST, IN the mid-1940s, New York intellectuals excitedly greeted existentialist ideas. *Partisan Review* devoted itself to translations of the writings of the leading French existentialists. As early as 1945 it had published Jean-Paul Sartre's "The Case for Responsible Literature." By the spring of 1946 it had produced an issue devoted to French life and writing. Sartre's "Portrait of an Anti-Semite," from his larger project *Anti-Semite and Jew*, appeared in this issue, as did "The Provincial Portrait Gallery." In another issue *Partisan Review* published his "The Root of the Chestnut Tree." Fiction by Simone de Beauvoir and Jean Genet, along with Camus's "Sisyphus" and "Hope and the Absurd in the Work of Franz Kafka," also graced the pages of *Partisan Review*. In addition to this flurry of articles by and

about the leading French existentialists, the journal published, between January and June 1948, large chunks of Sartre's *What Is Literature?* Nearly every issue contained reviews of works by Sartre, Beauvoir, and Camus. Not to be outdone, in 1947 the journal *politics*, edited by Dwight Macdonald, published a special French edition, highlighting Camus's "Neither Victims Nor Executioners," Beauvoir's "Eye for Eye," and Sartre's "Materialism and Revolution." *Yale French Studies* dedicated an issue in 1948 to French thought and literature.

Initially the New Yorkers recognized that French existentialism resembled their own ideas. After all, both the New Yorkers and the French were politically engaged, emerging out of battles with totalitarian opponents. Many of the New York intellectuals considered themselves battle-scarred veterans of anti-Stalinist warfare. The existentialists, especially Sartre and Camus, had a certain romantic luster attached to them thanks to their work with the French Resistance. They had managed to uphold humanistic ideals in the face of horror. The New Yorkers, moreover, agreed with existentialism's preference for the concrete over the abstract, the contingent over the absolute. Each group accepted writing as a political activity. In writing, as Sartre argued, the author declared himself for or against the age. A chastened spirit, a sharp edge of pessimism, defined both groups, along with an emphasis on the difficult responsibility inherent in absolute freedom. Daniel Bell spoke for his generation of New York thinkers: "Ours, a 'twice-born' generation, finds its wisdom in pessimism, evil, tragedy, and despair."[15] The New Yorkers maintained, perhaps because of the popular press coverage, that existentialists threatened to make a fetish of despair. Yet both groups embraced a tragic sense of life in the face of totalitarianism and the Holocaust, and they prided themselves on jettisoning antiquated and naive notions of progress.

Despite these affinities, within a few years of the introduction of existentialism in America, most New York intellectuals had cooled toward existentialism in general and strongly dismissed Sartre and Beauvoir in particular. Typically, art critic Harold Rosenberg, while making existential terms central to his influential essays, refused to pledge allegiance to existentialism. Indeed, he attempted an end run, proclaiming the originality of his own ideas and further noting that he had actually influenced Sartre.

Most New York intellectuals were unwilling or unable to engage existentialism fully. Hannah Arendt, a political philosopher, European émigré, and former student of Martin Heidegger, possessed the ability to decipher existentialism for New Yorkers, but her contributions failed miserably. She preferred to linger on abstruse Kantian categories rather than to bring alive the sweep of existentialism. William Barrett, a professor of philosophy at New York University and an editor of *Partisan Review,* published "What Is Existentialism?" in that journal in 1947 (the article was reissued as part of a pamphlet in 1948). These opening gambits only revealed the inability of most New York intellectuals to comprehend the relevance of existentialist thinking. Arendt and Barrett largely ignored Sartre and inflated Heidegger. Ironically, they found it easier to overlook Heidegger's support for Nazism than Sartre's complex engagement with Marxism. Even if the New York intellectuals of the late 1940s had desired a fuller accounting with existentialist philosophy than the bits and pieces of works translated from Sartre and company in *Partisan Review,* they would have been stymied by the unavailability of the seminal work of Heidegger, *Being and Time* (not translated into English until 1962), and of Sartre, *Being and Nothingness* (not translated until 1956). Yet the very style of the New Yorkers precluded any deep coming to terms with existentialism since, in the words of Irving Howe, they opted for a "style of brilliance" marked by "peacock strut, knock-out synthesis," a style that "celebrated the idea of the intellectual as anti-specialist . . . the writer as roamer among theories, as dilettante connoisscur, as *luftmensh* of the mind."[16] Such an approach undermined any sustained analysis of existentialism, leaving the philosophical logic of existentialism to professional philosophers.[17]

More than abstract intellectual affinities among groups of intellectuals determine the reception of ideas, especially from one cultural context to another. Reception is caught up in issues of symbolic capital, political implications and context, as well as cultural styles and personality conflicts. Intellectual networks are crucial. While Sartre and Beauvoir had built an intellectual network in Paris that assured the dissemination and dominance of their ideas, in New York they were less successful and engaged. On their part, Sartre and Beauvoir simply imagined New York intellectuals as shallow and America as too optimistic a land to be receptive to existential despair. The New Yorkers shook their heads in angry disbelief at the French existentialists' political Stalinism and lack of respect for the modernist monuments of literature. Also, if the postwar years represented the coming of age of American thought and culture, then the need to defer to French or European models had lessened; the symbolic capital of the Old World had depreciated in value. All of these issues, connected with personality clashes, distanced Parisian from New York intellectuals. The initial reception of existentialism in America, then, largely ran aground on the shoals of cultural and personal politics, and the specifics of existentialism got lost in the process.

5 BETWEEN 1946 AND 1948, under the aegis of the French Ministry of Culture, Sartre, Beauvoir, and Camus visited the United States to give lectures, grant interviews, and meet with American intellectuals. Only a handful of American intellectuals—Lionel Abel, William Barrett, Hannah Arendt—spoke French fluently, and the French visitors had poor English-language skills. By 1948, as the crisis of the Cold War intensified, the over-all perspective of the French intellectuals would be measured against the depth of their independent anticommunism, their comprehension of America's mission in the Cold War, and their literary tastes. According to such criteria, the New York intellectuals found the French to be dangerously naive and opinionated. In turn, the French, especially Sartre and Beauvoir, considered the New Yorkers narrow in their anticommunism and literary appreciation.

Sartre first visited the United States in mid-January 1945 for a five-month stay. The Office of War Information in Washington had asked for a repre-sentative group of French journalists to visit the United States. Camus, then editor of *Combat*, asked Sartre if he would represent the journal. Accord-ing to Beauvoir, Sartre had approached the journey with high expectations: "I've never seen Sartre so elated as the day Camus offered him the job of representing *Combat*." As Beauvoir recalled, America meant for both of them the "jazz, cinema and literature [that] had nourished our youth, but it had always been a great myth to us as well."[18]

Better known in America as a Resistance figure than as an existentialist, Sartre arrived with little reputation as a philosopher and literary presence. But in his first American publication, "Paris Alive: The Republic of Silence," he announced existential imperatives in all but name: the Resistance fighter, "in his freedom in choosing himself, . . . chose the freedom of all."[19] Sartre's visit got off to a rocky start when he complained about America's excessive influence on French politics. Forced to defend his comments lest he un-dermine postwar French-American relations, he maintained his right to an independent view while affirming his "spirit of deep friendship for the United States."[20]

During this visit Sartre spent little time with American intellectuals. In-stead he fell in with the French exile community and pursued a passionate relationship with Dolores Vanetti, once an actress in Paris, now living in New York and working for the French Office of War Information. Love and jazz seemed more on Sartre's mind than the opening up of a beachhead for ex-istentialist philosophy on American shores. No doubt, as well, his opinion that Americans were overly optimistic and materialistic led him to see America as an unlikely venue for the recruitment of disciples to the exis-tentialist cause.[21]

In the winter of 1946 Sartre returned to the United States as the celebrated leader of existentialism. *Time* magazine exclaimed, "The literary lion
of Paris bounced into Manhattan last week."[22] In contrast to the previous
trip, this time Sartre lectured at Harvard, Yale, Princeton, and Columbia
universities. He had an important luncheon meeting with a select group of
Partisan Review intellectuals: editors Philip Rahv and William Phillips, accompanied by Lionel Abel and Hannah Arendt. He impressed the New
Yorkers with his "veritable volcano of words," according to William Barrett.[23]
While the New Yorkers deplored his praise for what they considered to be
the nihilistic criminality of Jean Genet, goodwill prevailed, and in 1946 *Partisan Review* published two stories by Genet.[24]

Differences about literature now took a back seat to the political differences between Sartre and the New Yorkers. Sartre's politics antagonized the
New York anticommunist intellectuals. Phillips found Sartre "in the impossible position of trying to go with the revolutionary tide and still maintain his
independence and critical sense."[25] Sartre and Beauvoir had decided at this
time that existential action needed to be connected with a mass movement
to effect change. While cognizant of the shortcomings of traditional Marxism, Sartre believed that the working class (and later colonized people)
marched with the force of historical circumstance. Thus his "third way" position made him view the Soviet Union as a corrupted workers' state and
Marxism as problematic because of its materialism. But he viewed the Soviet Union as a necessary counterbalance to the expansionist imperatives
of American capitalism in Europe and around the world. To the New Yorkers, Sartre too often apologized for Stalinism. Years later, Abel referred to
Sartre's philosophy and his turn away from existentialism as an inevitable expression of his "Metaphysical Stalinism."[26]

If some disdained Sartre for his Marxism, a few others in New York rejected him for his existentialism. J. Alvarez del Vayo, European editor for
the *Nation,* regarded the existential emphasis on the human condition, on
human solidarity against the forces of evil, as vapid political blather. Sartre's
excessively individualist, pessimist, and irrationalist philosophy undermined,
for del Vayo, any identification between existentialism and the proletarian
movement: "History becomes a carrousel of human events, or rather of
human accidents, turning round and round without ever reaching a destination."[27] In a similar manner, old-school Stalinist cultural arbiter V. J.
Jerome condemned existentialism as a "mystic hodge-podge," nothing more
than "petty-bourgeois anarchist self-exaltation."[28] Of course, at this point
Sartre had yet to publish the full text of *The Critique of Dialectical Reason*
(1960), in which he attempted to reconcile his existentialism with his Marxism, much to the detriment of the former doctrine.

During his visit Sartre showed good sense in keeping himself aloof from political discussions with his enemies on both sides of the divide. He did find an enthusiastic audience among New York's Francophiles. Under the sponsorship of the avant-garde surrealist magazine *View,* he lectured on the state of the French theater at Carnegie Hall to an overflow crowd that included artist Marcel Duchamp and "people from the 57th Street art world."[29] While the 57th Street art crowd and the editorial board of *Partisan Review* might have been in close physical proximity, they were separated by enormous differences of interests and thought. Nonetheless, a variety of intellectuals wrote for both *View* and *Partisan Review. View* published pieces by political writers such as Lionel Abel, Meyer Schapiro, and James T. Farrell. Moreover, in 1946 and 1947 there appeared in the pages of *View* an article by critic Wallace Fowlie on "Existentialist Theater," as well as translations of work by Sartre and Genet and an excerpt from Camus's *The Stranger.* The politics of existentialism, however, engaged the editors of *View* less than the cultural prestige and trendiness of existential thinkers such as Sartre. John Bernard Meyers captured the vogue quality that existentialism had for some in the *View* crowd:

> "I think, said Charles one afternoon, that Surrealism is on its way out."
> "And what is on its way in?, I asked."
> "Existentialism, Honey. Existentialism."[30]

Sartre resisted identification with existentialism as an intellectual fashion, believing that his ideas would be diminished through such commodification. Moreover, he fretted that existentialism might wilt in the bright sun of American optimism and naiveté. His essay "A European Declaration of Independence" (1950) found that American accounts of existentialism reduced it to a simple expression of the suffering of Europeans during and after the Second World War. This gave it an ephemeral edge at the very moment when Sartre wanted to link existentialism with what he considered to be the historical trends described by Marxism. Angered by political and cultural tensions between European and American intellectuals over the Cold War, Sartre opened up with both barrels, proclaiming America shackled to technological determinism, capitalist profits, and a numbing mass culture.[31] He now explicitly connected his political agenda to his cultural critique. Europe must gain its autonomy from both the United States and the Soviet Union, "instead of being batted back and forth between them." Only then would European culture be renewed. By 1950, when American intellectuals increasingly viewed the world as divided between the democratic ideals of the United States and the totalitarian principles of the Soviet Union, Sartre's foray into the cultural politics of the Cold War only assured that his voice would not be taken seriously, his existentialism corrupted by his politics.[32]

Beauvoir had more extensive contact than Sartre with American thinkers and writers during her visits to the United States in the late 1940s, but it made little difference. She arrived in New York in the spring of 1947 for an extended American tour—in the words of the *New Yorker,* "the prettiest Existentialist you ever saw," the "No. 2 existentialist."[33] Though she despised what she saw as American materialism, Beauvoir adored much in American cultural life, especially American jazz. While in the United States she engaged in a passionate love affair with Chicago novelist Nelson Algren, whose interest in the seamy side of life, hard living, and left-wing politics appealed to her.[34]

According to William Phillips, American intellectuals wined and dined Beauvoir, seeking to make her feel at home in America. But she shocked them with her "dogmatic, even truculent" ideas. Her "quick, facile, almost ready-made" ideas made Phillips "suspect the authenticity of her existentialism because she was so glib about it." "I once asked her, half-jokingly, what kind of angst she felt most, and she replied, with the heartiness of an athletic woman, that she felt none at all, she was happy and well adjusted, never even missing an hour of sleep. I said nothing, but wondered about the anxiety the Parisian existentialists talked about and what connection it had with the anguish of someone like Kierkegaard."[35] Phillips neither expected nor wanted to see the anguished struggle of the modern intellectual writ large in Beauvoir's mien, but he and other Americans resented her assertions about America and American thinkers. "She seemed," according to William Barrett, "like a traveler carrying an invisible visa form in which all the main items had already been entered and she had only to fill in a few blanks."[36] Indeed, the New York intellectuals became so frustrated with her that, male and female alike, they adopted a patronizing and sexist attitude toward her. After hearing Phillips's complaints about Beauvoir's views, Hannah Arendt chided him for failing to think of Beauvoir as a woman rather than as a thinker: "One occasionally flirts with women, she reminded me," Phillips recalled; "one does not only discuss deep questions. I still do not know whether this was a comment on de Beauvoir or me, or on both of us."[37]

First in an essay, "An Existentialist Looks at Americans" (1947), published in the *New York Times Magazine,* and then more fully in a book, *America Day by Day* (translated in 1953), Beauvoir reflected on her travels in America. She evaluated the inner and outer lives of Americans according to "Existential criteria": does America permit individuals to "justify their existence" and to find "valid reasons for living"? Given her disdain for materialistic America, Beauvoir answered in the negative. Americans were dynamic and ambitious for material wealth instead of the "great things" in life. Anticipating arguments that David Riesman would make popular in *The Lonely Crowd* (1950) and that American critics of the shallowness of American life had long posited, Beauvoir found that, existentially speaking, Americans were afraid of freedom, unwilling to engage in high-level discussions of serious ideas, childish in some ways, and unable to trust themselves. Yet she held out hope for the next generation of Americans who might yet become aware of "'the tragic sense of life' and the responsibilities incumbent on a great country."[38] In addition, Beauvoir skewered American thinkers as narrow-minded, unwilling to entertain the possibility of the literary talent of those outside their own canon. American intellectuals were also, according to Beauvoir, atrophied in their "violent hatred for Stalinism." Her discussions with Americans quickly degenerated because "they spoke so heatedly that they did not listen to me, and I did not understand them very well." The New York intellectuals she met were rigid, both in their international and their literary politics: "They themselves were sterile; that was the heart of the matter and why, with few readers and no political influence or passion, they hated life, not only in literature but everywhere they met it."[39]

Suffice it to say that such opinions did not endear Beauvoir or French existentialism to New York intellectuals. Phillips remarked that Beauvoir comprehended the United States simplistically, as nothing more than "an imperialist country in the death throes of the class struggle."[40] Critic and novelist Mary McCarthy, renowned in New York intellectual circles for the lash of her critical whip, depicted Beauvoir as a culture vulture—someone slumming, constantly on the prowl for the "real" American experience, whether it be food or human suffering. McCarthy noted that for Beauvoir, America was, "so to speak, already a past, a gelid eternity of drugstores, juke boxes, smiles, refrigerators, and 'fascism,' and . . . [the typical American] is no longer an individual but a sort of Mars man, a projection of science fiction. . . . Such a futuristic vision of America was already in Mlle. de Beauvoir's head when she descended from the plane as from a space ship, wearing metaphorical goggles." Existentialist truisms and trite Marxism rendered Beauvoir's vision of America a simplistic caricature, an act of misinformation and bile.[41]

6 CAMUS'S MEETINGS with New York intellectuals went better than those of Sartre and Beauvoir, and he had the good sense to keep private his deeply negative impressions of America. The New York intellectuals regarded Camus's politics as aligned with their own anti-Stalinism, and they warmed to him personally. The question of his relation to the existen-

tialist movement concerned the New Yorkers, but few of them cared how Camus's notion of the absurd differed from the Sartrean concept, or comprehended the politics of the French intellectual scene and how they divided Camus from Sartre. Camus generally distanced himself as much as he could from existentialism, fearful that he would be reduced to a footnote to Sartre.[42] Arendt appreciated Camus, referring to him as "one of those young men from the Resistance . . . absolutely honest and has great political insight." She found Camus to be a new type of European, "at home everywhere." In contrast, she described Sartre as "much too typically a Frenchman, much too literary, in a way too talented, too ambitious."[43] Phillips concurred that Camus was more handsome, more reserved, more open to casual talk, and more in tune with the New York intellectuals' revulsion against Stalinism.[44] Likewise, Barrett found Camus's political views to be instilled with "elementary feelings of decency" joined to his being "wonderfully appealing in his sheer modesty."[45]

In the spring of 1946 Camus delivered an important lecture, "The Human Crisis," at Columbia University in New York.[46] The lecture effectively summed up his politics of moderation and revolt. Camus opened with the "spiritual experience of my generation" facing an absurd world, a world sadly saturated with destruction and death (20). He sought to make this culture of death concrete by offering his audience verbal snapshots of the human despair connected with wartime collaboration and resistance. Torture and political murder, Camus warned, had survived the specific setting of the Second World War: "The poison is not gone . . . we all bear it in our very hearts . . . we are all responsible for Hitlerism" (22). If the "Human Crisis" reared its ugly head as part of the human condition bequeathed to modern men and women, then Camus, in the face of the "cult of efficiency and distraction," needed clarity: "We want to see the human condition as it is" (30). Modern individuals exist "in a world without values," except for those exerted by the "will to power," the God of historical necessity, and the faceless bureaucratic rationales for torture and destruction (26).

To combat these realities, Camus proposed his philosophy of revolt: "We must fight against injustice, against slavery and terror, because it is these three scourges which impose silence on men, fence them from one another, make them indistinct to one another" (28). Thus revolt must be directed against "all forms of realistic and fatalistic thinking" (28), "the death penalty throughout the universe," and the prioritization of politics over morality (29). Camus counseled an ethical stance whereby individuals created "positive values" through a "universalism . . . [by] which all men of good will may find themselves in touch with one another" (29). Out of individual despair in a collective age, individuals came together with a core of shared values that allowed them to revolt against the dehumanization and absurdity that constituted the human condition.

In the view of Beauvoir and others, Camus's conclusions rang true, but only in an empty sense; of course, countered Beauvoir, we must revolt against injustice, torture, and the absurd. But while Camus validated his politics of revolt in terms of the creation of values, Beauvoir and Sartre increasingly rooted existential commitment in the realm of historical forces and identification with the masses. These "abstractions" struck Camus as part of the problem to be confronted and overcome by the individual in revolt. To Beauvoir, these entities concretized individual revolt, drew individuals into movements for change, and recognized that while it was best to be "neither victim nor executioner," to use Camus's well-known phrase, under certain concrete circumstances, in the messy means-and-ends realm of politics, choices might have to be made that violated abstract moral desires. For Beauvoir, ends might overcome means. For Camus, to choose in this manner opened the door to the death camp. Beauvoir denounced Camus's universalism and moralism as insulating him from really hard choices: his "reaction to the contradictions of the political situation was to detach himself from it."[47]

Dwight Macdonald, who had broken with *Partisan Review* and formed his own journal of opinion, *politics,* in 1944, identified with Camus and the choices that arose out of a chastened moral perspective. In a long and influential essay, "The Root Is Man," arising out of his conversations with Camus and published in the spring and summer of 1946 (around the same time Camus delivered his talk), Macdonald took stock of the human condition after the destruction of the Second World War, the explosion of atomic bombs, and the failure of Marxism.[48] Political ideologies, the lifeblood of his generation, Macdonald now maintained, had led to orgies of mass destruction. The individual must be content to exist without "either Certainty or Directives" (99). Truly radical thought, Macdonald proclaimed, viewed human nature as both good and evil while remaining skeptical about the claim of "science to explain things beyond a certain point" (100). Values must be built with attention to the concrete "sphere of human, personal interests, and in this sense, the root is man" (100). Macdonald urged a politics of moderation, based on decentralization of authority, pacifism, and anarchy.[49] "We must," he announced, "reduce political action to a modest, unpretentious, personal level—one that is real in the sense that it satisfies, here and now, the psychological needs and the ethical values of the particular persons taking part in it" (209).

Macdonald, along with Camus, criticized the bureaucratic logic of the

modern permanent war state, dismissed the utopian pretensions of technological progress and Marxian science, and rejected the confidence and
complacency of the emerging corporate liberal state. He sought to free the
individual from being reduced to a "cell in the social organism" (102). Yet
Macdonald was honest enough in the difficult years after the war, and just
before the onset of the Cold War, to wear his perplexity on his sleeve:
"Whether Free Will exists or not, it thus seems necessary to behave as
though it did" (197). This meant, in the language of chastened perceptions,
not an end to politics but a new form of political engagement, anchored in
the recognition that political activity must be based upon ethical values. In
tones that harkened back to Emerson and that mimicked Camus, Macdonald wrote, "I think each man's values come from intuitions which are peculiar to himself and yet—if he is talented as a moralist—also strike common
chords that vibrate respondingly in other people's consciences" (197). Macdonald adopted a gadfly politics in the wake of the "end of ideology": "What
seems necessary is thus to encourage attitudes of disrespect, scepticism,
ridicule towards the State and all authority, rather than to build up competing authority" (213). Such perceptions, as Camus maintained, led not to
passivity but to a commitment to personal integrity and new, smaller political formations (212). Thus for both Macdonald and Camus, "individual actions based on moral convictions have *greater* force today" (212).

Macdonald wanted to work closely with Camus in forming precisely this
type of small activist group. But as historian Gregory Sumner notes, Macdonald's desire to collaborate with Camus on a "Europe-America Groups"
project, which would bring together European and American intellectuals
dedicated to nonviolent resistance, foundered. In part, Camus failed to pursue the idea and got involved in his own political squabbles in Europe.[50]
Macdonald never developed his vision into a coherent politics, although he
did resurface in the 1960s as an opponent of the war in Vietnam. Later he
distanced himself from Camus, claiming never to have been able to read
Camus's seminal works on revolt, *The Rebel* and *The Myth of Sisyphus*. In
1956 he announced, in what was at best a caricature, that his sense of being
an American gave him a fuller perspective on life than Camus and the existentialists: "I am beginning to realize I have been an optimist all my life without ever realizing it. The world of bringing up children seems not to exist
in Camus and de Beauvoir."[51]

7   IN A HOST OF essays Sartre tried to demonstrate his love for American literature, perhaps hoping to garner support among the American
literary intelligentsia. If so, he missed his mark miserably. The more he
praised certain American authors, the deeper the rift between him and

American intellectuals. Sartre would come to be seen as another apologist for retrograde proletarian literature. The New Yorkers would be forced to battle against Sartre's literary canon as they had done ten years earlier against other challengers to their own appreciation for European high modernism.[52]

In "American Novelists in French Eyes" (1946) Sartre enunciated most fully his own canon of the greats of American literature: William Faulkner, Ernest Hemingway, John Dos Passos, Erskine Caldwell, and John Steinbeck. At other times Richard Wright and James M. Cain entered the pantheon. The gritty realism and social criticism of these writers appealed to Sartre and Beauvoir. Sartre found the lack of psychological depth in some of these authors' characters a breath of fresh air, an antidote to the French overreliance on subjectivism and psychologism. Indeed, these writers have "produced a *technical* revolution. . . . They have placed in our [French writers'] hands new and supple instruments, which allow us to approach subjects which heretofore we had no means of treating: the unconscious; sociological events; the true relation of the individual to society, present or past."[53]

Yet as Sartre made clear, the new French writers would not mimic the Americans; instead, they would adapt American techniques of the novel to French tastes. Thus Camus uses Hemingway's style as "the best way to express his philosophical experience of the absurdity of the world." Likewise, Beauvoir employs Faulkner's rupturing of time as a means to other ends. The new French novels, Sartre argued (no doubt thinking of his own, Beauvoir's, and Camus's wartime productions), will be better adapted to the "less brutal" French taste, which in turn may reacquaint American readers with the "eternal youth" that is to be found in the "'old' Faulkner."[54] Beauvoir expressed similar opinions of American literature. She related her dismay when, at a New York cocktail party, an intellectual explained to her that the French "craze for American literature disgusted him. He accepted Faulkner; but Hemingway, Dos Passos, Caldwell, Steinbeck—these were all journalists, just realists. And to translate James Cain, [Horace] MacCoy [*sic*] and Dashiel Hammett must mean that we took Americans for barbarians."[55]

Beauvoir got it right on this score. American intellectuals were aghast at the literary canon of French existentialists. At this particular moment, the New Yorkers believed that they had finally achieved hegemony as critics, warding off challenges from the left and dismissing middlebrow pretenders to literary value. Their antagonism toward the literary views of the French grew out of earlier battles over the canon, against those whom the *Partisan Review* crowd considered to be hack critics for the Popular Front of the 1930s or Stalinists of the 1940s.

The literary nationalism of Popular Front–era critics, as varied as Vernon

L. Parrington, Van Wyck Brooks, Archibald MacLeish, and Granville Hicks, had celebrated an American cult of experience, had been too attentive to class conflict, and had been overly focused on literary realism. In contrast, Lionel Trilling enunciated the view of *Partisan Review* critics in finding much of American literature to suffer from a lack of philosophical depth and character development, too close attention to a mysterious entity called "reality," and hostility toward "evidence of imagination and creativeness."[56] Philip Rahv largely agreed with Trilling, preferring to worship at the feet of European masters but acknowledging, against Popular Fronters, that American writers such as Henry James had recognized that a spirit of "romance and reality and civilization" could be found in America. Rahv averred that James in his fiction had "never faltered in the maze of these contraries; he knew how to take hold of them creatively and to weave them into the web of his art. And the secret of their combination is the secret of his irony and of his humor."[57] Appreciation for these ironies and combinations, for Trilling and Rahv, was beyond the grasp of the Popular Front critics and their literary favorites. Any sense of evil and despair residing in Steinbeck, for example, struck the New Yorkers as shallow.

In addition, postwar New York intellectuals wanted to distance themselves from popular and middlebrow culture, which they viewed as lowering literary standards, producing a kitsch mentality, fostering conformity, and playing into the hands of communism. As critic Andrew Ross has demonstrated, New York intellectuals regarded the ideology of the Popular Front as a Stalinist aesthetic. Thus when Sartre and Beauvoir trotted out their litany of American literary greats, the New York intellectuals bristled with political and aesthetic indignation. Rather than a cult of experience, as desired by Sartre, Rahv preferred novels of ideas, a modernist "Paleface" literature.[58]

The New York intellectuals, as critic Harvey Teres remarks, "tended to make European culture and politics the measure of all things."[59] While the New York critics had initially helped bring renown to the French existentialists, they soon found it necessary to undermine their credibility as literary critics and novelists, lest their own critical acumen and values become diminished. Thus by the late 1940s, New Yorkers subjected the works of the French existentialists to a barrage of criticism. While some of it was political in nature, much of it was based upon the New Yorkers' deep-seated animosity toward the literary politics that the French represented. To save the monuments of European modernism, the New Yorkers would have to destroy its latest incarnation, French existentialism.

Partisan Review critic Elizabeth Hardwick dismissed Sartre's novel *The Age of Reason* as a mediocre piece of writing in which "literary naivete . . .

clings to every page." The technique of the work, she wrote, "is particularly crude," no doubt a reference to the "crude" style of writing that Sartre and Beauvoir found peculiarly American. Indeed, Sartre failed to meet the standards of modernism and tragedy upheld by the New York intellectuals: "For some reason, Sartre will not look the psychological ambiguities and motivations in the eye. Nor does he deal adequately with tragic, universal problems, preferring instead to get lost in mundane details of his sordid characters' lives." Indeed, Hardwick categorized Sartre as insufficiently existentialist because his novel failed to offer itself as a "significant parable of the human condition."[60]

Not only did French existentialist novels crudely ape the work of second-rate American social realist writers, they also failed to deal adequately with ideas. Rahv and the *Partisan Review* crowd craved novels of ideas, but they did not want them, or literary innovation and technique, subsumed into a philosophical and moral agenda. Thus social theorist James Burnham found Beauvoir's *The Blood of Others* a failure: "The philosophical problems, never fused to the concrete, are diluted into platitudes, a name-brand flavoring for pulp-level tripe." Although Burnham valued Camus's *The Plague,* he rejected the novel's moralizing as too explicit and "somewhat banal." To be more successful, Burnham lectured, Camus would have needed to have "more confidence in his own myth which, if the artist's work is completed, is able, in its own way, to speak for itself."[61] Edmund Wilson, dean of American critics, felt that Sartre, like Steinbeck, while possessed of "undeniably exceptional gifts," was guilty of squandering them with a naive realism that in fact made "actual human experience" seem less real. The only value Wilson could perceive in the philosophy of existentialism—which he found to be a rather traditional exposition of man's inherent freedom and need for engagement—was that it would be useful in fighting Marxism and the theology of dialectical materialism.[62]

Better than anyone else, William Barrett summed up the New York intellectuals' aesthetic and political distance from Sartrean existentialism. Trained as a philosopher but with a keen literary bent, Barrett in two essays, "Talent and Career of Jean-Paul Sartre" (1946) and "The End of Modern Literature" (1949), passed judgment on Sartre as both a philosopher and a writer. The earlier essay, a review of Sartre's still untranslated opus *Being and Nothingness* and two of the novels from his *The Roads to Freedom* trilogy, denigrated Sartre as a prisoner of renown who produced work of inferior quality in order to maintain a public presence. Sartre had fallen prey to a leftist "compulsion to be *engagé.*"[63] From the anti-Stalinist political perspective of the New York intellectuals, this marked the demise of Sartre as a serious thinker and artist.

According to Barrett, Sartre suffered from "the immaculate rightness of his first draft." Barrett found the seven hundred pages of *Being and Nothingness* marred by "extreme naivete and positive obtuseness." Of course, Barrett failed to recognize that the "compulsion to be *engagé*" that accompanied Sartre's fame had nothing to do with the length of *Being and Nothingness,* since he had composed that work well before becoming famous. Sartre's novelistic primitivism reflected "the influence of the American novel . . . banal and meaningless conversations, characters wandering in and out. . . . American fiction is the African sculpture of French writers." Echoing the canonical assumptions of the New York intellectuals, Barrett concluded that "these last novels of Sartre are grim reminders that one cannot read Steinbeck and Dos Passos as great novelists with impunity."[64] Years later, in his intellectual autobiography *The Truants,* Barrett remained rankled by Sartre's pantheon of American literary figures. Sartre and Beauvoir had seemed "to swallow in one indiscriminate bolus all our 'tough-guy' literature . . . and out of this amalgam they constructed an America of the imagination which they took for the real America—a country more eerie and violent even than we really are."[65]

Barrett also engaged Sartre's philosophical project in these early reviews. While Barrett praised Sartre's understanding of the contingency of existence, which Barrett later stressed in his popular text, *Irrational Man* (1958), he preferred Heidegger's phenomenology over Sartre's Hegelian and idealist metaphysics. In addition, again returning to a preference of the New York intellectuals, Barrett ridiculed Sartre's "frivolous and presumptuous" dismissal of the Freudian unconscious. While Barrett appreciated that Sartre rejected the unconscious in order to open up the realm of choice for the individual, he maintained that freedom of action became meaningful only when the complexity of the situation, of the possibilities and historical contexts of action, were enumerated. Thus Sartrean psychology proved to be "thin and puerile."[66]

In 1949 Barrett evaluated Sartre's *What Is Literature?* (newly translated in a Philosophical Library edition). Barrett's review attested to New York intellectuals' interest in Sartre, but also to their distance from him and his ideas. Barrett marveled at Sartre's ambition and range. Sartre composed "with the Zeitgeist breathing hotly down his neck."[67] But in his call for a literature of engagement, Sartre sought to distance literature from the modernist dead end of art for art's sake. Serious writers, in the wake of the Second World War and the atomic bomb, Sartre contended, must address the issues of the time or become irrelevant. While Barrett agreed somewhat, he dismissed Sartre's overly schematic and simplistic reductionism. Sartre's vehement hatred of the bourgeoisie led him, according to Barrett, to dismiss as irrelevant such modernist masters as Proust, Flaubert, and Joyce. For Barrett these masters of modern consciousness, while not politically *engagés* in the Sartrean sense, were great artists who could, in a few passages of observation, dissect the zeitgeist of their era better than "second-rate" novelists such as Dos Passos or Richard Wright. Proust offered "a profounder study of the breakdown of a social class than anything given us by proletarian or 'socialist realist' literature," while Joyce's *Finnegans Wake* confronted "the destruction of the whole civilization."[68]

Sartre's literary identification with the Popular Front mentality of the 1930s pushed his work toward the dangerous realm of the middlebrow, another bogeyman for the New York intellectuals. Barrett, reflecting on the political experiences of the anti-Stalinists, spoke of the lesson learned: Marxist simplifications of literature into works that are either politically useful or politically distant affronted both revolutionary and aesthetic ideals. Sartre's desire to break from the tradition of great literature pointed in the direction "of a lower and less ambitious level." Sartre appeared to be "aiming at the second-rate" so that he might popularize his ideas by cooperating with the burgeoning mass media. Barrett warned that Sartre's conciliation between mass culture and literature would result in a "watering down of content."[69]

8 REJECTION OF the existentialists among New York intellectuals coexisted with unacknowledged acceptance of many aspects of an existential perspective. While they outwardly dismissed French existentialism, in their creative work and criticism they adopted many of its essentials. Such ambivalence can be seen in novelist Saul Bellow. In most of his public pronouncements Bellow raged against the dire effects of French existentialism on literature. He chortled that in the late 1940s Richard Wright had tried to convince him that phenomenologist Edmund Husserl was "indispensable reading for all writers." The notion of the creative writer having to turn to a dense Germanic philosopher struck Bellow as ludicrous. While Bellow admitted that he kept up with existentialist ideas, especially when he resided in France in the late 1940s, he considered Sartre a "con" for his Stalinist apologies and hatred of the bourgeoisie.[70]

Most important, Bellow hated it when his own work was associated with, or reduced to, the school of existentialism. As many literary critics have shown, existential themes can be detected in most of Bellow's novels.[71] His first novel, *The Dangling Man* (1947), had definite affinities with Sartre's *Nausea*. The main character of Bellow's slim volume leads an inauthentic existence. He plays at life as if it were a waiting game, as evinced in his willingness to dangle until he is drafted. Finally, in a fit of affirmation, he makes a choice, takes a stand, and declares that he will cease to be a bystander and enlist in the army.

Bellow disliked the intellectual pretensions and language of existential pessimism. Herzog, one of his characters clearly modeled on an image of the New York intellectual, calls philosophers of the abyss and nihilism "pip-squeaks of the Wasteland." Herzog reduces the existentialist slogan to "God is no more but Death is." Rahv interpreted his friend Bellow's take on existentialism thus: "Herzog protests vehemently against the seeming profundities of the modern cult of pain and suffering. Himself in a state of extreme anguish, he needs no theories to rub it in."[72]

But even without recourse to theories, Bellow's characters confront existential concerns. For all of his emphasis on alienation, death, and the absurdity of existence, Bellow remains a writer of hope, capturing the American existential demand for a dauntless attitude. This is his home-grown brand of existentialism, straight out of the immigrant streets. Defying what he considered to be the overly bleak landscape of the modern world explicated by Sartre, Eugène Ionesco, and others, Bellow announced, "After nakedness what? After absurdity what?" After all, the issues of guilt, anxiety, and death, Bellow stated, were hardly the exclusive property of existentialists. The American writer had to be concerned with absurdity and alienation, as well as politics. But the most important responsibility of the writer was to bolster the human spirit, to have characters who have achieved a sense of maturity by the conclusion of the novel.[73] Bellow's views and those expressed by Sartre in *What Is Literature?* actually paralleled one another. Aesthetic values did not exist apart from political commitments; in Bellow's opinion, Sartre lacked the quality of balance.

Bellow's character Sammler, in the novel *Mr. Sammler's Planet* (1970), a survivor of the Holocaust now cast adrift as an old man in violent New York City, comes to an existential understanding of the human condition. His view encompasses both a hard-core realism and a sense of human sympathy: "the belief that there is the same truth in the heart of every human being, or a splash of God's own spirit, and this is the richest thing we share in common." But while acknowledging this hope, Bellow also has Sammler admit, "I wouldn't count on it." You shouldn't count on it, says Bellow, but don't wallow in that recognition.[74]

Hence, while New York intellectuals rejected the literary theory and personal politics of the French existentialists, they hardly refused to traffic in their own brand of existential thinking. This can be seen even in Lionel Trilling, the quintessential New York intellectual of the postwar years. As with Bellow, these are affinities rather than direct influences. After all, French existentialists, no less than New York intellectuals, worried deeply about the demise of the gods of Marxism and history, the role of the intellectual, and the formulation of an ethical position. Trilling's novel *The Middle of the Journey* (1947) can be read as a persistent rumination on these themes.[75]

The existential setting of the novel is apparent: The character John Laskell, slowly recovering from a near-fatal illness, has faced the reality of his own death. Out of this experience he emerges as a twice-born sick soul. He cannot hold to the religious certitude of the others in the book—either Gifford Maxim (modeled on Whittaker Chambers), the former communist now a religious convert, or the Crooms, communist fellow travelers agog with an innocent and dangerous belief in progress and the innate goodness of the working class. Laskell comes to the position that one can, within limits, make choices in one's life, which is in essence to accept moral responsibility. No less than the characters in Camus's *The Stranger* or Sartre's *Nausea,* Laskell confronts the abyss. In the context of an extreme situation, in which he confronts death and comes to a full consciousness of existence, Laskell finds an ethical position that permits him to participate in a struggle to improve the human condition. But he faces the battle with a sobered sense of possibility, becoming a Camusian rebel of moderation.

9 AMONG THE New York intellectual crowd, art critic Harold Rosenberg made himself most at home with existentialism, although he rarely uttered the word. His existential sensibility was unbeholden to Paris communiqués. Indeed, as he claimed, his own writings may have influenced Sartre's ideas. Born in Chicago in 1900, a poet and drama and art critic connected to the *Partisan Review* crowd, Rosenberg had deep connections to the New York School of painters. Blessed with a jaunty prose style, he became an influential art critic. Existential ideas framed the gestures and motives of abstract expressionism that Rosenberg discussed in his important article "The American Action Painters" (1952). This article inaugurated the term "action painting," which came to define the style of a wide variety of painters ranging from Jackson Pollock and Franz Kline to Mark Rothko and Willem de Kooning. In coining this term, Rosenberg managed to attach the work of painters to the emerging existential zeitgeist while also distancing himself from the more formalist criticism of his chief rival, Clement Greenberg. If Greenberg largely placed abstract expressionism within the internal history of painting, Rosenberg situated it within the space of the painter striving for self-realization. In adopting the language of existentialism, Rosenberg picked up on statements already being bandied about by the artists themselves and by other critics. As de Kooning said, speaking for himself and other artists in New York at this time, "We weren't influenced di-

rectly by Existentialism, but it was in the air, and we felt it without knowing too much about it. We were in touch with the mood."[76]

Rosenberg never called himself an existentialist, in part because he wanted to be seen as an American original, a "Coonskin" critic. In contrast to the "Redcoats," who imposed with ill effects their assumptions on reality, "Coonskinners" were "sharpshooting individuals," outsiders, open to possibility. In terms of painting, Rosenberg proclaimed, "Coonskinism" expressed "itself in the form of 'free' abstract expression."[77] Such dichotomies had polemical rather than analytical purchase. But at the outset, Rosenberg compromised his own originality by borrowing categories from Philip Rahv's precursor essay, "Paleface and Redskin" (1939). Rahv had posited a split in the American literary canon between the "Palefaces," writers of "drawing room fictions," and the "Redskins," writers of energy and "tragic failure." Thus Rosenberg's "Redcoats" might be analogous to Rahv's "Palefaces," and his "Coonskinners" to Rahv's "Redskins."[78]

Rosenberg paid careful attention to the currents of the art scene while resisting appropriation by any existing school of criticism or philosophy. He sought to maintain his own identity and realize himself in the act of criticism. In "The Stages: Geography of Action," an essay published in 1947, Rosenberg presented existential images of the scene of action, of the notion of a drama in which the actor faces a situation. His language might have been taken straight out of Sartre's still untranslated *Being and Nothingness:*

> The hero is he who has the power to return to the stage after he has been carried off—the power to be resurrected. He holds himself in readiness in the darkness, until events happening above give him his cue to break forth again into the light. . . . Since, however, the visible stage is all, a void appears at the end of each man's performance, as the abyss at the end of the sea appeared before the fifteenth-century mariner. Once this void has been sensed, how desperately the actor clings to the one stage! For he knows that the time will come when he will be driven from it forever. Then he will be turned to nothingness.

This fear of the abyss, of the nothingness, Rosenberg proclaims, leads the actor into a state of "ontological anxiety" wherein existence takes on meaning only when one is performing on the stage. Such performances, however, resist the inauthentic, because the actor seeks "to make sure that the part one plays will really be one's own."[79]

Certainly the language and assumptions of this piece are existential. In a fascinating footnote, Rosenberg noted that this article had been translated into French as "Du Jeu au je" and published in Sartre's journal of opinion,

Les Temps modernes. Rosenberg stated that Sartre's play *Les Mains sales,* commonly translated as *Dirty Hands,* found "its motives" in his own article. Thus we encounter a reversal of the presumed transatlantic crossing of intellectual influence. Here the flow is from the Coonskin Rosenberg to the Frenchman Sartre. When Rosenberg had his piece reprinted in a collection of essays in 1967, he announced, lest anyone think him a camp follower of existentialism, "My discussion of *Hamlet* could scarcely be identified with Existentialism, since it followed up on a portion of an essay published more than a decade before the Existentialist movement began." Thus is rendered obvious the anxiety of influence, Rosenberg's fear that he might be transformed into a Redcoat of criticism.[80]

The influence may well have flowed as Rosenberg recounts it. In an early essay, "Character Change and the Drama" (1932), Rosenberg had discussed *Hamlet* in terms that informed the later essay, which Sartre might well have read or discussed with Rosenberg while in New York in the winter of 1946. Sartre wrote *Dirty Hands,* one of his most important plays, around Christmas of 1947, while he and Beauvoir were on a working vacation.[81] In this play Sartre's anti-Stalinism is at its strongest, but he also reveals his appreciation for the complexity of political action in a world where choices are often unclear and consequences often unintended. Sartre's "hero" is "alien to the spirit of his age" and "torn by contradictions." Much of Sartre's personality and politics as they stood in 1947 are to be found in the main character.[82] But the play came to be associated with Cold War–era anticommunist animus. As Sartre's politics shifted and he embarked on his own search for a "third way," he attempted to suppress performances of the play in Vienna and New York. By 1948 he increasingly identified himself with the Parti communiste français (PCF), and the play's careful dissection of the twists and turns of Comintern policy proved an embarrassment to him.

To trace the themes that may have influenced Sartre, let us begin with Rosenberg's 1932 essay. In that piece Rosenberg presents Hamlet as a character with "all the qualities required for action" but without an "identity structure" for action.[83] Hamlet, as "man thinking," cannot act. He becomes a "hypothetical actor who has wandered by accident upon a stage" (147–48). In order to act, to kill the king, Hamlet requires a new identity, which comes to him only after a near-death experience. Out of such a boundary situation, Hamlet gains a "capacity for action." He is "transformed from the image of a personality into that of a dramatic identity, he has found at last his place in the play" (149).

The same themes reappear in the "Stages" essay of 1947 that presumably influenced Sartre. Here Hamlet is described as inauthentic, "obsessed by the sense of being an actor . . . of falsifying himself through what he does and says. His self-consciousness exceeds his role and blocks his performance of it." Only through a "change in the situation," as Hamlet confronts death in the form of the ghost, can the "gap between the actor and his action" be overcome.[84] The ghost grants Hamlet revenge as a motive for action. But action cannot follow immediately. According to Rosenberg, Hamlet must "become passive for the sake of action, mystified for the sake of exactness, a 'dull and muddy-mettled rascal' in order to play the role of hero" (86). After returning from his voyage and after the attempt on his life, Hamlet moves from "play acting to self" (90). Reborn, Hamlet's "identity is no longer in question and he no longer hesitates about his feelings or his capacity for action" (100). For the remainder of the play he chooses to act, aware of contradictions but willing to do the deeds with the weight of historical consciousness upon his shoulders:

> In becoming equal to the plot Hamlet experiences the nostalgia of the transcending hero for human accident and self-contradiction. Upon his return from England his misery is no longer that of violent vacillation between is and seems, expressing itself in tortured monologues and angry wit. . . . [It] has a tone of detachment and farewell. . . . The anguish of the re-born Hamlet is accompanied by a sad feeling of inevitability. . . . The drama in which the living man attempted in vain to seize his life as particular to him concludes by proclaiming the utter irony of human existence. (101–2)

The basic dramatic plot of Sartre's *Dirty Hands* and the problems the main character Hugo confronts very much resemble the problems Rosenberg outlined in his analysis of *Hamlet*. Sartre's play takes place in an Eastern European country in the early days of the Second World War. An underground communist group works against the Nazis and their collaborators. Hugo and his wife Jessica are ineffectual bourgeois intellectuals. Hugo wants an assignment that will win him the respect of his comrades and that will define him to himself and to his wife as worthy. To use the language of Rosenberg's essays, he feels himself to be play-acting: "I live in a stage set."[85] Hugo and Jessica are unformed, searching for an identity and looking for love and power in others to give them direction. Both will find it in the powerful figure of Hoerderer.

A man of action and commanding intellect, conversant with power, Hoerderer enjoys manipulating others. His rise to power, however, ends abruptly when party officials label him a counterrevolutionary and recruit Hugo to assassinate him. Hugo accepts the assignment but, Hamlet-like, delays the act. When he does finally kill Hoerderer, he acts from jealousy of the moment rather than from political conviction. Hugo later learns of the absurdity of his act: The party has repudiated its previous line, claiming now that Hoerderer was not a deviationist. All that remains to put all of the pieces back in the puzzle is to have Hugo accept this revision and repudiate his action. If he refuses to do so, then he will be killed. The absurdity of the situation proves to be too much for Hugo to countenance. In his first real decision, he chooses death over a life based on deception. He opts to embrace his fate and, in the process, to honor Hoerderer: "A man like Hoerderer doesn't die by accident. He dies for his ideas, for his political program; he's responsible for his death. If I openly claim my crime and declare myself Raskolnikov and am willing to pay the necessary price, then he will have the death he deserves" (247).

In choosing death, Hugo chooses himself; when he declares himself "unsalvageable" to the party leaders, he creates an identity. He becomes, in Rosenberg's terms, an actor in his own play. He becomes at once heroic and authentic. He faces the existential situation, and he acts. However much (or little) Rosenberg's terminology may have influenced Sartre in the composition of *Dirty Hands*, both thinkers attempted to develop a lexicon for authentic action in a world of deception.

A similar desire for authentic action can be seen in the terms Rosenberg employed in his famous existential description of the abstract expressionists in "The American Action Painters" (1952), which analyzes no particular works of art, nor mentions any painters by name. Instead Rosenberg attempts to stake out the territory, to merge his theory with a manner of expression, hoping that neither of them will harden too quickly into a dead style.

"At a certain moment the canvas began to appear to one American painter after another as an arena in which to act," wrote Rosenberg; "what was to go on the canvas was not a picture but an event." The nature of this event had nothing to do with traditional theories of representation, of capturing an "object actual or imagined."[86] Painting transformed itself into an act, a "mood," a "surprise" in which the aesthetics of traditional art are subordinated to the "gesturing with materials" by the artist (26). The act of painting becomes synonymous with the biography of the artist, or with the realization of the actor in his choice of roles. In a sweeping gesture of intellectual history, one that captured the eclectic nature of the abstract expressionist painters, Rosenberg announced, "It follows that anything is relevant to it [the new painting]. Anything that has to do with action—psychology, philosophy, history, mythology, hero worship." The only thing excluded from significance to the work of painting, wrote Rosenberg, was "art criticism." The critic now appeared as a "stranger" to the new work, which departed from certain styles and forms, which self-creatively took to "living on the canvas" (28).

Painting as dramatic enactment meant for Rosenberg "the way the artist organizes his emotional and intellectual energy as if he were in a living situation. The interest lies in the kind of act taking place in the four-sided arena, a dramatic interest" (29). Thus in this drama, the painter is transformed into an "actor." The actions or gestures of this actor are best interpreted by the "spectator" through a new "vocabulary of action: its inception, duration, direction—psychic state, concentration and relaxation of the will, passivity, alert waiting. He must become a connoisseur of the gradations between the automatic, the spontaneous, the evoked" (29).

This language fits well the style of Jackson Pollock. Pollock became a sensation in the art world when he began to work on large canvases, off the easel, with his drip-and-spatter mode of painting. He became a painter of the automatic and the spontaneous, expressing himself through his acts on the canvas. Pollock, a type of existential man in the popular imagination, exuded a new artistic sensibility. Critic Robert Goodnough wrote of him, "Of course anyone can pour paint on a canvas, as anyone can bang on a piano, but to create one must purify the emotions; few have the strength, will or even the need, to do this."[87] Critic Irving Sandler noted that "the moods of Pollock's 'drip' paintings partake of two contrary states of consciousness—ecstasy and anxiety, although more often than not they embody the former."[88] Rosenberg centered this tension, between the "private Dark Nights" of the artist and the liberation of painting, in "a desperate recognition of moral and intellectual exhaustion . . . [and] the exhilaration of an adventure over depths in which he might find reflected the true image of his identity" ("American Action Painters," 31).

Rosenberg announced that the painter had finally parted with past artistic styles and "decided to paint. . . just TO PAINT." At this "big moment," the "gesture on the canvas was a gesture of liberation, from Value—political, esthetic, moral" (30). Value derived from the creative act itself, from the authenticity inherent in the actions that the artist has "gesticulated upon the canvas," from the novelties that he has found, and that have found him, in a burst of spontaneous creation (31). In essence, the painter placed himself in a situation, one that required action for expression. The terror of this dangerous situation became the anguished stuff inherent in abstract expressionist art, according to Rosenberg.[89]

Rosenberg viewed the "personal revolts" of artists against specific schools and styles of painting as central to the action painter. Art as action rested on the enormous assumption that the artist accepts as real only that which he is in the process of creating. To drive home this point, Rosenberg quoted from Kierkegaard: "Except the soul has divested itself of the love of created things. . . ." With this quotation, Rosenberg seemed to be acknowledging Mark Rothko's view, based on his reading Kierkegaard, that the artist approaching the blank canvas confronts an extreme situation, predicated upon risk and choice. The artist struggles against "the anguish of the esthetic" lest he foreclose open-ended possibilities by confinement to an already defined style of painting. This existential struggle means that the artist "must exercise in himself a constant No" ("American Action Painters," 32).

Rosenberg's essay strikingly transformed the act of painting into the revolt of the artist. And the value of that revolt, he seemed to argue, was aesthetic and gestural—the personal expression and interaction of the artist with the materials and the canvas. Out of that interaction emerged an authentic work of art, an existential expression of freedom. The artist need not answer to the critic, for the "vanguard artist," like the alienated figures of existential literature and philosophy, "has an audience of nobody" except himself in the moment of creation (38).

Rosenberg's existential take on abstract expressionism does not bring one very far in terms of understanding the particulars of the art work. "Action painting," he later wrote in *The Anxious Object* (1964), "solved no problems." Yet this was a measure of its success, its refusal to follow a political or popular agenda. Indeed, the radicalism of the action painter resided in his refusal to participate in traditional politics. Instead, the "American painter discovered a new function for art as the action that belonged to himself." Out of this "struggle for identity," the artist "took hold of the crisis directly, without ideological mediation."[90]

Thus by the early 1960s, Rosenberg's Kierkegaardian turn had come to completion. "In Greece," he wrote in *The Anxious Object,* quoting Kierkegaard, "philosophizing was a mode of action" (38). The action painters, for Rosenberg, were existentialists aware that the anxiety of the modern age resisted traditional utopian solutions such as Marxism. Although abstract expressionists might have lacked apparent "radical subject matter," such as the Spanish Civil War or class struggle, in their art work they returned "the metaphysical point to art" by "confronting in daily practice the problematic nature of modern individuality" (40). Even if the painters of the action school had grown rich, even if their work had been co-opted by the very commercial culture that signaled the death of individuality, the anxiety that adhered to the created object in the moment of its creation remained for Rosenberg a signal achievement, "the artist's drama of creation within the blind alley of an epoch" (44). That blind alley to which Rosenberg alluded was the sum of modern life, the horrors of the Second World War, the Holocaust, the atomic bomb, the commercialization of culture, and the development of mass culture. Upon the despair of the modern world the action painters had, for a brief moment, shone an anguished and original beacon of creative hope: "In that it dared to be subjective, to affirm the artist as an active self, Action Painting was the last 'moment' in art on the plane of dramatic and intellectual seriousness. The painters in this current have kept to the tradition of the human being as the ultimate subject of painting. All art movements are movements toward mediocrity for those who are content to be carried by them. The premises of Action Painting, however, are still valid for individual beginnings" (46–47).

THE HIGH INTELLECTUAL seriousness, the "individual beginnings" of the abstract expressionists, the anguish and tragedy that informed their work, and that of the New York intellectuals, for that matter, did not wear well for long. By the 1960s the solemn metaphysical concerns and artistic styles of the abstract expressionists had come under attack by new styles of painting and performance. The spontaneity that had originally been part of abstract expressionism had hardened into a style, transformed into objects of veneration and commercial value. In reaction, performance artists took to the streets to question the authority and seriousness of art, to make art that lived only for the moment of its creation. And with the rise of camp and pop art, the high existential seriousness of the artist working out his own personal turmoil in relation to the canvas seemed at best an antiquated notion. As Susan Sontag phrased it, "There are other creative sensibilities besides the high seriousness (both tragic and comic) of high culture and of the high style of evaluating people. And one cheats oneself, as a human being, if one has respect only for the high style of culture."[91]

The worst of the New York intellectuals' nightmares, an elite embrace of popular culture, had come to pass. While existentialism cannot be held responsible for this, New Yorkers considered it part of the problem, as a philosophy caught up in radical politics and popular culture. Their personal interactions with Sartre and Beauvoir only furthered their alienation from existentialism, despite their affinities with the ideas it contained. Although New York intellectuals, with the exception of Rosenberg and a few others, strongly rejected French existentialism, a growing clamor for it was heard on American campuses throughout the 1950s and 1960s, and professors and publishers refused to turn a deaf ear. As a result, books tumbled from presses explaining the essentials of existentialism and at the same time creating a canon of key texts that would define the tradition. Alas, that tradition would be drawn in rather unimaginative form, ignoring the existential thinking of Americans in favor of a discourse limited to Europe.

Chapter Seven

The Canon of Existentialism

1 IN THE POSTWAR YEARS, American philosophers created a canon of existentialism. Canons exclude as much as they include; they define what is relevant and what is beside the point. They answer questions such as, Which philosophers should be included in the canon of existentialism? Who are the precursors of Sartrean existentialism? Does Sartre build upon that legacy or reject it? Should existentialism be seen in the atheistic terms of Sartre or the religious terms of Kierkegaard? Could both coexist under the name of existentialism?[1] Whereas in France the line between existential philosophy and literature was usefully blurred,[2] initial American canonizers tended to push French literary existentialism to the periphery. Professional philosophers in America, as historian Ann Fulton contends, established the validity of existentialism as a philosophical position and the relevance of Sartre's phenomenology to the Continental tradition and to the empiricism of Anglo-American philosophy.[3] These concerns had not been important in France or Germany, where existentialism was instantly perceived as part of the tradition of Continental philosophy.

Publication in 1956 of Walter Kaufmann's anthology *Existentialism: From Dostoevsky to Sartre* transformed the canon of existentialism in America to include literature as well as philosophy. Thanks to Kaufmann, certain essential texts came to define the existential canon, now available in a single volume suitable for classroom adoption. Indeed, Kaufmann's work has remained in print since its initial publication. Yet Kaufmann, along with nearly all analysts and anthologists of existentialism, kept it narrowly anchored in the European philosophical and literary tradition. This ensured that existentialism would be viewed as an export to America. American precursors were all but forgotten, except in the important work of Hazel E. Barnes. With ardor and conviction, Barnes argued for an affinity between the thought of William James and that of European philosophers, thus accepting, at least implicitly, the conclusion that since the existential attitude is part of the human condition, American thinkers were existential long before the doctrine received full explication and fame in the hands of Sartre. Finally,

Barnes attempted to steer existentialism away from its presumed pessimism toward a greater sense of possibility and individual responsibility, even flirting with optimism, themes that might be expected to resonate more deeply with American readers. She answered most fully the question, After existential recognition of the despair of modern existence, what?

2   EXISTENTIALISM in America moved from vogue to canon in little over a decade. While professional philosophers played an important role in establishing the canon, scholars with an uneasy relationship to academic philosophy made existentialism available to a wider, nonacademic audience. Initial expositions of existentialism for a highbrow audience came from philosophers, most of whom had a certain cachet from having studied in Germany with Martin Heidegger and Karl Jaspers.

Perhaps more than any other figure in the postwar era, Hannah Arendt linked the culture of Weimar Germany with that of the New York intellectuals. A German-born Jew, Arendt had studied with Heidegger and been intimate with him; Jaspers directed her doctoral dissertation. During the war she had been involved in refugee relief efforts, finally escaping from France to the United States. She quickly established herself as a force in New York intellectual circles. Critic Alfred Kazin remarked that Arendt "became vital to my life . . . for the *direction* of her thinking . . . for the personal insistencies she gained from her comprehension of the European catastrophe. She gave her friends . . . intellectual courage before the moral terror the war had willed to us."[4] She joined such cultural capital with a personal power that "bristled with intellectual charm, as if to reduce everyone in sight to an alert discipleship," recalled Irving Howe. "Rarely have I met a writer with so acute an awareness of the power to overwhelm."[5]

Although it would be an oversimplification to claim Arendt as a full-blown existentialist, existential themes informed her work. In her monumental *The Origins of Totalitarianism* (1951) she documented, in both a metaphysical and a historical manner, the destruction that had followed the decline of the nation state and the rise of imperialism. In this crucible, nation states such as Germany and Russia had developed into totalitarian regimes. With Erich Fromm, Rollo May, and others, Arendt argued that the appeal of these totalitarian states rested on their promised solutions to the chronic loneliness, alienation, and malaise of modern men and women. Thus the existential problems of the anxious individual lurked at the heart of totalitarianism.

Arendt's specific interpretations and the sweeping structure of her arguments were less important to postwar American intellectuals than the nightmarish, numbing vision that she painted. The category of class, once so central to the social theories of intellectuals, had been demolished by the alienation of individuals from their own class and by the power of the totalitarian state to transcend class boundaries. In postwar America, appeals to class were often viewed as divisive and counterproductive, helping to create the orgies of destruction that made the totalitarian turn all the more confounding and frightful. Everyone, it now appeared, shared the human condition, with its attendant joys and sorrows.[6] In a state of "existential despair," human beings came face to face with choices between the seductive allure of totalitarianism and the uncertain freedom of democracy.

Arendt's sociological concerns, her philosophical background, and her position within the circle of New York intellectuals made her the perfect candidate to explicate existentialism for an American audience. In 1946 she published two essays, "What Is Existenz Philosophy?" and "French Existentialism," which appeared respectively in *Partisan Review* and the *Nation*.[7] Although the essays were less than effective, they helped set the terms of debate over the canon of existentialism in America.

"What Is Existenz Philosophy?" placed existentialism within the tradition of German philosophy going back to Kant and Schelling, both of whom had helped establish "the *autonomy* of man" (40). But in the hands of Kant, "*the* philosopher of the French Revolution," freedom was problematic: "While Kant made Man the master and measure of Man, at the same time he lowered him to a slave of Being" (41). Thus opened up the problem of how to raise man to heroic stature through the exercise of freedom. Heidegger (as well as Nietzsche) had devoted himself to this task, albeit in troubling ways.

Arendt argued that Heidegger's philosophy could lead to a dangerous egoism: "What is at stake for this Being in the world is, finally, nothing else than to maintain himself in the world" (49). Escape, through resoluteness, from the intense anxiety of being thrown into this world, of having to face nothingness, arrives in Heidegger's attempt to overcome man's "radical separation" (50) from others. Arendt observed that Heideggerian problems with the concept of the self led toward an "Over-self, in order to make a transition from the fundamental guilt, grasped through resoluteness, to action" (51). Clearly Arendt considered this an unprofitable response to alienation and totalitarianism.

In contrast to Heidegger, Jaspers's vision of modern philosophy staked out the "ways it must travel if it is not to get stuck in the blind alley of a positivistic or nihilistic fanaticism" (55). Jaspers's existentialist philosophy abandoned the egoism that had its roots in the excesses of romanticism and pushed men into a community (akin to the concept of a *polis* that would later be central to Arendt's own political philosophy), through which "they hunt neither the phantom of the Self nor do they live in the arrogant illusion that they can be Being generally" (56).

Arendt's essay on *Existenz* and the German philosophical tradition demonstrated her erudition and settled some personal philosophical scores. But it generated little discussion and did not lead to a boom in interest in either Heidegger or Jaspers. In the postwar years the attention of Americans focused on French existentialism. Arendt acknowledged this in "French Existentialism," a less philosophically dense and more wide-ranging essay. Arendt took seriously the work of Sartre and Camus. French existentialism consisted of two key concepts: *l'esprit sérieux* and the homelessness of man. *L'esprit sérieux*, central to Sartre's still untranslated *Being and Nothingness*, referred to how individuals adopt an inauthentic stance with regard to life. Rather than accepting the freedom to create oneself, to develop an identity, the individual usually sank into what Sartre referred to as a mode of being-in-itself *(en soi)*, a perspective predicated on "bad faith," something frozen and artificial. Arendt, however, ignored Sartre's *Being and Nothingness* for her illustrations of inauthenticity, instead employing references to Kafka's novels, to Camus's character Meursault in *The Stranger,* and to the characters in Sartre's "brilliant" play *No Exit.*

Arendt next outlined the concept of homelessness, a term particularly apt for her, since she had been a displaced person during the Second World War. She discussed how Camus's concept of absurdity arose out of the poor fit between man and the world. She then contrasted Camus's concept of the absurd with Sartre's stress on the superfluous, contingent, *de trop* nature of man's being-in-the-world, as illustrated by the chestnut tree episode in *Nausea*. There Sartre had juxtaposed the rootedness, the thingness, of the tree in contrast to his protagonist's contingent nature. To be is to live in absurdity; everything exudes this absurdity and is part of the contingency and aloneness of human existence (227).

Arendt asked readers to view French existentialism as more than "just another fashion of the day." Based on a "definite modernity of attitude," French existentialism courageously refused to turn to the past for inspiration or nostalgia (227–28). Instead, heroically and rebelliously, it engaged the problems of the world. Yet Arendt detected a hint of nihilism in French existential philosophy. Jaspers's communal existentialism needed to be melded with the insights of French existentialism into the inauthentic modes of human existence. Everyone shared the human condition.

In her two essays Arendt paid her respects to existentialism's philosophical pedigree and contemporary relevance. Each essay, however, suffered from its own defects. Encumbered with erudition, the piece on German existentialism proved impenetrable. Without a firm grounding in Sartre, the essay on French existentialism lacked depth and authority. Yet in 1946 Arendt had initiated a process of canon formation, one that situated existentialism in German thought. Others would quickly follow in her wake.

3 IN 1948 Marjorie Grene published *Dreadful Freedom: A Critique of Existentialism,* a book that helped develop the existential canon in America. Although Grene included one chapter on Kierkegaard and another on Karl Jaspers and Gabriel Marcel, most of the book centered on the work of Heidegger and Sartre. Although one commentator wished that Grene had jettisoned her "fascination" with Sartre, the book was actually one of the first sustained commentaries on Sartre in relation to Heidegger published in America.[8]

As an upstart philosophy, existentialism attracted outsiders. Women such as Grene, by choice and necessity, played a significant role in formulating the existential canon in America.[9] Fresh out of graduate school and looking for a teaching position in philosophy in the midst of the depression, Grene remembered being told, "Goodbye, you're a bright little girl, but nobody gives jobs to women in philosophy."[10] Her own choices also undermined her career trajectory. She later claimed that she had "composed a dreadful slapdash dissertation" on Kierkegaard and *Existenzphilosophie* (360). Grene further stated, "I had little if any sympathy for that particular gloomy Dane."[11] Yet at the time Grene was obviously drawn to Continental philosophy (especially Kant). She claimed to be unenthusiastic about existentialism, despite having studied in Germany with Heidegger in 1931 and Jaspers in 1932. Why did she pursue existentialism so far in advance of almost all American students of philosophy and then later denigrate her interest in it? Grene maintained that "it's easier to write about philosophers one doesn't believe" (358). Perhaps, but one senses here a retrospective judgment, insufficient to compel a young person to travel to Germany to study with Heidegger or to pursue a dissertation on Kierkegaard. Rather, she must have been drawn to existential questions.

In *Dreadful Freedom* Grene described existentialism as a "penetrating statement of our old disheartenment, a new expression of an old despair."[12] Existentialism looked squarely into the face of the dread that arrives with the recognition of freedom and responsibility. Despite its "clever sophisms or well-turned phrases," existentialism represented "the impassioned realization of the utter loneliness and dread of our being-in-the-world, the sense of all that it means to be 'condemned to be free.'"[13] While Grene respected this turn toward the reality of dread, she did not share the philosophical logic of existentialism, nor did she believe that the confrontation with dread occurred solely on the individual level. Grene's attraction-repulsion syndrome continued to define her work on existentialism for nearly two decades after her initial exposure to existentialist thought.

Given her ambivalence about existentialism, Grene attempted early in her academic career to move away from Martin Heidegger and company. At Radcliffe, "in reaction against existentialism," she studied the revolutionary work in philosophical logic then being pursued by Rudolf Carnap and the Vienna School (360). In 1937–38 she "managed to get to Chicago as a half-time assistant in order to participate in Carnap's research seminar (this time because I *was* a woman: they said, 'We're supposed to be a liberal department, and we've never hired a woman, so let's try this one')" (360–61). Six years later, dismissed from her position at the University of Chicago, Grene had cooled to logical positivism. Thereafter, until the mid-1960s, when finally hired by the University of California at Davis, Grene survived as a freelance philosopher, armed with the "thought [that] I should do anything more or less respectable I was given a chance to do" (361).

Existentialism evolved into Grene's unavoidable field of expertise; throughout the 1940s and 1950s, publishers demanded that she produce books on this "hot" subject. Resentment seeped into her work: "I loathed existentialism" (361–62). Existentialism, ironically, allowed Grene's academic anguish to find an outlet in a profession closed to her gender. While her work reads as a sustained critique of existentialism, it also takes existentialism seriously.

Grene, like all philosophers, situated existentialism within the context of philosophical tradition. She made some initial, tantalizing references to its connection with American pragmatism's theory of knowledge, based on experimentalism and experience. But she regarded pragmatism as distinct from existentialism in that the former was dedicated (at least in the work of John Dewey) to an empirical ideal of science. In contrast, she connected existentialism with the Continental tradition of Cartesian rationalism and Kantian critique, as well as with Kierkegaard's criticism of Hegelian categories.[14]

In *Dreadful Freedom* Grene described existentialism as "a brilliant statement of the tragic dilemma if not of man, at least of man in our time," remarkable for its "relentless, even extravagant, honesty in the rejection of easy solutions or apparent solutions" to the problem of man (14). Grene applauded much in the existentialist emphasis on revolt and responsibility. She also focused on how a sense of being-in-the-world, of "thrownness" (a Heideggerean concept), had placed man in the unique position of being challenged to live authentically in an absurd world. Writing in the aftermath of the Second World War, Grene took the tragic sensibility to heart. She dismissed American pragmatism as "afraid to face evil," as having "nothing positive beyond the pleasant desire to make things comfortable" (27). In contrast, existentialism's emphasis on meaninglessness, contingency, and death all pointed in the direction of a Kierkegaardian dynamic that might lead to a more chastened view of life and to a "renewal of philosophic vision" (29).

Grene disdained the social implications of Heidegger's philosophical ontology. She discussed how, in both Heidegger and Sartre, the lonely individual confronts a "dreadful freedom." Community seems impossible, as it had for Arendt. In Sartre, all human relations exist as contests of domination—each individual seeking to reduce another individual to the status of an object. According to Grene, Heidegger's conception of freedom foundered on the problem of "our existing-together-with-others outside the conventional and unauthentic level of existence." Grene maintained that Heidegger offered "next to nothing" to lessen our loneliness unto death. He failed to imagine how individuals might develop a sufficient sense of empathy or even pity for others to construct a viable community. This results in an ontological alienation from others (69). The same critique applied to Sartre. Grene found Sartre's recently delivered talk, "Existentialism Is a Humanism," to be a "sugar-coating," a refusal to face the logic of his position on intersubjective communication (73). Sartrean freedom all too often exists only for the individual without concern for the social implications of his or her act (74). Such views, based upon a metaphysics of domination, struck Grene as, "to say the least, depressing" (87).

4 MANY EARLY American analysts of existentialism were offended even more than Grene by Sartre's atheistic, bleak universe. Popular and accessible books by Ralph Harper (*Existentialism: A Theory of Man* [1948]), Helmut Kuhn (*Encounter with Nothingness* [1949]), Kurt Reinhardt (*The Existentialist Revolt* [1952]), and James Collins (*The Existentialists* [1952]) all attempted to mute Sartrean existentialist challenges to religious belief.[15] These writers were well grounded in philosophy and theology. Kuhn, a professor of philosophy at Emory University, and Reinhardt, a professor of Germanic languages at Stanford, were German-born. Reinhardt had studied with both Husserl and Heidegger in Germany before coming to the United States in 1928. Collins, a professor of philosophy at St. Louis University and an adherent to the system of Aquinas, had taken his Ph.D. at Yale with Charles W. Hendel.[16] Harper served as both a rector at St. James's Church in Monkton, Maryland, and a sometime lecturer at Harvard University in the English Department. These writers framed existentialism as a doctrine of "dreadful freedom," with happiness or transcendence possible only

through religious faith. At the same time, as philosophers, these authors did much to erect an existential canon for their readers.

By the late 1940s nearly everyone agreed on the names that should dominate the canon of existentialism: Kierkegaard, Nietzsche, Heidegger, Jaspers, Sartre, and Marcel. To create a canon, however, required more than consensus on which philosophers belonged to it. Analysts needed to thematize existentialism into a set of propositions. Collins, who wrote frequently on Kierkegaard, uncovered five essential themes to existentialism:

1. Philosophy was a subjective adventure, necessary for life.
2. Philosophy required the development of a descriptive metaphysics.
3. Philosophy must recognize the presence of "man in the world."
4. Existentialism promoted a particular relationship between "man and fellow man." And, most important,
5. Existentialism had much to say concerning the relationship that might exist between "man and God."[17]

Reinhardt upped the ante, finding nine themes in existentialism:

1. Subjective truth
2. Estrangement
3. Existence and nothingness
4. Existential anguish and nothingness
5. Existence and the "Other"
6. Situation and "limit situation"
7. Temporality and historicity
8. Existence and death
9. Existence and God[18]

Both presented existential existence as marked by the estrangement of the individual from his or her life, by a sense of nothingness and anguish. Out of confrontation with the temporal nature of community and history, salvation arrived through a Kierkegaardian doctrine of faith.

Whatever formula they concocted to explain existentialism, these authors all battled the demon of Sartrean atheism. Reinhardt wrote as a "matter of compelling personal urgency" (*Existentialist Revolt*, vii), and he deplored Nietzsche's attempt to displace God: "In the case of Nietzsche his own ego usurps in the end the vacated throne of God" (117).[19] In contrast, Kierkegaard's "authentic individual" was responsible to himself, to his fellow men, and to God. For Kierkegaard, the "ethical mode of life is transformed into the *religious* mode of life when, with a contrite heart, man chooses himself as *guilty* and hopes for divine forgiveness" (56).

According to Reinhardt, Sartre shared Nietzsche's atheism and his evil individualism. Sartre, the "Ape of Lucifer" (156), presents an "apodictic postulary denial" of God (166). Nothing can be found to "support the postulate of Sartre that the existence of God is a logical and ontological impossibility" (170). With Sartre dismissed as illogical, Reinhardt celebrates Jaspers's more moderate humanistic existentialism and Marcel's religious existentialism: "The Christian thinker is always an 'existential' thinker in the sense that he is not concerned with abstract and universal ideas and essences that bear no relation to actual life" (242).

In similar fashion, Kuhn transformed the nothingness central to Heidegger and Sartre into an opening for religion: "The incomprehensible fullness of meaning and reality, God alone . . . is the rightful claimant to the role of the saving destroyer."[20] Out of the "encounter with nothingness," Kuhn argued in tones reminiscent of Kierkegaard and Barth, the individual confronts his or her own "remoteness from God" (xv). The problem with modern existentialists such as Nietzsche, Heidegger, and Sartre is that while they correctly posit the "encounter with Nothingness," their ideal of transcendence "does not issue in the new childhood of faith but in the hardened masculinity of the superman" (xix). In the end, Kuhn warned, "the Nothingness which the Existentialist encounters is the shadow of the repudiated God" (xxii).

James Collins's *The Existentialists* found existential questions in Augustine, Pascal, and Kant, as well as in the usual candidates Kierkegaard, Nietzsche, and Husserl. Alas, Nietzsche "proves to be a guide down a dark path."[21] In contrast, Husserl, with his phenomenological quest for exact description of things, proves valuable. Collins joins Kierkegaard and Husserl in a Thomist sense: "The great problem confronting the existentialist movement is whether a synthesis is really possible between Kierkegaardian content and Husserlian form, between individual existence and purified universal essence" (30). Collins turns to this problem in his examination of Sartre on "the relation between essence and existence, moral law and human freedom, consciousness and being" (40). Sartre's philosophy is confused; his "myth of the In-itself," while working to support atheism, leads to the "verge of irrationalism" (56). Sartrean "absurdity is not in the nature of being but is a conclusion following upon an aboriginal and systematically developed atheism, integrated with an autonomous phenomenological method" (79). Thus while Sartre makes a real contribution in the "analysis of human action," his entire philosophical edifice is rhetorical, doomed to fall given the absence of moral law in Sartrean existentialism (79).

Unlike the other analysts, Harper opened his work, *Existentialism: A Theory of Man,* with a frank admission of partisanship: "I am writing as an existentialist, not as a spectator of existentialism."[22] His "dynamic existentialism," which is "at heart religious," opposed nihilist excess. But Harper chose to derive his existential formulations from a little-known late-nineteenth-century French Neo-Scholastic theologian named Pierre Rousselot. In Rousselot, Harper believed he had found "a dynamic theory of love and human energy which seems to supply the crucial insight for the explanation of any existential theory of man" (18). Rousselot's "loving intellectualism" stressed "apprehension over volition." And this type of intellect was "itself a power, a movement, a form of life, energy." The form that this energy took, Harper claimed, was that of love or caring; awareness was composed of "willing (desire, energy), possessing (intellect) and feeling (emotion)—all three" (112–13). Apparently Harper thought that this psychological perspective opened the way to a transcendental, spiritual notion of personhood devoid of the nihilism and materialism often associated with existentialism. This led him to an "interiorized scholasticism" that ends up "in the disclosure of our want; it is the want of self which is translated as a want of God" (128).

These religiously oriented books on existentialism were accessible, but unsuccessful. They easily lost their readers in the arcana of Thomistic philosophy, failed to link philosophical and literary existentialism, or, in the case of Harper, oddly attempted to include a little-known thinker in the canon of existentialism. Finally, the religious devotion of these works limited their appeal. The French atheistic existentialists—Sartre, Beauvoir, and Camus—were on the rise. Popular culture and highbrow culture alike recognized a need to encounter them fully. The anxiety of existence demanded a fuller, fairer hearing, in the halls of both philosophy and literature.

5   BY THE EARLY 1950S, as historian Ann Fulton demonstrates, some professional philosophers had moved from profound skepticism to begrudging but serious interest in existentialism. Increasingly, books and articles in professional journals placed existential ideas within the mainstream of the philosophical tradition.[23] John Wild's *The Challenge of Existentialism* (1955) was especially important in this regard.[24]

A professor of philosophy at Harvard, Wild respectfully dissected existentialism. He found that, as formulated by Kierkegaard, Heidegger, Sartre, and others, existentialism suffered from severe limitations as a coherent philosophy: it lacked a "philosophy of nature," it rejected the "principle of sufficient reason" (the willingness to describe facts as given without asking "the question *why?*"), and it had gaps in metaphysics and epistemology (179). Existentialist ethics, while usefully emphasizing the concrete and the empirical, pushed the "assertion of freedom to such lengths that it becomes fantastic and unbelievable," verging on anarchy, "moral relativism and irrationalism" (183–84). Nevertheless, Wild maintained that existentialism might actually save both philosophy and the Western world from extinction at the hands of totalitarians.

The analytic revolution in American philosophy, based on logic and science, disdainful of ultimate questions, seemed to be "bankrupt" (3). Analytic philosophy, in Wild's image, "is like a man who becomes so interested in the cracks and spots of dust upon his glasses that he loses all interest in what he may actually see through them" (10). The narrow, scientific language of professional philosophy was dangerously divorced from the affairs of men. Philosophy had once been concerned with the pursuit of wisdom; now it sought to avoid concrete experience (15).[25]

In the era of the atomic bomb and the Cold War, Wild wanted thinking individuals everywhere to search for a philosophy that could engage their deepest longings and needs. Much to his chagrin, the ideology of Marxism, with its grand historical sweep and totalizing imperative, responded all too readily to such needs. Marxism dealt with the empirical reality of man, in contrast to the rarified discourse of analytic philosophy. Wild worried about Marxism winning the ideological battle against Western democracies. Hence the West needed a philosophical perspective that would allow its most cherished ideals to be supported—and existentialism, far more than analytic philosophy, appeared up to the task.

Existentialism, in contrast with Marxism, vitally concerned itself with "the freedom and dignity of the individual person" (25). Out of this empirical and philosophical concern, existentialism appeared to Wild as an antidote to both analytic and Marxist philosophies. But in order for existentialism to be philosophically valuable, it had to fit within Wild's notion of a philosophy of the future, based upon his own perspective of phenomenological realism. Thus he wanted the total chaos and contingency often stressed by the existentialists to be replaced by order in the cosmos: "What we wish to know ultimately is not an order that we have invented, but the order that is really there." Better to base theory "on the wider and firmer grounds of that real structure" than upon the shaky foundations of existentialist subjectivity (204–5).

6 WILLIAM BARRETT'S *Irrational Man* (1958), still in print, introduced many Americans to existentialist philosophy. One individual remembered reading Barrett's volume forty years earlier as a high school student: "This stuff really made sense. Still does."[26] Unlike Wild's work, limited to an audience of philosophers, Barrett's book helped establish, for intellec-

tuals and the public at large, the philosophical relevancy of existentialism. It also widened the canon of existentialism to include literature. Like Wild, Barrett employed existential philosophy as a battering ram against both analytic philosophy (a *"déformation professionale"*) and Marxist ideology.[27]

Long before 1958, Barrett had played a major role in the explication of existentialist ideas. In the pages of *Partisan Review* and then in a short volume of essays largely culled from that journal, *What Is Existentialism?* (1947), Barrett had attempted to demonstrate the philosophical sweep of existentialism.[28] While respecting Sartre greatly for his multifaceted talents, Barrett preferred Heidegger as a philosopher. Barrett's status as a bona fide academic, professor of philosophy at New York University and a New York intellectual, granted him a certain cachet, which transformed *Irrational Man,* despite its shortcomings, into one of the most popular works on existential ideas penned by an American.

Like Wild, Barrett most appreciated existentialism when it attacked positivism and Marxism. Both views blurred the "unique facts of human personality" in favor of abstract historical forces and necessities. Existentialism raged against such "thin and oversimplified" perspectives (*Irrational Man,* 19). Defensively, some professional philosophers were troubled by what they saw to be an undercurrent of disdain for logic itself in Barrett's work.[29] Such readings missed Barrett's desire to oppose the twin dangers of abstract reason and uncontrolled irrationality.[30]

Although Barrett had, by the time of the publication of *Irrational Man,* long broken with his radical past, he remained committed to aspects of Marxist critique and terminology, finding "bourgeois society in a state of dissolution" (30). The modernist shock of recognition "touches a sore spot, or several sore spots, in the ordinary citizen of which he is totally unaware" (38). In Hemingway's fiction, for example, experience undermines abstraction. Modern art, in the lonely stick figures of sculptor Alberto Giacometti or the absurdist plays of Samuel Beckett, "begins and sometimes ends, as a confession of spiritual poverty. That is its greatness and triumph, but also the needle it jabs into the Philistine's sore spot, for the last thing he wants to be reminded of is his spiritual poverty" (40). Recent works of literature, Barrett remarked, reveal "the violent contrast between power and impoverishment"; they are composed in the face of "the terror of the atomic bomb which hangs over us like impending night. . . . The bomb reveals the dreadful and total contingency of human existence. Existentialism is the philosophy of the atomic age" (57).

In *Irrational Man,* passionate analysis coexisted with attempts to draw a wide-ranging genealogy of existentialism.[31] Barrett quickly wended his way through Hebraic notions of man confronting God and issues of justification and faith in the Book of Job. In this confrontation—which was central in Kierkegaard—Barrett found that "the features of Hebraic man are those which existential philosophy has attempted to exhume and bring to the reflective consciousness of our time, a time in which as a matter of historical happening the Hebraic religion (which means Western religion) no longer retains its unconditional validity for the mass of mankind" (69).

In the longest section of the volume, Barrett offered chapters on Kierkegaard, Nietzsche, Heidegger, and Sartre, all marked by a lucid writing style, hit-and-run analysis, and strong opinions. His chapter on Kierkegaard provided a pastiche of biographical information, analysis of the history of religious devotion, and emphasis on the themes of intense individualism, the necessity of choice, and faith in Kierkegaard's writings. Kierkegaard, as Barrett understood him, believed that "the individual is higher than the universal" (149). This insight became a benchmark for other existentialists. Emphasis on the individual and the revolt against Hegelian abstraction logically led the reader into a chapter on Nietzsche. While Barrett neatly connected Nietzsche with classical thought, he neglected to mention existentialism even once in the entire chapter. The essential argument of the chapter appears to be that despite Nietzsche's heroism in challenging the pieties of rationalism, he took his revolt to dangerous extremes, prefiguring our own fate, our Faustian bargain with the "frantic dynamism" of modernity that verges on the psychotic (182).

Heidegger's thorough immersion in the history of philosophy and his distance from analytic philosophy most impressed Barrett. Heideggerian themes of dread and death, mood and feeling, anxiety and guilt, transformed philosophical reflection, bringing it back to the problems of men while framing such discussions in a philosophical vocabulary moored in sophisticated and poetic discussions of ontology. In his celebration of Heidegger, Barrett followed Arendt's earlier suggestions.

Barrett found Sartre's work fascinating but inferior to Heidegger's. While he agreed with Sartre that existence preceded essence, he felt that Sartre reduced the issue, as well as the question of Being, to a Cartesian dualism. Sartre failed to understand how Heidegger's concept of Being overcame the dualism inherent in the concepts of the *en soi* (the inert thing-in-itself) and the *pour soi* (the for-itself, transcendent being) at the center of Sartre's philosophical phenomenology. In the end, the problem with Sartre was that his notion of "freedom *is* demonical. It is rootless freedom." This view opened Sartre up to all kinds of naive (pro-communist, in Barrett's interpretation) politics (233).

The question that hovers over the entire book relates to the fascinating title, *Irrational Man*. Certainly, as Barrett indicates, existentialism opposed

Enlightenment notions of abstract reason. While there are hints of a revolt against reason in the existentialists, Barrett never established that existentialism develops either an image or a philosophy of irrational man. After all, Barrett condemned Sartre in part for his Cartesian rationalism.

In the end, Barrett found existentialism most valuable for its tragic vision of human life. Existential man remains an unfinished project. In contrast to the hubris of totalitarian regimes and the confidence of liberal planners, existentialism recognizes that man's existence is precarious, often caught up in extreme situations that reflect the tumultuous nature of modern living. Existentialism, then, does not fully reject the Enlightenment; it simply tells us that there is both light and darkness in man. By carrying this knowledge in both his heart and his mind, modern man might possibly be able to construct a better world. Such is the message of Barrett's *Irrational Man*.

7 THE PUBLICATION in 1956 of Walter Kaufmann's collection of primary sources, *Existentialism: From Dostoevsky to Sartre*, marked the single most important moment in the popularization of existentialism in America.[32] The volume was, and continues to be, a tremendous success. By 1968 it had already gone through twenty-eight printings, serving as the main passage for most undergraduates into the constructed world of existentialism. As a sophomore at Princeton in 1970, Gail Finney remembered that she "devoured" the volume, "which inspired further reading, and thought. I had found a way of thinking with which I could wholly identify."[33] Kaufmann's anthology signaled a shift in the interpretation of existentialism. It disdained the moral and religious fervor that earlier anthologists had brought to their reading of existentialism. The publication of this source book no doubt facilitated the introduction of existential thinkers and ideas to a wide audience, but the organization of the work and Kaufmann's lengthy introduction also perpetuated the view of existentialism as a strictly European phenomenon.

Kaufmann brought great authority to his analysis of existentialism. Born in 1921 in Freiburg, where Heidegger taught, Kaufmann came to the United States in 1939, fleeing the Nazi Holocaust. He attended Williams College and served in the United States Army Air Force and military intelligence during the Second World War. After the war he received his Ph.D. from Harvard. At the time when he published his anthology, Kaufmann was a professor of philosophy at Princeton University and author of a path-breaking philosophical resuscitation of Nietzsche.[34] Kaufmann used the term "existentialism" to describe how Nietzsche's aphoristic and experimental philosophical style achieved unity and coherence. The grounding of philosophy in a concrete experimental method, which Kaufmann associated most with

Nietzsche and Sartre, became the rule of thumb by which he evaluated the thinkers presented in his anthology.

Kaufmann's introduction to the volume and the samples of existentialism that he chose all designated existentialism as part of the European philosophical tradition. Moreover, Kaufmann defined the tradition as essentially German: the nine thinkers he discussed included four Germans, one Dane working within the German philosophical tradition, and one Czech writing in German. Camus, while included along with Sartre, was represented only with the brief tale "The Myth of Sisyphus." Kaufmann's selections and his introduction make clear that he intended to appropriate existentialism as a discipline of European philosophy. Yet he also inched existentialism away from the tradition of philosophy by associating it to such a degree with literature. As already noted, Kaufmann's book came in the wake of a host of works by professional philosophers attempting to place existentialism within the framework of the Western philosophical tradition. However, Kaufmann, who shared Wild's and Barrett's animus toward the dangerous abstractions of analytic philosophy, celebrated the literary power of existentialism. Thus philosophy and literature are equally well represented in his collection.

The work begins with a long selection from Dostoevsky's *Notes from Underground*. The next two chapters are predictable, featuring Kierkegaard and Nietzsche. A selection from Rilke's *The Notebooks of Malte Laurids Brigge* and a few pieces from Kafka make clear Kaufmann's literary bent. Jaspers and Heidegger return the reader to philosophical issues before Sartre is introduced, represented by fiction, some philosophy, and criticism. The work concludes with Camus, who up until Kaufmann's anthology had been absent from the canon of existentialism. Thus of the nine thinkers presented in this anthology of existentialism, three (Dostoevsky, Rilke, and Kafka) are writers of fiction and two (Camus and Sartre) inhabit the worlds of both fiction and philosophy, with only four (Kierkegaard, Nietzsche, Jaspers, and Heidegger) being associated strictly with philosophy.

Kaufmann found the heart of existentialism to be a rejection of membership in "any school of thought," a refusal to accept any "body of beliefs" or system of thought as adequate, and a further rejection of "traditional philosophy as superficial, academic, and remote from life" (12). While all of these themes were articulated most clearly in Kierkegaard, Kaufmann condemned Kierkegaard as a "befuddled thinker," aggressive but not deep, unable to make clear, analytical distinctions, and given to overwrought outbursts of passion (16).

To Kaufmann's mind, all of Kierkegaard's strong points, and none of his defects, could be uncovered in Nietzsche, who brilliantly combined passion and critique without discarding reason. Kaufmann most wanted to demonstrate that Nietzsche might be considered an existentialist while at the same time existing above existentialism. Far too "multifarious" (22) a thinker to be reduced to an exemplar of existentialism alone, Nietzsche avoided the one-sided fascination with dread and death that dominated much of existentialist thought. Why, then, include Nietzsche in a volume on existentialist thought? "Existentialism without Nietzsche," Kaufmann explained, "would be almost like Thomism without Aristotle." But one must also recognize that "to call Nietzsche an existentialist is a little like calling Aristotle a Thomist" (22).

The remainder of Kaufmann's introduction to the first major American anthology of writings on existentialism analyzed existential themes in Heidegger, Jaspers, and Sartre, mainly on the basis of how well these thinkers interpreted or built upon Nietzsche. Kaufmann departed from this script only in the concluding pages of the introduction, where he addressed a problem specific to the current state of academic philosophy. Repeating a now common complaint, Kaufmann found British and American philosophy to be "superficial and trivial. . . . [They have] managed the rare feat of being frivolous and dull at once" (50). Through existentialism, philosophers might come to realize that "a philosophy has to be lived" (51). Yet the necessity for the lived experience, for the passionate and concrete engagement with issues, as exemplified by Kierkegaard, must be balanced with clear, strong arguments, as Nietzsche had achieved.

Kaufmann's volume would have been better titled *Existentialism through Nietzsche*. But in its combining of European philosophy and literature at the heart of existentialism, it set the stage for future anthologies.

8 ANTHOLOGISTS LARGELY excluded American thinkers from the tradition of existentialism. Given Kaufmann's adoration of Nietzsche as the fount of all modern philosophical and literary insight, he might at least have included in the existential canon the American writer whom Nietzsche himself most adored: Emerson, that "perfervid individualist" who so resisted confinement to any philosophical school. The problem with Kaufmann's description of existentialism is not that he creates a tradition as such, but that he limits the tradition to reflect nothing more than his own Eurocentric philosophical pedigree.

William Barrett had already addressed this issue in *Irrational Man*, albeit in oblique fashion. With other commentators, Barrett rejected the possibility of an American existentialist tradition. In a familiar argument for American exceptionalism, Barrett upheld the myth—then central to the discipline of American Studies—of America as a land of innocence and possibility, of a people singularly unresponsive to the life of the mind. Thus, although vaguely part of the "human condition," existential thought was a European import. The former fact explained its long history, the latter its present exemplification. Sartre's morbidity spoke to the modern European condition, expressive, at first glance, of a particular historical and geographical climate, one largely alien to optimistic Americans. How, then, to account for the overwhelming American fascination with existentialism in the postwar years?

In part the vogue of existentialism was simply a continuing manifestation of the American hunger for European ideas, no matter what their specific content. This may be seen as an example of what Michael Lind has called American "Europhilia," the point of view whereby everything European is taken seriously but American cultural life is denigrated.[35] But, it must be remembered, at this cultural moment American art and culture (and industry and ideology) were gaining confidence, beginning to see themselves as on the cutting edge. While European existentialism opposed "our native youthfulness and optimism," according to Barrett, conditions in America were changing.[36] Yes, Americans had yet to "live through the crucial experience of human finitude." Europeans, in their doctrines of existential dread and anxiety, were breaking "the path that America itself will have eventually to tread."[37] Existentialism pointed at America's present and her future, but it was alien to her past.

Most of the anthologies of existentialism published during the 1960s in the wake of Kaufmann's volume also presented it as a European phenomenon, and a literary one. No longer would anthologies of existentialist writings be composed only by philosophy professors for philosophy courses. Literature professors Frederick R. Karl and Leo Hamalian produced *The Existential Imagination* (1963), a volume of readings from Shakespeare to Sartre that stressed alienation, estrangement, concern with the authenticity of the self, and the presence of death and the absurd as the defining facets of the imagination.[38] Indeed, its book jacket announced, "apart from the ideas, the stories and selections are entertaining and rewarding works of art in themselves. *The Existential Imagination* is not only philosophy but storytelling at its best." Here the familiar sat next to the less well known—Kafka with the Marquis de Sade, Dostoevsky with Villiers de l'Isle-Adam, Samuel Beckett with Stanislaw Zielinski. The age of existentialism as a purely philosophical tradition had vanished, thanks paradoxically to Kaufmann's anthology.

Yet in the entire kingdom of the "existential imagination," not one American author emerged. The editors of *The Existential Imagination* explained that America and England had failed to produce existentialist literature because of an optimistic, practical, can-do national attitude (18–19): "With some exceptions" (the editors avoid mentioning Melville, Hawthorne, Crane, and many others) "American fiction is not existential in mood" (28). Why, then, would a volume of European writings in an existential idiom be of interest to American readers? Because Americans had, at last, in the postwar years, encountered the absurd and contingent nature of the world (31).

Literature professor William Spanos's *A Casebook on Existentialism* (1966) hinted at an American presence by including a selection from Hemingway's "A Clean Well-Lighted Place" in the section on literature, alongside the work of eight European writers.[39] Europeans dominated the section on philosophy, with the exception of an excerpt from Paul Tillich's *The Courage to Be* (a work Tillich composed while in America). In the concluding paragraph of his introduction, Spanos did allude to authors who might also be included in the existential paradigm, and some of them were American: Ralph Ellison and Archibald MacLeish, an unlikely pairing.[40] As in all of the anthologies, the presumed authority and authenticity of the European existential imagination drowned out American existential voices.

The bulging reader *The Worlds of Existentialism* (1964), edited by philosophy of religion professor Maurice Friedman, also failed to acknowledge any significant American presence in existentialism. It did, however, expand the canon ever so slightly.[41] A section on "Forerunners" went from Heraclitus of Ephesus to the Bible, with stops to present Jakob Boehme, Blaise Pascal, and the Hasid Rabbi Nachman before moving on to Schelling, Feuerbach, and other more familiar figures. But Friedman wisely included a few pages from Herman Melville's *Moby-Dick*. He also revised the canon to include material from Jewish theologian Martin Buber, a particular passion of his. Elsewhere, in sections dealing with "The Existential Subject," "Intersubjectivity," and religious issues, the roster of thinkers remained overwhelmingly European. Only in the final section, "Existentialism and Psychotherapy," could Americans be found: a couple of pages from sociologist Helen Merrell Lynd about shame and the search for identity, as well as work by existential and transactional psychologists such as Rollo May, Leslie H. Farber, and Carl Rogers. Thus while Americans might now be seen as making a contribution to existentialism through therapy, they were absent from the history of existentialism.

9 "THE DISCOVERY OF French Existentialism," remembered Hazel E. Barnes, marked "a turning point in my intellectual life."[42] Somewhat by chance, somewhat by plan, Barnes embarked in 1948 on her lifetime quest to make French existentialism central to the discourse of American intellectual life. Rather than attempting, like Barrett and Kaufmann, to establish Sartre as the dead end in a grand tradition of German philosophical reflection, Barnes pushed the Germans aside to create space not

only for Sartre but for Beauvoir and Camus as well. Her refiguring of the canon of existentialism would come to dominate popular American conceptions of existentialism in the 1960s. Moreover, Barnes presented French existentialism in a new light. As she recalled in her memoir, *The Story I Tell Myself,* "I strongly emphasized the optimistic aspects of Existentialism, though I took pains not to overlook what many persons saw as its dark side" (162).

One day in 1948, after teaching a philosophy class at the University of Toledo, Barnes was approached by a student with a question: "What is this Existentialism everybody is talking about?" After a fumbling answer that "it seemed to me to be a somewhat sensational attitude toward life and a philosophy of defeatism and despair," Barnes realized that she had been simply repeating "others' judgments" (143). She went to the college library and bookstore and began to devour works on existentialism in English translation. "The Existentialist writers," she realized, "Sartre most of all, even at the start, 'spoke to my condition'" (144).

Chance soon coincided with desire to propel Barnes to the forefront of Americans working on existentialism. She decided to turn her reading into a course, one of the first in the United States devoted to existential philosophy and literature.[43] Next, Barnes began to work on a larger study of French existentialism. Soon after taking a teaching position at Ohio State University in 1951, she wrote about her proposal to the editors at the Philosophical Library, the press responsible for many early translations and studies of French existentialism. After she had explained her background— Ph.D. in classics and philosophy, experience translating Greek and Latin, an ability to read French—the editors asked Barnes if she would be interested in translating into English Sartre's most important work, *Being and Nothingness.* She accepted the assignment quickly, perhaps rashly. After all, she was expert neither in French nor in modern German or French philosophy. But she "set to work" with an openness to the task and a recognition that undertaking to do the translation would vastly deepen her own comprehension of Sartre (150). As the undertrained Walter Lowrie had translated Kierkegaard in the 1930s, so a similarly undertrained Barnes translated Sartre in the 1950s.

Barnes succeeded with Sartre, as Lowrie had with Kierkegaard, because she possessed a feel for him and an identification with his critical ideas. Her success at translating Sartre, despite academic quibbles that ensued over particular terms that she had chosen, can be traced to her ability to capture the mood of his work more than his technical language. As Barnes indicated, she wanted to get it right, of course, but she also wanted to convey Sartre's style. In any case, her translation of Sartre made available to an academic public his major philosophical statement, and academic interest burgeoned.[44]

Barnes stalked larger game than translation. She wanted to translate the mood of French existentialism into an American idiom that would be as useful for others as it had been for herself. She did this by respecting technical philosophy while embracing literary expressions of existentialism. She decided also that the political valence and ethical importance of existentialism deserved a fuller accounting than other analysts had given to it. Finally, she realized that French existentialism flowed well into the existing streams of American pragmatism.

Barnes remembered that as a child, at the behest of her father, she would memorize passages from William James's essay "Habit." In this essay, part of his larger *Principles of Psychology* (1890), James is at his most Victorian. Although he wavers as to whether or not the individual can slough off habits once they have become ingrained, the upshot of the piece is that individuals are responsible for their fates and that habits are modes by which individuals organize the messy aspects of life. Indeed, habit becomes a creative response to the "booming, buzzing confusion" of the universe.[45] In later years Barnes found herself drawn to James's philosophy for what she believed were its essentially existential imperatives.

James and the existentialists shared many themes and concerns. James and Sartre each began with an essentially problematic premise: that the universe is without inherent order or logic. This recognition can be debilitating, but it can also open up the possibility for each individual to take responsibility for his or her actions in the face of this "dreadful freedom." Actions are choices, and the choices that we make constitute the sum total of our lives. Both James and Camus, in Barnes's judgment, revolted against the absurd nature of existence. The meaning of life, for James, comes from "pugnacity," our willingness to struggle for things we consider to be useful. We are also blessed with "curiosity," which keeps us engaged with the world, and a sense of "honor," a need to contribute. These imperatives, Barnes found, are similar to the ideals that Camus stressed, especially his emphasis on the necessity for the "absurd man" to be honest with himself. Out of such self-scrutiny, for Camus, comes a consciousness of man's condition and, concomitantly, a desire to endure in the face of the absurd.[46]

James and Sartre were most importantly joined, in Barnes's view, by their shared phenomenological psychology.[47] Each presented consciousness as active; consciousness defined itself against nothingness. In Sartrean terms, as explained by Barnes, consciousness existed "in the world; and like the world it is the object of consciousness."[48] The Sartrean notion of consciousness is consciousness of something, of an object. Consciousness constantly involves itself in creation; this brings the individual face to face with the anguish of nothingness. "Anguish before the future," wrote Barnes in an early explication of Sartre's views, "comes when I realize that the self which I will be in the future both is and is not the self which I am now. . . . A nothingness has slipped into this relation [between the present self and the future self] and there is nothing to prevent that [future] self from choosing then what now I do not want that future self to choose. It will be free in the future to choose as it pleases."[49] This is, in essence, a view of the self in Jamesian terms as consciousness directed toward the world, a self that is in process.

In Barnes's opinion, "Pragmatism prepared the American reading public for Existentialism."[50] To be sure, as Barnes posited, the affinities between a pragmatic and existentialist view of consciousness, of moral responsibility, of the nature of meaning and truth, were real (despite the different philosophical pedigrees of the two movements). But at the historical moment when existentialism burst upon the American scene, pragmatism was essentially moribund, associated with a looseness of exposition and terminology. Professional philosophy had by and large moved beyond pragmatism into analytic philosophy. Although some philosophers, such as C. I. Lewis, worked out of a pragmatic perspective, the particulars and language of their work were far removed from those of James and even John Dewey. So in effect it might be fairer to suggest that the introduction of French existentialism, with the help of Barnes's efforts, helped pragmatism to make a comeback—to become linked, as it would later in the work of Richard Rorty, with a European philosophical perspective.[51] Barnes, unlike Kaufmann, did not celebrate the German philosophical tradition, nor did she seek to validate Nietzsche above all others. A partisan of French existentialists, she helped popularize French existentialism in the 1960s among university students.

Barnes especially championed Simone de Beauvoir. Today, debate rages in the circles of existentialism about Beauvoir's role in the development of critical existential concepts. For some analysts, Sartre did not originate the insights that Beauvoir followed but rather appropriated ideas that she had already set out in her literary work and conversations.[52] Barnes's position in this matter was typically open, even before the question had been raised fully: "I do not at all preclude the possibility that de Beauvoir has contributed to the formation of Sartre's philosophy. I suspect that his debt to her is considerable."[53] Who had the idea first mattered little to Barnes. She clearly considered Sartre to be the philosophical giant, developing most systematically the implications of existentialism. Yet Barnes greatly respected Beauvoir as a figure in the early women's movement (she praised *The Sec-*

ond Sex and emphasized its connection with the work of Sartre on bad faith and anti-Semitism), a novelist of ideas, and an ethicist of distinction in *The Ethics of Ambiguity* (1948).

Indeed, in some ways not fully grappled with by Barnes at the time, Beauvoir loomed as the more appealing philosopher and exemplar. In *Being and Nothingness,* conflict, objectification, and inauthenticity dominated Sartre's vision of human interrelations to the near exclusion of examples of good faith. In Beauvoir, despite her recognition of the problem of others (one that had perplexed James as well), there operates an almost Kantian imperative that rendered the abstract concrete. The ambiguity of Being remains, making ethics more of a method than a philosophical absolute. Beauvoir rejected a priori ethics in preference for an existential ethics recognizing that the individual "exists only by transcending himself, and his freedom can be achieved only through the freedom of others. He justifies his existence by a movement which, like freedom, springs from his heart but which leads outside of himself."[54]

Barnes explained these ideas most fully in *An Existentialist Ethics* (1967). In good pragmatist fashion, she sought to evaluate the consequences of existentialism for ethics in light of present-day problems. The work was more than a simple exegesis of Sartre's and Beauvoir's ethical discussions. While Barnes's emphases were distinct from theirs, she believed that one must think through and with Sartre and Beauvoir. After all, the function of Sartre's work "is to show man his reflection as in a mirror, a magic mirror which images potentiality as well as the actual."[55]

Barnes sought to transform the pessimistic elements of existentialist doctrine into a humanistic perspective. In this endeavor she in effect returned to Sartre's much maligned attempt at a simple exposition of existentialism in his lecture "Existentialism Is a Humanism," delivered in Paris in 1946 and translated into English in 1948 as *Existentialism.* In this work Sartre stressed that "man is anguish," crippled by the "forlornness" and "despair" that arise from the fact that he is condemned to be free.[56] Yet Sartre announced this view to be "optimistic, since man's destiny is within himself. . . . [Existentialism] tells him that the only hope is in his acting and that action is the only thing that enables a man to live" (42). Alongside recognition of this responsibility to act, to make one's life, is the further notice that in choosing oneself, one also acts within the context of others, in accord with a desire to improve the human condition. In this existential humanism, man is not considered as an end, because that would be inauthentic, a positing of man as a fixed entity. Existential humanism, as outlined by Sartre, served to "remind man that there is no law-maker other than himself, and that in his forlornness he will decide by himself; because we point out that man will fulfill himself as man, not in turning toward himself, but in seeking outside of himself a goal which is just this liberation, just this particular fulfillment" (60).

Barnes revised Sartre most fully in her willingness to develop his concept of bad faith. She viewed bad faith as more than a problem in one's relations to others, in how one presented oneself to others as a fixed entity, an *esprit sérieux*. For Barnes, bad faith began with the individual's relation to himself or herself, and it influenced relations with others. Barnes imbricated the self fully in the social fabric of personal interrelations. Realizing that bad faith could not be banished by total self-consciousness and honesty, she engaged in all of her work the "existential paradox" that since "everyone is free . . . everyone is totally responsible."[57]

Figures and movements as diverse as the radical individualist Ayn Rand, the novelist and essayist Norman Mailer, the New Bohemians (Beats), and Zen Buddhists fell under Barnes's gaze in *An Existentialist Ethics*. She rejected Rand's objectivism as "foolishly rationalistic" and dysfunctional as a social philosophy.[58] Rand's world celebrated the Sartrean precept that "hell is other people" rather than attempting to go beyond this recognition to a new form of human community. Barnes identified more with Mailer's hipster (albeit rejecting the violent edge associated with him) and the Beat's "aesthetic delight in the other's personalizing eccentricities" (166). Yet the vision of the Beat and hipster, wrote Barnes, was limited to a male vision, with women relegated to the sidelines as earth mothers or exemplars of "antediluvian . . . femininity" (167). Barnes thus used Sartre's concept of inauthenticity, of fixed character, in the service of the then developing women's liberation movement.

From her existential humanist perspective, Barnes also analyzed the new student radicals, finding that "in their better manifestations" the "New Radicals have bridged the gap that separated Sartre from Camus. They have refused to sacrifice purity of principle to ideological commitments." In their acceptance of the heroism inherent in the act of rebellion, and in their constant battle over questions of means and ends, they struck her as exemplifications of Camus's ideal of the rebel (200). Moreover, the New Radicals were *engagés*, committed, and unbeholden (as Sartre had come to be) to a relatively inflexible Marxist ideology. Barnes followed Sartre and Beauvoir in many matters, but she refused to sanction their increasing emphasis on historical necessity, support for the Soviet Union, and anti-American diatribes.

Barnes's humanistic existentialism prevented her from viewing the New Radicals as bona fide existentialists. She dismissed elements of "anti-intellectualism and irresponsibility," which she found to be "characteristic of the apolitical, more nihilistic rebels" (206). While Barnes was not very specific about who these rebels were, she did, in the end, identify with the new student radicalism that was then exploding on American college campuses against speech codes, in support of the civil rights movement, and in opposition to the war in Vietnam: "I believe that I can discern in the New Radicals more hope for a positive moral rebirth in American society than in any other sector of today's world" (207).

Almost as a warning to the excesses of student rebellion, Barnes presented her own vision of what one could draw from the existential canon of Sartre, Beauvoir, and Camus that she had been laboring to develop. Most important, for Barnes, was a "concept of responsible freedom." Passion and commitment were keys to existentialism. How, she asked, to reply to the point raised by Walter Kaufmann about the authenticity of the passionate commitment of a Nazi to hatred? Rather than discussing Sartre's *Anti-Semite and Jew*, with its emphasis on the self-hatred and inauthentic nature of the anti-Semite, Barnes proposed that the true existentialist makes choices and takes action. Such choices and action may be good or bad, to be sure. But even "more sacred" to existentialism's emphasis on choice, action, and passionate commitment is its imperative (found most fully in Beauvoir) to not "treat others as objects, denying and abusing their freedom, perhaps killing them in the name of the true Faith" (299). Of course, this elided the question, since ethics begins with the recognition that conflicts arise when there is more than one person in the world.

Here, in essence, Barnes celebrates a Niebuhrian and Camusian view of the necessity of action tempered by the recognition of the tragic and limited nature of certitude. While Sartre may have abstractly assented to this formula, in practice his need for political engagement often overcame his political judgments. For Barnes, one must act, certainly, in accord with a vision that increased the overall fund of human freedom, without confusing that end with means antagonistic to it. Radical freedom meant radical self-questioning: "Only if the choice is renewed, without being accompanied by the refusal to put everything into question, does it remain existentially pure" (299–300).

In a very determined manner, Barnes helped shift the canon of existentialism. In previous analyses and anthologies, many penned by religious conservatives or guilty refugees from a previous radicalism, French existentialism had existed mainly as a depiction of the alienated, absurd landscape of the modern condition. The solutions of existentialists, especially Sartre and Beauvoir, were rejected out of hand because in the 1960s they were increasingly associated with Marxism and third-world liberation movements. Other analysts pushed the French aside in favor of a German religious existential tradition that seemed—in many thinkers, if not in Nietzsche—more open to religious solutions and to a politically unengaged search for pure Being. But Barnes would have none of this. While some might claim that an existentialist ethics implied no particular political position, Barnes, in pragmatic fashion, asked readers to think about the commitments of Sartre, Beauvoir, and Camus to women's rights, to racial equality, and to greater freedom. She attempted to create an appreciation for the politics of French existentialism within an American context. As she phrased it in *The Literature of Possibility* (1959), "It has always seemed strange to me that in discussions as to whether or not there is any positive philosophy of value in existentialism, both critics and defenders have almost universally ignored the constructive work of Sartre and de Beauvoir with regard to the oppression of minorities and the psychology of racial prejudice" (66).

OTHERS WERE ALSO aware of the particular political and racial valence of French existentialism. In the work of African-American novelists Richard Wright and Ralph Ellison, in the Hipster ideal of Norman Mailer, and in the early effusions of the New Left and the women's movement, the nexus between French existentialism and human liberation would be fully recognized and appropriated, becoming in the process part of the American conversation of existentialism.

1948–1968

*Realizing an
Existential Vision*

Chapter Eight

"Cold Rage": Richard Wright and Ralph Ellison

1   A CRITICAL MOMENT in the saga of Antoine Roquentin, the protagonist of Jean-Paul Sartre's first novel, *Nausea* (1938), occurs when he is "plunged in a horrible ecstasy" as the truth about the nausea that afflicts him is painfully revealed. Roquentin, an aimless historian attempting to write a biography of a nobleman, exists inauthentically; he seeks meaning in someone else's existence rather than in his own. As he comes to this realization, Roquentin confronts the root principles of Sartrean existentialist philosophy: "The essential thing is contingency. . . . To exist is simply *to be there.*" Rather than signaling the giddiness of freedom, this realization translates into despair, for men "are *superfluous,* that is to say, amorphous, vague and sad."[1]

To end the novel on this note would have been to give in to tragedy, to pose a problem without a solution. Instead, in the closing pages of this ceaselessly philosophical tome Sartre trumpets the initial blast of an existentialist resolution of possibility. Evaluating the sad contours of his life, Roquentin finally begins to hear, perhaps for the first time, the melody and words of a jazz song. He begins to feel: "A glorious little suffering has just been born, an exemplary suffering" (174). The liberating words to the song begin to intrude past the nausea, through the depths of nothingness: "Some of these days / You'll miss me, honey" (175).

The song plunges Roquentin into a reverie about the identities of the songwriter and the singer. The songwriter he imagines to be a Jewish man, a "clean-shaven American with thick black eyebrows" living in New York City, while the singer must be a "Negress." Through their art, the Negress and the Jew "have washed themselves of the sin of existing." Listening to this music of creation, Roquentin comes to feel "something I didn't know any more: a sort of joy" (176–77). Armed with a sense that one just might, through the energy of creation, be able to "justify" one's existence, Roquentin sees the image of himself at the dock of absurdity fade from view. He determines to act to create himself.

Jean-Paul Sartre had, without realizing it, linked together African-American blues and existentialism. While the link may be appropriate, his specific references are mistaken. One imagines that marvelous character in Ralph Ellison's essay "The Little Man at Chehaw Station" reading Sartre's riff on the blues and laughing at how he had managed to get it so right and yet so wrong. The Little Man is the trickster, the American autodidact, lurking behind the scenes ready to pounce upon unwarranted pretension or sloppy artistry.[2] He would have admonished this Frenchman Sartre to get his facts straight, especially if he intends to mess with the blues. The writer of "Some of These Days" was an African-American comedian and vaudevillian named Shelton Brooks, and the singer in the recording that Sartre references was almost certainly not a "Negress" but a Jewish woman, Sophie Tucker, known as "the Last of the Red Hot Mamas," who made the number her signature song in 1910.[3]

2   THOUGH ROOTED IN the African-American experience, the blues, like existentialism, claims both universal relevance and historical specificity. They dance quite well together, as Richard Wright and Ralph Ellison discovered. The depth of African-American suffering, according to Wright, transformed itself into "America's Metaphor."[4] Wright once said, "When the feeling of the fact of being Negro is accepted fully into the consciousness of a Negro there's something universal about it and something that lifts it above being a Negro in America." This "double consciousness," first made famous by W. E. B. Du Bois, brought with it a responsibility and a challenge. Thus lamented Wright, "Oh, will I ever have the strength and courage to tell what I feel and think; and do I know it well enough to tell it."[5] To tell it to himself and to the world became Wright's existential quest, allowing him the chance to transcend his despair, to escape the "exile from himself."[6] By combining the blues and existentialism, he and Ellison sought to capture the particular beat of the African-American experience and to render it in the idiom of the human condition.

"How those French boys and girls think and write; nothing like it exists on earth today," recalled Wright. Existential writers, he continued, were united by a "humanistic passion to defend the dignity of man."[7] Ellison once stated, "If I were to identify myself as an existentialist writer, then it would be existentialism in terms of André Malraux rather than Sartre. It would be in terms of Unamuno, let's say, without the religious framework, rather than Camus' emphasis."[8] Here Ellison flirts with the existentialist tradition while avoiding committing himself to a precise relationship, in a manner typical of his independent streak, his unwillingness to be reduced to any fixed identity.

Yet Ellison identified himself with existentialism, and he established its presence in African-American life: "There *is* an existential tradition within

American Negro life and, of course, that comes out of *the* blues and spirituals."[9] In similar fashion Wright proclaimed, "Now Kierkegaard is one of the great writers of today." But Wright read Kierkegaard as a comrade in despair, a fellow belter of the blues. Wright once assured his friend C. L. R. James "that he was reading Kierkegaard because everything that he read in Kierkegaard he had known before."[10] After talking with his friend Constance Webb about existentialism, Wright began to recite "existential" passages from his autobiography, *Black Boy* (1945). The pages he recited spoke of anxiety and pain, of situations in which one is forced into an inauthentic mode of being.[11]

Wright's pathos depended upon the gritty realism with which he evoked the pain and inauthenticity forced upon African Americans. This, according to James Baldwin and Ellison, diminished Wright as a novelist because it led him to focus on the pathology rather than the diversity and complexity of the African-American experience. In a devastating review, "Everybody's Protest Novel" (1949), Baldwin found that the failure of Wright's early fiction lay "in its rejection of life, the human being, the denial of his beauty, dread, power, in its insistence that it is his categorization alone which is real and which cannot be transcended."[12] Ellison agreed, calling for writers to capture, in a daring experimental style, the internal rhythms of creativity and freedom of African Americans. Moreover, Wright stood condemned by Ellison for the "boot-legging of philosophy" into fiction, which did a disservice both to philosophy and to fiction.[13]

There is some truth to these charges. Wright was a powerful if unimaginative naturalist, and his novels were designed, in part, to protest social injustice. Yet as he once yelled at James Baldwin, "What do you mean, *protest!* . . . *All* literature is protest." Wright considered it impossible to write a novel about African-American life in racist America that failed to register protest.[14] In contrast, Ellison wore his philosophical erudition and sources more lightly. When making philosophical allusions, Ellison carried them off with a touch of the comic that eluded Wright. Thus in *Invisible Man,* Ellison writes, riffing on Kierkegaard, "But I am an orator, a rabble-rouser—Am? I *was,* and perhaps shall be again. Who knows? All sickness is not unto death, neither is invisibility."[15]

Yet despite their stylistic differences, Wright and Ellison had much in common, both in their lives and in their work. Each began as an outsider, on account of race, early poverty, and geographical distance from centers of culture. Wright's *Black Boy* relates his struggle to find a voice and his consuming wish to flee the provincialism of the racist South. But even in the dark days of his Southern existence, he found a glimmer of freedom in books. Access to the public library became a trope of escape; books may not set one free, but they do help their reader to imagine freedom and to rebel against the iron fist of racial oppression. Reading transported Wright out of his narrow world: "My days and nights were one long, quiet, continuously contained dream of terror, tension, and anxiety."[16] Ellison, who always sought to upset staid presumptions, announced that deep pockets of culture are to be found everywhere, even in the South and his native Oklahoma. He recalled his music teacher at Tuskegee Institute, deep in the Black Belt, who proudly displayed on her piano a score signed by the Italian composer Busoni.[17] Yet both Wright and Ellison needed to escape to Northern centers, to Chicago and New York, to establish themselves as part of a community of writers. Out of these commonalities Wright and Ellison forged a friendship, with Ellison even serving as best man at Wright's first wedding.[18]

Like almost all African-American intellectuals coming of age in the depression era, Wright and Ellison came within the orbit of the Communist Party of America. According to the account they both offered during the Cold War era, their years in the Communist Party constituted a dark age from which they emerged slowly into the light of serious writing. In Wright's view, the Communist Party sought to subvert his intellectual and artistic freedom for its own particular purposes. "He talks like a book," said one African-American communist of Wright, and that, Wright said, "was enough to condemn me forever as 'bourgeois.'"[19] Ellison recalled how members of the party "sneered" at Wright's "intellectuality . . . and dismissed his concern with literature and culture as an affectation."[20]

Some historians take a more positive view of the relation between African-American writers and the Communist Party. Literary historian William J. Maxwell finds the Communist Party in Harlem to have been nonauthoritarian, in fact often open and supportive of African-American artists. Other scholars argue that the party greatly helped the cause of black civil rights and organized African-American workers, no matter what the national and international directives from the Comintern. The influence of the Communist Party on African-American intellectuals is probably less distinguished. While the party did offer, as Jerry Gafio Watts notes, an institutional framework for African-American intellectuals to come into contact with committed and successful white writers and a variety of party organs in which to publish, it also had a deadening effect on the quality of their writing. Membership and commitment came at a price; writers, especially African Americans, were supposed to represent "their people" in a politically useful, artistically determined manner. Departures from this version of socialist realism drew penalties ranging from warnings about deviationism to expulsion from the party, which meant the end of literary friendships and publishing connections.[21]

Wright and Ellison came to disdain the Communist Party because, as writer Saunders Redding put it, "communism did not allow for the play of individual thought and initiative. It had no warmth in it."[22] Wright agreed. He broke from the party around 1943 in the name of artistic freedom, although he had been relatively uncoerced by the party powers. After all, Wright's naturalistic style was *de rigueur* for party stalwarts, and he felt more comfortable with didacticism over experiment in his fiction.[23] Separation from the party did allow him in his novel *The Outsider* (1953) to consider fully the implications of the existential nature of the human condition, as well as to capture the machinations of the party elite. But this did not mark a break with his earlier writing. After all, as Granville Hicks noted, Wright's classic work of "protest fiction," *Native Son* (1940), concerns a "search for meaning" as much as does *The Outsider.* But Wright's "search for meaning" pertained to matters of both politics and the soul.[24] Ellison's break with the Communist Party, his coming out from the underground, arose from his visceral disdain for the party aesthetic. He defined his fiction by its blues idiom, its jaunty steps in the direction of literary creativity and stylistic experiment. Yet politics remained central to Ellison's fiction; he was, after all, writing about the experiences of a black man in racist white America.

An existential stance made it easier for Ellison and Wright to see themselves as heroic individuals, resisting Communist Party directives but still committed to literature and social change. This independence brought down upon them the ire of the party faithful. Thus Lloyd Brown excoriated the "one-man-against-the-world theme" of Ellison's *Invisible Man* as not only partial but part of "the anti-Communist lie that Ellison tells" in a novel that "is profoundly anti-Negro."[25] In practice, existentialist politics and fiction, no less than philosophy, prided themselves on their antiabstractionism, on their close connection with the rhythms of reality. More important, the existentialist ethos—the concern with human freedom—is always constrained, quite contrary to bourgeois ideals of progress, by its heavy burden of tragedy and limitation. Responsibility, not self-aggrandizement, defined French existentialism. As Wright recalled from a conversation with Sartre in 1947 (soon after Sartre had sketched his ideal of the committed writer in *What Is Literature?*), "Sartre is quite of my opinion regarding the possibility of action today, that it is up to the individual to do what he can to uphold the concept of what it means to be human."[26]

3 FREED FROM THE clamps of the Communist Party, Wright in *The Outsider* and Ellison in *Invisible Man* dissected the perfervid possibilities of freedom. Acknowledging communism to be the God that had failed, attracted more to the rhetoric and categories of Kierkegaard than to

the content of his religious faith, Wright and Ellison began to struggle with the existential nihilist tradition. Although they had broken from the regimentation and collectivism of the Communist Party, neither Wright nor Ellison became an apostle of individualism in the American grain, or of Russian anarchism, or of any other "ism." Wright's freedom consisted in his desire to remain politically engaged, to continue to rip at racism, and also to wrestle with the possibilities of freedom and individuality. Wright had learned a lesson about himself and collectivism: his communist comrades "had never been able to conquer their fear of the individual way in which I acted and lived, an individuality which life had seared into my bones."[27]

The existential nihilist tradition, exemplified in the work of Dostoevsky, especially his *Notes from Underground,* explores the possibility of a world where all the props for God and science, morals and mores, have crashed to the ground. In this bleak universe walk characters whose existence is totally free but for whom that freedom elicits terror rather than elation, passivity rather than activity: "It is best to do nothing! The best thing is conscious inertia!"[28] Self-loathing, despair, disdain for authority, alienation, and the lonely sense of impending death are the rocks scattered across the existential nihilist landscape. In its best moments, the literature of this tradition clearly articulates the malaise of modern existence without celebrating it. Thus in Dostoevsky, the glimmer of God slashes through the darkness; in Samuel Beckett, the resolve of the human spirit eases the loneliness of the absurd.

Wright and Ellison work through the limits of nihilism toward an existential sense of commitment and human solidarity. Ellison remarked that he connected his Invisible Man, "ever so distantly, with the narrator of Dostoevsky's *Notes from Underground,* and with that *I* began to structure the movement of my plot, while *he* began to merge with my more specialized concerns with fictional form and with certain problems arising out of the pluralistic literary tradition from which I spring."[29] As Ellison indicates, he (and Wright as well) is not content to claim a single precursor or tradition. Each has supped too fully at the table of humanistic existentialism and political reality to be satisfied with despair. Each must hold out for himself, and his readers, a sense of transcendence, a possibility of hope. For Wright, this imperative is reflected in his attempt to have Cross Damon, his outsider, recognize that sense of human meaning in a world where existence precedes essence and requires human interaction. Hell may often be other people, but hell is definitely red hot when other people are banished from our lives. Ellison's Invisible Man may exist on the periphery, may retreat to his underground lair, but he learns at the end of the novel that his existence will take on meaning only when he climbs up from below into the human family.

"Perhaps that's my greatest social crime," reflects the Invisible Man at the end of the novel: "I've overstayed my hibernation, since there's a possibility that even an invisible man has a socially responsible role to play."[30]

Although *The Outsider* and *Invisible Man* are both existential novels, flowing out of an extensive dialogue with the particular problems of black America and the existential problems of the human condition, they are structured quite differently. Wright's novel wears its philosophical armor in a sometimes weary, didactic style. Wright lets us know that he has read Kierkegaard, Sartre, and Beauvoir. Existentialism defines the work—sometimes to good effect, oftentimes not. In contrast, Ellison does not flaunt his existentialism. It is deeply enmeshed in the blues ideology that informs the novel. Ellison is the consummate artist, someone who believes that artistry must not take a back seat to message. This kind of artistry is what novelist and critic Albert Murray has in mind when he speaks of "the fundamental condition of human life as being a ceaseless struggle for form against chaos, of sense against nonsense." This is the human condition, the essence of a blues and existentialist life of heroic improvisation.[31]

4   RICHARD WRIGHT was an existentialist before he knew such a thing existed. According to his friend Margaret Walker, Wright was "close . . . to existentialism all his life. . . . [He] had lived with dread and despair. . . . [The] circumstances of black life in America were so bleak and tragic, and fraught with bitter, unrelieved suffering, and absurdity that only existentialist philosophy could give meaning to it."[32] Wright's *Native Son* and *Black Boy* gave "meaning" at least to some aspects of the black experience in America, without recourse to an explicitly existentialist idiom. But once Wright confronted the work of writers in the existential tradition, he was hooked; like Molière's Jourdain, he realized that he had been speaking prose his entire life without knowing it. Between the mid-1940s and early 1950s, Wright entered fully into a dialogue with European currents of existentialism, weighing its insights against his experiences as a black man in America and the world view that he had formed out of those indignities. He never confronted a choice of either existentialism or black life; he sought to bring the two together to speak to the universal problems of human existence and to the specific realities of African-American oppression.

Wright found in Fyodor Dostoevsky an early model for the writer grappling with the problem of the human condition. Around 1940 Wright began gobbling up Dostoevsky's fiction. "Foremost among all the writers who have influenced me," he wrote, "in my attitude toward the psychological state of man is Dostoevsky."[33] In 1960 Wright called Raskolnikov, the protagonist of *Crime and Punishment,* "one of my heroes."[34] Raskolnikov tests the limits of freedom and experiences the guilt of trying to be above morality. Wright exulted in the fever pitch of Dostoevsky's characters, in their living on the edge as outsiders, willing or forced to challenge with their lives the polite assumptions of their society. As the African-American religious thinker and literary critic Nathan A. Scott, Jr., puts it, Dostoevsky proclaimed as his own the modern world of the "lonely soul" and succeeded in "charting its hitherto unexplored recesses with the bravery and depth of insight of the true tragic poet." Indeed, Dostoevsky "performs a fierce surgery upon the modern soul."[35]

The escape from self and society and the guilt that comes with that freedom are the key themes of a story by Wright with the Dostoevskian title "The Man Who Lived Underground" (1944). "Emotionally," Wright's underground man "hovered between the world aboveground and the world underground."[36] Wright's protagonist, identified only once by name during the story, flees from the police after being forced to confess to a murder he did not commit. He escapes into the sewer system, wandering through its dark, cavelike structures. Occasionally he emerges to pilfer a radio from a shop or to rob a safe. He commits these crimes but feels no guilt for them or for the innocent people who suffer as a result. Maybe the beating of the boy accused of stealing the radio "would bring to the boy's attention, for the first time in his life, the secret of his existence, the guilt that he could never get rid of."[37] But Wright's underground man is consumed with guilt for the crime he has *not* committed. This most Dostoevskian of sagas ends with the underground man confessing to his crimes, trying to reveal the nature of his actions to policemen who cannot and do not want to fathom the depths of his soul. He threatens their sense of order, and he is executed in cold blood.

In the 1940s Wright discovered in French existentialism some answers to the "secret of experience" and representations of the "guilt that he could never get rid of." He first learned about existentialism through his friend Dorothy Norman. Norman, a wealthy patron of the arts and an important photographer, was intellectually lively and well connected. In 1938 she founded the journal *Twice a Year*, which she edited until 1948, publishing work by Kafka, Anaïs Nin, Sartre, Beauvoir, Camus, and many other writers. The journal also served as a forum for work by leading antifascist writers. Norman met Wright in 1944, and they quickly became friends. At her soirées he encountered important intellectuals such as Hannah Arendt and Paul Tillich.[38] Through Norman, Wright came into contact with Sartre, Beauvoir, and Camus.[39]

Thanks to literary historian Michel Fabre we can with some certainty reconstruct Wright's initial readings of French existentialist texts. Wright read Sartre's important essay "Anti-Semite and Jew" when it was published in

Partisan Review in 1946. He next read Sartre's *Existentialism* in 1947, and between 1949 and 1951 he read many of Sartre's novels and plays, including *The Chips Are Down,* a novel in some respects similar to *The Outsider.* He read Camus's pessimistic essay "The Crisis of Man" in *Twice a Year* in 1946, followed by *The Stranger* and *Caligula* in 1947. He read *The Plague* in 1948. While personally close to Beauvoir, according to Fabre, Wright read only one of her works, *The Second Sex,* with care.[40] In the case of Beauvoir, the influence was more from Wright to her, as she perceived in Wright's model of African-American oppression and psychological damage a means of understanding the oppression of women.[41]

Wright interacted with the French existentialists at a most opportune moment. In the late 1940s Sartre sought through his "third way" politics to steer clear of both the Soviets and the Americans while remaining politically committed. He increasingly engaged with struggles around the world against colonialism, and he had not quite yet become an apologist for the Soviet Union.[42] Wright too sought a third way and increasingly came to identify with anti-imperialist struggles. Wright had rejected the Communist Party with insight and vehemence. But in doing so he had cut himself off from a host of literary and political connections. This sense of loneliness was, of course, only exacerbated by his leaving the United States for France in 1947. Luckily he fit comfortably into existentialist circles in Paris.

This comfort, in the minds of some critics, undermined Wright's fiction, cutting him off from his roots and draining his writing of its passion and intensity of experience. These problems are seen to undermine the success of Wright's novel *The Outsider.* First, some condemned the novel as philosophically ponderous and irrelevant to African-American struggles in the South, the struggles that had been the lifeblood of Wright's creative universe. Second, the novel struck some as derivative, owing too much to Sartre's *The Chips Are Down.*[43]

On the first point, some old friends of Wright believed that his exile in France and immersion in European existentialist texts had harmed his writing. Arna Bontemps claimed that Wright "did his best writing when he was unhappy, when he was angry, when he was under tremendous tension." If Wright's happiness hindered his creativity, then he was crippled further by his interest in existentialism. Writer Saunders Redding proclaimed that "existentialism is no philosophy that can be made to accommodate the reality of Negro life." In Redding's dichotomy, Wright thought as an existentialist but lived as a Negro.[44] Granville Hicks, in a very favorable review of *The Outsider* as the "first consciously existential" novel composed by an American author, admitted that Wright had abandoned sociological and racial analysis for a more general excursion into the human condition.[45] Critic

Steven Marcus charged that Wright had failed to universalize his African-American hero; instead he "simply denies the Negro's experience and reality."[46] Wright fueled this view by writing on the jacket notice for *The Outsider* that his "hero could be of any race."[47] Yet other analysts discover in the novel a strong sense of racial injustice, with Wright unmasking racism in all of its insidious forms. Unfortunately these analysts in turn quickly dismiss the existential, universal pretensions of the novel to focus on racial politics: "*The Outsider* must be seen against this background of anti-colonialism, anti-fascism, and anti-racism."[48]

The Outsider shuttles back and forth between the particular and the universal, the passionate and the philosophical. While Margaret Walker correctly refers to the novel as the "most autobiographical," hence most particular, of Wright's works because it deals with his experiences of alienation, poverty, new beginnings, and the Communist Party, it also attempts to subsume particular experiences into a universal, philosophical framework.[49] Wright had found Camus's novel *The Stranger* "devoid of passion. . . . What is of course really interesting in this book is the use of fiction to express a philosophical point of view."[50] Wright wanted passion and philosophy to merge in *The Outsider*. Thus he employed the oxymoronic expression "cold rage" twice in the novel to convey the melding of passion and thought in the acts of Cross Damon, a bridging of the gap between emotion and reason that defines his character but fails to absolve him of guilt and responsibility.[51]

As for the second complaint about *The Outsider*—that it was derivative—the similarities between it and Sartre's largely forgotten novel *The Chips Are Down* (originally conceived as a screenplay) are insignificant in both a philosophical and a literary sense. Although Wright was intently reading existentialist works by the time he went to Paris in 1947, he had begun work on his novel well before this time.[52] Sartre's novel appeared in an English translation in 1948. Also, the theme of *The Chips Are Down* is hardly unusual. Beauvoir wrote to Sartre in 1947 about seeing a film version of Hemingway's *The Killers*: "Once again dead people coming back to earth, and there's exactly your gimmick."[53]

Sartre's novel is about second chances, much like the second chance that Wright's protagonist Cross Damon gets. But there the similarities end. Sartre's characters Eve and Pierre are given a reprieve after their deaths because in the strange world of the afterlife they find that they were meant to love each other. Returned to earthly existence for twenty-four hours, they must demonstrate that their love can be realized absolutely and uncompromisingly. If not, they must return to the realm of the dead. While Eve and Pierre do love one another, they are burdened with their past, with their social class and connections. They must attempt to break free of those webs that have defined their lives. Alas, there are no opportunities to clean the slate after the fact. What's done is done. As Eve so existentially phrases it, "The chips are down, you see. One can't take back one's bet."[54]

Cross Damon, the protagonist of *The Outsider,* also grasps at a second chance. A troubled young postal worker, unhappily married with children, Cross is having an affair with an underage woman who is pregnant with his child. He drinks too much and contemplates suicide. Without prospects, waiting for death, he exists in existential despair. "Death" comes, but in the most unanticipated, opportune manner. In a case of mistaken identity, Cross Damon is declared dead, the victim of a train crash. He decides, in a giddy moment of freedom, to allow his death to stand and to create for himself a new identity. Unlike the characters in Sartre's novel, each of whom acts in good faith and with an eye toward humanity, Damon proceeds without scruples; his freedom is nihilistic and absolute. It leads to his committing murder, and eventually to the suicide of the one he loves. Only at the end of the novel does Damon come to the realization that he has wasted his second chance.

For Wright, failure is not inherent in the quest as it is for Sartre. In *The Chips Are Down* and in his play *No Exit,* Sartre maintains that we are our acts; nothing can be changed. In contrast, Wright assumes that Damon erred only in the degree of his attempt to remake himself apart from humanity. Damon represents nihilism, but at the moment of his death he comes to recognize his mistake: "The search can't be done alone. . . . Never alone. . . . Alone a man is nothing. . . . Man is a promise that he must never break."[55]

The Chips Are Down and *The Outsider* both traffic in existential themes, but they part company on the potential for personal transcendence. Sartre's novel is clearly in step with themes that run throughout his early philosophical works. Existence precedes essence, and the individual is free to create himself and the world. The choices one makes, however, authentic or not, cannot be changed. Transcendence comes through action and projects. Sartre does not concern himself with religious issues. Anxiety accompanies freedom and responsibility—nothing more, nothing less. While Sartre's emphasis on choice resembles the dialectic of faith in Kierkegaard—and Sartre did borrow psychological categories from Kierkegaard for use in *Being and Nothingness*—it differs from religious existentialism in the essential limits of the choice. For Sartre, given his metaphysics, to take the leap into religion is an act of bad faith; illusion overcomes the responsibility to act freely.

In a sense, Wright agrees with Sartre. He considers religion a dead option as well. But *The Outsider* depends so much upon the psychological and religious structure of Kierkegaard that it becomes a work of secular religion. Wright proves himself more conversant with Kierkegaard's writings than with Sartre's. Kierkegaard's *The Concept of Dread* was "almost a daily companion" of Wright's, according to one of his friends.[56] Wright's work feels distinctly different from Sartre's—at once more constrained and more hopeful. Wright is far superior to Sartre as a novelist, and his eye for psychological detail is more attuned to Kierkegaardian inflections than it is to Sartrean postures. Yet Wright is a novelist, rather than a philosopher. Thus he is a *bricoleur,* someone who takes bits and pieces of philosophy and psychology from wherever he finds them; consistency of the thought concerns him less than how well that thought propels his novel.

5   As noted earlier, Wright carefully read Kierkegaard and Dostoevsky, two writers who fit well into the tradition of religious existentialism. Each one, after his own minute dissection of the malaise of modern man, opts for the leap into faith and salvation. Wright structures the path of Cross Damon, from dread to despair to decision, in the same manner. A "mood of bleak dread" defines Damon, but he cannot share with anyone else "the nightmare that was his life."[57] In writing *The Outsider,* Wright borrowed much of his discussion of anxiety or dread from Kierkegaard's *The Concept of Dread,* translated by Walter Lowrie. In fact, book 1 of *The Outsider,* called "Dread," opens with an epigraph selected from Kierkegaard's work: "Dread is an alien power which lays hold of an individual, and yet one cannot tear oneself away, nor has one a will to do so; for one fears what one desires" (1).

In Kierkegaardian terms, one method, albeit a futile one, of attempting to alleviate the horror of despair is to live aesthetically. In "The Seducer's Diary" Kierkegaard describes this approach to life as the Don Juan syndrome, a flitting from one pleasure to another without real satisfaction. The individual staves off anxiety in the face of emptiness by chasing after some particular object of desire. The gaining of the object only renews the sense of anxiety, and the quest begins anew. Kierkegaard describes the seducer in terms that also apply with precision to Wright's Cross Damon:

> He who goes astray within himself does not have such a large territory in which to move; he soon perceives that it is a circle from which he cannot find an exit. . . . I can think of nothing more tormenting than a scheming mind that loses the thread and then directs all its keenness against itself as the conscience awakens and it becomes a matter of rescuing himself from this perplexity. The many exits from his foxhole are futile; the instant his troubled soul already thinks it sees daylight filtering in, it turns out to be a new entrance, and thus, like panic-stricken wild game, pursued by despair, he is continually seeking an exit and continually finding an entrance through which he goes back into himself. Such a person is not always what could be called a crim-

inal; he very often is himself frustrated by his own schemes, and yet he is stricken with a more terrible punishment than is the criminal, for what is even the pain of repentance compared with this conscious madness?[58]

In many ways Damon exemplifies the Kierkegaardian seducer. Driven by his need to create an identity, ultimately hobbled by his own nihilism and by the murders that he commits with increasing regularity, Damon finds himself without an "exit." Unlike the judge in Kierkegaard's parable, whose life is based upon universal ethical injunctions, or Abraham, the Knight of Faith, who lives according to commands from God, Damon lives as an aesthete, according to values that he creates himself and with relatively little concern for the needs and rights of others. This form of existential nihilism has its allures, especially when Damon reflects back on the life he had led previously, a life distinguished only by its constant dread. But his new life, which in Kierkegaardian terms is aimless and soulless, results in new, deeper forms of anxiety and despair that cry out for a religious solution. Although Damon feels little apparent guilt at his murder of an old friend and his later killings of a proto-fascist and a communist, he wraps himself up in a web of deceit. When he confesses his crimes to Eva, the woman he loves, her shock pushes her to suicide. This death, which he has caused, sends Damon, the seducer and murderer, into a new state of being: despair.

In Kierkegaardian terms, despair differs from dread, although Wright frequently muddled the distinction. The "Dread" with which Wright deals in book 1 of *The Outsider* is the anxiety of everyday life. Damon's dread can often be connected with specific details of his life: his troubled relationships, his religious upbringing. By contrast, his sense of despair is more generic. It hits him especially hard, compared with his post office buddies, because he possesses acutely refined sensibilities and a highly reflective self-consciousness. He refuses to lose himself in the realm of the inauthentic, or in what Sartre would call acts of bad faith. Unprotected by bad faith, Damon lives in dread. He gains a chance to go "beyond freedom" but quickly encounters new sources of anxiety and guilt.[59]

In book 4 of the novel, "Despair," Damon finally hits bottom. His suffering goes beyond dread to include numbing feelings of helplessness and guilt. Now, burdened by his acts of murder and his compromised love for Eva, he becomes consumed by guilt. The "godlike power" (317) that he had earlier been able to exercise without a second thought no longer protects him from himself. Instead, the burden of godlike absolute freedom only drives home Damon's loneliness and his absolute inability to resolve his problems.

In Kierkegaard, this teetering on the edge of the abyss is the existential religious moment just before the individual, aware of his or her sinfulness and without hope, takes the leap into faith and salvation. In a more secular sense, Damon takes a first step on the road to salvation when, driven by guilt, he seeks a confessor. District attorney Ely Houston is a logical candidate for the role. A hunchback (like Kierkegaard) and a devotee of Nietzschean ideals, Houston understands Damon's nihilism and shares his fascination with absolute freedom in a world without divine sanction. As Houston puts it, "My greatest sympathy is for those who feel that they have a *right* to break the law." Houston appreciates the will to power but chooses, in a heroic act of self-abnegation, not to exercise it. He has gained insight into the mind of the modern nihilist without himself expressing anything other than abstract, intellectual sympathy with the position. Houston lives vicariously, in the realm of the mind. He is a voyeur, reveling in and revolting against Damon's willingness to go "beyond freedom" into pure nihilism. But Damon will not play Houston's game; he needs to confess to Eva, the one pure being in the novel. Unfortunately, Eva cannot accept his admission of deceit and murder. Damon's decision to share his deepest secrets with her brings him back into the human community, but at a terrible cost. Eva's leap into suicide leaves Damon without human connections, his only option being to take his own leap, either into death or into a new life.

Wright takes another Kierkegaardian religious term as the title of the final book of *The Outsider:* "Decision." Damon has now wasted his second chance at life, has committed multiple murders, and carries a crushing burden of guilt. In Wright's resolutely secular universe, a religious leap of faith to redemption through Christ is impossible. And a third chance for Damon to establish a new identity and life seems foreclosed and absurd. To bring matters to a conclusion, Wright has Damon shot by his enemies in the Communist Party. Revealingly, they execute him not because he threatens them in a doctrinal sense but because they simply cannot comprehend what makes him tick. As unknown, alienated man, Damon is the incomprehensible, monstrous face of modernity.

At the moment of his death, Damon makes a full accounting with the mistakes of his life. In his underground existence, he had attempted to be a god and to set himself apart from others. In many ways his perceptions of the world were thoroughly existential, though nihilistic: "Maybe man is nothing in particular. . . . Maybe that's the terror of it. Man may be just anything at all" (172). For Damon, the world lacks inherent meaning; existence appears to be an absurd relationship between the desires of men and the reality of nature. The problem for him, and for the existential nihilist tradition, is that when such insights are taken as absolutes, without regard for consequences and responsibility, disaster ensues. Neither religious solutions nor liberal ideals of progress speak to Wright. As Damon comes to realize, human existence, without any metaphysical support structures, is hell. In a reversal of the overused Sartrean equation that "hell is other people," the life of Cross Damon reveals that hell is being without other people. And in a reversal of another Sartrean dictum—that "man is a useless passion"—Damon recognizes that "man is all we've got" (585).

In the years during and after the composition of *The Outsider,* Wright pursued on a world stage a politics of noncommunist radicalism, identifying himself with African nationalism and condemning white racism and colonialism. While Michel Fabre sees Wright in these years as moving beyond his "period of existential doubting," the imperatives of existentialism remained with him. In his radical manifesto *White Man, Listen!* (1957) he continued to identify himself with the underground mentality, welcoming the sense of "aloneness" as perhaps the "natural, inevitable condition of man." Asked by a young woman if his ideas "make people happy," Wright responded, "My dear, I do not deal in happiness; I deal in meaning."[60] And, as Wright well knew, that search for meaning, for Cross Damon and himself, brought the individual into the terrain of the existential.

6   IN THE NOVEL *Invisible Man* (1952) and in the many interviews and essays collected in the seminal volumes *Shadow and Act* (1964) and *Going to the Territory* (1986), Ralph Ellison presented the blues and existentialism as complementary forms of expression: one can hear music in existentialist philosophy and read philosophy in the music of the blues. The philosophy of blues music expresses the existential realities of everyday life. Wright too acknowledged this connection. At critical points in *The Outsider,* the blues and jazz music serve as expressions of modern alienation and transcendence. For Cross Damon, "blue-jazz" captures his "sense of estrangement" (178). While the blues is the specific vernacular expression of African Americans—rooted in the experiences of the middle passage, slavery, the lost hopes of Reconstruction, and the great migration to the North—the content of the music escapes strict confinement to African-American experience. Indeed, blues narratives are rarely explicit about racism. More commonly, the blues centers around problems of love, estrangement, and loneliness. It relates the sadness of love gone cold, of living without hope, and of life's treacheries. These conditions are overcome not through metaphysical speculation—as is the case in Sartre—but through the celebration of the reality of the pain and its transcendence through irony.

The blues, according to critic Albert Murray, must be understood in terms of something more than its lyrical content. In fact, the words of blues songs are often so mumbled and muttered as to be incomprehensible. Yet in the familiar pounding rhythms of the blues can be found a secular form of salvation, a momentary release in the ecstasy of the dance. The blues enthusiast dances both with and against the devil. As Ellison has expressed it, "The blues is an impulse to keep the painful details and episodes of a brutal experience alive in one's aching consciousness, to finger its jagged grain, and to transcend it, not by the consolation of philosophy but by squeezing from it a near-tragic, near-comic lyricism." In words that might apply with cunning veracity in the *Invisible Man,* Ellison notes that "as a form, the blues is an autobiographical chronicle of personal catastrophe expressed lyrically."[61]

The relationship between the blues and existentialism rests upon both abstract affinities and specific circumstances. First, for African Americans, existentialism's vocabulary of dread, absurdity, and death captures the tempo of their experience, both in the Jim Crow South and in the Northern states to which many migrated. Second, for Ellison, the use of existentialist terminology, as employed in the interviews and essays, provided him with cultural capital, the imprimatur of being in a conversation with a European philosophical and literary movement. Since common themes mark the languages of existentialism and the blues, this rummaging around in traditions allowed Ellison to avoid being reduced to his worst nightmare: a writer of black protest fiction. Existentialism permitted him to confront the human condition. Conversely, his blues idiom helped him to record the experience and day-to-day realities of the black community. Third, for Ellison, no less than for Richard Wright, the turn to existentialism related to his break with the literary politics of the communist movement in the United States in the 1930s and 1940s. Out of this break with party discipline and theory, Ellison gravitated not only toward existentialism but toward a form of existentialist heroism wherein the individual, rather than the race or class, became, despite certain limitations, the lonely possessor of responsibility for his fate.

A will to master and to mix diverse traditions dominates Ellison's work and thought. Ellison employed existentialism and the blues to capture African-American particularity and to universalize it, both through subject and art, so that his work might express (in a way that Sartre's Roquentin could only dream about) "man's triumph over chaos."[62] Ellison understood that "the human condition varies for each and every writer just as it does for each and every individual. Each must live within the isolation of his own senses, dreams, and memories; each must die his own death. For the writer the problem is to project his own conception eloquently and artistically. Like all good artists, he stakes his talent against the world."[63]

In interviews and essays, Ellison has acknowledged his literary ancestors. When pressed about the blues folklore that informs so much of *Invisible*

Man, he responded that obviously he was attuned to the African-American tradition. His musical background in the blues and jazz was immense, and he could easily wax nostalgic remembering the blues energy of his fellow Oklahoman Jimmy Rushing. The African-American blues tradition was mediated and transformed by Ellison into a different art form by its dialogue with European modernism. After all, he noted, it was thanks to the influence of T. S. Eliot and James Joyce that he became "conscious of the literary value of my folk inheritance."[64] Ellison cherished being able to mix and match diverse cultural traditions.[65]

Writing in *Partisan Review* in 1958, Ellison acknowledged the complexity of his background, in part as a ploy to avoid confinement within any single tradition: "My cultural background, like that of most Americans, is dual (my middle name, sadly enough, is Waldo)."[66] Here Ellison plays in a trickster, ironic mode, admitting that he is both African-American and American, especially blessed, or cursed, with the odd name if not the legacy of Ralph Waldo Emerson. Like Emerson, Ralph Waldo Ellison draws on traditions while also setting himself up as one of the rank of Poets, who—in the words of Emerson—are "liberating gods, they are free, and they make free."[67] Or, as Ellison quotes from André Malraux, "All poetry . . . implies the destruction of the relationship between things that seems obvious to us in favor of particular relationships imposed by the poet."[68]

The celebration of freedom, Emersonian or existential, powers Ellison's work. During his artistic apprenticeship in the 1930s, well before Sartre and Camus had become the sentinels of an existentialist sensibility in America, Ellison was already "aware of Kierkegaard and Unamuno." Yet it was André Malraux, more than anyone else, who became associated in Ellison's mind with existentialism. Ellison marveled at Malraux's heroic stature as the writer making history and art while participating in the Spanish Civil War.[69] He transformed the Malrauxean ideal of heroism into the stuff of art and everyday life.[70] Finally, Ellison's friend, novelist and blues critic Albert Murray, documented the fascination with Malraux and existential heroism that each of them connected with African-American blues: "André Malraux might well have been referring to the blues and the function of blues musicians when he described the human condition in terms of ever-impending chaos and declared that each victory of the artist represents a triumph of man over his fate. That he was addressing himself to fundamental implications of heroism should be clear enough."[71]

Some critics deride Ellison's existential heroism, his struggle for self-definition and individual artistry, as both politically counterproductive and naive. Jerry Gafio Watts takes Ellison to task for being "obsessed with the issue of individual freedom." Watts claims that Ellisonian existentialism prioritizes the individual over the community, strips away the historically specific and enduring context of racism, and ultimately undermines group solidarity. To Watts, Ellison sinks "too deeply into the quagmire of bourgeois liberty."[72] Years earlier Irving Howe had voiced similar complaints, condemning Ellison's heroic individualism as "a moral and psychological impossibility" for African Americans in racist America.[73]

Watts and Howe drew the line too boldly between protest fiction and individual freedom. To be sure, Ellison prioritized artistic creativity over social message. And, after his negative experiences with the Communist Party, he preferred to dance to an individual rather than a collectivist tune. He wanted his fiction of heroism, even when tinged with irony, to critique racism and power. But this must be done in a manner that avoided naturalism that reduced characters to ciphers of social forces. In existential language, Ellison opted for choice and freedom on the part of the individual. Yet in order to exercise judgment, the individual had to come of age, shed the blinders of convention and bad faith. Even when composing in a comic mode, Ellison proved adept at capturing the daily indignities confronted by African Americans. His fiction rivets attention on the concrete, on the individual in the act of rebellion or acquiescence. As the Invisible Man eventually comes to recognize, only by coming into the open air of self-consciousness does collective solidarity become a possibility.

7   *Invisible Man* presents the tale of a nameless young African-American male coming of age after the First World War. The existential valence of the novel derives from the Invisible Man's inauthenticity; he clings to the role of the good student on the road to Booker T. Washington–like self-improvement and respectability. Clothed in this false suit of identity, the Invisible Man is constantly baffled and battered by circumstances, as if he were experiencing someone else's fate. So long as he has this perception, he is absolved from responsibility for his own fate. Paradoxically, the bright light of the day blinds him to the racism and absurdity of modern America; only when he is underground does he achieve self-consciousness. But this recognition comes at the cost of loneliness and alienation. Thus at the conclusion of this novel on race and the human condition, the Invisible Man decides to leave his underground lair (shades of Dostoevsky and Wright).[74] Chastened but unbowed, he enters into the light to challenge the absurdity of racist power and the power of absurdity. By making the choice to emerge, the Invisible Man takes responsibility and proclaims the relevance of his own experiences, and his own humanity, for others: "Who knows but that, on the lower frequencies, I speak for you?"[75]

A blues refrain opens up the novel in a very important manner. In the prologue the Invisible Man announces his desire to hear at once "five recordings of Louis Armstrong playing and singing 'What Did I Do to Be So Black and Blue'" (1929). The Invisible Man respects Armstrong "because he's made poetry out of being invisible. I think it must be because he's unaware that he *is* invisible." The narrator explains that the power of Armstrong's music and of his invisibility comes from "a slightly different sense of time, you're never quite on the beat." This being ahead of or behind the beat allows one to "slip into the breaks and look around. That's what you hear vaguely in Louis' music" (8).

Ellison taps the same beat in his novel, invoking and playing on Armstrong's music. First, he references a particular Armstrong recording of "What Did I Do," and an unusual one at that. Like most blues songs, this work expresses suffering, poverty, and isolation: "empty beds," "ain't got a friend." Most of these lyrics, as Armstrong sings them, are slurred, as if to maintain invisibility. But the recording puts a challenging emphasis on color: Armstrong can very clearly be heard to sing, "My only sin is in my skin / What did I do, to be so black and blue?" In an act of double signification, the nature of a musical form (the blues) and the suffering of a particular race (the black) are reflected in the idiomatic expression for being bruised (black and blue).

Taking its cue from Armstrong's blues, the initial chapter of Ellison's novel narrates the horrible and absurd experiences the Invisible Man suffers at the Battle Royal.[76] At this point the Invisible Man cannot perceive the reality of the world; he is inauthentic, uttering empty lines memorized from Booker T. Washington and the psychology of racial uplift. He gushes with pride about winning a scholarship to attend an African-American college. Summoned to address the town's leading white citizens who have bestowed this honor upon him, the Invisible Man is humiliated and put in his place. He is thrown together with a group of rougher black boys and, for the pleasure of the white audience, put through a number of exercises in absurdity and degradation: being made to try to hit one another while blindfolded, being forced to gaze upon a naked white woman and to dive for coins resting upon an electrified surface.

Surviving these indignities, the Invisible Man, now literally black and blue from the ordeal, recites his speech while swallowing his own blood, symbolic of the blood of his race shed by the white man. The reward for his acquiescence appears, at first, to be unproblematic. He receives a fancy leather briefcase and a scholarship to attend the black college. "I was so moved that I could hardly express my thanks. A rope [an ironic reference to lynching] of bloody saliva forming a shape like an undiscovered continent drooled upon the leather and I wiped it quickly away. I felt an importance that I had never dreamed" (32). These hard-won objects figure later in the novel, when during a riot in Harlem the Invisible Man "escapes" into a sewer. Now, surrounded by absolute blackness, he tries to burn both his possessions (his high school diploma) and his illusions so that he may at last find true illumination.

Existentialist and blues perspectives recur throughout *Invisible Man*. In a well-known analysis, critic Houston A. Baker, Jr., shows that the chapter dealing with the sharecropper Trueblood is an extended blues refrain, brimming with recognition of the weaknesses of the flesh, allusions to castration, the acceptance of tragic responsibility, and not a small dose of jiving for financial benefit.[77] Trueblood rapes and impregnates his daughter one cold night when she joins him and his wife to sleep in the warmth of a single bed. In this act, Trueblood is both a willing participant and a victim of circumstance. "Trueblood's true consciousness," observes critic Steven Marx, "is of the ambivalence at the heart of his destiny."[78] Despite this ambivalence, Trueblood in his own manner comes to take responsibility for what has transpired, and he fashions the experience into an extended blues meditation. Most important, the blues connects with an existential recognition and acceptance of one's fate and the implications of one's acts. As Trueblood recounts it, "All I know is I *ends up* singin' the blues. I sings me some blues that night ain't never been sang before, and while I'm singin' them blues I makes up my mind that I ain't nobody but myself and ain't nothing I can do but let whatever happen, happen" (66). Trueblood decides to return home and face his wife and daughter. In a show of the individualistic heroism of everyday life that Ellison so admired, he accepts his fate and his responsibility to his family.

To sing the blues, one must wrestle with the heavy burden of consciousness. Throughout much of the narrative, the Invisible Man cannot sing the blues because he fails to penetrate the veil of convention, to comprehend the absurdity of his condition. Having lost his scholarship, he arrives in New York City with a letter from Bledsoe, his college president, that he is confident will procure him employment and enable him to earn sufficient funds to return to school. His troubles at college began when he allowed a white benefactor to the college to stray into a saloon where African-American uplift did not exist. He thus violated one of Bledsoe's rules: never let the white person peek behind the veil of black respectability. In retaliation, Bledsoe crafts a "letter of recommendation" for the Invisible Man that ensures that he will be denied employment. By nature dangerously trusting, he dutifully makes the rounds with this letter, ignorant of its contents.

Just prior to learning the actual nature of the letter, the Invisible Man happens to meet someone named Peter Wheatstraw (evidently named for the real-life blues singer Peetie Wheatstraw). Like so many of the African Americans in the novel, Wheatstraw appears to be insane because he is without illusions. But knowledge must be puzzled out of life. Wheatstraw engages the Invisible Man with questions flavored with Southern humor and blues language. He pushes a cart full of architectural plans. When the Invisible Man asks where he got the plans and why he carries them around, Wheatstraw explains: "Plenty of these [plans] ain't never been used, you know. . . . Folks is always making plans and changing 'em" (172). Thinking of the letter of recommendation that he carries, the Invisible Man responds, with the ardor of the uninitiated, "You have to stick to the plan" (172). That, as he will soon find out, is the essence of his problem, which is part of a more profound problem: realizing that what is regularly offered as the truth is in fact bogus. Indeed, the Invisible Man has the text in front of him at every moment, but he is unable or unwilling to read it. In addition to failing to read what is in front of him, the Invisible Man has difficulty hearing what is said to him: "You're going too fast," he complains to Wheatstraw. Wheatstraw responds in the signifying language that Henry Louis Gates, Jr., finds central to African-American discourse: "Okay, I'm slowing down. I'll verse you but I won't curse you—My name is Peter Wheatstraw, I'm the Devil's only son-in-law, so roll 'em!" (172–73).[79]

In his excellent analysis of the Wheatstraw episode, Pancho Savery notes that the actual Peetie Wheatstraw was known as the "Devil's Son-in-Law." For Savery the identity of Wheatstraw as a blues singer is less important than what both he and Trueblood represent through their association with the blues: the continuity of the black tradition.[80] They attest, through their songs, to the reality of American racism and human suffering as well as possible responses to these facts of the human condition. The blues images and characters that populate the novel, then, are designed to establish a tradition (of acknowledgment and resistance) and to presage the coming to knowledge and the self-fashioning of identity on the part of the Invisible Man.

What will be the form of knowledge and identity assumed by the Invisible Man? It is here in the novel that existentialism and the blues assert themselves most forcefully. Prior to achieving self-knowledge, the Invisible Man must engage a parody of existential nihilism in the character of Rinehart. In some ways reminiscent of the hipster figure later celebrated by Norman Mailer, Rinehart is described variously as protean, chaotic, a phantom lover, a man of multiple, ever-shifting identities. He thrives on the chaos of creation. Attempting to describe him, the Invisible Man suddenly comes to enlightenment about himself and the nature of the world. Rinehart, the Invisible Man finds, "was a broad man, a man of parts who got around. Rinehart the rounder. It was true as I was true. His world was possibility and he knew it. He was years ahead of me and I was a fool. I must have been crazy and blind. The world in which we lived was without boundaries. A vast seething, hot world of fluidity, and Rine the rascal was at home. Perhaps *only* Rine the rascal was at home in it. It was unbelievable, but perhaps only the unbelievable could be believed. Perhaps the truth was always a lie" (490). As in the gospel line, "I was blind but now I see," the Invisible Man gains second sight. But what he sees, about himself and the world, proves unsatisfying. He escapes by fleeing underground.

There is, to be sure, a certain sense of comfort in invisibility underground. The Invisible Man's cavern is festooned with lights, powered by energy that he steals from the electric company. But the lights are blinding, preventing him from seeing himself. In contrast, Rinehart does not have an identity problem, paradoxically, because he does not have an identity. He is protean energy personified, albeit without direction. In his underground exile, the Invisible Man may never burn out, but he also cannot feel any warmth. In hibernation he, like Rinehart, avoids social bonds. The problem now confronting the Invisible Man is existential: what identity will he choose to present to the world, knowing full well that the world is indifferent to him?

Freedom equates with a state of becoming, a coming to awareness of the essential absurdity and alienation experienced by man as being-in-the-world; this means, above all, a recognition that man exists within the context of a community. As critic Cushing Strout remarks, "Ellison puts an existentialist's emphasis on knowing who one is as a condition for freedom, but for him that discovery is not only personal but communal."[81] The story of the Invisible Man reflects in comic and ironic fashion on this developing self-knowledge. The events that confront the Invisible Man are different in style from those that enmesh Sartre's Roquentin, yet both characters attempt to fashion a plan of action in the face of nothingness. But freedom, existentially considered, comes with costs. Absolute freedom, as Ellison makes clear in the character of Rinehart, is tantamount to blind fury. Freedom requires that once the clouds of illusion dissipate, hopelessness and inactivity do not follow. That would constitute only one piece of the puzzle of life: knowledge without a commitment to activity in the face of absurdity is unheroic, from Ellison's existentialist perspective. Out of the depths of existential and blues despair comes the responsibility to act, to claim in some small way responsibility for one's existence. Ellison thus transforms themes drawn from the blues cultural tradition into a philosophical statement that places ultimate responsibility—artistic and otherwise—in the hands of the individual. In roundabout fashion, then, Ellison's Invisible Man gains the opportunity to be the Malrauxean existential hero. This turning point occurs when the Invisible Man announces his intention to end his hibernation: "Perhaps that's my greatest social crime, I've overstayed my hibernation, since there's a possibility that even an invisible man has a socially responsible role to play" (572).

IN BOTH WRIGHT and Ellison, existentialism performed a host of functions. It offered them a language of engagement, a philosophical grounding to confront the vicissitudes of the human condition without forfeiting the specifics of the African-American milieu that served as the foundation for their writing. In so doing, existentialism supported a blues ideology and political analysis. It offered a current vocabulary that allowed Wright especially, but also Ellison, to connect their fiction of the black experience to a wider philosophical movement. Both Wright and Ellison engineered this act of appropriation on their own terms, rather than those of Sartre, Camus, or the Communist Party. Existentialism's ultimate appeal consisted in its ability to confront the essential question of art, the "meaning of life," the crushing reality of death, and the need to channel the "cold rage" that defined the existence of the artist and of the African-American experience. Others, such as Norman Mailer and Robert Frank, would similarly alight upon the affinities between the horrors of modern existential life in general and the particulars of African-American experience. Mailer especially failed to recognize that existential nihilism imprisoned, rather than liberated, the black person in America.

Chapter Nine

Norman Mailer's Existential Errand

1 NORMAN MAILER liked to spar with Jean-Paul Sartre in the boxing
ring of his mind. Mailer considered Sartre a worthy adversary, perhaps
the only thinker in the world who could match him as a novelist, essayist,
and public intellectual. Mailer admired the jab of Sartre's dialectical intellect, so subtle that "he could peel a nuance like an onion." But Sartre could
not go the distance, in Mailer's view, because "he had no sense of evil, the
anguish of God, and the possible existence of Satan."[1] In contrast to Sartre's
belief "that life is an absurdity," Mailer proclaimed that "for me life is meaningful but everything in the scheme of things will drive us to seeing things
as absurd. We could hardly be more different. He is an atheist and I'm not."[2]
Mailer believed there was a meaning to be discovered behind the pasteboard mask of reality, a truth to be wrested, a battle for good to triumph over
evil. Whatever their ultimate theological differences, Sartre and Mailer
shared a desire, as expressed by Mailer, to effect "a revolution in the consciousness of our time."[3]

Thus Mailer confronts Sartre and the anxiety of influence. He takes the
Sartrean position—expressed in Sartre's *What Is Literature?*—that the
writer must engage the age. But he distances himself from Sartre in an intriguing fashion. Sartre had in 1950 proclaimed the shallowness of Americans' sense of evil, but now Mailer turns the tables on him, announcing that
in fact Sartre himself lacked a sufficient sense of evil. Through a theologi-
cally charged sense of evil and political commitment, Mailer sets off to produce his revolution in the consciousness of his time.

After graduating from Harvard in 1943, Mailer fought in the Pacific during the Second World War, determined to use his experiences to write a
great war novel. In the 1950s he created for himself a persona of the writer
as rebel, a sort of modern antinomian. Thus in an era when America defined
itself according to its gross national product, suburban sprawl, and consensus ideology, Mailer worked overtime to set himself apart. To a sexually repressed America, he depicted sexuality in raw, hard terms. To a self-satisfied
America, he presented characters teeming with anxiety. To a complacently

religious America, he promoted a passionate and violent counterfaith. Against the American ideals of the corporate manager and family man, he celebrated the hipster and murderer. To those who viewed America on an upward spiral, he counterposed a nation in a state of decline, being eaten away by a moral cancer. He wanted to be, through his fiction and essays, a voice in the wilderness, a writer shaking the foundations of his era. The language and philosophical formulations that he employed would always be "Mailerian," individualistic to the extreme, but the general outlines of his perspective belong to the existential tradition.

Mailer pronounced himself, in no uncertain terms, an American existentialist. From the late 1950s through the 1970s, he returned repeatedly to forms of the word "existential." In *The Presidential Papers* (1963), *Existential Errands* (1972), and many of his interviews, he used the term to suggest "a situation where we cannot foretell the end."[4] He spoke of "existential" heroism, of "existential" acts such as marching on the Pentagon, of the "existential" nature of interviews, and of the "existential" confrontations of prizefights. He referred to his film *Wild 90* as "existential." He considered acting the most "existential" of endeavors because the actor "deals with situations like love, sex, disaster and death, all those accidents and ultimates whose ends are by their nature indeterminable."[5] He searched the horizon for existential sightings, finding them in varied places. In the figures of Martin Luther King, Jr., and John F. Kennedy he discovered individuals poised to "create a new reality which would displace the old psychological reality" of racism or presidential passivity. He went so far as to call Kennedy an "Existential Hero" in his essay "Superman Comes to the Supermarket" (1960).[6] In his near obsession with the term *existential*, perhaps Mailer sought to accomplish what he called that most "exceptional" of things: "to introduce a new idea into America," an idea that would be thoroughly grounded in his own grand ambitions and insights.[7] An existential consciousness, for Mailer, betokened a new reality for postwar America, a reality untainted by conformity and complacency.

Did Mailer have a clue about what he was doing in bandying about the term "existential"? Did he possess any sustained knowledge of existentialism? The depth and provenance of his existentialism are unclear. Mailer admitted that he had read little of Heidegger and only a smattering of Sartre. He possessed even less knowledge of Christian existentialism as outlined in the work of Tillich, Bonhoeffer, Jaspers, and Marcel. His biographer Mary V. Dearborn maintains that Mailer's knowledge of French existentialism came mostly from reading William Barrett's *What Is Existentialism?* in the late 1940s.[8] In response to a review of Dearborn's book, Mailer remembered "reading *Being and Nothingness* over many weeks and arguing in my mind with Sartre for years."⁹ Yet as we shall see, he had delved more deeply into Kierkegaard.

In the end, the question of the degree of Mailer's engagement with the primary texts of existentialism is academic. Suffice it to say that he may well have read *Being and Nothingness*. As a youthful member of the *Partisan Review* circle, he no doubt encountered the writings of Sartre, Beauvoir, and Camus. And given the degree of interest in Kierkegaard in the late 1940s and early 1950s, thanks in part to Auden's anthology of Kierkegaard's writings, Mailer probably read some of this material as well. In any case, he had an unerring ear for the cultural conversation of his era. Even lacking a thorough grounding in existentialism, Mailer proved quite adept at delineating what he viewed as the essential problems of existentialism as currently being developed by Sartre. Existentialism provided Mailer with a new vocabulary in which to express his well-established notions about life as marked by a Manichean struggle between the forces of good and evil, the necessity to experience sin in order to be saved, and the blurred line between sin and salvation. Moreover, his use of existential terminology pushed him into a world of experience and action.

We do have some idea of the time frame and circumstances of Mailer's embrace of an existential vocabulary. In "The White Negro" (1957), one of his most infamous effusions, Mailer had presented a vision of the demimonde, a celebration of life on the edge as lived by those outside the law: Negro hipsters, pimps, drug addicts, and murderers. These existential psychopaths or hipsters acted with nihilistic freedom in an orgy of destruction. This struck Mailer as a valid response to the conformity, consumerism, and repression of mainstream American culture in the mid-1950s. But the Mailerian hipster evolved into the existentialist hero. Mailer explained this shift in terminology: "I came to use the words existential and existentialism rather than Hip. Hip, I knew, would end in a box on Madison Avenue."¹⁰ Although he had from the very start associated a certain theological or religious imperative with the hipster's quest for authenticity and intensity of experience, Mailer needed to develop a fuller theology, one in which existential imperatives would be supported in the world of everyday experience. Perhaps he also wanted to distance himself from the hipster ideal that was then associated with certain aspects of Beat culture. Or, conversely, perhaps because of the sophistication and popularity of existentialism, Mailer suddenly emerged with his own version of an existential theology. But the essential ideas of the existential struggle against death and of the individual's need to define himself against the age in an authentic manner—these notions had long been central to Mailer's work as a writer.

In retrospect, the first two decades of Mailer's work, from publication of

The Naked and The Dead (1948) well into *The Armies of the Night* (1968), revolve around an existential concern with the problem of evil. In Mailer's universe, the Devil is afoot, and God is under siege. God and the Devil wage this battle by proxy, through the actions of human beings on each side of the divide. Mailer wanted to express this religious, Manichean cosmology in existential terms. His notion of the forces of good versus evil, albeit intended for radical purposes, greatly resembled the either/or rhetoric of Cold War liberals.[11] Hipster heroes, soldiers representing all walks of life, and individuals struggling to find themselves command his attention. In the background, informing all of their struggles, is the effort to transcend evil, to fight against the Devil. In the act of defining themselves, Mailer's heroes make choices that have an effect on others. Even his most outrageous conception, the hipster, becomes a religious and existential luminary, a transcendent creature wailing against Mailer's three C's of death: conformity, consumerism, and cancer, all the Devil's pride. Through his apotheosis of violence and life at the edges, the hipster transforms himself into a force for good, a life force keeping the Devil at bay.

2 MAILER'S INITIAL encounter in print with the idea of the absurd and other existential themes occurred in May 1956. In his last column for the New York *Village Voice,* an alternative paper that he had helped found, Mailer worried about the importance and meaning of Samuel Beckett's play *Waiting for Godot,* which had just opened in a New York production. In this stark, absurdist drama, two characters play a waiting game—for truth, for life, for God. The play can be read as a commentary on a world without meaning, on the transitory nature of existence. Yet it can also be viewed as an expression of how, in the face of nothingness, the human spirit manages to keep hope alive, how it struggles to endure.

Without having seen or read the play, his knowledge of it based solely on reviews and word of mouth, Mailer dismissed it as enunciating a "view of life . . . most attractive to those who are impotent. So I doubt if I will like it, because finally not everyone is impotent, nor is our final fate, our human condition, necessarily doomed to impotence." A few days after the column appeared, after reading the play twice and actually viewing the production, Mailer repented, finding Beckett's work to be "about impotence rather than an ode to it." Despite its bleakness and "hopeless" aspects, he now admitted that the play succeeded as a work of art.[12] Mailer was tentative with his praise partly because of his reaction to a Beckett interview he had read earlier that week in the *New York Times.* There Beckett had appeared to stress the themes of impotence and ignorance, placing them at the heart of his work. From this Mailer concluded that the play was "the latest touchstone in social chi-chi. . . . Most of the present admirers of 'Godot' are, I believe, snobs, intellectual snobs of undue ambition and impotent imagination, the worst sort of literary type, invariably more interested in being part of some intellectual elite than in the creative act itself" (321).

In coming to terms with Beckett's masterwork, Mailer confronted some of his own demons concerning impotence and the meaning of existence.[13] The Beckett essay occupies a suggestive position in *Advertisements for Myself* (1959), Mailer's bravura commentary upon his own intellectual and artistic development. It comes at the end of the third section of the book, right before the section that features his most important and controversial essay, "The White Negro." I am not saying that Mailer's encounter with Beckett's absurdist, existential landscape moved him to write "The White Negro." In earlier *Village Voice* articles he had already elucidated some essentials of his philosophy of the hipster rebel. But by grappling with Beckett, by positioning himself in opposition to the impotent "chi-chi" wails of "withered puffballs, balls blown passively through life" (322), Mailer had formulated his new vision. This new view of transcendence through heroic transgression, this ideal of "the destructive, the liberating, the creative nihilism of the Hip" (325), constituted the core of his American existentialism.

But well before Mailer expressed his "mature" view of transcendence in "The White Negro," he had already engaged issues raised in the review of *Waiting for Godot:* good versus evil, potency versus impotency, hope versus despair. These oppositions appear throughout his early novels. In his first two novels, *The Naked and the Dead* (1948) and *Barbary Shore* (1951), Mailer depicted a nihilistic world marked by the exercise of power. The crushing weight of political and military authoritarianism is relieved only by irony and absurdity. Power and planning go awry, thanks to the chaos of nature and pure luck. And, as we shall see, in essays and in two other novels that sandwich "The White Negro," in *The Deer Park* (1955) and *An American Dream* (1965), Mailer developed his particular version of transgressive-theological existentialism based on the hero engaging in cathartic violence in behalf of a beleaguered God.

3 AT AGE TWENTY-FIVE, home from the war, Mailer published his immensely successful debut novel, *The Naked and the Dead.* The Second World War served as a backdrop for this excavation of the exercise of naked power. On a small Pacific island, American forces attempt to dislodge the Japanese from their entrenched position. Cummings, the American commanding officer, is a sadistic proto-fascist, a Nietzschean superman of the mind. Yet for all of his power and tactical brilliance, the absurdist reality of war intrudes on his plans. Convinced of the necessity for major naval

support to launch an assault upon the Japanese position, Cummings leaves the island to request logistical help from his superiors. While he is away, his second in command, the plodding, unimaginative Major Dalleson, without forethought but with immense of amounts of luck, manages to rout the enemy. Meanwhile, Sergeant Croft, who personifies the primitive will of physical power, attempts Ahab-like to lead his soldiers in a maniacal quest up Mount Anaka. To achieve this end, he deceives the liberal Captain Hearn, who dies as a result. But Croft's vision of conquering the mountain through an act of sheer will is stolen from him when, as he clutches for the summit, a nest of hornets is unleashed, forcing the survivors to scurry back down. Absurdity piles upon absurdity, for it turns out, unbeknownst to Croft and his men, that the climb occurred after the Japanese had already been defeated.

Mailer's emphasis on the absurdity of war, as demonstrated in the utter inability of men to control external events and the forces of nature, suggests an existential focus. There coexists with this bleak emphasis a respect for individual heroism, even when it proves to be an absurd endeavor. Soldiers Goldstein and Ridges attempt to save the life of Wilson, a severely wounded comrade. They trudge with him through a landscape of unrelenting heat and despair, fixed on their goal of making it to the safety of the shore. The monotony of the trek is broken by Wilson's anguished cries for water, which his comrades know they must not give him, for a drink would be fatal to a man with a stomach wound as terrible as his. Finally, Ridges gives in. His thirst quenched, Wilson dies, and the rescue mission has ended, absurdly, in failure.

In addition to exploring the absurdity of human endeavor, Mailer depicts in *The Naked and the Dead* a modern world marked by alienation, isolation, and the looming specter of totalitarianism—all themes that defined the discourse of intellectuals in the 1950s. In the "Time Machines" sections of the novel, vignettes reminiscent of the flashbacks in John Dos Passos's *USA,* Mailer attempts to show the illusions under which each of the soldiers was raised, the hurts they have absorbed and nourished, and the numbing sense of limitation that they cannot shrug off. In Sartrean terms, Mailer's characters act in bad faith, fixed in terms of what they represent rather than of what they might become. Imprisoned in the chambers of their histories, the soldiers are passive. Thus a soldier named Roth, in the tones of the characters in *Waiting for Godot,* cries out to his comrades, who are isolated from him in a host of ways, "I can't go on, I can't."[14] Faced with the need to make a leap across a mountain precipice, Roth feels "dread" and "anxiety," his fate framed in the vocabulary of existentialism. When the time comes to make the leap, the Kierkegaardian assault, Roth recognizes that while he wants to jump, "his body knew he could not make it" (665). But *not* to jump is impossible. Impelled by social pressure and his own bitterness, "his exhausted body propelling him too feebly," he ends up clutching at "nothing. . . . In his fall Roth heard himself bellow with anger, and was amazed that he could make so great a noise. Through his numbness, through his disbelief, he had a thought before he crashed into the rocks far below. He wanted to live. A little man, tumbling through space" (666).

Standing in contrast to this "little man" clutching absurdly at the spark of life are the totalitarians Croft and Cummings. They are men of action and resolve, conversant with power and history and willing to take the risks that make life something more than the cancer of slow death that was a central theme in Mailer's existentialist ontology. Croft's totalitarianism is almost Darwinian. Relentless in his determination to prove his physical audacity, to act ruthlessly, and to impose his will by force of power, Croft moves easily through the world of "nature red of tooth and claw." Yet he is not a superman in any sense, since with but one crucial exception he is a tool of his superiors, a good soldier who has been trained to follow orders. Croft's totalitarianism, then, is that of the jungle. But his powers are eclipsed in the mechanized and bureaucratic world that Cummings dominates.

Conversant and comfortable with ideas, Cummings understands the movement of history and the play of power: "The only morality of the future is a power morality, and a man who cannot find his adjustment to it is doomed" (323). Aware that "the natural role of twentieth-century man is anxiety" (177), Cummings manipulates the isolation of modern men to capture them for potential mass movements that would meet their psychological need for direction and belief. The general, and men of leadership like him, move the chess pieces of humanity around, occasionally sacrificing some of them in causes that satisfy the bureaucratic rationale of the totalitarian state.

In many ways Cummings exemplifies the ideas then current in the sociology of totalitarianism, captured in works such as Erich Fromm's *Escape from Freedom* (1941). In miniature, the battle of wills between the liberal Hearn and the fascist Cummings mimics the real struggle then going on in the world of politics. Cummings crushes Hearn by forcing him to stoop down and pick up a cigarette. In time, Cummings will translate his power over the individual into an equal power over the mass: "He would find it. There had been a time when Hearn had resisted him too. And his elation, suppressed until now, stimulated him" (326). Cummings's exercise of power, however, is bureaucratic and nihilistic, beyond good and evil; thus, in a sense, it is empty, devoid of values or of greater ends.

4 ALTHOUGH MAILER'S next novel, *Barbary Shore,* takes place in the confining quarters of a rooming house in Brooklyn, it deals with issues similar to those of *The Naked and the Dead:* the power of the state, the weakness of the individual, the failure of will, and the decline of hope. As in Beckett, these issues form a landscape of impotency and gloom. Mailer referred to this work as the "first of the existentialist novels in America."[15] Critic Norman Podhoretz agreed with Mailer about the existentialism of *Barbary Shore,* finding that everything in the novel "seems to hang on the will of the people involved."[16] For critic Richard Poirier, the main character of the novel "is an American hip existentialist almost by default—long before 'The White Negro.'"[17] Mailer considered even the reception of *Barbary Shore* to have been existential because of how reviewers savaged the book and reduced it to a mere footnote in cultural history.[18]

The novel is organized around a series of existential situations. The weakly drawn main character, Mickey Lovett, is a war veteran, an amnesiac, and a writer. A man without a history, Lovett does possess the will to create in the present—a perfect existential character thrust into a hothouse of ideas and intrigue. In the Brooklyn boardinghouse where Lovett resides, landlady Beverly Guinevere exemplifies the America ideal in decline. She represents the lascivious modern world of consumerism, the allure of the flesh; her life is modeled upon Hollywood dreams and kitsch notions. She is not really in an existential state of becoming; she is fully formed by the messages of her culture. Her seductiveness makes her both appealing and dangerous to the existential development of other characters in the novel.

The protagonists in this existential battle, a battle perhaps over the future of humanity, are, first, McLeod, an important operative in the communist movement before the Second World War who during the war went to work for the United States government. A chastened Marxist, of sorts, he is believed to have stolen a small, never identified object from the government. Another character, Hollingsworth, represents the banality of evil. He wants this object returned, although it is unclear in whose interests he operates. In the midst of an endless series of dialogues about crushed hopes and human possibilities, a situation is created whereby McLeod finally seems to capitulate to Hollingsworth's demands for the object. In so doing, he relinquishes hope for a revolutionary future. But instead of giving the object to Hollingsworth, McLeod opts to entrust it to Lovett: "So the heritage passed on to me, poor hope, and the little object as well, and I went out into the world."[19]

Action does not ensue on Lovett's part. He plays a waiting game, as "the blind will lead the blind, and the deaf shout warnings to one another until their voices are lost." Although McLeod may hope that Lovett will "be alive to see the rising of the Phoenix," the atmosphere and conclusion of the novel suggest not the possibility of revolutionary salvation but rather the futility of waiting impotently on false hopes, like the characters in *Godot* (223). Even when the individual is thrust into an existential situation, the impotency of action, the absurdity of social movements, seems to reduce him to a cipher, a man without a past but also without the ability to impose his will on the future.

Barbary Shore captures Mailer's frustrations with American politics of the 1950s. In 1948 he had been a supporter of Henry A. Wallace, whom he perceived to be a man of the left, or at least a dissenter against emergent Cold War corporativism. Mailer had also been attempting, in the manner of Sartre in the 1940s, to maintain an independent political course, one that opposed Marxist collectivism and Stalinism while also rejecting American imperialism and material realities. After *Barbary Shore,* Mailer moved from an overriding concern with politics to a focus on culture, but he remained a radical in his cultural politics.[20] Driven by existential imperatives, Mailer cried out for authenticity against the emergent liberal consensus of the era. Clearly he wanted a way out of the morass of American culture. His solution, however problematic, appeared in his essay "The White Negro."

5   "THE WHITE NEGRO" should be read as a jazz riff, a daring existential foray into a new consciousness. Mailer begins with the terrain familiar not only to Beckett and Sartre but to the New York intellectuals as well. Themes of death and rebellion, conformity and creation, predominate. The Second World War had "presented a mirror to the human condition which blinded anyone who looked into it."[21] In the face of mass destruction, of new, faceless forms of annihilation, modern men and women suffer "from a collective failure of nerve" (338). This insight obviously parallels those of Schlesinger's *The Vital Center,* although Mailer desires a vital center for culture *and* rebellion in a time of despair: "Our collective condition is to live with instant death by atomic war, relatively quick death by the State as *l'univers concentrationnaire,* or with a slow death by conformity with every creative and rebellious instinct stifled (at what damage to the mind and the heart and the liver and the nerves no research foundation for cancer will discover in a hurry), if the fate of twentieth century man is to live with death from adolescence to premature senescence" (339). Mailer refuses to rest with this set of unsatisfying alternatives. His solution will appear in the figure of the existential hipster, the rebel psychopath who acknowledges and lives under the sign of death. The hipster chooses to be creative, albeit in an often destructive manner.

The existential hipster has arrived at "the only life-giving answer [which] is to accept the terms of death, to live with death as immediate danger . . . to set out on that uncharted journey into the rebellious imperatives of the self" (339). If Mailer had stopped with this designation, his hipster would have fit well with the notion of the existential hero as a figure confronting death in its various forms, refusing at all times the stultifying succor of bad faith. But while Mailer admitted affinities between his hipster and existential images of man, he refused to join the circle of French existentialism.

Mailer found French existentialism, with its rejection of the unconscious and its Cartesian temperament, a tepid philosophy that welcomed alienation "without ever feeling it at all" (341). The French had developed a philosophy of alienation that was aloof from its own assumptions, aware of absurdity but without a religious or passionate sense of purpose that would propel the individual beyond that absurdity. Mailer's existential hipster, in contrast, stood ready to strike at any moment, an individual with an existential, more than an intellectual, awareness of the nature of man (341–43).

Despite his protestations, Mailer shared much with Sartre in terms of intellectual range and artistic reach, as well as politics. And both of them were fascinated with the underbelly of polite society, raging against the bourgeois culture that had spawned them. Moreover, Mailer's image of the hipster closely mirrored Sartre's presentation of the thief, sexual predator, and writer Jean Genet.[22] Thus for the pugnacious Mailer, the closer he came to French existentialism the more he needed to distance himself from it.

Mailer celebrated the psychopath as existential hero. He discovered exemplars of the hip existential mentality in drug addicts, jazz musicians, and oppressed African Americans. Drawing on some insights that his friend psychologist Robert Lindner had developed, Mailer hailed the singular "private vision" of the psychopath. The psychopath, in his frenzied search for stimulation, for intensity of experience, embraces the reality of his death and transcends it (albeit momentarily) through acts of rebellion, acts that are often childlike, murderous, "dark, romantic," but always creative and dynamic: "His inner experience of the possibilities within death is his logic." In the psychopath, then, we see a philosophy of movement and process, growth and change, new challenges constantly being met, the individual testing the possibilities of life by flirting with the omnipresent reality of death (342–43). In his embrace of violence as catharsis, Mailer admits that he has a "masculine argument" designed to distinguish his existential hipster from the "feminine" mystical thinker (342). Like the Beats, Mailer excludes existential possibilities for women; his vision is gendered and narrow. Creativity and transcendence are male, stasis and tradition are female, for Mailer as much as for Sartre. In his vehement rejection of middle-class values, Mailer promotes a vision of the male as sexual libertine, inhabiting a world in which women serve the sexual needs of men who are embarked on paths of self-discovery and liberation.

For Mailer, the American Negro incarnated the psychopathic hipster personality. He intended this as praise. The Negro, in Mailer's terminology, had been transformed into the psychopathic hipster through centuries of oppressive social conditions. The psychic circuits of the Negro had been formed under a reign of terror, of horrible acts of violence and discrimination:

> Knowing in the cells of his existence that life was war, nothing but war, the Negro (all exceptions admitted) could rarely afford the sophisticated inhibitions of civilization, and so he kept for his survival the art of the primitive, he lived in the enormous present, he subsisted for his Saturday night kicks, relinquishing the pleasures of the mind for the more obligatory pleasures of the body, and in his music he gave voice to the character and quality of his existence, to his rage and the infinite variations of joy, lust, languor, growl, cramp, pinch, scream and despair of his orgasm. (341)

This was, to put it mildly, a highly controversial interpretation that perversely transformed the data of discrimination into the prerequisites for a deeper, existential freedom. In the minds of some of his critics, most famously James Baldwin, Mailer badly misunderstood the survival mechanisms that African Americans had been forced to adopt in white America. The rigors of their existence in the face of racist white power were not a source of joyous transcendence but a daily grind of humiliation and suffering. When Mailer chose to slum it with drug addicts, pimps, pushers, and psychopaths (whether black or white), Baldwin found him and others of his ilk (such as Jack Kerouac in his reflections about the "true" life of the Negro) absurd and naive. As to Mailer's musings about the sexuality of blacks, their ability to achieve more powerful orgasm because of their proximity to death, Baldwin thought it sick to "malign the sorely menaced sexuality of Negroes in order to justify the white man's own sexual panic."[23]

In point of fact, Mailer was following a line of inquiry with a long, controversial history. As historian Eric Lott has demonstrated, whites constructed an identity for themselves based in part upon differences posited between them and the Other, in this case the African American. Built into the very sinews of that construction was a powerful combination of disdain mingled with desire.[24] Mailer, then, seems to have been playing with a representation of the African American—as carefree, sexually liberated, and hip—that already existed within the construction of both black and white identities. Although Mailer stereotyped the African American in a manner that fit all too easily into white racist perceptions, he also developed an analysis of the blues and hip that resonated within black culture.

After all, Mailer's description of the blues and jazz—as arising out of black suffering, as capturing the experiential realities of the black condition in white America, and as a means of transcendence and spiritual escape—resembles black critic Albert Murray's insightful depiction of the blues, but with a critical distinction. For Murray, the blues is existential because it is "a statement about confronting the complexities inherent in the human situation and about improvising or experimenting or riffing or otherwise playing with (or even gambling with) such possibilities as are also inherent in the obstacles, the disjunctures, and the jeopardy. It is also a statement about perseverance and about resilience and thus also about the maintenance of equilibrium despite precarious circumstances and about achieving elegance in the very process of coping with the rudiments of subsistence."[25] But for Murray, as for Ralph Ellison, while this is part of the African-American condition and culture, it is also inherent in the human condition. More important, Murray refuses to reduce the blues or black life to mere pathological categories.

In contrast, Mailer composed for polemical purposes rather than for nuance. He appropriated the image of the Negro as sexual libertine not to deny him his humanity but to celebrate the possibility of existential freedom. In doing so, he froze identity for the African American, an act of bad faith akin to that of the racist's search for a fixed identity for the object of his scorn. Unfortunately, Mailer downplayed acts of quiet resistance and necessary submission, of the humanity of complex individuals attempting to cope with the black experience in Jim Crow racist America.

Mailer's vision of the hipster derived also from his observations of the New York jazz scene during the 1950s. Black musicians lived on the edge with their music, creating an idiom that grew out of both their freedom and their confinement. Their style seemed to fit the negative stereotypes of the racist mind while also rejecting dominant values through new modes of dress and expression. The jazz musician represented Mailer's hipster ideal: the spontaneous and creative individual mocking the expectations of white conformist society.[26]

Mailer probably learned much about the language of hip, existential rebellion from Anatole Broyard's essay "A Portrait of the Hipster," which appeared in *Partisan Review* in 1948. Broyard's essay fascinates for a number of reasons, beyond its import as a precursor to Mailer's later, more famous rendition. Broyard, a Greenwich Village fixture, had a lightning-quick mind along with a penetrating style and grace. Well known around the Village for his deep comprehension of black culture, Broyard marvelously imitated the style, the walk, and the glare of the hipster Negro. In his memoir of life in Greenwich Village, Broyard presented a raucous account of sexual experiment, intellectual stimulation, and the necessity of distancing oneself from family connections. But as critic Henry Louis Gates, Jr., has revealed, Broyard was born an African American; he passed for white in an act of concealment and reinvention. Broyard was a reversal of Mailer's White Negro: the Negro as White Hipster.[27]

According to Broyard, the hipster developed the language of jive to deal with anxiety. "Articulateness is a . . . cause of anxiety"; thus the language of jive or hip by its very inarticulateness serves to "cut the world down to size. . . . In a vocabulary of a dozen verbs, adjectives, and nouns he [the hipster] could describe everything that happened" (721). Hip language, Broyard claimed, consisted of aggression, sexual metaphor, and irony. The hipster carried "his language and his new philosophy like concealed weapons" in order "to conquer the world" (722). Through style, dress, and music, the hipster created a counterculture, with values opposite those of the dominant culture. Anticipating Mailer's celebration of the criminal psychopath, Broyard noted that the hipster "was an underground man, requiring especial adjustment to ordinary conditions; he was a lucifugous creature of the darkness, where sex, gambling, crime, and other bold acts of consequence occurred" (723).

Broyard anticipated Mailer's frame of mind. He noted that "intellectuals *manqués*" naturally embrace the hipster: "Ransacking everything for meaning, admiring insurgence, they attributed every heroism to the hipster. He became their 'there but for the grip of my superego go I.' He was received in the Village as an oracle; his language was *the revolution of the word, the personal idiom.* He was the great instinctual man, an ambassador from the Id. . . . He was an interpreter for the blind, the deaf, the dumb, the insensible, the impotent" (726). Alas, wrote Broyard, such celebration co-opted the hipster, who then "grew moribundly self-conscious, smug, encapsulated, isolated from its source, from the sickness which spawned it. . . . The hipster—once an unregenerate individualist, an underground poet, a guerrilla—had become a pretentious poet laureate" (727).

Mailer's "The White Negro" built upon the image that Broyard celebrated while adding to it the notion of the psychopath as a way of safeguarding his hipster against easy co-optation. Mailer's hipster was not a Beat, in the manner of Jack Kerouac or Allen Ginsberg. Beat rebellion struck Mailer as too tame, too predictable, without sufficient edge. Thus in detailing the psychology of the psychopathic hipster, Mailer stressed antisocial emotions and urges. Psychopathic violence became a search for the "apocalyptic orgasm," hipster therapy, a Reichian mode of growing and letting go of self-hatred and self-repression (347). The hipster vented his deepest urges, marked at once by "infantile fantasy" and violent rage (346). Only by expressing these desires could the psychopath transcend the conformity and death of the world.

In one of his more unfortunate effusions Mailer announced,

> I obey the logic of the extreme psychopath—even if the fear is of him-self, and the action is to murder. The psychopath murders—if he has the courage—out of the necessity to purge his violence, for if he can-not empty his hatred then he cannot love, his being is frozen with im-placable self-hatred for his cowardice. (It can of course be suggested that it takes little courage for two strong eighteen-year old hoodlums, let us say, to beat in the brains of a candy-store keeper, and indeed the act—even by the logic of the psychopath—is not likely to prove very therapeutic for the victim is not an immediate equal. Still, courage of a sort is necessary, for one murders not only a weak fifty-year old man but an institution as well, one violates private property, one enters into a new relation with the police and introduces a dangerous element into one's life. The hoodlum is therefore daring the unknown, and so no matter how brutal the act, is not altogether cowardly. (347)

If this be the sum total of Mailer's American existentialism, then it is deeply problematic, at least in its initial expression in "The White Negro." Hazel E. Barnes found Mailer's effusions to be a form of "nihilistic fulfillment," a spirit "contrary to that of any writer associated with existentialism."[28] Indeed, the Sartrean existentialist, for all his presumed Cartesianism, presents a much hardier ethical ideal. His existential isolation is tame in comparison with the raging isolation of his American counterpart. Sartrean existentialism pushes outward toward political engagement against pure nihilism. Mailer has rhetorically placed himself in a no man's land. Action replaces impotence, to be sure, but at the cost of human solidarity. All Mailer seems to offer are fleeting orgasms and the fury of destructive rage. Such vitalism and inten-sity become obsolete at the very moment of their expression, and the junkie's quest for ever more intense experience begins anew. Thus Norman Pod-horetz observes that the hipster, in reaction to the hypocrisy of the domi-nant culture, retreats "into a private world of his own where everything, in-cluding language, is stripped down to what he considers the reliable essentials."[29] But these essentials are insufficient; the spiral of inwardness can lead only to self-destruction.

Mailer recognized this, of course. In "The White Negro" he did attempt to gloss such elements in his existential logic. He talked about the language of hip as essentially creative, a language of movement that believed that "to swing is to communicate, is to convey the rhythms of one's own being to a lover, a friend, or an audience, and—equally necessary—be able to feel the rhythms of their response." For Mailer "the conception of the learning process as dug by Hip is that one cannot really learn until one contains within oneself the implicit rhythm of the subject or the person" (350). Yet Mailer admitted that hip morality meant "to do what one feels whenever and wherever it is possible . . . to open the limits of the possible for oneself" (354).

Mailer wanted to move beyond nihilism. Along with Beauvoir, he posited the need for an existential ethics: "In widening the arena of the possible, one widens it reciprocally for others as well, so that the nihilistic fulfillment of each man's desire contains its antithesis of human co-operation" (354). It remained murky, at best, as to where one might find "human co-operation" in the beating to death of the candy-store owner. Certainly Mailer fails at this stage to acknowledge an ethics of responsibility because he is so wildly intent on promoting individual catharsis as a means to overcome the deadening effects of postwar American conformity. But his nihilism takes an intriguing turn when he increasingly argues that individuals can act in behalf of God in a struggle with the Devil. The Devil, for Mailer, personifies institutions of conformity, modes of repression, cancers that inhibit individual growth. By striking out, violently, against such entities, the rebel pushes toward the creation of "the catharsis which prepares growth" (355).[30] The hipster, in Mailer's view, thus functions as a truly religious existentialist: "To be an existentialist, one must be able to feel oneself—one must know one's desires, one's rages, one's anguish. . . . To be a real existentialist (Sartre admittedly to the contrary) one must be religious, one must have one's sense of the 'purpose'—whatever the purpose may be—but a life which is directed by one's faith in the necessity of action is a life committed to the notion that the substratum of existence is the search, the end meaningful but mysterious" (341).

6 MAILER'S STRONGEST fictional expression of the existential hipster is the character Marion Faye in *The Deer Park,* published two years before "The White Negro." Some critics have found Faye to be the key character in *The Deer Park,* even though he appears in only a handful of pages in the novel. Nathan A. Scott considers him to be an essentially religious figure because he is "committed, with something like a monastic rigor, to the disciplines of the *via negativa.*"[31] Faye's hipster world is defined by "acts of violence as the catharsis which prepares growth." A pimp, an individual of strong convictions, Faye refuses to entertain illusions about himself. He em-

bodies all of the emerging concerns of Mailer's American existentialism: the fascination with death and transcendence, the notion of living without bad faith, the cathartic aspects of violence, and the liberating world of pimping, drugs, and sexual licence. All of these aspects of the Mailerian world of existentialism are brought together in Faye by Mailer's odd theological perspective.

Faye is a Kierkegaardian figure. Mailer has stated that his theology of the battle between good and evil might be helpful in "leading people back to Kierkegaard." According to Mailer, "Kierkegaard taught us, or tried to teach us, that at the moment we're feeling most saintly, we may in fact be evil. And that moment when we think we're most evil and finally corrupt, we may, in fact, in the eyes of God, be saintly at that moment." This Kierkegaardian perception, Mailer claims, helps diminish our "fundamental arrogance."[32]

In *The Deer Park* Mailer explores the emptiness of the aesthetic ideal, a theme that Kierkegaard had discussed in the section of *Either/Or* called "The Seducer's Diary." (The park of the novel's title is both a place where assignations were conducted in the France of Louis XV and a park that figures prominently in *Either/Or.*) Kierkegaard described the aesthetic ideal as the desire to "accomplish the task of living poetically," of "discovering the interesting in life."[33] As the narrator remarks of the "seducer" Johannes, "For him, individuals were merely for stimulation; he discarded them as trees shake off their leaves—he was rejuvenated, the foliage withered."[34] Yet satisfaction eludes the seducer in search of aesthetic stimulation; the pleasure of each orgy of possession fades rapidly, supplanted by a need for new stimulation. A peripatetic search for satisfaction becomes an end in itself, one that is finally empty. This, in bare outlines, is the reality and fate of Marion Faye, the psychopathic hipster. Blessed with the passion of the seducer, Faye has an almost religious need to transcend the mundane. He yearns to live authentically, without bad faith (he is honest with himself). And, most important, Faye exists in what Mailer calls "a state of extreme awareness," a state akin to religious devotion.[35]

Like so many of the male characters in Mailer's early fiction, and indeed in much of his writing in general, Marion Faye drifts. The abandoned child of a self-centered actress/celebrity and (perhaps) a mysterious Middle Eastern prince, Faye is a deeply introspective young man. As a child he wanted to be a priest. Another character in the novel describes him in essentially Kierkegaardian terms as "just a religious man turned inside out." In a dream sequence, Faye appears as "Father Marion," a saint in hell.[36] With Faye, Mailer seems to be testing aspects of his emerging theological position, which may be reduced to the equation that in order to be truly saved, one has to have drunk deeply at the well of sin. The most important aspect of

Mailer's theology at this point is its passion and vitalism. Here, in his own fashion, Mailer touches the pulse of debates then raging about American religion. The complacency that Will Herberg charted in American religious devotion, the easy vicissitudes of faith, are shunted aside by Mailer. A fundamentalist of sorts, he presents a world marked by a stark dichotomy, good and evil locked in battle. While Mailer, like Nietzsche, inverts traditional values, he retains religious passion. Those who live close to the abyss, who battle against the conformity of American culture, they alone are near to religious ecstasy and existential transcendence.[37]

Faye wants to transform himself into a saint of sin. He believes that "the world is bullshit. That's why people want a dull life" (17). Rigorously honest about himself and his ability to overcome any obstacle, he announces that there is no pleasure greater than a "conquered repugnance" (146). Armed with these insights, Faye constantly seeks to test himself, to experience life at the edge, to place his needs above those of others, to live a Kierkegaardian life of passion, and to refuse polite conformity. He is, to a degree, a modernized, hip version of Kierkegaard's aesthetic personality on the road to becoming a Knight of Faith.

Faye is a complex aesthete. Much of the time he searches for experience, for transcendence and pleasure. But he must also force himself, through his doctrine of "conquered repugnance," to do certain things less for pleasure than to prove to himself that he is capable of doing them. In the words of critic Diana Trilling, Faye wants a "purposeful, as opposed to purposeless death. Faye is not God the Father, but he is unmistakably in training to be God the Son. Dying for us, the Hipster becomes our savior."[38] In this quest Faye must, according to Mailer, force himself to be cruel, thus going against his inner wishes.[39]

Toward the end of the novel Faye tries his hand at controlling another individual. In this he parallels the Kierkegaardian seducer, who plays upon the affections and needs of his prey only to betray them once he has captured her attention. As Johannes puts it in "The Seducer's Diary," speaking about his beloved Cordelia, "Soon the bond of the engagement will be broken. She herself will be the one who dissolves it, in order by this dissolution to captivate me even more, if possible, just as flowing locks captivate more than those that are bound up. If I broke the engagement, I would miss out on this erotic somersault, which is so seductive to look at and such a sure sign of the audacity of her soul."[40]

In a somewhat similar fashion, Faye plays on the emotional weaknesses of Elena, deciding at one point that a greater challenge than to seduce another person would be to manipulate her into wanting to kill herself. Faye seeks what Mailer in another context referred to as the connection between the psychopath and the saint: "A murderer in the moment of his murder could feel a sense of beauty and perfection as complete as the transport of the saint. (And indeed this was the root of the paradox which had driven Kierkegaard near to mad for he had the courage to see that his criminal impulses were also his most religious.)"[41] Faye attempts to achieve this sainthood by conquering his "repugnance" at the idea of causing the death of another. At first Faye protests to himself against the inhumane act of manipulation that he contemplates. The louder the protest, the more necessary it becomes for him to act, to prove to himself that no sin is too large for him to commit. Alas, Faye feels emotional attachment, even guilt; he is relieved when he finds that Elena has chosen not to end her life. Ravaged by mixed emotions, he acts kindly toward her and toys with his own suicidal tendencies, resulting in a traffic accident and his going to jail for carrying an unregistered weapon. This complex character, in a frenzied search for existential transcendence full of religious intonations, rebels against the conformity of comfort. He charges into unexplored realms of the soul, all in a brutally honest and apparently amoral fashion.

7   MAILER'S THEOLOGY, first outlined in *The Deer Park* and in "The White Negro," is predicated on the existential recognition of death as a boundary situation. Mailer also contends that God becomes strong only when individuals passionately engage in a struggle against evil. God and the Devil are constantly at one another's throats in Mailer's Manichean universe, yet the lines between good and evil are blurred. This Kierkegaardian perception is at the heart of Mailer's existential theology. Mailer maintains that the struggle against evil—sometimes referred to as the cancer of conformity—offers the only possibility of transcendence or rebirth through a religious, existentially charged experience. He presents his characters as versions of Kierkegaard's Abraham, acting out of faith and instinct that their acts will be sanctioned as just.

Mailer believed that it is the intensity of freedom under the shadow of death that defines existence. Once the reality of our individual demise has been recognized and felt, then it must be resisted. Out of such recognition and action arises the possibility of existential freedom, the freedom of the hipster that Mailer naively associated with African Americans. In fact, Mailer's rejection of French and German existentialism, as he understood them, hinged on his sense that they proclaimed death to be meaningless: "Existentialism is rootless unless one dares the hypothesis that death is an existential continuation of life." For Mailer, essence does not precede existence, but it does live on after existence, through the migration of the soul into new possibilities of Eternity.[42]

Mailer thus demanded an existentialism wider in scope than the concrete situations of the present; he wanted a future-oriented existentialism, a vision of transcendence that extended beyond the limits of the corporeal body or the absurdity of life. European existentialism ran aground, he believed, on the "uninhabitable terrain of the absurd."[43] In *The Naked and the Dead* Mailer recognized the absurdity of man's existence, but he could not imagine that it was futile or meaningless to fight the good fight against evil. Such struggles, Mailer posited, defeated the absurd and gave meaning to existence. To have a particular valence, his views needed to be understood within the context of a schema larger than that of Sartre and Heidegger, a universe in which such struggles had a metaphysical logic behind them. This logic, however mystical, became the essence of Mailer's existential theology.[44]

Circling back a bit, Mailer had first hinted at his existentialist theology in the 1956 essay on *Waiting for Godot*. In a charitable yet strong reading of Beckett, Mailer proposed that the playwright might actually be attempting something quite radical, beyond mere critique, something that inched toward a religious sensibility. According to Mailer's theological interpretation of the play, the character Lucky possessed Christ-like features. Thus, Mailer thought, Beckett might be restating the Christian ideal that only through caring for the "most degraded" does redemption become possible. In addition, Mailer posited yet "another and richer possibility":

> I believe Beckett is also saying, again consciously or unconsciously, that God's destiny is flesh and blood with ours, and so, far from conceiving of a God who sits in judgment and allows souls, lost souls, to leave purgatory and be reborn again, there is the greater agony of God at the mercy of man's fate, God determined by man's efforts, man who has free will and can no longer exercise it and God therefore in bondage to the result of man's efforts. At the end, Vladimir and Gogo having failed again, there is the hint, the murmur, that God's condition is also worse, and he too has come closer to failure—when Vladimir asks the boy in the closing minutes of the play what Godot does, the boy answers: "He does nothing, Sir." Godot, by implication, lives in the same condition, the same spiritual insomnia, agony, limbo, the same despair of one's fading powers which has hung over the play. ("Public Notice," 324)

By the late 1950s, then, Mailer had clothed his hipster ideal in theological trappings. He became as God-saturated as Herman Melville had been a century earlier. In 1964 Mailer wrote, "I have some obsession with how

God exists," with His power, with His limitations, indeed, with His fate as "an embattled existential creature."[45] God, in Mailer's theology, battled constantly with the Devil:

> If there is any urgency in God's intent, if we are not actors working out a play for our salvation, but rather soldiers in an army which seeks to carry some noble conception of Being out across the stars, or back into the protoplasm of life, then a portion of God's creative power was extinguished in the camps of extermination. If God is not all-powerful but existential, discovering the possibilities and limitations of His creative powers in the form of the history which is made by His creatures, then one must postulate an existential equal to God, an antagonist, the Devil, a principle of Evil whose signature was the concentration camps, whose joy is to waste substance, whose intent is to prevent God's conception of Being from reaching its mysterious goal.[46]

Mailer's God engages in existential battle with the Devil, but with at best only some "mysterious goal" in mind. This jibes with the Kierkegaardian perception that God's ways are incomprehensible to mortals. Yet the critical question, given the incommensurate distance between man and God remains: What is man's role in this existential contest? Mailer maintained that just as God and the Devil battle, so does man somehow struggle in God's behalf. As man overcomes evil and transcends conformity, he strengthens God. In essence, God and man, when engaged in existential battles, wage a war for the good and the continuation of their beleaguered souls.

In a 1959 interview, building on ideas he had hinted at in "The White Negro," Mailer sketched what he called his "Theology of Hip." He reiterated his central beliefs: "Hip conceives of Man's fate being tied up with God's fate."[47] Mailer claimed to believe "that God is in danger of dying" because the Devil was winning the struggle. Yet, he suggested, when men succumbed to the conformity and torpidity of modern American life, God suffered as much as they did: "I believe there is a way in which a man's personality can die before his time; if one's death isn't dramatic, if one is extinguished day by day by the society in which one lives, then one loses one's chance of eternity."[48] This recognition fitted with Mailer's emphasis on passionate action and engagement: "The moral consequences of this are not only staggering, but they're thrilling; because moral experience is intensified rather than diminished" ("Hip, Hell, and the Navigator," 33).

This perception became a feisty mantra in Mailer's theological ramblings. In essence, his cosmology saw the success of God in fending off the attack of the Devil and his minions as dependent on the activities of individuals.

Indeed, at times Mailer suggested that God could even cause pain and suffering for individuals because "God Himself is engaged in a destiny so extraordinary, so demanding that He too can suffer from a moral corruption, that He can make demands upon us which are unfair" (think here of the demand that God placed upon Abraham, as rendered in Kierkegaard's *Fear and Trembling*), "that He can abuse our beings in order to achieve His means, even as we abuse the very cells of our own body" (33). At other times Mailer persevered in the more charitable view that "God is not all powerful. He's merely doing the best He can."[49]

The 1959 interview represented a muddled but intriguing attempt by Mailer to develop an ethical and religious component for his particular brand of existentialism. He wants to resolve the ethical dilemma opened up in "The White Negro" whereby action is celebrated without apparent direction, in the hope that pathological violence will be somehow better than the organized violence of the state. Mailer's metaphysics of hip presents an existentialist rationale for authenticity as necessary to the victory of God over the Devil and the salvation of man's eternal soul. But his pleas fall short as ethical imperatives, because he is vague about what constitutes an ethical act. All too often Mailer describes the ethical as that which contributes to growth. Growth, moreover, Mailer oddly maintains, is quantifiable, discernible in the cellular structure of the individual.[50] Yet this notion does nothing to define moral activity, nor does his emphasis on fighting against the Devil. As Mailer admits, he wants to emphasize a Kierkegaardian lesson, that the dividing lines between the saint and the sinner are often indistinct and possibly insignificant, even in the eyes of God.[51]

This would seem to lead Mailer to a Sartrean position that favors authenticity over inauthenticity. The essential ethical import of an existential act, then, comes from its being conscious and passionate. Although Mailer never responded directly to this possibility, one of his interpreters has attempted to outline how Mailer might avoid mere vitalism and solipsism. According to Robert Solotaroff, Mailer would define an act as immoral or unethical if it diminished the individual's power to grow. Thus, in any given situation the choice not to grow is defined as immoral and linked to the diminution of the individual and, ultimately, of God. The Devil, in this Mailerian equation, thrives from nongrowth, and he sometimes appears as a spectral presence representing moral lethargy. As Solotaroff sums it up, "For Mailer, the truth or reality of a particular context" (or the action demanded by an existential situation) "lies in its ability to provide energy to a particular human being at a particular point in his life."[52] But this does not begin to resolve the problem of how to define a moral and ethical act.

Mailer's solipsism founders, despite his claims about biology and God. And it does not improve on Sartre's ethics, prior to or after his Marxist period. Beauvoir, perhaps, comes closer to an ethical imperative, if not a solution, when she proclaims in *The Ethics of Ambiguity* (1948), in terms that Mailer would have been able to appreciate, that "a life justifies itself only if its effort to perpetuate itself is integrated into its surpassing." Then this struggle for freedom overcomes the nothingness at the core of being and links the individual to the human community, to the "will for universal solidarity." Thus, for Beauvoir as for Mailer, "each finite undertaking must also be open to the totality of men."[53]

Mailer believed that the presence of a religious schema in his American existentialism elevated it above the existentialism of Heidegger and Sartre. These thinkers erred in proclaiming that "man must lead his life as if death is meaningful even when man knows that death is meaningless." If this is the case, then Mailer wonders why "man should bother to be authentic" at all: "Existentialism is rootless unless one dares the hypothesis that death is an existential continuation of life, that the soul may pass through migrations, or cease to exist in the continuum of nature (which is the unspoken intimation of cancer). But accepting this hypothesis, authenticity and commitment return to the center of ethics, for man then faces no peril so huge as alienation from his own soul, a death which is other than death, a disappearance into nothingness rather than into Eternity."[54] Hence the question that eats at Mailer: Why be authentic, or ethical, if we cease to exist when we die? In contrast to the European existentialists, then, Mailer's emphasis on a soul, a soul that continues to live even after we physically perish, strengthens the imperative to be authentic. Our actions in life determine the survivability of our immortal souls. Thus growth in this life contributes to the growth of the soul, which in turn aids God in His struggle with the Devil.

But does Mailer resolve this issue? Does his interpretation of the meaning of death appreciably revise French existentialism? Mailer frames the issue to indicate an enduring struggle for the soul, a never-ending battle between God and the Devil. If this is the case, then surcease is never to be found; authenticity will never be resolved, choices will forever be presented. Thus we are back at the same point posited by Sartrean existentialism: that we are projects, beings in a state of becoming. The value of authenticity, for Sartre, is that we act with conscious awareness of the contingency of existence, the necessity and complexity of choice and, with it, the heavy weight of responsibility for our actions. All that Mailer's theology adds to this equation is an extension of the field. The struggle continues unabated, in death just as in life.

8 MAILER PRESENTED his fullest account of an existential theology of hip in the novel *An American Dream*. The problematic and the heroic aspects of his existential theology both appear in this fascinating, if ultimately unsatisfying, work. Some critics mistake this work as a piece of realistic fiction or as a crazy quilt of sexual ideas run amok. Tom Wolfe dismissed it as a novel with "all these gods, devils, and orgasms running around, like some Methodist minister who has discovered orgone theory and, with a supreme ecumenical thrust, has decided to embrace both John Wesley and Wilhelm Reich."[55] Richard Lehan better understands the novel as "an existential allegory—an examination of the self overcoming dread in its open-ended journey into an understanding of primitive and psychic energy."[56] In this sense *An American Dream* exemplifies themes already broached in "The White Negro" and *The Deer Park*.

The protagonist, Stephen Rojack, a war hero who has killed other men, is an "existentialist psychologist," author of a book on death. He is also a television personality and former congressman. Above all else, he is a soul in the process of disintegration. Separated from his wife, Deborah, and toying with the idea of suicide, Rojack rushes to see her. He still loves her deeply, although, as he recognizes, his motives are at best mixed: "I had loved her with the fury of my ego."[57] She rejects him, punishing him with tales of lovers present and past. In a rage, he strikes her, and they battle. Deborah's strength is amazing; the fighters appear to be evenly matched. But Rojack finally chokes the life out of her. His decision to kill is influenced by many factors: the force of circumstance, the history of deep-seated antagonism between him and Deborah, and his sense of participating in a bitter fight against evil in the universe. Mailer attempts to recreate the moment in Camus's *The Stranger* when, in the blinding light of the Algerian sun, Meursault "decides" to shoot the Arab on the beach. Rojack's mind says to him, "Hold back! You're going too far, hold back!" He tries to stop, "but pulse packed behind pulse in a pressure up to thunderhead. . . . [My] mind exploded in a fireworks of rockets, stars, and hurtling embers, the arm about her neck leaped against the whisper I could still feel murmuring in her throat, and *crack* I choked her harder . . . I was floating. I was as far into myself as I had ever been and universes wheeled in a dream" (31).

Rojack creates himself by means of this murder, which permits him to push out against the confines of a slow death into conformity. Deborah's death is at once a catharsis for him and a triumph of the forces of good over evil. Mailer depicts this existential act, this hipster breaking with the boundaries of good and evil, in the most favorable light. The murder of Deborah, who represented the essence of his compromise or death in life, rejuvenates Rojack.[58] He returns to a state of grace and childlike innocence: "I was weary with a most honorable fatigue, and my flesh seemed new. I had not felt so nice since I was twelve" (32). This catharsis through murder recalls Mailer's discussion on the liberating power of murder in "The White Negro." In both cases, murder allows the killer to encounter levels of experience generally unknown: "Murder, after all, has exhilaration within it. . . . The exhilaration comes I suppose from possessing such strength. Besides, murder offers the promise of vast relief. It is never unsexual" (8). As in "The White Negro," the search for authenticity and strength, the resolve to act, the quest for the ultimate orgasm, explodes in a celebration of murder.

To make Rojack's act an expression of freedom and a strike against the Devil, Mailer must characterize Deborah as evil. He describes her as "an artist with the needle" (17), meaning both that she can stab with her words and that her allure is addictive.[59] Rojack's only means of escape, of establishing his own sense of authenticity and freedom, is through murder. Deborah personifies the power of evil, which Mailer identifies as feminine: she "had been in touch with the moon and now had the word. She had powers . . . the power to lay a curse" (22). Rojack decides that Deborah "was not incapable of murdering me" (25). He recalls that Deborah once stated, "I'm evil if truth be told. But I despise it, truly I do. It's just that evil has power!" (36).

Here again Mailer's themes are Kierkegaardian. The lines between good and evil are indiscernible, and this applies equally to Deborah and to Rojack. In Deborah "goodness was imprisoned by evil." The two coexist powerfully within her. Echoing Mailer's own musings about the nature of good and evil, Rojack states, "She was evil, I would decide, and then think next that goodness could come on a visit to evil only in the disguise of evil: yes, evil would know that goodness had come only by the power of its force. I might be the one who was therefore evil, and Deborah was trapped with me" (37).

Rojack's battle with Deborah continues even after her death. In the novel, as in Mailer's existential theology, souls wage war after the death of physical being. Rojack realizes that "Deborah would be there to meet me in the hour of my death" (40). On the heels of this recognition, Rojack decides that he must not allow himself to be jailed, for imprisonment exterminates the soul. Energized in the immediate wake of the murder, Rojack makes his way to the maid's room, where he engages with her in sustained sexual intercourse described in metaphors of sin and salvation, the Devil and the Lord.

The details of the remainder of the novel are unimportant, except insofar as they allow Mailer to continue playing with themes of innocence and salvation. Mailer's text evokes the American dream, the ideal of rebirth, of what Richard Slotkin in another context calls "regeneration through violence."[60] Cherry, the most weakly drawn character in the novel, represents innocence and redemption. Rojack truly loves her, and he fends off rivals such as Shago Martin, a potent black hipster, modeled on jazz musician Miles Davis.[61] Cherry has experienced evil and sin, but she has managed to reject suicide and to cherish life. Her soul, according to Mailer, has remained intact and has grown. When she dies her soul continues, even granting to Rojack certain magical powers that allow him to win big in Las Vegas.

Having now violated the premises of realistic fiction, Mailer further embellishes the story with elements of his familiar existential theology of God against the Devil. Rojack enlists on the side of God, but without any certitude. At one point he announces, "On occasion, I'm vain enough" to believe that "I am a solicitor for the Devil" (236). Solicitor or saint, Rojack's rejuvenation arises from his existential experiences with dread and death, with action and murder, and from the choice for life as against confinement. If in the process moral limits have been traversed, then so be it. For Mailer, the existential hipster cannot be confined by the presumptions of polite society, by the numbing certitude of ethical admonitions. With Kierkegaard, Mailer would celebrate the Knight of Faith, the individual like Abraham who believes in the absurd but acts out of the irony of faith.[62] In such a world the individual acts by the passionate purity of his heart alone.

9   A FINAL STATEMENT of Mailer's giddy existentialism, brought down from the heights of theology to the realm of political change, can be found in his classic work of engaged journalism, *The Armies of the Night* (1968). In his earlier collection of essays, *The Presidential Papers,* Mailer had posited an elitist existentialism whereby existentialist heroes such as John F. Kennedy chart and change the course of history, or individuals such as boxers Sonny Liston and Floyd Patterson are thrust into the ring in an existential situation. In *The Armies of the Night* Mailer deals with a mass phenomenon, the protest against the war in Vietnam. This mass act of civil disobedience, culminating in a march on the Pentagon, captured the existential anguish of a generation, as well as Mailer's own. Yet Mailer puzzles over the significance of the event: "The March on the Pentagon was an ambiguous event whose essential value or absurdity may not be established for ten or twenty years, or indeed ever."[63]

Throughout the work Mailer presents himself as confronting a situation that is existential in that "we do not know how it is going to turn out." The march on the Pentagon induces existential dread because "the government doesn't know either" what will happen (48). Yet Mailer mixes existential situations together. When at one point he commandeers the stage and acts as a raucous master of ceremonies, he finds himself in an existential situation as well. He refers to himself as "The Existentialist" (50) as he struggles with his ambiguous relation to celebrity and with his wariness of other writers, especially poet Robert Lowell.

As Mailer contemplates the existential dilemmas that are driving the march on the Pentagon, he feels a mixture of awe and disdain for the younger generation, the shock troops in the assault. Positively, he identifies with them because they are existentialists, entering into unknown territory. And they are hipsters in that they "lust for apocalypse" and reject middle-class sobriety. Yet they also repel Mailer because of their "lobotomies from sin . . . their innocence," and above all their use of LSD, which he refers to as "a devil's drug—designed by the Devil to consume the love of the best, and leave them liver-wasted, weeds of the big city" (44). Mailer apparently felt that LSD deadened the mind, acting as a chemical analogue to middle-class conformity.

A more important message than Mailer's admonitions on drugs—he is a bourbon man himself—struggles to be expressed in *The Armies of the Night*. At the end of all the bluster and posturing and drunken revery, Mailer comes finally to achieve a state of existential grace. He had described such a moment earlier, as it occurred to Rojack, when "God writhes in his bonds. Rush to the locks. Deliver us from our curse. For we must end on the road to that mystery where courage, death, and the dream of love give promise of sleep" (317). Mailer experiences something similar at the march on the Pentagon. He comes to realize that he has acted with authentic conviction: he participated in and was arrested for an act described in precise and existentially compelling terms, "transgressing a police line as a protest against the war in Vietnam" (159). At this moment, at the precipice of transgression, Mailer acted existentially. He faced the absurdity not only of his own action but of the entirety of the war. And, with Camus's Sisyphus in mind, we might imagine that at this moment, Mailer was happy.

MUCH HAD CHANGED in America since Mailer first engaged the national consciousness in 1948 with his vociferous attacks on the conformity of Cold War culture. By the 1960s a new generation had arisen to join in his critique of that culture. Mailer and this new generation would share certain elements of an existentialist perspective, certainly in terms of choice and commitment. But the student radicals would jettison the idiosyncratic theology of Mailer's hip saints, and would reject much of his macho posturing. Such a divide probably pleased Mailer, since it allowed him to retain his status as an outsider, constantly agitating against the status quo. Like his existential heroes, Mailer's errand required that he speak to the consciousness of an age without being part of it.

Chapter Ten

Robert Frank's
Existential Vision

1 PHOTOGRAPHER Robert Frank captured an existential mood in his series of photographs *The Americans* (1959), taken while he traveled across the United States in the 1950s. Although he was associated with the Beats, Frank's sensibility was darker, more existential, and less raucous in its celebration of freedom. A somber edge frames his art work; he pictures American society as alienated, steeped to the bone in violence and apathy. He believed, with Norman Mailer, that African Americans, to the degree that they were consigned to living outside of the dominant society, were somehow endowed with the ability to experience a freedom that was paradoxically denied to whites. Although this kind of dichotomy often gives way to racist stereotyping, primitivism, and romanticization, Frank's photographs refused, in the end, to allow matters to rest so easily. His depictions of African Americans managed to document the chains of their segregation and oppression in Jim Crow America. His work is grounded in a reality that he refused to obscure.

Critic Susan Sontag once remarked that Frank's photographs, with their burden of violence, desolation, and death, present America as the "grave of the Occident."[1] Yet this does not exhaust Frank's vision. *The Americans* offers another set of possibilities: a vision of phoenixlike redemption. The logic of his images, in both placement and content, presents a typically existential accounting with death. Indeed, death and despair may be said to litter the highways of Robert Frank's America. Among the debris, in the lives of outsiders not confined to the bourgeois logic of success, Frank finds an incipient critique and possible solution. Each individual must begin, as Frank did, with an examination of reality in order to confront the existential givens of the world. Out of such knowledge of society, and of the self, transcendence might be possible. In Frank's estimation, this meant confronting racism in American culture, as well as the belief that freedom comes through creation, both of art and of identity. With Samuel Beckett, Frank recognized that the artist has the responsibility to chronicle alienation and despair. In the process of creating an art that captures reality, the artist is in essence transcending that reality, creating a monument to the human spirit, to the redemptive powers of human freedom in the face of despair.

2   FRANK'S AMERICAN journey began in 1947 when he arrived from his native Switzerland. Born in 1924, he had grown up in an almost unreal world. While the Second World War and the Holocaust engulfed Europe, Frank was relatively protected in his homeland. Situated on the edge of destruction, the young Jew not surprisingly developed a sense of distance and alienation from his surroundings. Beat writer Joyce Johnson, who knew Frank from Greenwich Village days, has described him as possessing a blend of "European dourness and pessimistic wit." These qualities allowed him to cultivate a sense of self and a compassion for people. As he explained, "It made me less afraid and better able to cope with different situations later because I lived through that fear. Being Jewish and living with the threat of Hitler must have been a very big part of my understanding of people that were put down or who were held back."[2]

Frank made his initial mark as a fashion photographer, work that allowed him to earn a living but failed to satisfy his artistic needs. He wanted an escape, and he sought it in fine-art photography. Before he began working on *The Americans* in 1955–56, Frank had already staked out his territory. In photographs taken in Brazil, England, and Spain between 1947 and 1952, he had captured images of alienation, loneliness, mass culture, violence, and death; these concepts were already associated with images of the open highway and the movement of the automobile. As an existentialist, Frank wanted to depict the human condition, albeit in a manner different from his mentor, Edward Steichen. In America, Frank realized that vision by presenting the dilemmas of modern men and women in their starkest form. Spiritual poverty, he would demonstrate, resided most fully alongside material wealth.

Frank's existential sensibility arose not only out of his experiences as a Jew in Switzerland during the war but out of his reading of existentialist works. "I read all the early books by Sartre, the 'Roads to Freedom' novels," he said. "It helped me, it strengthened my determination." But it did not turn him into a political activist like Sartre or Camus: he didn't "become involved," he explained, because he was "suspicious of groups and rules and authority."[3] Such suspicions would blunt the explicit political messages of his photographs, but they would not dim the light that he cast on the anomie of modern America. "I always felt that the way you live—that's my political statement, that's what I am; that's who I am."[4] And being who he was required a sense of commitment: "Life for a photographer cannot be a matter of indifference. . . . It is important to see what is invisible to others."[5]

Frank always had a "feeling of being outside." He wanted to capture what was around him without making his presence felt. Ironically, his outsider sensibility conferred on him the distance and the invisibility necessary to get into the crevices of culture, to capture moments that eluded others or that seemed insignificant. His art required no communication or connection with others: "I wouldn't have to talk with anyone. . . . [I would be] just an observer." Frank wanted to be the photographer on the move, seizing the moment through an "instantaneous reaction to oneself."[6] His self-professedly personal vision emphasized feeling over ratiocination. To a degree, the gesture, the moment of the artist in the throes of creation, resembled the ideal of action painting as enunciated by Harold Rosenberg. And through his art Frank, like Jack Kerouac, searched for self and subject. Kerouac maintained that this peripatetic, in-motion attitude and style had rendered Frank shadowlike and at times invisible to his photographic subjects. Moreover, Frank's desire to use photography to express himself mimics the aesthetic of Beckett, with his proclamation that "best would be no words at all." Like Beckett, Frank wanted to present the alienation in his subjects, and also to grapple with his own. And he desired through his photography to universalize his own experiences, to capture the human condition, and to offer a broadside critique of the American dream.

To achieve these goals, Frank needed first to distance himself from Steichen's upbeat photographic portrait of the human condition. In an immensely popular exhibit, *The Family of Man,* Steichen brought together images that depicted the diversity and humanity of people from around the globe. Steichen wanted his exhibit to overcome American exceptionalism, to break down international boundaries in order to foster better foreign relations and to avoid a nuclear holocaust. Frank worked with Steichen on this project, and some of his own images appeared in the exhibit.[7] Steichen's exhibit, even when it managed to include images with depressing or harsh content, remained resolutely optimistic and sentimental, awash in humanity.[8]

In contrast, Frank sought in his photography to depict the despair and alienation of the human condition. "I just didn't agree with his [Steichen's] sentimentality about photographs any more," stated Frank. "I was aware that I was living in a different world—that the world wasn't as good as that."[9] In such a world, Frank sought to achieve transcendence through art, yet he shared his subjects' sense of anguish. He wanted to overcome despair, rather than to wallow in it, but he refused to do so in any cloying or sentimental manner. He wrapped himself in a vision of freedom; his Sartrean road to freedom began with his individual choices and needs. This constituted, as Frank phrased it in a Guggenheim Fellowship application, the "vision in his mind."[10]

The desire to realize a "vision in his mind" linked Frank with Jack Kerouac and the Beat movement. Both Kerouac and Frank had endured long periods of frustration before finding a publisher willing to commit to their respective works, *On the Road* (1957) and *The Americans.* The first time Kerouac encountered Frank's images he stated, "You got eyes." Kerouac quickly agreed to write the introduction to an American edition of *The Americans.* Their collaboration and friendship would continue through a planned photo essay of a road trip the two took to Florida, and through the film *Pull My Daisy* (1959–60), a "Spontaneous Documentary" about the Beats filmed by Frank with narration by Kerouac.[11]

For both Frank and Kerouac, existence was characterized by change, movement, and speed. Kerouac's *On the Road* perfectly captured the kinetic nature and possibility of postwar Beat liberation and rebellion. The character Dean Moriarity, based on Neal Cassidy, thrived on fast cars, amphetamines, and open highways. Experimentation and living in the moment emerged as Beat ideals, part of a "culture of spontaneity."[12] According to psychologist Robert J. Lifton, Beats craved "experiential transcendence," a state in which the present moment is lived with "such great intensity that time and death are, in effect, eliminated."[13] Such moments were often the product of danger or drugs. While the Beat individual felt alienated, he or she reveled in that outsider status, wearing it as an emblem of coolness. Unlike the existentialist, the Beat did not work through a perspective of anguish and dread. Instead, the Beat, somewhat unproblematically, proclaimed his or her freedom, freedom to take to the road or to become part of the urban netherworld.

Thus despite their rejection of American consumer culture and the suburban ideal, Beats remained upbeat about America. With their precursor Walt Whitman, they embraced the multitudes, identified with the pioneer spirit, and proclaimed their own individuality. To be sure, some Beat writing, such as Allen Ginsberg's haunting poem *Howl* (1956), thrust deep into the heart of the emerging American culture of containment, but other Beat writers seemed unconcerned with the political landscape of 1950s America, with the horrors of racism, with the specter of McCarthyism, or even more generally with the despair and alienation inherent in the human condition. Kerouac's writings present alienation with a happy, rebellious face. Like Mailer, Beat writers identified only with what they viewed as the liberating aspects of African-American life. Thus Kerouac, mesmerized by the ideal of the exotic Other, wrote of his throbbing desire to be an African American: "In the Denver colored section, wishing I were a Negro, feeling that the best the white world offered was not enough ecstacy for me, not enough life, joy, kicks, darkness, music, not enough night."[14]

Frank's existentialism and his personality combined to keep him anchored in his own despair and artistic vision. He chose to be an angry outsider, alienated from the American consensus: "I believe that it's good to be angry if you're an artist . . . . The anger will make you work harder to produce things that will contain more conviction."[15] This helped give his photographs their hard edge of critique, even as he flirted with aspects of the primitivism that Mailer and Kerouac celebrated. But in a fundamental way Frank could not be satisfied with simplistic notions of transcendence, for he had experienced too much pain in Europe. Ginsberg realized this when he noted in Frank and his photographs a "quality of loneliness."[16]

3 FRANK'S PHOTOGRAPHIC style featured tilted horizon lines and, in some of his prints, a hazy quality—quite distinct from the standards of photographic practice and perfection defined by *Life* magazine. Through style, Frank captured movement and spontaneity; in the manner of abstract expressionist painters he managed to freeze the immediacy of the moment. In the abstract expressionists Frank found support for his own vision and style: "They were people who really believed in what they did." They "reinforced my belief that you could really follow your intuition—no matter how crazy or far-off or how laughed at it would be. You could go and make pictures that were not sentimental. You could photograph what you felt like."[17] To make these types of pictures, Frank used a lightweight 35 mm Leica camera that helped him move and shoot rapidly, "from the hip," without the encumbrances that had weighed down Walker Evans, for one.[18] Unlike Evans, Frank refused to wait days for the proper lighting situation. More important than the perfectly composed scene for Frank was his own immediate response to what he saw. In a sense, Baudelaire's description of the *flâneur*, as expressed and interpreted by Walter Benjamin and Susan Sontag, perfectly captures Frank's existential, modernist style. As Sontag puts it, the photographer generally appears as "the solitary walker reconnoitering, stalking, cruising the urban" (and, for Frank, the rural, as well) "inferno," impelled onward by the "seamy corners" of the city.[19] Frank's existential imperative as a photographer, then, was to be beholden to no one, to explore unrepresented, subterranean subjects and to place his personal imprimatur on all he encountered. And every place that he turned in postwar America, he saw the mark of death.

Frank presents his existential, death-saturated vision in the series of five photographs nestled side by side in the middle of *The Americans*. The logic of these photographs replicates in miniature the volume's larger poetic vision of the intermingling of life and death. In "U.S. 91, Leaving Blackfoot, Idaho," Frank's shot of the interior of a car captures two intent, grimly serious young Native American men about to begin their auto journey. This image is followed by "St. Petersburg, Florida," an evocative study of elderly people sitting on two benches whose posts seem to recall the marker lines of a highway. In the background of this image, counterposed to the rootedness of those players in the waiting game of death, is a car—perhaps the one carrying the Idaho youth—streaking off to new horizons and possibilities.

But the next image fixes our attention on the death-in-life waiting of the old and the frenetic movement of the young. This is the famous photograph "Covered Car—Long Beach, California." In the shadow of two palm trees, and in front of what might well be described as a Bauhaus crypt, is a tarp-shrouded car, immobile and dead. In this image Frank examines the interplay of two symbols of the American dream, the car culture and the utopian ideal of California, and finds each of them imbued with death. He dashes the expectation that the tarp might be lifted and the car reborn in the next photograph, an image of a covered body, the victim of an accident, alongside the road of dreams and song, Route 66.

The final photo in this montage returns us to the road and thus opens up once again a set of possibilities. "U.S. 285, New Mexico" is an ode to the existential juxtaposition of life and death. Like so many of Frank's photographs, it serves as a testament to French critic Roland Barthes's observation that photographic images invoke death with tremendous vigor.[20] In Frank's image, the road stretches forever into the night; the lanes of the highway suggest escape, speed, and freedom while also evoking danger. In the passing lane one can glimpse, ever so faintly, the outline of an oncoming car, its headlights barely visible. Here as in the other images, freedom shares the road with death, possibility with demise. The photographs express the endless road of life, especially those moments when we are in the passing lane, traveling fast, faster, fastest. And yet as we seek to avoid inertia and complacency, we must always be cognizant of that other car, the car of death, immobility, old age, coming toward us. Like Mathieu in Sartre's *The Age of Reason,* which he greatly admired, Frank recognized that freedom means more than simply avoiding commitments.[21] We must continue forward into an existential engagement with life.

In *The Americans* Frank painted a landscape of relentless despair. As Kerouac put it, he had "sucked a sad poem right out of America onto film."[22] Reviewers rejected the pathos of *The Americans,* condemning the book as a token of Frank's one-sided, personal, pessimistic vision of life. *Popular Photography* columnist Arthur Goldsmith found Frank's vision "too marred by spite, bitterness, and narrow prejudices, just as so many of the prints are flawed by meaningless blur, grain, muddy exposure, drunken horizons, and general sloppiness."[23] Later students have acknowledged the depths of sadness and the problematic quality of the photographic technique in the work and have contrasted it, usually unfavorably, with the relatively benign, respectful treatment of the poor in Walker Evans's photographs from the 1930s, especially in his masterwork *Let Us Now Praise Famous Men* (1941). This comparison juxtaposes the hopes and expectations for change in depression-era America, in the period of the Popular Front, against the malaise and despair that marked Frank's postwar atomic-age America.[24]

To be sure, one cannot overstate the tremendous, almost numbing sadness that defines Frank's photographs. Out of a total of about sixty photographs depicting faces in *The Americans,* only a handful capture a smile or indicate any sense of happiness or adjustment. And even then the smiling person is often situated next to a dour individual, or the smile is patently false, as in the wonderful shot of the young television performer whose artificial grin is rendered even more so by being reproduced on the television monitor next to the stage set. Even happiness appears to be mere artifice in a consumer society.

Frank's vision is pessimistic, existential, and in a sense politically engaged. He refuses to hide the despair that he uncovers beneath the surface of official and public forms of optimism in postwar America. Yet, as we shall see, this is not a nihilistic end point for Frank; it is the beginning of his vision. Frank objected strenuously to the false image of America then being trumpeted by politicians and pundits. He despised the dominant visions of the 1950s with their naive suggestions that happiness could be found through consumer spending, military buildups, and the social status quo. Frank recalled being terribly troubled by McCarthyism during this period, and he believed that it had polluted all aspects of American life. His photographs of the American political landscape capture this feeling.[25] *The Americans* is dotted with self-important petty politicians shown suppressing a yawn or surrounded by tattered flags and campaign signs. A pervasive sense of violence stalks Frank's pictures, as in his representations of taut cowboys wound up and ready for a fight. When depicting workers, Frank presents them as sad and alienated, gloomy and anonymous, in all-night diners, elevators, buses, and bathrooms. His vision resurrects the loneliness that Edward Hopper had captured decades earlier, but with more of a critical edge. In a photograph of a Detroit factory, the workers' faces are indistinct, blurred, wonderful analogues to the speeding assembly line that enslaves them and turns them into machines.

Frank turned an ironic eye on the contrasts between the deep political and spiritual sickness of Americans and the liveliness of the material artifacts that surround them. "Bar—Las Vegas, Nevada" captures the naked loneliness of American life. A young man steps up to a jukebox; he appears languid, deadened, oblivious to the world surrounding him. The jukebox, in contrast, is alive. One imagines it revving up to reverberate with the strains of a lively beat. The man, not the jukebox, is the material object, the dead machine.[26]

White Americans were, for Frank, the walking dead. He makes this apparent in his photograph "Charity Ball—New York City." A woman socialite, gaudy in jewels, decked in lifeless fashion, and without a smile—indeed, her grimace evinces only the severest ennui—accepts on her cheek the kiss of a man whose long fingers wrap around her cold shoulders in a Dracula-like embrace. Even when America's upper crust are depicted as smiling, as in "Cocktail Party—New York City," they seem to be courting death: their wealth does not free them but only seems to weigh them down. From Frank's photographs one might surmise that the blood of America had been sucked out of it by a materialistic, alienating, absurd culture. Frank operated on the periphery of this culture, the existential photographer reacting to, and capturing, the deadening absurdity that he viewed.

4 IF FRANK HAD merely piled image upon image of desolation and despair, he would have been no more than an existential nihilist at best. But in fact he felt that he had to give his audience, and himself, something more than a diseased body biding time until the undertaker came to claim it, and in this he had something in common with Sartre. Sartre's *Nausea* offers us a stinging sense of alienation and despair, a rumination on the failure of history and progress to provide us with absolute meaning, yet in the end the novel sounds a note of hope. Through art, through the creative spirit, transcendence is possible. This is the message that Hazel E. Barnes too hammered home in her more optimistic works on existentialism. In the same manner, Frank's images attest to the desire to survive through art. In the specific content of his work as well he presents an alternative, albeit shaky, strategy of transcendence. He does this through his willingness to identify with the plight and possibility of the African-American experience in racist America.

African Americans represent for Frank authenticity and possibility. In this respect he follows in the footsteps of Norman Mailer and Jack Kerouac, who celebrated the primitive freedom they associated with African Americans. In this equation, precisely because African Americans are consigned to the periphery of American society and to the constant reality of violence, they are endowed with existential recognition and freedom. They are constantly in a boundary situation, living in the shadow of death and apart from the conventions of the larger American society. Because they occupy the liminal spaces at the border of respectability, African Americans, unlike whites, are not alienated from themselves, are able to exhibit emotions and spontaneity. They are not imprisoned by modern American conformity and consumerism.

Although Frank's depiction of African Americans comes dangerously close to a modern version of minstrelsy or primitivism, he manages to pull back from the brink by recognizing that he is projecting his own needs and fantasies upon them. He does this sympathetically, to be sure, because he feels strongly that he is also an outsider, by birth, religion, and sensibility, to the mainstream of American society. Yet he also knows, and condemns, the social and political realities of oppression in the era of Jim Crow segregation in the South and racism in the North. Frank refuses to remove African Americans from the complexity of their historical context. Like Ellison, who railed against reducing the African-American experience to a sociological or psychological exercise in pathology, Frank captured African-American expressions of outsider freedom while also recognizing the bars constructed by white Americans to imprison them. His images avoid the all-too-easy rendering of heroic or impoverished African Americans in the agitprop style of the Popular Front. Instead, Frank documented the ambivalence, irony, and pathos of the black experience while still finding within the blues idiom that had been asserted by Ralph Ellison and Albert Murray a sense of the possibility of existential transcendence.

Of all the subjects depicted in *The Americans,* only the African Americans show emotion, evince deep feelings, convey an appearance of authenticity. The dangerously simple dichotomy of black feeling/white unfeeling or black freedom/white slavery is communicated most clearly in the structure that Frank uses to organize his photographs. In "San Francisco," Frank has clearly disturbed the peace and quiet of a black couple who were sitting on a hillside enjoying a beautiful view of the city below. The woman and man react to Frank's intrusion—his vaunted invisibility fails him here—with disdain and obvious anger; he has violated their privacy.[27] The next photograph in the book, "Belle Isle—Detroit," shows some white people who, while in a setting as idyllic as the previous shot of San Francisco, seem oblivious to Frank's presence and equally unaware of the beauty of their surroundings. In another photograph also entitled "Belle Isle—Detroit," Frank depicts a moving convertible full of young black boys enjoying the cool breezes on their bare chests, perhaps anticipating or still reveling in the joys of the beach. Their freedom arises from their organic and natural relationship to nature. In contrast, an elderly couple in the photograph "Detroit" sit in an enclosed hardtop automobile, unmoving in heavy traffic. They seem less angry than numbed by the wait.

Other photographs in *The Americans* return to the liveliness of African Americans. In one photograph Frank depicts a black baby next to a jukebox;

unlike the passive young man depicted before a jukebox in the photograph discussed earlier, the baby in this image is joyful and kinetic. Even in the shot of a large black woman sitting on a chair in an open field, the image in the collection in which a black person is pictured as most alone, the woman places a jaunty hand on her hip. Her smile positively illuminates the surrounding landscape. Alone but not alienated, she lives in the moment.

Existential thinking thrives on the recognition of death. This knowledge is a prerequisite to the expression of freedom. Not surprisingly, as already noted, scenes of death abound in Frank's *The Americans.* In these images African Americans confront death defiantly, existentially. In "Funeral—St. Helena, South Carolina" a group of young black males lean against their freshly shined automobiles. There is less a sense of grief in this shot than one of intense boredom, an unwillingness to let death interfere with the enjoyment of life. Another photograph of the same funeral juxtaposes the cold stiffness of the corpse in his coffin with the movement of the living. Death is acknowledged, but the necessity of moving beyond it, of getting on with one's own life, is stressed.

Without Mailer's obsessiveness, Frank also depicts nonwhites as sexually vital and passionate. In *The Americans* whites embrace with hard grips, suggestive of a death struggle or of conjugal necessity. Desire is absent. Frank prefers the sexual freedom of the outsider. His marvelous image "New York City" shows three black or Puerto Rican women (probably transvestites). They are aware of Frank's presence; this is no candid shot. Instead of retreating from the camera, they strike a sexual pose. One caresses her own face; another thrusts out a hip. In the background the third woman covers her face, but not in a modest attempt to hide or to seek anonymity; the gesture is mocking and provocative, the fingers of her hand spread wide across her face.

The intensity that Frank imputed to African Americans and other outsiders with regard to sexuality extended to his depiction of their religious experience as well. Religion in 1950s America, as Will Herberg had noted in *Protestant-Catholic-Jew,* had been reduced to a polite ritual, a social requirement of a conformist culture. In his rejection of this tame ideal, Frank, thankfully, avoided pat shots of black spiritual enthusiasms. He instead focused on a white-robed black preacher clutching a cross as he prays by the shores of the Mississippi River. The significance of this ritual is unclear, but the man's intense emotion is etched on his face. The next photograph depicts the literal hardening and deadening of religious zeal that occurs, as well as the affinities to commercialism that emerge, when it is translated into traditional symbolism. In the image of St. Francis, Frank photographs a stone statue of a priest carrying a cross. This priest is situated on a pedestal above the ground, seemingly preaching dead words to a cold modern world of gas stations and government office buildings.[28]

More than Mailer, Frank recognized how limitations on black rights constrain the possibilities of true, existential freedom. Frank traveled the terrain, soon to begin to crumble, of Jim Crow America. The cover photograph of the Aperture edition of *The Americans* perfectly denotes the reality of black life. In this image we see the faces of a number of people through the open windows of a New Orleans trolley. The pain and despair in the face of one black man immediately draws our attention. He is framed by the window sashes of the vehicle as if by the bars in a prison with no exit. Exiled, with the other black passengers pictured, to the back of the trolley, he is trapped in the social realities of the segregation era.

The most poignant and ambivalent expression of racial realities in *The Americans* is the photograph "Charleston, South Carolina." A richly black-skinned nurse, clothed in regulation white uniform against a background of blurred white streets and institutional white walls, holds a very pale white baby. The immobile child stares straight ahead, perhaps peering off into the future. It has a sagacious look well beyond its years, as though it realizes that its close relationship with this black woman, this surrogate mother, is foreclosed by the pressing realities of socially regulated duration; the process of distancing may already be occurring. The attitude of the black nurse is uncertain. Though she holds the baby close, her look is not directed at the child, whose reality seems alien to her. The woman seems lost in thought as well. Perhaps she too is contemplating her separateness from the child; perhaps she is contemplating the foreclosed future of her own children as against the expansive possibilities of the white child in her arms.

FRANK'S EXISTENTIAL vision, then, begins and continues with a sense of despair, with alienation abounding. Like Ahab, Frank is "always looking for the truth, and the truth can't be captured."[29] But his existential insights, although drenched with despair, refuse to wallow in it. Instead, Frank suggests that the feelings and emotions of African Americans are positive goods, correctives to the enclosures of white American society. He understands that this strange freedom is problematic, an outgrowth of the dialectic of slavery and repression. Black authenticity comes with a price. African Americans live in constant jeopardy. Death and oppression place them in boundary situations. This allows them, like soldiers on the battlefield, to experience the possibility of transcendence.

In contrast, Frank maintains that whites are enslaved, alienated from their feelings, living without recognition of their own despair, of their own imprisonment in the culture of the Cold War. They live inauthentic lives and refuse to acknowledge the thin line separating them from annihilation, be it through conformity, atomic destruction, or political witch hunts. Frank avoids arguing that whites should act more like blacks (the line of Mailer and Kerouac); rather, he seems to imply through his photographs that all Americans need to escape from the prison of modern society. Blacks must be liberated from the shackles of segregation, and whites must be liberated from conformity and spiritual alienation so that they may live more authentically. In its emphasis on death and despair and its notions of transcendence, Frank's existential photography takes him to the possibility of an authentic life; it brings him to the edge of wisdom.[30]

1960–1993

Postwar Student and Women's Movements

Chapter Eleven

Camus's Rebels

1 In 1965, AT a University of Wisconsin teach-in on the war in Vietnam, spellbound activists listened to a talk by Germaine Brée on Albert Camus. A French Resistance activist and friend of Camus, Brée had been teaching at the University of Wisconsin for five years. Facing "a thousand or so militant students," she spoke of Camus's imperative of commitment—the possibilities it offered and the responsibilities it demanded. As Brée recalled, "All felt" that Camus "was a great model for the times." James Gilbert, a student activist attending the lecture, marveled at "the idea of the world being absurd," since it left space for students like him to "carve out some sort of commitment within that absurdity. . . . Just like *Catch-22* with a political ending!"[1]

Students turned to Camus frequently and passionately. As Serge Doubrovsky put it, "Reservations or hostility either toward Camus's person or his work are virtually unknown on this side of the Atlantic. . . . Students throw themselves upon these texts with an insatiable hunger."[2] Camus was a thinker graced with accessible prose and philosophy, made even more appealing by his compassion and commitment. Connected with Sartre, Beauvoir, and existentialism, he seemed a heroic figure, having been editor of the French Resistance paper *Combat* during and after the Second World War. Camus struggled in his writings with the questions of suicide, commitment, and rebellion. His voice was tested and true. His observations were those of a man of the left, but they came with a skepticism toward all metaphysical systems and political certitudes. A chastened but still engagé rebel, Camus figured as someone with whom you might enter into a productive dialogue. In Hayden Carruth's novel *After the Stranger* (1965), Aspen, a reclusive painter, is drawn out of his melancholy and loneliness by imaginary conversations with Camus. After an initial conversation Aspen notes, "Camus is fine. I mean the man as well. Quality of gentleness, humaneness, a sort of detachment. And humor, more than I had expected. Never sufficiently remarked before the extent to which the impersonal view is prerequisite to the compassionate view."[3] In many ways Camus became the philosophical radical of choice for the New Left generation of activists and thinkers.

In the 1960s and later, Camus dominated the consciousness of radical students. Todd Gitlin, an activist with Students for a Democratic Society (SDS), remembered that not only did his fellow students imbibe "the intellectual air of existentialism," but his undergraduate roommate had announced that his reading of Camus's *The Myth of Sisyphus* "had saved him from suicide."[4] Ken Sawyer read Camus's *The Stranger* as a fifteen-year-old, and his other works of fiction and philosophy soon thereafter. Over three decades later, after graduation from Harvard Divinity School and twenty-seven years as a Unitarian Universalist minister, Sawyer realized "that Camus was the most influential person in my life of thought, not because he said things novel to me, but because he gave voice to my deepest beliefs and feelings."[5] Another student from the 1960s, reflecting back on his college reading of Camus, remarked, "As our century closes with its deluge of trivia, celebrity, religious subterfuge, and political cant, Camus' simple appreciation of the 'benign indifference of the universe' and his place in it has more relevance than ever for me."[6] Betty Denitch, after arriving in Berkeley in 1959 to attend graduate school, joined the Young People's Socialist League as "a sort of existential gesture." At the time, she recalled, "I was reading Camus, and I thought, well, you can't hope much will come out of it, but still, what do you do with your life?"[7]

For a generation coming of age in the 1960s, confronting the civil rights movement and the war in Vietnam, Albert Camus perhaps more than Jean-Paul Sartre offered intellectual inspiration and guidance.[8] Of course, Sartre remained an important presence, through his anti-imperialist rhetoric and work in war crimes tribunals against acts committed by the United States in Vietnam. His influence, however, slanted more toward the radical left, especially as it emerged with the breakup of SDS in late 1968 and early 1969. Sartre's introduction to Frantz Fanon's *The Wretched of the Earth* (1961) evoked the incendiary rhetorical romance of revolutionary violence: "The match is put to the fuse . . . the torrent of violence sweeps away all barriers."[9] Political philosopher Adolph Reed remembered looking at a copy of the book "that my parents had around the house. Sartre's wild introduction was properly cathartic."[10]

Sartre remained a presence among the New Left. Marcus Raskin, an activist and one of the founders of the Institute for Policy Studies, proclaimed that Sartre's "life taught us how we should be and live in the world. He embodied the profound paradox that to *escape* our existential loneliness we are called to responsibility to the world and to be responsible for what we neither control nor necessarily understand."[11] Even Jerry Rubin, soon to gain fame as a leader of the Yippie faction of the New Left, quoted Sartre at a New York City antiwar rally in 1966: "Sartre calls the Left in America 'the accursed of the earth' because of the difficulties it faces in this nation." Rubin argued for more than "mere protest. We must begin the politics of radical alternatives."[12] Elisabeth Israels Perry, as a young assistant professor in the late 1960s, faced an existential crisis of conscience. Told that she must take a loyalty oath in order to continue teaching, Perry refused after reading Sartre in preparation for a lecture in her Western Civilization class. She announced her conviction in class, wrote an article for the student newspaper, and helped get the faculty mobilized to defeat the loyalty oath requirement. Sartre's ideal of commitment no matter what the cost hit a nerve with her: "If people like me, without children, then, with really nothing much to lose but a job, didn't stand up and say no to this insidious stupidity, no one would."[13] But by and large Sartre does not figure as centrally as Camus in the memories of most radicals of the 1960s. Perhaps SDS leader Tom Hayden captured the contrast most honestly and simply: "I struggled with Sartre's *Being and Nothingness* and found myself preferring Camus."[14]

Whether one preferred Camus to Sartre, reading either of them did not in and of itself cause students to tumble out of their comfortable beds at the university and go to Mississippi to organize voting-rights drives. But as with Perry, it did help to cement a decision, to push one forward. Radicals identified with the existential heroics of the Resistance or of French postwar political struggles. Camus's ideas and attitudes mattered to student and faculty radicals. And as with earlier European existentialists, the ideas of Camus were assimilated into American traditions of radicalism. Thus while historian, pacifist, and activist Staughton Lynd applauded Camus's ideas of commitment, he cobbled together his own native American tradition of radical commitment and ideas, with William Penn, Tom Paine, Thomas Jefferson, and William Lloyd Garrison taking center stage.[15]

Students felt drawn to Camus for a host of reasons. Some, paradoxically, found him the essence of cool but also the exemplification of passionate commitment to ideals. This difficult balancing act appealed to many young radicals in the 1960s. His translator Justin O'Brien recalled of Camus, "In his person, as in his writings, he established at once a fraternal relationship with those he was addressing and no one could remain impervious to his boyish smile."[16] And he was dead, killed at an early age in an absurd traffic accident. Thus he existed as a romantic figure but one who could not, unlike Sartre, personally intervene and perhaps alienate others with his positions. The power of his image was as compelling as the beauty of his books and essays. The existential malaise (Meursault in *The Stranger*) or existential heroism (Rieux in *The Plague*) of his fictional characters seemed to students to capture their own predicament. In his works on confronting the absurd (*The Myth of Sisyphus*) or on the necessity of rebellion (*The Rebel*), Camus offered texts for young Americans in the process of figuring out how to express their anger, frustration, alienation, and rebellion. To be sure, the actions they often took, as Tom Hayden later realized, went against the grain of Camus's essential moderation. But for young Americans in search of a role model, Camus—a romantic combination of philosopher and literary figure, of activist and intellectual—fit the bill. Students identified with his injunction to resist the absurd and to fight oppression. In this world all that defines us as humans, all that connects us to humanity or the human condition, is our willingness, no matter the odds, to stand up for something. Only by such a commitment do we push aside the absurd, if only for a moment. And only by such a commitment do we escape the imprisonment of alienation and find human solidarity.

Camus's appeal extended beyond the cohort of young people on college campuses in the 1960s. Robert F. Kennedy, in the painful wake of his brother's assassination, turned in his late thirties to Camus for moral guidance. Kennedy gained from his sleepless-night readings of Camus's essays, novels, and plays a sense of fatalism, tragedy, and the absurd. He jotted down lines from Camus in his notebooks; he scribbled extensive marginalia in his copies of Camus's books; he quoted him in his speeches. As Kennedy's sense of responsibility toward the poor increased, he came to abhor the poverty of Appalachia, the South, and the urban ghettoes. His views found succinct expression in Camus's words: "Perhaps we cannot prevent this world from being a world in which children are tortured. But we can reduce the number of tortured children."[17] Indeed, at a campaign stop in Indiana, Kennedy saw signs reading, "KENNEDY AND CAMUS IN 1968." Kennedy claimed that his rejection of capital punishment arose out of his reading of Camus's "Reflections on the Guillotine."[18] Camus did not radicalize Kennedy, but he did help him comprehend a politics of the possible based on a commitment that grew out of despair. Armed with these new insights from Camus, Kennedy's black-and-white dogmatism lessened, his sense of mission deepened. He became something of a fatalist, a respecter of the absurd. Such sharp existential recognitions did not plunge him into a stupor of apathy or self-indulgence. Added to his already considerable energy, existentialism suggested to Kennedy that he must define himself through his actions, by his courage to act within an absurd world.

A younger generation of students shared Kennedy's passion for Camus's writings. Those in college during the 1960s were perhaps the last generation for whom books made a difference. This "last generation of a reading and writing society," according to literary historian Philip D. Beidler, created a "mythic consciousness" of itself and of the world largely though a disparate group of texts, books that were read, underlined, borrowed, lent, and taken to heart. The canon of "semi-official" authors and texts that were definitive for this generation is staggering in its diversity, ranging from J. D. Salinger's *The Catcher in the Rye* (1951) and Joseph Heller's absurdist *Catch-22* (1961) to the fantasies of J. R. R. Tolkien and Kurt Vonnegut's dissection of the absurd logic of destruction, *Slaughterhouse Five* (1969).[19] Yet all of these volumes offered a critique of American institutions and assumptions, all recognized the absurd and "phony" excuses of those in power.

An existential perspective, whether enunciated by Camus or by Sartre, proved to be the philosophy of choice of a generation of college students. Existentialism spoke to their feelings of alienation, their rebellion against authority, their frustration with absolutes, and their concerns about a culture of conformity. Older adults recognized this fact. J. Glenn Gray, chair of the Philosophy Department at Colorado College, noted in 1965 that "existentialism is capturing the students" of today. The existential thinkers students confronted in their classes brought home to them both the tragedy and the absurdity of their existence.[20] Walter Kaufmann, who did so much to make existentialist texts familiar in *Existentialism: From Dostoevsky to Sartre*, correctly predicted that students and younger faculty on the nation's campuses would be drawn to the existential ideal of engagement.[21]

2 UP UNTIL THE 1960s Sartre had overshadowed Camus, in part because of his status as the leader of the school of French existentialism and his prominence as a philosopher and literary figure. Popular and academic analysts of existentialism engaged with Sartre rather than with Camus. Moreover, Camus's own attempts to distance himself from existentialism rendered him harder to place, even though he was commonly, and correctly, grouped with the existentialist school. Hazel E. Barnes considered him to be an existential thinker. Indeed, she wrote to him, "In many instances I felt that it was you who had developed more fully themes which they [Sartre and Beauvoir] suggested, you who have on occasion provided answers to their questions." Camus replied to Barnes that while comfortable with being considered an "existential" writer, he did not want to be confined to being a member of a school of literature and philosophy called "existentialism." Instead, he wanted to retain his sense of independence, his own perspective.[22]

Camus communicated to a generation of students a message as lean and simple as his prose: The relation between man and the world is absurd. Alienation is part of the human condition. Death must be resisted. In defining ourselves, we must move beyond mere inwardness toward commitment to values such as justice and humaneness. Even when less than precise about what constituted these values, Camus argued that a committed intellectual or student made choices—without certitude, perhaps, but with the weight of responsibility. Success might prove elusive, but heroism defined the struggle. The myth of Sisyphus, condemned to an absurd existence of pushing a boulder to the top of a mountain only to have it roll down again and then repeating the ritual *ad nauseam,* became Camus's parable of heroism. Camus found inspiration in the notion that however empty Sisyphus's gesture might seem, it remained meaningful. The choice to live, to take responsibility, to act in an invariably hostile world, captured the odd beauty of the rebel who rejected absolutes but believed in the value of working for the betterment of humanity. One must act as if one's actions mattered. This would be the credo for Robert Moses in Mississippi.

Moses recalled that when he was in jail "this last time," for organizational activities on behalf of the Student Non-violent Coordinating Committee (SNCC), he "read through *The Rebel* and *The Plague* again."[23] Literally as well as figuratively, Moses took Camus's words with him onto the dangerous Mississippi roads to organize voting drives for disfranchised African Americans in the 1960s. He found in Camus an attitude that helped him understand and resist racist injustice and oppression. In Camus he discovered a fellow traveler struggling to maintain a principled humanity.

In his turn to Camus and existentialism, Moses followed a long line of African-American thinkers and artists. The existential themes of a tragic human condition and dauntlessness in the face of despair had appealed to Richard Wright and Ralph Ellison. Their blues idiom had easily accommodated the anguished swing of existentialism. Martin Luther King, Jr., six years older than Moses, moored much of his theology in the existentialism of Paul Tillich. An existential notion of man's "finite freedom" constituted for King "one of existentialism's most lasting contributions," a starting point for comprehending religious faith and social injustice. King appreciated existentialism's emphasis on anxiety and estrangement as part of the human condition. Despite its "fashionable" popularity, King found in existentialism "certain basic truths about man and his condition" that corrected an all-too-easy optimism. In his stirring "Letter from a Birmingham Jail," which he composed in 1963 after being arrested for demonstrating against segregated public accommodations, King invoked Tillich's notion that "sin is separation." Therefore, "is not segregation an existential awareness of man's tragic separation, his awful estrangement, his terrible sinfulness?" Given the weight of such recognition, King felt that he must "disobey segregation ordinances, for such ordinances are morally wrong."[24]

Born in 1935 in New York City, Robert Moses was one of a handful of African-American undergraduates at Hamilton College in the 1950s. He earned a master's degree in philosophy at Harvard in 1957, unable to continue the doctoral program because of family demands. Working as a high-school teacher in New York, Moses was transformed by learning about the Greensboro sit-in demonstrations that were undertaken in 1960 by black students against segregated facilities in the South. He went south in 1960, first working in the offices of the Southern Christian Leadership Conference in Atlanta, determined that the following year he would become involved in organizing African Americans in Mississippi to register to vote. This decision would change his life and that of many others.

By all accounts, Robert Moses had a remarkable blend of courage and conviction. According to Ernest Nobles, a farmer who knew Moses in Mc-Comb, Mississippi, "Poor Bob took a lot of beatings. . . . I just couldn't understand what Bob Moses was. Sometimes I think he was Moses in the Bible."[25] Although he often disagreed with Moses on tactics and style, activist Cleveland Sellers recognized that he was a "culture hero" to white students as well as to the black activists who joined the Freedom Summer activities of 1964: "There was something about him, the manner in which he carried himself, that seemed to draw all of us to him. He had been where we were going. And more important, he had emerged as the kind of person we wanted to be."[26]

One white civil rights volunteer said that Moses "starts . . . from a position that he is living on borrowed time."[27] "The thing was not how you're going to die," remarked Moses, "but how you're going to live."[28] Such observations, of course, reflect the distinctively existential quality of his courage. Moses felt that existentialism helped him navigate not only the shoals of the racist oppression of the Mississippi delta but also the unsettling problems of power and participation in the movement against that oppression. On both counts, he found insight in Camus's writings.

A committed reader of Camus, Moses studied Camus's *The Rebel* and *The Plague* as well as shorter works such as *Neither Victims nor Executioners*.[29] "I read a lot of Camus," he stated to Robert Penn Warren. "The main essence of what he says is what I feel really close to—closest to."[30] Moses identified with the character of Dr. Rieux in *The Plague*. Courageous and dedicated, Rieux is no fanatic. A chastened figure, unwilling to ignore the plague that surrounds him, he determines to oppose it. Perhaps not unlike Robert Moses, Rieux is a hero without pretensions. As to the meaning of the plague, to the desire of men and women to return from exile, Rieux "was thinking it has no importance whether such things have or have not a meaning; all we need consider is the answer given to men's hope." Thus "if there is one thing one can always yearn for and sometimes attain, it is human love."[31]

This need to give love, to express love in the face of hatred and fear, this desire to act with courage and honor, defined Moses as a civil rights activist. Sally Belfrage, a Freedom Summer volunteer, recalled that in the midst of a talk Moses "stood pondering something, quite still." The troubling issue was the racial tensions then beginning to erupt within the movement itself. Finally he found his voice by invoking Camus: "There is an analogy to *The Plague* by Camus. The country isn't willing yet to admit it has the plague, but it pervades the whole society. Everyone must come to grips with this, because it affects us all. We must discuss it openly and honestly. . . . If we ignore it, it's going to blow up in our faces."[32]

In addition to finding a literary analogy for problems within American society, Moses also discovered in the work of Camus a sensitivity to political questions about the relation between means and ends, as well as insights concerning the human condition. The nihilism of the lonely individual of Camus's first novel *The Stranger* gave way in *The Plague* to social solidarity. As Camus had expressed it in response to criticism by Roland Barthes, "If there is an evolution from *The Stranger* to *The Plague,* it is in the direction of solidarity and participation."[33]

The Rebel, Camus's philosophical companion piece to *The Plague,* takes up the subject of rebellion in an absurd world. Through the act of rebellion, man creates both for himself and for others: "I rebel—therefore we exist."[34] Rebellion against death, through an upholding of principles, is heroic and necessary. When carrying out such acts in the name of absolutes (either metaphysical or historical), the revolutionary rebel mistakenly obeys "the law of spiritual imperialism, he sets out in search of world conquest by way of an infinitely multiplied series of murders" (103). Thus in Camus's aphoristic analysis, "Absolute good and absolute evil, if the necessary logic is applied, both demand the same degree of passion" (125), and both lead to the realization that "the real passion of the twentieth century is servitude" (234). For Camus, "The principles that men give to themselves end by overwhelming their noblest intentions" (240).

Camus developed his concerns and insights in the harsh light of the age of totalitarianism. He wrote also in recognition of the nihilism of the modern age, a recognition at once necessary and daunting. He addressed the question of how to persevere in the face of such knowledge. In addition, Camus defined himself against Sartre's increasingly strong identification, in the late 1940s and 1950s, with the forces of history.[35] Sartrean existentialists were "subjected for the moment," according to Camus, "to the cult of history and its contradictions," to the view that "there is progress in the transition from rebellion to revolution and that the rebel is nothing if he is not a revolutionary." The problem with the revolutionary position, hitched to the shooting star of history, is that "every revolutionary ends by becoming either an oppressor or a heretic" (249). In response, Sartre rejected Camus's position as a politics of quietism: "You are no longer anything but an abstraction of revolt."[36] In contrast to Sartre, Camus willingly accepted the role of independent heretic, yet he wondered how to remain engaged against oppression without succumbing, as he put it in *The Rebel*, to "cowardly conformism" (280).

Camus also worried about how the rebel could avoid becoming the oppressor, about whether the rebel's critical knowledge of the problems of nihilism and revolution could allow him to act instead of becoming frozen in self-doubt and hesitancy. In the face of such existential knowledge, Camus counseled rebellion that is anchored in "thought that recognizes limits" (294) and that does not, in the name of absolute freedom and justice, "demand the right to destroy the existence and freedom of others" (284). In essence, Camus recommended a "philosophy of limits" (289), chastened by the rebel's recognition that everything is a question of balance, of constantly negotiating against absolutes: "Thus the rebel can never find peace" (285).

Peace eluded Camus in his own life. In the 1950s, as the Algerian war for independence deepened, Camus set himself apart from other French intellectuals in condemning the use of revolutionary violence in that conflict. He viewed the battle in concrete terms, worrying that abstract calls to violence would lead to an orgy of murder in the name of a righteous cause. Moreover, according to critic Edward Said, Camus identified so strongly with France that the assumptions and presumptions of colonialism blinded him to the reality of the Algerians' oppression. Yet Camus maintained, perhaps naively, that accommodation and balance between ends and means could be attained. His position of extreme moderation, tinged with the pain of being part of the struggle, of fearing the demise of a French presence in Algeria, undermined his intellectual authority in France.[37] But it had little effect on his American reputation as a champion of commitment in the name of justice.

Armed with the sober recognition that revolutionary calls for absolute order translate into regimes of death and oppression, Camus championed engagement with acute sensitivity to suffering. All we can do, he writes at the conclusion of his rumination on rebellion, is "to learn to live and to die, and, in order to be a man, to refuse to be a god." In this manner, at this "meridian of thought," the Camusian rebel comes "to share in the struggles and destiny of all men" (306). In so doing, the rebel strives to be neither a victim nor an executioner. Here, in essence, is the philosophy of the rebel that shaped Moses's thinking and actions while a member of SNCC. Moses did not attempt to work through on paper the dispute between Sartre and Camus. He adopted Camus's solution in action and philosophy: to rebel with a sense of moderation, avoiding the extremes of either utopian dreams or authoritarian promises.

3   WHEN MOSES attempted to register African Americans to vote in McComb, Mississippi, during the summer of 1961, "philosophy collided with reality."[38] Moses developed an eclectic philosophy of Gandhian nonviolent direct action, with hints of Buddhist mysticism and Christian idealism and a strong existential bent. He upheld nonviolence as a tactical, rather than a religious, ideal. Along with Camus, he resisted absolute values. Under certain circumstances, and under the weight of chastened responsibility, violence could be employed. But in McComb in the early 1960s, Moses and SNCC supported nonviolence as the best tactic to use in registering African Americans to vote. Such action required great courage, for the SNCC organizers and the black citizens who were attempting to exercise their constitutional right were harassed, often beaten, and sometimes killed.

The question, which Camus had framed well for Moses, was this: How, in the face of the temptation to respond with violence and hatred, could the individual avoid being a victim or becoming an executioner? Moses had carefully read Camus's short essay *Neither Victims nor Executioners*. Originally published in 1946 in *Combat,* the French Resistance journal that Camus edited, the essay was translated into English by Dwight Macdonald in *politics* in 1947 before being reissued as a pamphlet by the activist journal *Liberation* in 1960.[39] In whatever form Moses encountered it, the essay moved him. In this piece Camus, who had initially favored the death penalty for collaborators, rethought his position on violence and retribution. While finding the absolute rejection of violence to be utopian, Camus announced that we must reject "a world where murder is legitimate, and where human life is considered trifling" (28). Ends, however just, must not be achieved through unjust means. The individual must avoid being a victim but also must not assume the self-righteous mantle of executioner. To achieve this balance might mean to "fight within History" (60) and in the process to assert the very value of humanism.

Moses worried too about how he, as an activist, might be seduced into becoming an executioner, someone willing to use any means to achieve ends that he considered justified. Despite the absurdity of the idea of African Americans in Mississippi in the early 1960s becoming "executioners," Moses noted that within the ranks of SNCC itself, such temptations were already beginning to play themselves out. Some black staff members of SNCC, he stated, took out their anger and frustration on white staff members; in effect, they adopted the superiority, authenticity, and attitude of the executioner. Moses spoke out within SNCC against this hardening of racial lines. As one activist remembered, Moses stated, "We are all victims of the plague of prejudice but must not make the mistake that the authorities in Camus' *Plague* made by resisting the recognition of the disease because recognition would have made action necessary."[40]

Moses invoked Camus frequently when enunciating his essential principles for action. Especially drawn to Camus's sense of tragic limitations but with a commitment to act, Moses argued against allowing the problematic nature of action to result in quietism, whereby you "subjugate yourself to the conditions that are and don't try to change them."[41] One must act, but always with a sense of walking a tightrope between asserting one's own rights and not denying the rights of others. In so doing, one battles for "humanitarian values." And, "if it's possible, you try to eke out some corner of love or some glimpse of happiness within. And that's what I think more than anything else conquers the bitterness, let's say."[42]

Moses, to a degree, successfully rejected absolutes and celebrated the necessity of building a community of activists. He led by example, in part by putting his body on the line. A capable, if reluctant, participant in the organizational structure of SNCC, he opposed top-down leadership models. He preferred a version of "participatory democracy" without charismatic leaders. In the late 1980s, when asked to comment on the leadership of Martin Luther King, Jr., Moses reiterated that the important issue was not "the emergence and success of an individual, but the emergence and success of . . . the movement as a whole."[43] In a sense, he muted his own authority within the movement. At meetings he often remained silent, allowing the discussion to meander without personally intervening. When he did speak, he spoke slowly and softly, and his words carried weight. Recognizing that he could easily sway others to his position by the force of his personality, Moses attempted to avoid celebrity, preferring participation in a community of activists sharing goals and a philosophy.

Did Moses's approach to organizing succeed? Some argue that his existential attitude and singular individuality undermined the movement. His SNCC colleague Cleveland Sellers disapproved of those in the movement whom he called "floaters." Such individuals—"philosophers, existentialists," and the like— were the "flamboyant faction," anarchic, undisciplined, and "'high' on Freedom."[44] To Sellers's mind, they wasted time on esoteric arguments when they should have been engaging in organization-building and disciplined action. Another activist, Bruce Payne, criticized Moses's "anti-leader style of political organization"; by failing to offer his own insights, Moses "deprived" others of "valuable counsel."[45]

Although rarely explicit about the issue, historian Clayborne Carson suggests that one reason for the problems within SNCC was unwillingness on the part of Moses and others to build a more structured organization. Moses in effect followed his own inner sense of rebellion rather than creating or adhering to a party line.[46] This observation has much in common with Sellers's criticism of the "floaters" in SNCC. Yet Carson also admits that "if SNCC staff members did not discover a means of reconciling their desire for social justice with their desire for individual freedom, neither have those of us who are able to reflect on such questions in more tranquil times."[47] Of course, according to Camus, such reconciliation is a process, a continuing tension, the mark of the rebel. It is a difficult legacy, but an inescapable one. By upholding the values of humanity, the rebel lessens his chances of abusing those precise values. Speaking of those who refuse to impose the sentence of death, Camus writes, "Knowing themselves to be fallible, they at least draw the appropriate consequences. And true justice is on their side precisely insofar as logic is not."[48] Moses and Camus believed that "the ideal lies between these two extremes—victim and executioner."[49]

As an organizer, Moses accepted that he and his colleagues in the civil rights movement would face danger. He suffered under the recognition that in a sense he helped create situations that resulted in the death of others. Without an absolute belief in either the force or the logic of history, and without any hint of metaphysical nihilism, Moses was buffeted by the winds of his responsibility for others. His activities in organizing voter drives in the South increased local tensions, sometimes with dire consequences. Herbert Lee, a farmer involved with SNCC, was murdered in cold blood by E. H. Hearst, a racist white official. "We knew in our hearts and minds," Moses stated, "that Hearst was attacking Lee because of the voter registration drive, and I suppose that we all felt guilty and felt responsible, because it's one thing to get beat up and it's another thing to be responsible, or to participate in some way in a killing."[50]

Three years later, in 1964, Moses remained shaken by the responsibility of having sent civil rights workers into the killing fields of Mississippi. As one activist remembered, "his head hanging, his voice barely audible, [Moses] tried to tell us what he feels about being responsible for the creation of situations in which people get killed." He offered rationales, which "don't satisfy him." Speaking soon after the murder of three civil rights workers, Michael Schwerner, James Chaney, and Andrew Goodman, Moses said that "he asks no one to risk what he himself will not risk. . . . Looking at us sitting in the same room where the 3 missing men had been last week, Moses almost seemed to be wanting all of us to go home."[51]

Immeasurable burdens weighed upon activists such as Moses and Camus. In his notebooks Camus had written, "I am not made for politics because I am incapable of wanting or accepting the death of the adversary." Yet Camus, no less than Moses, realized that "modern man is obliged to become concerned with politics. I am concerned with it, in spite of myself. . . . I have never been able to refuse any of the obligations I encountered."[52] In much the same spirit, Moses struggled on, Sisyphus-like: "When you spend all your time fighting evil, you become preoccupied with it and terribly weary," but "we're going to do the job we have to do."[53] Moses reeled under the hatred. "He used to get hurt every time anybody would look mean at him, literally," remembered Connie Curry. "I mean he would feel it, and you could imagine that kind of sensitivity in Mississippi where people wanted to kill him."[54]

In the end, Moses retreated, if only temporarily, from the struggle with SNCC. His work in Mississippi soon extended itself into the arena of national politics. He began to work as an activist against the war in Vietnam, and, most famously, in 1964 he attempted with Fannie Lou Hamer and others to challenge the all-white Mississippi delegation to the Democratic National Convention. Outmaneuvered, perhaps sold out by his ostensible allies, Moses underwent a crisis. At one point in the middle of a meeting he announced to his fellow SNCC workers that he intended to change his surname from Moses to Parris. He could no longer bear the burden of being seen, symbolically and in reality, as a Moses leading his people out of the desert.[55] Other changes were in the offing. Moses reversed his position on the role of whites in the civil rights movement. Then, hounded by his draft board, he took flight to Canada, where he worked at odd jobs before moving to Africa to teach mathematics and English. Weary though he might have been, Moses never abandoned the fight. When President Carter offered an amnesty program for war resisters in 1977, he returned to the United States, settling in Cambridge, Massachusetts, to set up an innovative program to teach math and computer skills to students in inner-city schools. The learning of such skills meant "empowerment" for the powerless, just as the striving for voting rights had been years earlier in Mississippi.[56]

4 TOM HAYDEN faced similar problems of means and ends, of freedom and responsibility, as a radical student activist in the 1960s. No less than Bob Moses, Hayden often interrogated these dilemmas through the writings of Albert Camus. No single individual, certainly not Hayden, typifies the New Left. But as the memories quoted at the opening of this chapter indicate, an existentialist attitude or mood was widespread within the ca-

pacious New Left movement. Hayden's struggle with Camus may have been deeper than that of others, but it replicated the experiences of many of his generation. To understand Hayden's emerging rebellion against injustice and inequality, a brief excursion into the sources of his anxiety, and the alienation of his generation, might be useful.

All social criticism, in the "modern sense," presupposes a sense of alienation. The New Left emphasis on alienation built upon earlier foundations. Randolph Bourne, Van Wyck Brooks, and Waldo Frank, to name only a few, had in the early years of the twentieth century bemoaned their alienation from culture and society; they promoted as a palliative their concept of "personality," the realization of a true selfhood within a newly formulated community.[57] In contrast to the orthodox Marxist theory of alienation, in which alienation was associated with the industrial worker being robbed of the fruits of his labor by the capitalist, much of the literature of alienation in America focused on the estrangement of the middle and upper classes, who felt "weightless" or cut off from the presumed march of history.[58]

After the Second World War, "alienation" and "estrangement" came to function as central terms in sociological, religious, and psychological analysis. As already noted, Reinhold Niebuhr posited the estrangement of individuals from God, while Rollo May captured the alienation of the individual in an age of mass society and totalitarianism. Criticism of alienation in American society could be relatively mild and without religious overtones, as in the work of David Riesman. While Riesman negatively depicted the other-directed personality as drab and conformist, without an inner gyroscope for direction, he also admired its social sensitivities.[59]

By the 1960s, the literature of alienation had became more pointed and diverse. No longer confined to the totalitarian past of Nazi Germany or the present of the Soviet Union, as it had been in the work of Fromm, Arendt, and May, alienation stalked the American landscape, part and parcel of modern life when the power of consumerism and advertising promoted a false sense of identity. An anchored, inner-directed self seemed out of reach. Theorists as different as C. Wright Mills, Herbert Marcuse, and Norman O. Brown agreed that alienation and estrangement defined the American corporate liberal state, also then referred to as the new industrial state.[60] New Left students borrowed this terminology, talking often about the "one-dimensional" nature of life in America, about sexual repression, about the stultifying nature of conformity in 1950s America, and about the ways in which power operated to impose consensus. Students depicted the modern mega-university as a factory designed to produce complacent components for the new industrial state and the war machine.

New Left theorists argued that the corporate liberal state had cast a spell on the citizenry. Individuals in postwar America, the argument went, were either alienated, conformist, or sexually repressed, sometimes all three. Recognition by the individual of his own alienation proved difficult, since the nefarious strategies of the corporate liberal state managed to parade conformity as normality and channeled consumerism into a mode of individual self-expression and material gratification. In both cases, co-optation resulted. As Herbert Marcuse phrased it, "Containment of social change is perhaps the most singular achievement of advanced industrial society."[61] Various modes of repression meant that the individual's confrontation with existential realities, with the authentic self in postwar America, became consigned to the realm of the neurotic or the exotic. Satisfaction was to be gained through consumption. Self-worth was defined according to one's ability to own material objects. The modern state loomed as a mechanism of totalitarian control, with alienation at the heart of the system.[62] The individual seemed to sleepwalk through existence.

Against this crushing reality, this "repressive tolerance," to employ Marcuse's term, a new generation of students protested, seemingly born tired of the demands for conformity in an age of affluence. Paradoxically, it seemed, the very forces that conspired toward repression gave birth to the possibility of rebellion.[63] In the heated vision of Norman O. Brown's popular, oracular imagery, out of sublimation and repression might arise the "Resurrection of the Body," a new libidinal freedom and energy.[64] From the economic wealth of the period, and the logic of consumerism, came new products to be consumed; rock and roll, youth-oriented movies, and other expressions of rebellion entered into the mainstream.

Excited by these theories and images of rebellion, frustrated by society's expectations for them, many young people demanded authenticity; they sought to establish a true self through commitment to a vital community dedicated to high ideals. Theodore Roszak, whose *The Making of a Counter Culture* (1969) did much to explain the phenomenon and the variety of youthful rebellion in this period, later pointed out the ironic role that the conformist market played in creating rebels: "The teenager was invented as a market. But the market dangerously intensified self-awareness in the adolescent years of life that most lend themselves to brooding introspection. A fateful development. Rebels who began without a cause might soon find more than enough to justify rebellion."[65]

Reasons for rebellion were everywhere to be found in the 1950s and 1960s. The Cold War and the nuclear arms race threatened the survival and solidity of American society. The Cuban missile crisis of 1962 evoked a sense of living on "the edge of destruction," as a popular song phrased it. To many young people, American ideals of democracy and freedom were compromised, if not obliterated, by the denial of civil rights to African Americans. The presumed comforts of conformity became deadening. New voices in American society, ranging from the Beats to Lenny Bruce, suggested in no uncertain terms that something was amiss with the American dream. When poet Allen Ginsberg intoned about the destruction of "the best minds of my generation," he spoke from personal experience, and he reached outward to touch the experiences of others. Many balked at the paradox of living in a land of individualism where attempts at free expression, spontaneity, and authenticity were denigrated as antisocial and procommunist. American power, increasingly consigned to the morass of Vietnam, proved to many the emptiness of the American ideal of beneficent democracy and freedom. Hardly surprising, then, that a generation would find reasons, both personal and political, to rebel. In a period when the personal increasingly became the political, the search for authenticity would have immense ramifications.

Whatever the causes of youth rebellion and its ultimate implications, much of the intellectual understanding of and language for alienation and rebellion came out of a dialogue with existentialism. A sense of the centrality of existentialism to the New Left can be gleaned from Doug Rossinow's excellent study of the students who came to radicalism at the University of Texas in the late 1950s and early 1960s. These young men and women, as Rossinow convincingly demonstrates, were fired by Christian existentialism and inspired by the civil rights movement. These forces worked in tandem to radicalize them as they embarked on their serious quest for authenticity and commitment.

Through organizations such as Christian Faith-and-Life Community (CFLC), Rossinow explains, University of Texas students came into contact with minister John Wesley Mathews, a rather charismatic existentialist, who had studied with H. Richard Niebuhr at Yale.[66] Under his guidance, and through readings of existential theologians such as Dietrich Bonhoeffer, Rudolf Bultmann, and Paul Tillich, students came to accept that religious salvation depended upon a sense of religious crisis that was projected outward. Estrangement from God was as alienating as estrangement from one's true self. These students read Kierkegaard, but they did not chart their spiritual development through him. Although some New Left students identified with Kierkegaard's language and his sense of urgency in spiritual matters, they distanced themselves from him in terms of politics. Kierkegaardian inwardness was a lonely dead-end street. One student at this time read Kierkegaard "front to back" and as a result came to despise leftist political commitments. As a friend of his later put it, "He reduced my politics to an existential gesture."[67]

In speaking of a "dissident Christian tradition" of activism, Rossinow maintains that it "encouraged young people searching for authenticity to intervene in the larger social world" (12). Out of this cadre at the University of Texas came some of SDS's early national leadership, Sandra "Casey" Cason along with Robb and Dorothy Burlage. All identified with the "dissident Christian tradition" and with the writings of Camus (36, 75). Students found in each tradition a similar set of concerns about commitment and authenticity: "The way to be human was to refuse to be complicit" (76). To be authentic, for this generation of radicals at the University of Texas, meant an existential religious commitment and engagement with the emerging civil rights movement.[68]

The radicalism of these students expressed their desire to be authentic, to avoid the trap that Sartre had captured so well in his novel *Nausea* and that figured centrally in his *Being and Nothingness* when he spoke of bad faith. Camus, in *The Stranger*, dealt no less powerfully with themes of estrangement and alienation. But most important, Camus attempted to move beyond alienation and meaninglessness to commitment and authenticity. Tom Hayden, and the student rebels he came into contact with at the University of Texas, would move into political engagement in the civil rights and antiwar movements.

5 TOM HAYDEN looked to Camus for inspiration and guidance. When he and fellow radical Sandra Cason were married in 1961 in Austin, their vows included selections from Ecclesiastes and Camus. Hayden also accepted, as he interpreted it, Camus's emphasis on rebellion, on the ethical demands upon the individual act, on the momentous decision to "choose justice in order to remain faithful to the world," however absurd that world might appear.[69] As his journey led him from involvement in the civil rights movement to actions with SDS, voter registration drives in Mississippi, demonstrations at Columbia University, and confrontation in the streets of Chicago in 1968, Hayden gauged retrospectively the logic of his rebellion in the language and terms that Camus had bequeathed to him. Sometimes he lived up to Camus's strictures; other times he fell short. At all times he regarded Camus as a role model and a moral exemplar.

Hayden appeared to be most Camusian when he was the rebel with a cause, tinged with a sense of doubt and tragedy. Doubt and a chastened sense of possibility are the bookends of Hayden's important career as an American radical. He began as an undergraduate beset with doubt but with a commitment to activism in spite of it. After a period when revolutionary excess sometimes got the better of him, Hayden returned to a more chastened sensibility. Indeed, this sense of a chastened self defines his memoir *Reunion* (1988), a work that is essentially a dialogue between him and

Camus, structured along the lines of Whittaker Chambers's coming to see the light in *Witness* and Ralph Ellison's Invisible Man coming out of hibernation. It is a book about the redemptive possibilities of self-knowledge.

Hayden, born in 1939, was a typical middle-class youth radicalized by the events of his era.[70] Perhaps he correctly traced this process of radicalization to the disjuncture between the politics and policies of America in the 1950s and 1960s and the ideals and values that were supposed to define them. In any case, the ideal of the rebel quickly captured the young Hayden's imagination as he devoured Kerouac's *On the Road*, read issues of *Mad* magazine, and identified with the cool rebellion of James Dean. While attending the University of Michigan as an undergraduate, Hayden immediately got involved with the student paper, the *Michigan Daily*. As a reporter for the paper, he traveled to Los Angeles for the Democratic National Convention in 1960, where he met Martin Luther King, Jr. In a retrospective moment of prophecy, Hayden relates in his memoir that King told him, "Ultimately, you have to take a stand with your life" (35).

The young Hayden knew that he must act but was uncertain about exactly how to proceed. In 1960, his senior year, as editor of the *Michigan Daily*, he offered advice to freshmen that was suffused with his own uncertainties. Hayden argued that he and his fellow students confronted "a world apparently without leaders, a world of vast confusion, changing cultures, strained by the nearness of total war, and it has been in such shape throughout the life of almost every student." In the face of such chaos, the responsibility of the "active student" is to "grope as he moves along his educational path through a myriad of surrounding tensions."[71] A year later, in an article published in, of all places, the fashion magazine *Mademoiselle,* Hayden announced his solidarity with the common suffering of humanity and with the Camusian ideal that "human life is invariably valuable." Young activists must uphold "ideology without illusions," by which he meant a chastened sensibility, a rejection of "emotionalism." He praised "calculated rebellion, which frees the impulse of outraged protest and harnesses it to practical programs."[72] In essence, Hayden was at this point in his life counseling a Camusian program of moderation.[73]

The fullest expression of Hayden's Camusian doubt mingled with a commitment to activism appeared in the essay "A Letter to the New (Young) Left" (1961). The essay anticipates, in many ways, ideas that would appear in the Port Huron Statement issued by SDS in 1962. Hayden is forthright regarding his doubt and his need for action. He opens with a quick survey of the emptiness of much "liberal philosophy," finding C. Wright Mills—an influence on him and the subject of his master's thesis—to be "appealing and dynamic in his expression of theory in the grand manner, but his pessimism yields us no path out of the dark." Without help forthcoming from Mills, Hayden and his fellow student radicals were left to "stand, limp, questioning, even scared."[74]

"How, then," Hayden asked, "shall we respond?" He answered hesitantly, by calling for a radicalism tinged with morality, a "reflective commitment" whereby "passion and our critical talents [combine] into a provisional position" (7). Combining classical American pragmatism with Camusian existentialism, Hayden warns against abstraction and absolutes and argues in favor of concreteness and activity. But he lacks the intrepid optimism sometimes associated with Deweyan pragmatism or Enlightenment empiricism. Instead, his tone is that of a weary traveler, someone who knows that a long road lies ahead and the final destination may prove to be out of reach: "Contrary to what our passions demand, our struggle will not be brief and cataclysmic—unless terminated in the roaring climax of nuclear war" (8).

At this stage in his intellectual and political evolution, Hayden's politics are Camusian, stressing engagement, commitment, and moderation: "Our gains will be modest, not sensational" (8). He admits his uncertainty ("I am beset by doubt at this point") but insists that "it is possible and necessary to begin to think and act—provisionally yet strongly—in the midst of our doubts." In terms that recall Camus's rebel, Hayden writes, "We must begin to see doubt, not as a reason for inaction. . . . We must see it as a reminder that infallibility is not the property of any single man, and moreover, that compassion for enemies is not simply a heroic show, but a manifestation of our deepest moral anxiety" (8). Although such Camusian sentiments became less pronounced in Hayden's writing as the chaos of the 1960s mushroomed, they did resurface in his memoir, composed in the 1980s. There he reaffirmed the value and necessity of acting with the sober sensitivity that comes from anxiety about the relation between means and ends.

These early ideas informed the critical text of the New Left: the Port Huron Statement, drawn up in 1962 by Hayden and approved by the members of SDS. Historians disagree about the intellectual thrust of this document. James Miller singles out the ideal of "participatory democracy" as its most telling moment. The roots of the concept of "participatory democracy," according to Miller, are found in "civic republicanism," exemplified by the writings of C. Wright Mills and John Dewey. Here is a vision of rational political discussion and activity in a community of common interests.[75] The problem, for Miller, is that these inchoate ideals coexist with others that he associates with Camus and existentialism. In Miller's view, by 1962 Hayden had demonstrated tendencies to succumb to "a kind of reckless existentialism," to a romanticism that would bring him, and many in the New Left, to an almost cultish identification with revolutionary leaders such as Fidel Castro, Ho Chi Minh, and Che Guevara. For Miller, Camus's ideals led to "a world of clashing wills and romantic heroes."[76] In contrast, Doug Rossinow sees "Christian existentialism" as a valuable presence in the Port Huron Statement, with its emphasis on commitment, breakthrough, and community, as well as on the power of love to overcome hatred and to establish authenticity.[77]

Both are right, although I have deep reservations concerning Miller's equation of Camus with "reckless existentialism." The Port Huron Statement is eclectic, and it does reflect the various sources and issues that were swirling around in the excited minds of Hayden and his comrades at this particular historical moment. The anticommunist sophistication that Michael Harrington wished for in the document was absent not simply because Hayden and his comrades were too young to have experienced the sectarian Cold War battles with Stalinism, but because they were in part reacting against the cant of Cold Warriorism that lay at the heart of American foreign policy in this period. The document does manage to balance a host of needs in a way designed, as Rossinow rightly insists, to propel students, and American society, toward commitment to erect a community based upon love and authenticity rather than racism, imperialism, and consumerism.

The Port Huron Statement, strong on critique, vague on solutions—hardly surprising for a manifesto—summed up an existential analysis drawn from the literature of alienation and authenticity. In Hayden's notes from March 1962, preparatory to the statement, he complains that those in power suffer from a "moral appetite . . . rendered arid." They are unable to respond to "the questions we [student radicals] think existentially important." What is necessary for the movement are individuals who "combine the capacity for intellectual honesty and clarity with the ability to persuade and accomplish." The radical, Hayden argues, must "become a creator and self-maker rather than a pitiless and buffeted thing unable to reach the forces that control."[78]

Rather than discussing these needs in the Port Huron Statement as part of an abstract human condition, Hayden presents them as embedded within the specific bedrock of American society. Because of the arms race, humanity teeters on the brink of destruction, and Hayden places much of the blame for this state of affairs upon the United States. The crushing fear of nuclear annihilation, combined with the routinization and automation of existence, lead Americans toward a conformist life. Echoing the analysis of Marcuse, Hayden finds that escape seems impossible since "the dominant institutions are complex enough to blunt the minds of their potential critics, and entrenched enough to swiftly dissipate or repel the energies of protest and reform, thus limiting human expectancies."[79] Anxiety translates into passivity; here we have the essentials of the existential critique already sounded in the 1940s and 1950s by Erich Fromm and Rollo May.

The section in the Port Huron Statement on "Values" calls for human beings to be allowed to find their authentic selves, and thus to be freed to grapple with the existential questions of "What is really important? Can we live in a different and better way?" (331). Despite the crushing logic of corporate liberalism, the omnipresence of the military-industrial complex, the dearth of serious public spaces for debate and dialogue—despite all of this, Hayden and the members of SDS maintain that

> men have unrealized potential for self-cultivation, self-direction, self-understanding, and creativity. It is this potential that we regard as crucial and to which we appeal, not to the human potentiality for violence, unreason, and submission to authority. The goal of man and society should be human independence . . . finding a meaning in life that is personally authentic. . . . This kind of independence does not mean egotistic individualism—the object is not to have one's way so much as it is to have a way that is one's own. Nor do we deify man—we merely have faith in his potential. (332)

Compare these sentiments with those expressed in *Neither Victims nor Executioners,* in which Camus declares himself against the dead-end politics of absolutes and in favor of world peace (disarmament is a key theme in the Port Huron Statement) and the formation of new and vital communities. For Camus, proper political thinking "refuses to justify lies and murder" (52); it seeks to expose the corruption and deceit of power and to bring about "lasting reforms which are the distinguishing mark of a revolution" (52). Camus offers up hope in man's ability "to shape a living society within a dying society. Men must therefore, as individuals, draw up . . . a new social contract which will unite them according to more reasonable principles" (55). The Port Huron Statement essentially expressed these very principles, with reasoned and impassioned opposition to American imperialism, racism, corporate greed, and denial of poverty. In the end, the Port Huron Statement, like Camus's recommendations, is a remarkably sober document, one thoroughly in the American grain of criticism and hopefulness.[80] Yet by the late 1960s, Hayden and others were facing in practice a Camusian dilemma: how to avoid being victims without becoming executioners.

6 AS HAYDEN reflected back on his opposition to the war in Vietnam and on the fight for racial equality and against poverty, he viewed his struggles in terms of the thought of Albert Camus. He structured his mem-

oir along lines similar to those of Whittaker Chambers's *Witness*, with Camus replacing Kierkegaard as the moral and ethical yardstick by which the protagonist—the Knight of Faith for Chambers, the rebel for Hayden—measures his progress. Hayden's SDS journey is not, as James Miller suggests, a narrative of "reckless existentialism" overtaking sober participatory democracy. It is, rather, about Hayden straying, or being pushed away, from the precepts of Camus, from strictures about the importance of not allowing means to pollute ends. It is about forgetting one of the essential components of an existential perspective: a chastened sensibility. That chastened sensibility, apparent in Hayden's writings up to the mid-1960s, got pushed aside in his rush to romantic radicalization. A new rhetoric and a nonexistential confidence in the absolute righteousness of the struggle against the machines of war and racism in America come to intrude into Hayden's world. Che replaces Camus. As his comrade Todd Gitlin phrased it, speaking for himself as much as for Hayden and others in SDS and the movement, "How could the organization that began by echoing Albert Camus and C. Wright Mills end with one faction chanting, 'Ho, Ho, Ho Chi Minh' . . . while members of the other waved their Little Red Books in the air . . . ?" The Revolution became "the ultimate alibi."[81]

Events contributed to Hayden's increasing radicalization. He had been beaten in Mississippi and was emotionally crushed by the assassination of John F. Kennedy. Although he deplored Kennedy's weakness on civil rights and his fondness for military solutions, Hayden identified with Kennedy as a charismatic leader capable of becoming a force for change in America. Escalation of the war in Vietnam embraced a mad logic of its own, one that peaceful protests and political action could not disrupt. The urban riots of 1967, the increasing militancy of the Black Power movement, the assassinations of Martin Luther King, Jr., and Robert F. Kennedy, and the repression of the Black Panther Party all pushed Hayden and other radicals toward revolutionary posturing and a desire for violent catharsis. Community organizing, such as Hayden had done with the Economic Research and Action Program (ERAP) in Newark, went up in flames with the riots. Hayden spoke of the riots as an act of rebellion, one that city officials were unable to understand. Drawing upon an image from Camus's novel *The Plague*, Hayden wrote that Newark city officials "must have viewed the riot as a plague for which there were no doctors, no medicine." Its nature not understood, the plague would have to run its course of violence and destruction. Hayden in 1967 did not valorize violence, but he did view it as a valuable tactic that could "contribute to shattering the status quo." But this is not the end, nor even a favored means for Hayden. Yet, still in keeping with the ideals of the Port Huron Statement and SNCC organizing techniques, Hayden calls for those in the ghetto to organize and to exercise power over issues such as "urban renewal and housing, social services, policing, and taxation." African Americans must "build a decent community while resisting racist power."[82]

Hayden's rhetoric has changed. He now quotes Castro, arguing that American students should be "guerrillas in the field of culture." With the escalation of the war in Vietnam, he calls, along with some in the New Left, for "bringing the war home" and for confronting the power structure. In the process, he celebrates revolutionary violence.[83] After his second trip to North Vietnam in 1967, Hayden increasingly endorses violence as an engine for social change.[84] His alienation deepens as he confronts a society that he and others have analyzed as all-controlling and inflexible, as able to manipulate the masses. He identifies more and more with a revolutionary vanguard; he believes that the time is ripe for revolution in America.[85] While coalition-building against the war continues, it is often seen as a futile gesture, a form of politics that is co-opted from the outset by "the system." Violent resistance becomes a romantic exercise in self-defeat and nihilism. As Hayden later admitted, he became "fascinated by the simplicity and power of the Molotov cocktail during those days in Newark" (*Reunion*, 165). Speaking to a New York audience about the forthcoming demonstrations in Chicago during the summer of 1968 against the Democratic presidential nomination of Hubert H. Humphrey, who was identified with the war in Vietnam, Hayden announced that protesters "should come to Chicago prepared to shed their blood" (297).

And shed their blood they did; they were attacked and routed by the Chicago police force. But the demise of the New Left continued apace because of its factional disintegration, its failure to align itself fully into coalitions with the labor movement, and the repression that it faced. This is not to suggest that the New Left altogether failed. It planted the seeds for a more open Democratic Party, for a deeper skepticism toward the government, for an ecological consciousness, and for an understanding of the role of the university within the military-industrial complex, to name but a few of its accomplishments.[86]

Tom Hayden emerged from his revolutionary period with a greater appreciation for the logic of Camus's moderation and a deeper disdain for his own excesses, and those of his comrades on the left. Indeed, throughout *Reunion* he invariably evaluates his activities through the perspective of Camus. Initially, out of discussions about Camus with his first wife, Hayden had come to understand the necessity of commitment. He uses Camus's terms to explain the meaning of being jailed for civil rights organizing in the South: "It was both a necessary moral act and a rite of passage into serious commitment. For individuals to break through the veil of fear that held people back from directly confronting the wall of segregation itself required raw courage and philosophical commitment" (70).

Camus helped Hayden come to realize, even if he was not always able to follow the directive in practice, that the individual rebel must act in the name of moderation and humane principles. Means must not be subsumed to ends; "genuine rebellion" should never fall victim to "mad revolt" (77). One acts without certainty and with a chastened sensibility. These Camusian, existential imperatives, as Hayden realized, are difficult ideals to realize. Acknowledging "a limit to rebellion for its own sake," he recognized that he lacked the desire to be a modern Sisyphus, "pushing the boulder up the hill over and over." As he admitted, "I wanted to win" (77).

There is nothing wrong, of course, with wanting to win, especially when the cause is just, like civil rights or ending the war in Vietnam. But when these causes come to be seen as absolutes that blur the ethical issues of tactics, then problems ensue. Revolutionary violence can become personal therapy, a search for catharsis. Rather than being the result of "reckless existentialism," such difficulties are caused by its opposite, a forgetfulness of the tragedy of the human condition. Young Hayden, like Bob Moses, had that sense of tragedy in the early 1960s, but it was beaten out of him, literally and figuratively, by the chaos of the times, and by his own enthusiasm and desire for success.[87]

In retrospect, Hayden regretted his excesses. He acknowledged that "the lure of violence and martyrdom were powerful subterranean forces in my makeup" (*Reunion,* 422). In giving in to these forces, Hayden betrayed his Camusian ideals. Camus "had warned against the politics of resentment." Camus recognized that in certain tragic situations, violence might be warranted. But he demanded that violent action be undertaken in good faith, without illusions and without absolutes. Once one gave into the "evil secretion" (297) that separated the rebel from the masses, even from the humanity of those he opposed, then the victim transformed himself into the executioner. In that vein, recalling the activists with whom he had worked on the ERAP project in Newark during the 1960s, Hayden praised those who had continued to be dedicated rebels doing community organizing. They were the true "soldiers of Camus" (170). In these former comrades Hayden saw realized the ideal of Camusian rebellion, a form of rebellion that "goes beyond the concepts of optimism and pessimism . . . finding itself in working despite odds. Its realism and sanity would be grounded in nothing more than the ability to face whatever comes."[88]

Reflecting in his memoir on his activities during the hubbub of the 1960s, Hayden recognized "how far many of us had strayed from the original disposition of the sixties. We had become isolated, self-enclosed in a universe of political rather than human life . . . [;] language turned to jargon, disputes were elevated to doctrinal heights, paranoia replaced openness." In the face of this recognition, Hayden "decided to recharge my commitment to ending the endless war. . . . Like Camus's Rieux in *The Plague,* I would focus on the pestilence of spiritual depression. I would assume that the average American still didn't know or feel what the plague of Vietnam was all about" (435–36). Thus the rebel returned to the roots of SNCC and Bob Moses, to the essence of Camus's solidarity with others, asserting himself in the process of education, of coalition-building, of striving to find values in a world of chaos and injustice.

7   IN HIS MEMOIR Hayden mentions one unlikely-sounding role model: Dustin Hoffman, "my hero from *The Graduate*" (377). The ideal of the existential rebel, albeit without explicit Camusian inflections, was expressed in a number of American films of this period, including *Cool Hand Luke* and *The Graduate,* both of which appeared in 1967. In each of these films the existential hero confronts an absurd world while managing to find moments of grace within it.

In the opening scene of *Cool Hand Luke,* a drunken Lucas Jackson, played by Paul Newman, is shown committing an absurd act of rebellion that he will pay for dearly: snapping the heads off parking meters. He offers no explanation for his act, only a shrug and a sense that there wasn't much else for him to do on a Saturday night in this nowhere town. Luke simply does not fit in. He is a war hero unable to adjust to civilian life, and the highly regulated prison in which he now finds himself is, not surprisingly, unbearable. He faces two initial obstacles. First are his fellow prisoners. They resent his independence, his defiance of their rules and hierarchies. Yet he wins their respect through absurd acts: refusing to stay down during a fight against a much stronger man, betting that he can eat an inordinately large number of eggs at one sitting. He becomes a hero for the other prisoners, a role that he does not seek. They begin to live through him a vicarious, inauthentic existence. Second, Luke riles the prison authorities with quiet but firm acts of insubordination and repeated attempts to escape. The prison warden famously characterizes Luke's problem as "failure to communicate," but the divide is a deeper problem of understanding, an inability to cross the abyss of meaninglessness that Luke confronts daily.

Luke understands that transcendence and escape are, at best, momentary. Freedom is equated with rebellion. While his comrades in the prison may delight in a photograph that Luke has sent them of him partying without a care with two beautiful women at a nightclub, Luke realizes that the image is not real. He has paid for such photographic proof of his happiness and freedom by the sweat of his brow. Alienation and rebellion alone define his existence. Like Sisyphus, Luke will not be broken. He exists, within his situation, on his own terms. He may be beaten, he may be abused, but he perseveres. In the end, against the disabling power of authority, Luke escapes again, knowing full well that when he is hunted down, he will be killed. He ends up in a church, mocking God, raging against His absence or His unwillingness to intervene on his behalf. In the church, Luke will be shot, figuratively crucified for his rebellion. But he dies unvanquished, an existential hero for our age.

An existential rebel of less heroic proportions can be found in the character of Benjamin Braddock in Mike Nichols's film *The Graduate.* A college graduate, a bright young man without any direction in life, Ben lolls about his parents' swimming pool and more or less stumbles into an affair with Mrs. Robinson, the mother of the young woman with whom he will fall madly in love. Until he makes the leap into true love, his life lacks meaning. Once he finds love, passivity gives way to purpose. Dauntless, he speeds in his Alfa Romeo sports car up the California coast to rescue his love, Elaine, who is about to be married into the security of upper-class America. In the church scene, we are again presented with images suggesting the hero's crucifixion. Benjamin whisks Elaine away from the wedding, and they escape aboard a city bus. Rather than a moment of triumph, it is a moment of recognition. Seated at the back of the bus, they sense that they have either made a mistake or simply been caught up in the rush of excitement, in the vitality of the act of rebellion. It is an absurd situation, a moment of nagging existential doubt. Indeed, as director Mike Nichols noted of that final scene, "I think that Benjamin and Elaine will end up exactly like their parents; that's what I was trying to say in the last scene."[89] Thus we return to the matter of Hammett's Flitcraft in *The Maltese Falcon:* existential rebellion cannot always overcome the power of the quotidian.

The significance of these films, in the context of the 1960s, was in how they confirmed the countercultural perception of American culture as empty, alienating, and inauthentic. Authority existed through raw power rather than moral right, through conformity rather than individual choice. In *Cool Hand Luke*, the villain is raw power: the power of the prison authorities creates a world that oozes repression and death. In *The Graduate*, the issue is not so much power as it is the emptiness of suburban life and of the prospects offered to young people. Nichols emphasizes the impossibility of Ben and Elaine escaping from the clutches of middle-class conformity. The pervasiveness of conformist expectations is captured in the famous party scene in which a friend of the Braddock family takes Ben aside to say that he has only one word for him, one word that he wants him to consider carefully: "Plastics." Offered as career advice, the word captures the manu-factured, mass-produced, inauthentic, unreal quality of the world that is the source of Ben's alienation and discontent.

THE EXISTENTIAL FILMS of the 1960s did not have to invoke French theory to drive home their point. They developed ideas already central to the youth culture of the 1960s, especially the quest for authenticity in a world of falsity, the need to overcome passivity with action, the desire to find meaning in life. Compared with the noir films of the 1940s, the situations in these films were more commonplace, less the product of nighttime intrigue or convoluted plot structures. In the case of *The Graduate,* the situations are absurd but hardly extreme. Although alienated, Ben is not a character from Dostoevsky. In keeping with the American film noir tradition, the ex-istential films of the 1960s depicted the problems of male heroes unwilling to buckle under to a set of expectations. The rebellions of women are rarely examined, although occasionally, in films such as *Diary of a Mad House-wife* (1970), one gets the sense of a woman confronting the abyss of mean-ing, the emptiness that Betty Friedan famously called "the problem that has no name." Such films are exceptions to the rule of male existential heroes. Yet existentialism became linked with feminism through the work of both Beauvoir and Friedan.

Chapter Twelve

Existential Feminists:
Simone de Beauvoir and
Betty Friedan

1 In 1975, two towering figures of postwar feminism finally met face to face when Betty Friedan traveled to Paris to engage in a dialogue with Simone de Beauvoir. Beauvoir and Friedan had both contributed mightily to the resurgence of a feminist program after the Second World War. Beauvoir's *The Second Sex* (1949), published in an English translation in 1953, and Friedan's *The Feminine Mystique*, published in 1962, had been bestsellers in America. Their works had transformed the lives of many women in America. Rosalind Fraad Baxandall, an activist in the student left and women's movement, recalled that "in high school *The Second Sex* was my Ann Landers. I read and reread every wilted page for advice."[1] Kate Millett acknowledged "a great debt to *The Second Sex*. I couldn't have written *Sexual Politics* without it."[2] "Almost every woman of my generation," wrote activist Sheila Tobias, "can remember where she was the day she first came across Betty Friedan's book *The Feminine Mystique*." After reading that book, Tobias admitted, "my sense of life's possibilities changed . . . and they have never been the same."[3] Susan Brownmiller recalled reading Friedan's book while working as a civil rights advocate in the Freedom Summer of 1964. Despite finding Friedan's focus a bit narrow, Brownmiller felt that "I'd seen myself on every page. *The Feminine Mystique* changed my life."[4]

The meeting between Beauvoir and Friedan proved to be chilly. For her part, Friedan found Beauvoir to be curt, distracted, and abstract in her thinking.[5] The more radical Beauvoir must have found Friedan hopelessly bourgeois in her unwillingness to cut to the quick of the systemic nature of the capitalist oppression of women. Moreover, Beauvoir no doubt bristled at Friedan's failure in *The Feminine Mystique* to properly credit her own path-breaking work on women's status, *The Second Sex*. Indeed, after the publication of Friedan's *The Second Stage* (1981), a work that questioned aspects of the women's liberation movement, the chasm between the two deepened. Beauvoir said that she "tossed that book in anger across my room."[6]

Predictably, analysts find the intellectual and political relationship of

Betty Friedan to Simone de Beauvoir highly complex and contested. Immediately after Friedan published *The Feminine Mystique*, reviewers, even those favorable to her ideas, jumped on her both for stealing Beauvoir's ideas and for simplifying them beyond recognition. According to educational theorist Diane Ravitch, "Mrs. Friedan's book represents little more than a rehashing and watering-down of many of the French writer's ideas."[7] A later assessment of Friedan's debt to Beauvoir was even harsher. In 1980 Sandra Dijkstra found Friedan weak in her comprehension of the analytic sweep of the concept of "sexual politics," guilty of a "shrinking of conceptualization," and beholden to a weak-tea liberal feminist agenda. Friedan was, at best, a Johanna-come-lately, a popularizer who stripped away the radicalism of Beauvoir's feminism to make it palatable to the bourgeois American audience of the 1960s.[8]

The divide between Beauvoir and Friedan seems unbridgeable but also curious. After all, if Friedan was so influenced by Beauvoir, how could her analysis be so deficient in comparison? Did Friedan simply appropriate the essential structure of Beauvoir's analysis for her own political, reformist purposes? In point of fact, both of them approach women's questions largely through an existential perspective. In the case of Beauvoir, this is explicit and obvious; in the case of Friedan, it is less so. While Friedan's existentialism could be viewed as yet another instance of cribbing from Beauvoir, this is not the case.

Friedan certainly read Beauvoir's *The Second Sex* and Sartre's *Existentialism* prior to composing *The Feminine Mystique*, copying out passages from both works. She seemed especially impressed with the emphasis in both books on the exercise of freedom. She copied out Sartre's famous dictum that "existence precedes essence" and remarked on the paradox that having freedom can make a woman incapable of acting.[9] Yet Friedan identified with the voluntaristic bent of the early existentialism of both Sartre and Beauvoir, a position that each of them later revised to emphasize more the context (political and economic) of the situation and the individual in relation to others. There is no indication from the relatively few notes that Friedan jotted down that she gained any theoretical structure or essential interpretive thrust from her reading of *The Second Sex*.

With Friedan, it is less than useful to search for intellectual precursors to explain her existential perspective. To be sure, she was acquainted with a great deal of psychological and philosophical theory, some of which she employed in *The Feminine Mystique*. She had come into contact with existential thinking first as an undergraduate at Smith College in the late 1930s and early 1940s, and then as a graduate student in psychology at Berkeley. In lectures given by Otto Kraushaar, an early explicator of Kierkegaard's philosophy, she encountered Nietzsche, reading *Beyond Good and Evil* for class. In her psychology classes she read Erik Erikson, Gordon Allport, Kurt Lewin, and Abraham Maslow, finding in all of them a "dynamic theory of personality" predicated on a rejection of absolutes and essences, an emphasis on the interaction between individual and environment, and the centrality of development for the individual. Prior to writing *The Feminine Mystique,* Friedan read Rollo May and Erich Fromm, gaining from them support for her own insights into the existential nature of modern anxiety and the psychological desire to flee from the demands of freedom into the dangerous arms of totalitarianism. After all, while she carefully read Fromm's *Escape from Freedom* before writing *The Feminine Mystique,* she had in 1940, while an undergraduate, already referred to the "psychological force" of totalitarianism's appeal to youth in Europe arising partly out of "a desire for security, mental security."[10] In sum, Friedan was thoroughly familiar with, if not learned in, the existential tradition.

Friedan once boasted, "I know that everything I know has come from my own experience."[11] Of course, her experience included her reading of Sartre and Beauvoir as well as her reading of Fromm and May. But she had both an agile and a confident mind, one able to leap into a thesis with abandon, in the process making it her own, no matter how much others might have already discussed it. This may well account for Friedan's suppression of Beauvoir in *The Feminine Mystique.* Rather than discussing where her own work differed from, or even expanded upon, Beauvoir's foundational text, Friedan consigned Beauvoir to the briefest, inessential reference. She refused to see herself in any sense as either an acolyte of Beauvoir or a footnote to *The Second Sex.*

Years later, under pressure from critics and interviewers, Friedan attempted to clear the air about her debt to Beauvoir, perhaps even to overcome what literary critic Harold Bloom has called the "anxiety of influence."[12] In 1975, reflecting on her failed dialogue with Beauvoir, Friedan announced, "I had learned my own existentialism from her. It was *The Second Sex* that introduced me to that [existential] approach to reality and political responsibility—that, in effect, freed me from the rubrics of authoritarian ideology and led me to whatever original analysis of woman's existence that I have been able to contribute."[13] An odd statement, since there is no indication of such an impact dating from the time when Friedan read Beauvoir, and certainly no indication of such influence in the pages of *The Feminine Mystique.* Especially interesting here is how Friedan acknowledges the shattering significance of *The Second Sex:* not for its feminism, but for its existentialism. Yet in the next breath Friedan retracts her praise for that work by stating that its overall effect on her was "so depressing that I felt like going back to bed." No catharsis resulted. Only after Friedan's concrete analysis of her own oppression, and that of other women in America, did she finally realize that the feminine mystique was "something that could be changed."[14]

In her memoir *Life So Far* (2000), Friedan explains that her appreciation for the existential comes not from Beauvoir's "depressing" *The Second Sex* but from her memoirs and novels such as *The Mandarins*. Friedan proclaims a rather mystical, almost *sui generis*, form of existentialism. She speaks vaguely of something that she calls her "Jewish existential conscience," which she believes helps explain her commitment to social justice and activism.[15] Whatever the sources of this commitment, they are complex and rarely pursued by Friedan. She has systematically attempted to establish herself as an existential thinker and to make her existentialism, if not prior to Beauvoir's, at least superior to it in terms of its attention to the concrete experiences of life. Thus Friedan sees Beauvoir's thinking as abstract and theoretical, in contrast to her own brand of pragmatic existentialism, fully in the American grain. Saul Bellow has his protagonist Augie March proclaim proudly, "I am an American, Chicago-born . . . and go at things as I have taught myself, free style, and will make the record in my own way."[16] In like manner, Friedan announces to the world that she is "an American pragmatist, 'Middle-American,' if you will, since I grew up in Peoria, Illinois." This, she tells us, contributed to her American existential sensibility, her feminism based not on theory but on her "own experience."[17]

Despite deep political differences, Beauvoir and Friedan share an existential perspective. Out of that existential attitude comes agreement between them about a particular vision of women's history and reality. Of course, in the case of Beauvoir the existentialism is obvious; after all, she was, along with Sartre, the key figure in postwar French existentialism. In fact, in the view of some interpreters Beauvoir had arrived at crucial elements of modern French existential thought before Sartre.[18] Although the sources of Friedan's intellectual kinship with existentialism are murkier, she has chosen to frame her own theory within its guiding assumptions. Not surprisingly, much of the criticism leveled at both Beauvoir and Friedan over the years is fueled by animus toward the existential elements of their work.

According to some critics, Beauvoir's feminism suffers from two chief faults. First, in the view of historian Ruth Rosen, Beauvoir's existential perspective "enshrined individual choice, not collective action."[19] Second, her existentialist ethics can be seen as undermining her ability to recognize that women can be transcendent rather than immanent beings without operating in the traditional male realm. For Beauvoir, men's activities alone seem to be existential, projecting themselves into the future. In this view, Beauvoir ignored women's ways of knowing, the heroism of women working and rebelling under constrained circumstances throughout history. She lacked a sense of woman-centered communities. Moreover, on the personal level, as her correspondence with Sartre reveals, Beauvoir too often belittled herself as a philosopher, holding up Sartre as the more serious thinker.[20]

Critics of Friedan's feminism, meanwhile, though acknowledging her importance in having sounded a clarion call to women to fight sexual oppression in the public realm, point out that she failed to link her feminism to a critique of capitalist oppression, to identify with women of color and the working class. Friedan's individualist feminism, some maintain, prevented her from acknowledging the importance of "sexual politics" as an analytic and interpretive device.[21] According to some of her opponents, Friedan gloried in her "hopelessly bourgeois" lifestyle and politics.[22]

Their shared existentialism bequeathed to both Beauvoir and Friedan a particular slant or attitude when they addressed the problem of Woman. As believers in the existential notion of the human condition, they easily conceived of women as a class or caste, an entity that could be both studied and theorized about in sweeping terms. Existentialism did not, of course, determine the specifics of their political positions on certain issues. Ideas and attitudes do not work in such reductionist fashion. But the existentialism of each writer influenced and limited her feminist analyses. With its emphasis on "dreadful freedom," existentialism demands that attention be focused on the individual, especially the singular individual on the brink of the frightening moment when she recognizes that choice is an option. In both Beauvoir and Friedan, the centering of attention on acts of individual conscience suggests that women's oppression, their reduction to the status of objects, can be overcome by acts of conscious recognition and choice.

While this perspective accepts—indeed, it places center stage—the reality of the social construction of the self, it also embodies a notion of the self as a process, a state of becoming. It assumes, at some level, a freedom of action, an ability to leap out of constraint. Such a leap does not necessarily result in comfort or realization of goals, but it does exemplify the freedom of the individual. And in this recognition, both Beauvoir and Friedan tend to focus more on the responsibility of the individual as implicated in her own oppression than might other analysts of woman's condition. Yet to their credit, both Beauvoir and Friedan move beyond this point, arguing that the individual, once she has achieved this recognition, reaches out to work with others in a collective effort to realize freedom for all.

Such a choice, for both Friedan and Beauvoir, actually increased the need for solidarity through work within a movement. Indeed, as Beauvoir had indicated in *The Ethics of Ambiguity* (1947; translated 1948), this personal choice, this existential leap, rather than taking one into a world of isolated, alienated beings (as sometimes depicted by Sartre), becomes the moment when an ethics of solidarity, of human connection, becomes possible. The recognition of one's own freedom leads to the realization that others too are individuals in search of freedom. The freedom of the individual, writes Beauvoir, "can be achieved only through the freedom of others. He justifies his existence by a movement which, like freedom, springs from his heart but which leads outside of himself."[23] While conflict among individuals is inevitable, the possible road to freedom through collective action is opened up. Woman is no longer immanent, she is now transcendent—both in and of the world.

2   THE FAMOUS WORDS Beauvoir uttered in *The Second Sex,* "One is not born, but rather becomes, a woman," have become the signature statement of social constructionist feminism.[24] These words announce that social customs and institutions, rather than biological necessity, fashion identity.[25] But when Beauvoir composed this statement, its resonance was proudly existentialist. "Existence precedes essence," Sartre had famously proclaimed in 1945.[26] Beauvoir and Sartre both held strongly to the existential imperative that men and women create themselves through constant acts of negation and transcendence. In making oneself in a universe without essential constraints, albeit restrained by historical conditions, the individual always retains a degree of choice. Even when placed in the most extreme of situations (like Resistance fighters being tortured by Nazis), the individual still has the heroic and frightening responsibility to make a choice (in this case, to choose to reveal information or to perish). Of course, not all situations are of such moment. But even in the rhythms of everyday life, Beauvoir and Sartre discerned the willingness of individuals to retreat from freedom, to avoid choices, by acting inauthentically. Many confused the role that they played with genuine individuality and responsibility. Freedom, both Sartre and Beauvoir averred, was no easy matter.

Existential concepts and imperatives define the structure and attitude of Beauvoir's *The Second Sex.* Existentialism, with its emphasis on the freedom of the concrete individual, powers her excavation of the history of women and the potential for their liberation. Beauvoir's use of existential theory for a project of women's liberation resembles the deployment of a blues existentialism against racism that we have seen in the work of Richard Wright and Ralph Ellison. As Margaret A. Simons argues, Wright played a role in helping Beauvoir come to understand the nature of the Other (the individual who is denied full human potential and reduced to an object) and to appreciate the psychological effects of oppression on both women and

African Americans.[27] Existentialism, by questioning the "givens," the polite presumptions of power and privilege, and by returning time and again to the ultimate questions of life, death, and the potential of freedom, must challenge the status quo.

Nowhere is this more apparent than in Beauvoir's *The Second Sex*. Beauvoir begins with the existential given that if existence precedes essence, then the individual is not confined by the straight-jacket of biological destiny or historical patterns. Beauvoir acknowledges, in a long and learned discussion of biological difference, that male and female are distinct in important ways. However, she concludes, "I deny that they [biological facts] establish for her [woman] a fixed inevitable destiny" (32). Rather, the truth is to be found in the contingent nature of history and the possible exercise of freedom on the part of the individual. Most important, Beauvoir emphasizes the existential ideal that each individual ultimately has a choice, even given the crushing weight of history. The individual always retains the freedom to rebel, to sacrifice her life, to define herself, if she is daring enough, through "exploits or projects" (xxvii) that are directed toward "an indefinitely open future" (xxix).

But alas, Beauvoir continues, rather than taking the dangerous but exhilarating road toward transcendence, creativity, and freedom, men and women submit to "a degradation of existence" (xxix), which Beauvoir characterizes in the Sartrean terminology of *Being and Nothingness* as a falling into "the 'en soi'—the brutish life of subjection to given conditions—and of . . . constraint and contingence" (142). This is the state of being that Beauvoir calls "immanence," a mythical existence based upon an unchanging view of the nature of woman. Most significantly, immanence appears to exist for Beauvoir as "a moral fault if the subject consents to it." If it is "inflicted" upon the individual, "it spells frustration and oppression. In both cases, it is an absolute evil" (xxix).

Woman, in Beauvoir's terms, is reduced to an object, to the Other. She often accepts her status as the Other as an act of bad faith, a way of avoiding the responsibility and anguish of freedom (268). Biological differences, as well as economic circumstances, help explain how and why man has imposed this status upon woman. But because the situation is historically situated, it is capable of reversal. The roots for Beauvoir's concept of the Other are Hegelian, resting in the master-slave dialectic, whereby the master needs the slave's resistance or relative freedom in order for the slave to be something more than a mere extension of the absolute will of the master. But the way in which Beauvoir employs the concept of the Other in *The Second Sex* coheres more with Sartre's ontology of conflict and the Nietzschean notion of the will to power. Beauvoir's world teems with struggle and domination.

Woman, as the Other, begins to exist "when man asserts himself as subject and free being" (79). The two human categories of man and woman are locked in struggle: "Each aspires to impose its sovereignty upon the other." Between independent beings, there is always a "state of tension" (61).

For biological and economic reasons, the result of this historical struggle has been the dominance of man over woman. Man is active, transcendent, involved in projects such as the invention of tools, the pursuit of adventure, the spoils of war, and the power of politics. Woman, in contrast, is limited by maternity and "closely bound to her body" (65). Woman works in the home, rears children, and limits her future. Beauvoir denigrates the role of housewife as one of sterile immanence—a type of living death. Her world, as defined by man and, often, as understood by woman herself, is limited. It is a mythical world that "justifies all privileges and even justifies their abuse" (255). In this world, woman "is considered to be mysterious in essence" (257). In her Otherness lies both her subjugation and her power.

Beauvoir's existentially colored ideas in *The Second Sex* intended to puncture essentialist, abstract, biological explanations for the condition of women. Gone are the clichéd excuses that consigned women to the realm of immanent beings rather than according them the status of transcendent beings responsible for their own growth and potentiality. And it supplied her with a heady existential language and agenda for liberation. Yet this existential core of *The Second Sex* at times evolves into its own kind of essentialism, one in which ultimate responsibility always appears to reside in the singular individual. The individual becomes complicit in her own oppression. Of course, Beauvoir, and Sartre for that matter, never intended to present this implication in such bold type. But the logic of their position in the late 1940s, growing out of both philosophical premises and the experiences of the Resistance, led to a voluntarism of striking and challenging proportions.

Nonetheless, for social constructionists such as Kate Millett in *Sexual Politics* (1970), Beauvoir figures as a feminist mother, pointing out how gender and oppression function as instruments of power in the texts of literature, the institution of marriage, and all byways of culture.[28] For feminists like Friedan, as caught up as Beauvoir in the tension between individual and society, and with an existential attitude, the key to liberation lay in the freedom of the concrete consciousness of the individual. While this perspective did not entirely discount the social constraints and circumstances imposed on women, it downplayed them, often shifting to the individual the onus of taking the action necessary to make liberation a reality. The problem for social constructionists in this view was not that the individual had to choose freedom. After all, a leap into recognition of oppression was part of the consciousness-raising central to feminism in the 1970s. Social constructionist radicals instead considered liberation within a group structure, as a collective rather than an individual project. By the 1970s, however, Beauvoir had accepted a Marxist feminist agenda, thus fitting individual liberation into a collective consciousness.

3 THE ESSENTIAL tension that informs Friedan's *The Feminine Mystique* is that between freedom and constraint. Like Beauvoir, Friedan struggles to grant agency to the individual while in the process suggesting that the individual assume responsibility for her own oppression. Friedan firmly believed that women in the postwar years were, as historian Elaine Tyler May phrased it, "homeward bound," contained ideologically and physically within the home.[29] While Friedan recognizes the constraints that have been imposed upon women, she also tends to elide those constraints and to posit that women—here understood by Friedan as college educated and bourgeois—can cast off the chains of the feminine mystique and become active in the world outside the home. But in order to achieve liberation and transcendence, women must first confront their real despair, recognize that they are unfulfilled, prisoners of the feminine mystique.

The sense of despair is real, and the problem that Friedan believed she faced—the problem of an inauthentic, empty existence—is compellingly rendered. By framing the problem that has no name in these terms, Friedan, no less than Beauvoir, leads her readers to a particular set of general conclusions. No matter how stiff the chains of oppression, how well structured the mystique, the individual woman is ultimately free. As she put it later, essentially borrowing the language of feminist consciousness-raising, "We must say yes to ourselves as women, and no to that outworn, obsolete image, the feminine mystique. We must stop denigrating ourselves, stop acquiescing in the remaining prejudices the mystique enshrines."[30] Freedom, in part, is a function of thinking differently.

But freedom to do what? Freedom to face the choice, the dreadful freedom that comes with the casting off of these chains. Like Beauvoir, Friedan recognized the anguish of freedom. Freedom demands courage and energy. It is hard, which helps explain why so many women retreat to the presumed safety of the household: "Not very many women . . . dared to leave the only security they knew."[31] Here Friedan evokes texts by Fromm and May on the anguish of, and escape from, freedom.

The greatest obstacle to American women's exercise of freedom does not appear to be economic or political constraints, or sexual politics, or even the unequal distribution of power within the public and private spheres. Instead, it was "the feminine mystique," a controlling myth or metaphor that imprisoned the American woman in the years after the Second World War.[32] The mystique—like Beauvoir's concept of the Other—is by definition mysterious. But out of its mystery comes its power. Indeed, the power of the mystique is such that it turns the oppression of women, the limitations upon their exercise of freedom and their realization of growth, into a "problem that has no name" (15). Freudians, functionalist anthropologists and sociologists, the intelligentsia, no less than the advertising and business establishment, all are implicated in a sustained attempt to produce an image of women that suggests that they can find fulfillment and happiness only within the home. On the basis of her research into popular women's magazines of the era, Friedan claimed that women were bombarded with images of themselves as homemakers rather than as active citizens or career women.[33] Women were expected to "glory in their own femininity," to be content as mothers and wives (15).

This agenda, in Friedan's view, offered a false bill of goods. The home was a prison, and educated women like Friedan were unhappy and underutilized as housewives and mothers. They felt unfulfilled, denied their potential for growth. Thus they turned inward, undermining themselves and punishing their families because of the frustrations they were not allowed to confess.[34] They are debilitated by "a strange feeling of desperation" (21). As one Long Island homemaker quoted by Friedan phrased it, "I just don't feel alive" (22).

Friedan frames the question of freedom in existential terms, in the language of identity and the psychology of alienation. She characterizes the postwar years as a time of retreat from commitment, a time when young men as well as women—in the face of McCarthyism and "after the loneliness of war and the unspeakableness of the bomb, against the frightening uncertainty, the cold immensity of the changing world"—sought escape from the dangerous reality of freedom. The home as a fantasy refuge fed into the feminine mystique, and a "pent-up hunger for marriage, home, and children was felt simultaneously by several different generations; a hunger which, in the prosperity of postwar America, everyone could suddenly satisfy" (183).

Friedan wavers about whether this stampede to the home was a forced option (thus a mark of oppression), a function of the powerful allure of the feminine mystique, or a choice freely arrived at. In her analysis, all three reasons are intertwined. To be sure, she understands the attraction of the mystique of the home—the ideal of safety from a world riven by competition and complaint. But the home, as Friedan emphasizes, became a place of pain. Life in the suburbs was something that women merely endured; they "adjusted to their role and suffered or ignored the problem that has no name. It can be less painful, for a woman, not to hear the strange, dissatisfied voice stirring within her" (26). But generally women failed to suppress such voices, leading to their double burden. Many women in the postwar years both worked outside the home and cared for children, without adequate support from either their husbands or the state. Many of those who had jobs were pushed out of them, forced to trade their positions as skilled laborers for positions defined by traditional gender expectations. There was, as Friedan herself experienced, a spirit of hostility against women in the workplace (185). Nonetheless, Friedan had the audacity to argue that many women took the easy way out after the war. They chose, perhaps in bad faith ("We found excuses," she says), to retreat to the home (186). They lacked the "courage to face" the possibility of their own freedom. The "American spirit fell into a strange sleep," and women too went into the home as a way of forgetting. Friedan's words on this matter are worth quoting at some length, for they reveal her sense that ultimate responsibility for the return of women to the home rested on the shoulders of the women themselves:

> All of us went back into the warm brightness of home, the way it was when we were children and slept peacefully upstairs while our parents read, or played bridge in the living room. . . . Women went home again just as men shrugged off the bomb, forgot the concentration camps, condoned corruption, and fell into helpless conformity; just as the thinkers avoided the complex larger problems of the postwar world. It was easier, safer, to think about love and sex than about communism, McCarthy, and the uncontrolled bomb. It was easier to look for Freudian sexual roots in man's behavior, his ideas, and his wars than to look critically at his society and act constructively to right its wrongs. There was a kind of personal retreat, even on the part of those most far-sighted, the most spirited; we lowered our eyes from the horizon, and steadily contemplated our own navels. (186–87)

Here we have, in synopsis form, Friedan's reading of the psychology of fascism, as rendered by Fromm, May, and others, applied to the woman question. Faced with the tensions of the postwar world, American women knowingly bought into the feminine mystique. This is akin to the thesis that German workers rushed to Hitler because his ideology of a glorious past and ambitious future offered them an escape from the dangerous present. The appeal of ideologies, in this view, is that they serve to propagate a mythical structure that gives meaning to lives that would otherwise be without direction. Alienation thus paves the way for a sense of purpose.

In no uncertain terms, Friedan blames the victims: "In the name of femininity, they [American housewives] have evaded the choices that would have given them a personal purpose, a sense of their own being." Then, quoting "the existentialists," she goes on to say that without choices there is no Being (i.e., personhood). Invoking Tillich and Sartre, she announces, "If you do not have the 'courage to be,' you lose your own being; in Sartre's [philosophy], you *are* your choices" (314, 436 n). Thus "the feminine mystique implies a choice between 'being a woman,'" which is a form of inauthentic existence (indeed, in a poorly chosen metaphor, Friedan likens the state of "being a woman" to that of being in a Nazi concentration camp), and "risking the pains of human growth" (317).

Human growth, as Friedan had learned from existential psychologists such as Abraham Maslow and Rollo May, is a necessity for the human being. Women must strive for "self-realization"—not through their roles as caregivers, which was as far as Maslow was willing to go, but as independent beings, with projects and commitments of their own (319–26). From Erik Erikson and David Riesman, excavators of the problems of the postwar male identity crisis, Friedan learned that only through meaningful work, work conducted outside the home, can one find self-realization and fulfillment. Only "in the service of a human purpose larger than themselves," and larger than the role of housewife, would women achieve a sense of real identity (333). Friedan ends by arguing for a liberal arts education for women as a means to self-knowledge and a step toward existential freedom. Then, like man, woman will be able to engage projects, to transcend her status, to learn "to think of herself as a human being first, not as a mother with time on her hands, and make a life plan in terms of her own abilities, a commitment of her own to society, with which her commitments as wife and mother can be integrated" (343). These words echo the conclusions of Beauvoir's *The Second Sex*.

4   DESPITE THE POWER of the feminine mystique as Friedan described it, by the early 1960s the time for change had arrived. Young women, she claimed, are now "responsible for their education"; they "do face a choice" (175). They are "becoming aware of an identity crisis in their own lives"; it is as if they were "waking from a coma" (79). They must decide: Will they choose adjustment, conformity, avoidance of conflict, therapy? Or individuality, human identity, education in the truest sense, with all its growing pains? This is essentially the same dichotomy that informs Beauvoir's *The Second Sex*, the juxtaposition of stasis and immanence with projects and growth. Friedan concludes that women can arrive at their own "self-realization" (334), at a sense of themselves as full human beings (344).

But there are problems with the way in which both Beauvoir and Friedan describe projects and growth. They invariably define projects in masculinist terms. As historian Mary Felstiner wisely observes, for Beauvoir, "deciding which activities to call transcendent, and which immanent, raises serious complications."[35] Such problems are not inherent in existentialism as such. But existentialism does work under the assumption that the individual exists fully through creative projects and commitments. Through undertakings such as these, nothingness is transcended, even if only for a moment's time. Unfortunately, the depth of such projects has been commonly connected not with ordinary acts but with the extreme situations of war, of political intrigue, of daring travel, of the casting off of identities. Since these options had historically been limited to the male realm, women's history, for Beauvoir and Friedan, was largely unmarked by transcendent acts of heroism.[36]

In her better moments Beauvoir realized that women could undertake transcendent and heroic acts in certain situations. In her novel *The Blood of Others* (1945), published at the time when she began work on *The Second Sex,* Beauvoir presents a story of a male activist, Jean Blomart, and a shopgirl, Hélène. Blomart is a leader in the Resistance. In his everyday acts he commits himself to a cause, and in the process, as he painfully realizes, he also takes responsibility for "the blood of others." Hélène, who is in love with Blomart, is a vain young woman who in the course of the novel evolves into an individual willing to sacrifice her life for the sake of a higher ideal. But her sacrifice can be seen as being to some degree compromised. She undertakes her act of transcendence in part to convince Blomart of her worthiness; she has perhaps acted less for the sake of the abstract ideal of freedom for others than out of love for a particular man. Nevertheless, through her work with the Resistance Hélène gains her identity: "She existed for something, for someone." In the midst of her dangerous work, in the warmth of her dangerous freedom, she is able to exclaim, "What a lovely night."[37]

In *The Second Sex* Beauvoir argues that even creative women are stymied by their lack of experience in the outside world. In her evaluation of the weaknesses of women artists in comparison with male artists, Beauvoir announced that unlike Kafka, Melville, Joyce, and Lawrence, "women do not contest the human situation, because they have hardly begun to assume it. . . . [Their] works for the most part lack metaphysical resonances and also anger." In sum, unlike great men, women have failed, or not been allowed, to climb the "loftiest summits" (711). Thus greatness has been a male feature, because great men "have taken the weight of the world upon their shoulders. . . . That is what no woman has ever done, what none has ever been *able* to do" (713).

Beauvoir did not sufficiently appreciate the heroism of women working against constraints in a limited fashion: surviving domestic violence, facing yet another pregnancy, managing to support a family. Such acts of everyday heroism evoke the existential heroism of Camus's Sisyphus, the rebel who grabs on to life even in the face of the cruel monotony of his endlessly repetitive labor. Indeed, the myth of Sisyphus is an apt metaphor for the acts of existential heroism of women on the stage of history. The homemaker's mundane fight against dirt is, in its essentials, an attempt to be a modern Sisyphus, to take pride in something, to overcome a situation. But despite the unrelenting, penetrating quality of her critique of housework and motherhood, Beauvoir fails to acknowledge this fact. The same might be said of Friedan.

Friedan limited herself to the plight of white middle-class American women. She ignored the struggles of working-class women and women of color to define themselves. Not all women in the period that Friedan wrote about were exiled in the home. In fact, more women than ever were working, albeit in jobs that were increasingly less skilled than a few years earlier. As civil rights activist Mary King recognized, while *The Feminine Mystique* "sent shock waves across American suburbs" in 1963, "it seemed irrelevant and marginal to us. . . . [It] was amazing to us that black women in the United States were not cited once."[38]

Nonetheless, Friedan's book was immensely popular, selling more than a million copies and issuing a clarion call for the second wave of the feminist movement.[39] It effectively brought women to a consciousness of their historical oppression. Friedan held that escape from oppression occurred with personal growth through projects outside the home. Unfortunately, under the sway of the feminine mystique, woman "exists only for and through her husband and children" (47). Housework is drudgery, monotonous, unsatisfying. It would be absurd for women to attempt to "try to make housework 'something more'" than it is (67). Housework must no longer be seen as a career, only as "something that must be done as quickly and efficiently as possible" (342).

Like Beauvoir, Friedan wanted women to step out of the home into productive, paid work. But unlike Beauvoir, she did not offer a biting critique of the capitalist nature of work. Friedan was a reformist, wanting women to have opportunities equal to those of men within the existing structures of power. Her solutions were reasonable but not revolutionary. Yet in the "Epilogue" to the 1997 reissue of *The Feminine Mystique,* Friedan supported a restructuring of society, with pay for work done in the home (a position that Beauvoir found insipid), a sharing of parental responsibilities, and less hierarchical arrangements in marriage and society. Women's education must not consist of inane courses about how to fill time or be better housewives. The only way in which women can hope "to reach full human potential [is] . . . by participating in the mainstream of society, by exercising their own voice in all the decisions shaping that society. For women to have full identity and freedom, they must have economic independence" (384–85). While Friedan never dropped her insistence on equality of opportunity for women, in the 1970s her work became increasingly appreciative of the plight of the housewife, of the value of the women who chose, or were stuck in, such an endeavor. In Friedan's new formulation, the family now figured as a "New Feminist Frontier."[40]

By the 1970s, Friedan's conservatism in the movement and her rejection of sexual politics—indeed, even of discussions of sexual identity—marked her as bourgeois and backward-looking. She had now come to identify herself with a reformist agenda through the organization of the National Organization for Women (NOW), tied to equality of opportunity in the workplace and an increasing respect for the family. In contrast, Beauvoir was now in her most radical period. Their differences of opinion surfaced when they met in 1975.

As she described it in her essay "A Dialogue with Simone de Beauvoir," Friedan began the discussion by acknowledging the important contributions both of them had made to modern feminism, "which I think we have both helped to influence by our books and through our thinking."[41] Having established herself and Beauvoir as feminist foremothers, Friedan also attempted to remind Beauvoir that until recently she had refused to identify herself as a feminist. Friedan spoke in radical tones early in the discussion, speculating that it might "be necessary to change the rules of the game, the very structure of work—the class separation of secretary-boss, nurse-doctor" (309). With this Beauvoir was in ready agreement.

Disagreement soon surfaced when Friedan suggested the value of placing "a minimum wage value on housework" so as to make poor and middle-class women eligible for "Social Security, for pensions, and . . . [for the equitable] division of property if there is a divorce." Much to Friedan's dismay, Beauvoir attacked this reformism. "It's keeping to the idea of women at home," replied Beauvoir, "and I'm very much against it" (311). The ever-pragmatic Friedan continued that it was only practical, since women continued to work within the home, and "their work should be valued at something." No, argued Beauvoir, such a vision is reactionary, linked to a notion that "women are doomed to stay at home." The choice of staying at home, she proclaimed, is no choice at all: "We don't believe that any woman should have this choice. No woman should be authorized to stay at home to raise her children" (311). The discussion between Beauvoir and Friedan soon ran aground. The divergence of their politics hid the deep affinities between their major works. Neither of them was able to recognize in the other a fellow traveler in the existential attitude.

5   THE EXISTENTIAL paths followed by Beauvoir and Friedan were almost preternaturally intertwined. Both of them wrote significant works on women. And both of them later composed large tomes dealing with the problems, and prospects, of old age. Beauvoir in *The Coming of Age* (1970) and Friedan in *The Fountain of Age* (1993) tackle what is, in essence, *the* existential problem: the proximity of death. But while they had once again been drawn to a similar set of issues and questions, their responses were utterly dissimilar. A heavy sense of pessimism and decline hovers around Beauvoir's work, while Friedan is almost euphoric, ecstatically happy about finding a "fountain of age."

Beauvoir's *The Coming of Age* is at once both her most existential and her most nonexistential work. It is existential in the obvious sense of confronting the closeness of death. In an actuarial sense, death is nearer to hand in old age; one is constantly aware of both the infirmities of the body and the proximity of the existential situation. Thus, Beauvoir writes, "like all human situations it [old age] has an existential dimension—it changes the individual's relationship with time and therefore his relationship with the world and with his own history."[42] But it does so in a constrained manner. Gone is the almost giddy sense of existential freedom. Now, following the line laid down by Sartre in *Being and Nothingness,* Beauvoir notes that death is that which is not experienced by the individual as anything else, since it cannot be retrospectively gauged; it is, in Sartrean terms, "the unrealizable" (291).[43]

Yet in a puzzling sense Beauvoir's pessimistic portrait of old age also seems nonexistential. She posits a situation that is not really a situation. At the point of old age, Beauvoir suggests (although she often contradicts herself), the individual recognizes transcendence as a chimera (361–62). The young person has hope, a sense that through projects he or she will prevail against the winds of time. The older person, closed in by the shadow of death and the weight of the past, becomes an immanent creature—a "practico-inert" (433), as she calls it, borrowing language from Sartre's *Critique of Dialectical Reason.*[44] But in framing the problem of old age in this manner, Beauvoir violates a principle central to her own work and that of Sartre: the heroic propensity of the individual to endure, to engage in projects, even in the project of simply living. As Camus understood far better, the very struggle to endure is a transcendent project, an act of heroism.

The Coming of Age works as a companion volume, in scope and method, to *The Second Sex:* as Beauvoir explains, it "envisages the condition of old people as I envisaged the condition of women in *The Second Sex*."[45] There is sweep and confidence to the volume. Beauvoir's learning is obvious and impressive. Moreover, this work has a sociological aspect to it that is absent in her earlier works. In this work she attempts a materialist interpretation of aging. She is attuned to the class issues involved. The poor suffer the most as they age, not only because they are often forcibly retired from jobs but also because they lack the financial means, and the cultural capital, to settle into a comfortable retirement. The wealthy, of course, fare better in this regard, but they too are haunted by aches and pains, a diminution of powers, and a sense of feeling redundant. But be the individual rich or poor, the prospects are desolate: "Leisure does not open up new possibilities for the retired man; just when he is at last set free from compulsion and restraint, the means of making use of his liberty are taken from him. He is condemned to stagnate in boredom and loneliness, a mere throw-out" (6). Despite its pessimism, the book was well received in France for its willingness "to break the conspiracy of silence" (2) that surrounded the question of old age. But Beauvoir later admitted, without elaboration, that she "was sorry to have written" it.[46]

The Coming of Age is, of course, charged with autobiographical undertones. Beauvoir composed her study of aging when she was in her late fifties and Sartre was in his sixties. While Beauvoir was, apart from the normal aches and pains, still quite vibrant, Sartre had been troubled with ill health for some time, his problems becoming particularly acute not long after publication of *The Coming of Age* in 1970.[47] As Beauvoir noted a year after turning fifty, "Death is no longer a brutal event in the far distance. . . . It has already begun."[48]

The proximity of death, the decline of creative powers, and the treatment of the aged as the refuse of society are the points Beauvoir emphasizes throughout the book. But her critique is somewhat at odds with itself. On the one hand, Beauvoir is nicely attentive to the plight of the working-class poor. She offers a good, albeit brief, sociological and economic analysis of their condition. It is a tale of horror, a biting exposé of facts that society would prefer to keep hidden. On the other hand, Beauvoir approaches the working class as the Other. She effectively captures their material plight, but she fails to penetrate to the core of their being. Not described in the correspondence, memoirs, and novels of the educated class, the inner lives of the working-class elderly remain hidden from Beauvoir. Their humanity, their struggle, their sense, perhaps, of indeed being engaged in projects to transcend their fate, is all but absent from *The Coming of Age*. This is not to quibble with the presentation of the material conditions of the aged poor as Beauvoir outlines them. She remains, however, on more comfortable terrain, like Friedan, when dealing with elites.

The great bulk of the volume is devoted to impressionistic narratives about how great writers, scientists, politicians, and others have confronted old age and death. The preponderance of the evidence that Beauvoir presents leads to the conclusion that old age has little to recommend it: "Old age reduces strength; it deadens emotion" (400). Scientific discoveries, for example, are the province of the young. The older scientist clings to theories that he or she developed long ago. For the scientist, old age is a rearguard action against diminishing powers of creativity and against challengers to theories that have become archaic. Moreover, many years of specialization in a subject robs the scientist of the intellectual breadth required to make intriguing contributions. The older scientist cannot keep up with the explosion of new data. All in all, Beauvoir contends, the aging scientist lacks prospects: "The weight of the past slows him down or even brings him to a halt, whereas the young generations break free from the practico-inert and move forward" (390). Thus the aged individual acts not in a transcendent fashion but in an absurd one, as an act of bad faith. Creativity vanishes, replaced by mere habit, which hardens into "a kind of ontological security" that ultimately becomes another form of anxiety (469).

Politicians, while they may have grown wise in some respects, also become cynical and frustrated as they age: "Their old age is a time of lost power and glory" (418). They see their accomplishments being corroded by the force of circumstances they can no longer control. Once retired from office, they lose their zest for being involved in the process of change, since their age brings home to them the obvious fact that they will not be around to witness the fruits of their labors: "The politician is created to make history and to be killed by history" (434).

In almost every endeavor associated with creativity, Beauvoir argues, a hardening of the arteries occurs. Even "the aged artist will not go much further than the point he has reached. There are some who twist and turn in a vain attempt to break out: all they achieve is self-caricature, not self-renewal" (409). But the problem with the aged artist goes beyond a mere diminution of faculties; the deeper problem is that an "old man's intellectual and emotional indifference may reduce him to complete inertia" (453). As mentioned earlier, Beauvoir seems to argue in *The Coming of Age* that existential transcendence through projects requires a sense of infinitude, common to the young but denied to the elderly. Working in the shadow of death makes it more difficult for the aged individual to transcend the situation. Aged artists face a "twofold finitude": "They are conscious of the shortness of their future and of the unique nature of the history which encloses them, a uniqueness that cannot be transcended" (409). Moreover, old age is a closed room with no exit: "Old people, even if they do believe in the future, the long-term future, do not reckon on being present when . . . change is brought about. Their faith does not protect them against disappointments in the present. Sometimes indeed they may lose it, and then the march of events, submerging them, seems like a denial of their whole existence" (413).

Beauvoir's conclusions seem contrary to the central tenet of French existentialism as she, Sartre, and Camus had earlier preached it. They had argued that it is in extreme situations, when death is at hand or when the nausea of inertia and immanence overwhelm, that the opportunity for escape and transcendence presents itself. Why, then, does Beauvoir present the aged artist as being so fully stymied by the shortness of time and the weight of the past? One might have expected her to argue that even in failure, the artist acts heroically in seeking transcendence through projects. Indeed, an illustration of this very point was near to hand, in the person of her friend Sartre. Riddled with ailments, criticized by his former Maoist comrades, his reputation in decline, Sartre nevertheless persisted with his monumental long-term project to subject Flaubert to an analysis that combined existentialism and Marxism. Whether or not Sartre succeeded in this project is beside the point. The important fact is that in tackling the project and surmounting the infirmities of age and reputation, he engaged in an existential act of great consequence.[49]

Like William James, who observed with regret that the plaster of habit had hardened an individual by age twenty-five, Beauvoir saw the self as limited by choices already made.[50] In old age, she argues, the individual invariably lives out the life that he or she has created or chosen. We are what we have made of ourselves; we are the sum total of our projects: "The truth is that a man's work can grow richer only in harmony with what it is and always will be" (409). This conclusion is hardly surprising, but it is overwhelmingly bleak—and existentially limited.

Beauvoir does, however, struggle against this conclusion. She praises the painter Pierre Auguste Renoir, who led a life of great richness in old age, and concludes from his example that when "a man is involved in some undertaking he will hate the death that annihilates it" (441). The key, then, is to continue with projects, even if they may never be realized. In perhaps her most optimistic consideration of the possibility of a creative old age, Beauvoir admits that "freedom and clarity of mind are not of much use if no goal beckons us any more: but they are of great value if one is still full of projects. The greatest good fortune, even greater than health, for the old person is to have his world still inhabited by projects; then, busy and useful, he escapes both from boredom and from decay. . . . His oldness passes, as it were, unnoticed" (492–93). But unwilling to linger in this land of the hopeful, Beauvoir immediately remarks that for such projects and creativity to be possible, the individual "must in his middle age have committed himself to undertakings that set time at defiance." Difficult enough, as she has relentlessly demonstrated, for creative artists with financial means; well nigh impossible for "the immense majority of human beings" who reside "in our society of exploitation" (493).

Beauvoir's lifetime of explicating existentialism, begun in the brave light of dreadful freedom, thus ends with an argument for stasis: "Liberty is frightening, and that is why the elderly man will sometimes refuse it" (489). True, of course, but no less for the elderly than for the young. Existentialism begins, and should end, with disdain for such a limited fate.

6 FRIEDAN'S *The Fountain of Age,* for all the bulk of its more than six hundred pages, is a thin work.[51] It combines anecdotal evidence with synopses of research studies on the old and the aging process. In many ways the work is a continuation of *The Feminine Mystique:* once again Friedan examines popular magazines, this time searching for signs of a youth culture and of the shunting off to the side of older people. Age becomes the new problem with no name. Friedan is determined to name the problem but also, more important, to dismiss it, to transform a mystique of debility and decline into a narrative of growth and wisdom.

Using the same existential language that she had employed earlier in *The Feminine Mystique,* Friedan describes life in *The Fountain of Age* as a set of choices. Evasion of choices, dismissal of autonomy and creativity in youth and in old age, has deleterious consequences for the mental and physical well-being of the individual. Thus individuals need "to step out into the true existential unknown of these new years of life now open to us, and to find our own terms of living it."[52] New roads or adventures will constantly open up to the aged. As Friedan puts it, "I glimpsed both the necessity and the possibility of intimacy and passionate sexual being/knowing beyond the dreams of our youth—the continuing necessity and possibility of making new existential choices in love, and of risking the existential pain, rage, and shame for as long as we choose to live" (259).

As she had done in *The Feminine Mystique,* Friedan studiously avoids confronting Beauvoir. There is but one reference to Beauvoir in the text, an aside that the feminism of writers such as Beauvoir and Germaine Greer no longer applies to the situation of women (264). Nonetheless, a critique of Beauvoir silently enters in the pages of *The Fountain of Age.* Once again,

Friedan attempts diligently to put a happy face on what Beauvoir would construe as a tragic situation. In old age, where Beauvoir sees suffering writ large, Friedan prefers to emphasize possibility and growth.

It is not that Friedan disagrees with all aspects of Beauvoir's view of aging. They agree, for example, that it is bad to shut the elderly away in nursing homes or institutions; that society allocates insufficient resources and care to the aged; that it is best for the elderly to remain as autonomous and creative for as long as possible. But whereas Beauvoir characterizes the process of aging and death as a painful part of the human condition, Friedan regards it as a myth constructed by a youth-oriented culture.

While Beauvoir does furnish some examples of aged writers and painters carrying on with their creative work, in general she emphasizes the decline in creative energy. Friedan, in contrast, refuses to acknowledge almost any negative aspect of old age. She effectively demonstrates that people deteriorate most quickly when their autonomy is challenged, when they are forced—with good intentions, as often as not—into situations that are deadening to the human spirit. But she is as deaf to issues of class and race in this work as she was thirty years earlier in *The Feminine Mystique*. Beauvoir's volume is lucid on the problems of class, on how workers are pushed out of jobs, forced into retirement without the resources to cope. The exploitation that for Beauvoir defines work continues after retirement; work and retirement are both part of a system of exploitation that must be abolished. While the reformist Friedan would no doubt agree that there are deficiencies within the working world that continue into retirement, she chooses to present a thesis of boundless possibility, to see only opportunities. Businesses err, she says, when they forsake older workers for younger ones. The problem with older workers is not that they cannot work well and be productive. It is, rather, that they are the victims of stereotypes, of the mystique of aging. Hence "the vicious circle: stereotypes regarding older employees' lower abilities, motivation, and learning capacity lead to restricted opportunities for training and development, and thus to 'obsolescence' and career stagnation, to blocked promotion ladders and career plateaus" (208–9).

The individuals who jump off the pages of Friedan's text are invariably just like her: vibrant, financially well-off individuals embarked on wonderful journeys, the best that money can buy. They go hiking in challenging terrain, travel to exotic places, engage in experimental living situations, soak up knowledge in Elderhostels. In Friedan's universe of aging, older people are in the process of discovering new possibilities, "new kinds of loving intimacy, purposeful work and activity, learning and knowing, community and care" (87).

Older people, Friedan argues, are different from younger ones, but not because they are weaker versions of their younger selves. Her argument seems to be that in the developmental process from youth to old age, some things may be lost but many others are gained. Thus, while she begrudgingly admits that some aged individuals do lose memory and strength, she argues that such losses are not inevitable; indeed, she seems to think that such declines are overstated, mainly a function of poorly designed tests (96, 108). Some members of the aged population do not function well, but they are individuals, Friedan claims, who have chosen, or have had the choice made for them, to withdraw from community and the exercise of autonomy.

For those able to maintain autonomy and community, the sky is the limit. Friedan defines aging in terms of wisdom, growth, and activity, as a period of great love and connectedness. The aged engage in an "affirmation of themselves, discovering new sources and directions for their own creativity and wisdom" (605). Friedan's vision of old age is nothing if not exuberant. Here, for example, she is discussing the political activities of the American Association of Retired People and the Gray Panthers:

> And through our actions, we will create a new image of age—free and joyous, living with pain, saying what we really think and feel at last— knowing who we are, realizing that we know more than we ever knew that we knew, not afraid of what anyone thinks of us anymore, moving with wonder into that unknown future we have helped to shape for the generations coming after us. There will not have to be such dread and denial for them in living their age if we use our own age in new adventures, breaking the old rules and inhibitions, changing the patterns and possibilities of love and work, learning and play, worship and creation, discovery and political responsibility, and resolving the seeming irreconcilable conflicts between them. (637)

It is a wonderful vision, the flip side of Beauvoir's existential pessimism. Even death loses its terror. The vision of death that Friedan develops is almost early Victorian, marked by a sense of going gently into the night after having lived a full life. Friedan admits that in her youth she had an existential fear of death: "I remember my own terror, as a teenager, when the realization first came over me that one day I would no longer be. The thought of death was unbearable to me" (543). But the "fountain of age" has brought calm to Friedan: Having witnessed the death of so many of her friends, she says, "I have felt, with increasing ease, that now familiar feeling of loss and sorrow, and yet that comfort, acceptance, at home with death. I have lost my terror and denial of death. I can live with its reality" (545). Death, she announces, borrowing a metaphor from biologist Lewis Thomas, can be a euphoric experience.

To be fair, there are many obvious truths in Friedan's work, as well as admonitions that are helpful, even if not easily realizable. Yes, it is better to be autonomous than dependent, better to be integrated into a community than isolated and alone, better to have wisdom than to persist in youthful brashness—and, most of all, better to have a choice in living and in dying. This is the crux of Friedan's existential optimism: choice allows the individual to grow and prosper, to remain fit and sharp. Borrowing from Stanley Elkins's work on slavery and Bruno Bettelheim's work on the concentration camp experience, she had argued in *The Feminine Mystique* that loss of control and the inability to have projects led women into a type of infantilization (91). She finds the same type of diminution being forced upon the elderly by the mystique of aging.

As already noted, the individuals who populate the pages of Friedan's work are vital and independent, but they are atypical. They are able to thrive precisely because they are engaged in existential projects. Beauvoir too believed that the absorption of the individual in projects was critical to growth and happiness, a way to battle the dread of freedom and the anxiety of death. But she was less sanguine about the possibilities when so many individuals were weighted down by horrible jobs, lack of resources, and the accumulated legacy of choices they had made, or evaded, in their earlier years. For Friedan and her wealthy informants, money never seems to be a problem, and the fund of educational capital seems only to increase with age. Creativity is a constantly expanding vista. None of the individuals she discusses are forced to work at McDonald's in order to supplement their meager pensions or Social Security. None of them have been forced to compromise their freedom by taking on responsibility for raising grandchildren. They and Friedan inhabit a utopian community where the exercise of choice is bountiful and joyous, where despair and anxiety are not part of the human condition or even of the social system. It is an appealing world of existentialism without any meat on its bones, something akin to what Ruth Rosen has called "therapeutic feminism." In Rosen's definition, therapeutic feminism is marked by a dismissal of social and economic oppression and a valorization of a woman's ability to overcome oppression through positive thinking. "If only she thought positively about herself," then any woman "could achieve some form of self-realization and emancipation."[53]

In *The Fountain of Age* as in much of her work, the inwardness of Friedan's vision forces her to see the world as she demands that it be, without anything standing in the way of her will to experience, her need to prosper. Rather than marking a stage of wisdom, her vision of old age evinces a continuing blindness, a continuing failure to see that lives often conflict and wills clash. Friedan cannot reconcile herself to, or even acknowledge, the existential truth that Beauvoir never jettisoned. While it is wonderful to affirm with one of her respondents, "I no longer need anyone's approval but my own" (335), Friedan seems not to recognize that this kind of freedom can become freedom without responsibility. It is a new version of rugged American individualism, at odds with Friedan's ideal of the community and wisdom that grace the lives of the aged.

BEAUVOIR AND FRIEDAN, two mothers of second-wave feminism, each coming from an existential perspective, remained at variance throughout their lives. Neither held a complete warrant on the truth. Each spoke of different truths while grappling as best she could with a critical existential question: How can an individual without projects, without an ability to transcend, be considered a free human being? Bringing this perspective to the plight of women in the postwar years, Beauvoir and Friedan both contributed mightily, each according to her own strengths and limitations, to the feminist movement. Their existentialism moved them to reject the absolutes upon which patriarchy rested most comfortably. Moreover, the existential imperatives of transcendence through projects helped them comprehend the horrible implications for women confined to the suburbs, for women denied the possibility of pursuing their own dreams. And in gazing at the ultimate existential situation, aging and dying, Beauvoir and Friedan wrestled with the implications of their notions of projects and transcendence for men and women on the cusp of a new millennium. Each of them engaged, with the help of existential terminology, the problematic nature of the human condition. If one is weighted too heavily with the baggage of pessimism and the other with the ballast of optimism, then it is all the sadder that the two of them were never able to engage in a meaningful dialogue. Each failed to recognize that while an existential attitude may begin with despair, it cannot end with either a resolute optimism or a profound pessimism. Growth comes through acts of transcendence, moments when the lock on the iron cage of the mundane is broken, when the "blue devils of nada" are pushed aside. These are ecstatic moments, as blues existentialists such as Albert Murray understand, all the more so because they are fleeting.[54] But they are not, as Beauvoir stressed, only the province of the young. The young may imagine that time is on their side, but the biting reality of existentialism is that individuals act and live most fully in a situation when they fully recognize the fact of their existence as mortal beings, fragile "boats against the current," as F. Scott Fitzgerald put it.[55] Within the constraints of the human condition, the individual, old or young, best in solidarity with others, endures.

Chapter Thirteen

Conclusion: Existentialism Today and Tomorrow

1 WHILE AT A cocktail party in the early 1990s, writer Herbert Gold lamented that it had become "old-fashioned and even passé to talk about the absence of existentialism" from contemporary culture: "Angst, anomie, existential despair, the death of God, if not now, when?" The entire existential vocabulary of his formative years in bohemian Greenwich Village had vanished.[1] Gold's worst fears about the demise of existentialism had already been captured in a scene from Woody Allen's film *Manhattan* (1979). The character Mary Wilkie, played by Diane Keaton, represents the position of hip New York intellectuals. After Woody Allen, essentially playing himself, proclaims his admiration for the films of Ingmar Bergman, Keaton's character rants, "So Scandinavian, bleak, my God, all that Kierkegaard. Right? Real adolescent, fashionable pessimism. I mean, the silence, God's silence, Okay, Okay, Okay. I mean I loved it when I was at Radcliffe, but alright you outgrow it, you absolutely outgrow it."

Outgrow existentialism? Hardly. Existentialism never died, nor has it faded away fully. It lives on, if in a tepid state, often reduced to a shorthand term for either teenage angst or yuppie nostalgia. Barely a day passes without the term appearing in newspapers or magazines, an easy adjective for summoning up a sense of anguish. Thus in the political arena, Eric Alterman can breezily refer to the "existential insult that voters delivered" in the November 1998 elections.[2] Senator Paul Wellstone from Minnesota proclaims that an upcoming budget battle will be "a really existential moment" for President Clinton.[3] The term pops up unexpectedly and casually in other aspects of American life as well. Existentialism, we are told in the entertainment section of the *Los Angeles Times,* is central to the sequel of the children's film *Toy Story.*[4] A critic praises Humphrey Bogart for his ability "to turn an existential mood into something irresistibly iconic."[5] A newspaper headline says of a comic strip, "Peanuts No Less Than Existential."[6]

The uneasy ubiquity of existentialism today renders it perhaps benign or even meaningless. Two recent cultural documents illustrate this fate. First, in the popular "Generation X" film *Reality Bites* (1994), the character portrayed by heartthrob Ethan Hawke is a brooding loner, given to chain-smoking cigarettes, hanging out aimlessly, and reading Heidegger's *Being and Time* at a luncheonette counter. He cops an existential attitude of ennui and alienation. Second, a two-page spread in *Vanity Fair* (December 1994) advertising Microsoft's Encarta '95 shows a picture of two young girls with the headline, "Forget Goldilocks and the Three Bears, tell us about Sartre." This is followed by an exchange between daughters and father:

> "C'mon Dad, tell us about Sartre and existentialism and his belief in the inescapable responsibility of all individuals for their own decisions and his relationship with Simone de Beauvoir," we pleaded as he tucked us in for the night.
>
> "Oh, all right," he said as he loaded the Microsoft Encarta multimedia encyclopedia into our personal computer and called up Sartre. . . .
>
> [If] we told you every single cool thing Encarta does, we'd be up all night and there'd be no time for Dad's bedtime stories about Sartre and the existentialists.
>
> After he kissed us goodnight, Dad said Sartre was fond of saying, "Man is condemned to be free." We told him he was free to keep us up as long as he wanted with stories about Sartre. He chuckled, turned out the lights, and said, "I think you two have had enough existentialism for one night."

Existentialism enough, to be sure. Such "lively" examples of existentialism in recent American culture attest, albeit paradoxically, to the living death of existentialism. Indeed, given the positive testimonials to the centrality of the experience of existentialism for American intellectuals over the last century and a half, one might wonder whether existentialism has met the worst fate that can befall an idea: to be at once fashionable and nostalgic.

2   WHAT HAPPENED TO existentialism? By the late 1970s existentialism had in many ways yielded ground, lost its potency in American culture and in the life of the mind. At the same time, it had become a shorthand form of expression. Perhaps its "vogue" had faded, at least in its French incarnation, after nearly four decades' centrality in American thought and culture. The language of anguish and dread that Herbert Gold considered the lifeblood of existentialism did not resonate well in a 1980s America that embraced the nostrums of Ronald Reagan and dashed madly after financial speculation and windfall profits. Yet existentialism had continued to seem meaningful during the economic boom of the 1950s.

One reason for the thinning out of existentialism may be that Sartre, so associated with it, began to lose favor with intellectuals and other opinion makers. Sartre's enthusiastic embrace of the radical left and his willingness to support reactionary communist regimes did not help his reputation, especially during the Reagan years, and perhaps the reputation of existentialism came to be tarnished as a result. In that unexpected bestseller *The Closing of the American Mind* (1987), Allan Bloom dismissed Sartre as the man "who had all those wonderful experiences of nothingness, the abyss, nausea, commitment without ground—the result of which was almost without fail, support of the Party line."[7] Within liberal and leftist academic circles, existentialism had, by the 1970s and 1980s, been pushed aside by deconstructionist and postmodernist theory.[8] A new generation of French philosophers, led by Jacques Derrida and Michel Foucault, challenged the assumptions and leaders of existentialism. In France, Sartre's reputation began to plummet in the 1970s. First, his attempted synthesis of existentialism and Marxism never took off; he failed to complete the second volume of his *Critique of Dialectical Reason*. But even if he had finished his project, it is doubtful that he and his thought would have carried the day. After all, structuralist anthropologist Claude Lévi-Strauss had already savaged the first volume of the *Critique of Dialectical Reason* as "contradictory in the one case and superfluous in the other."[9] In the wake of the structuralist and poststructuralist revolutions in France, Sartre and his existentialism were increasingly viewed as superfluous. Critics derided existentialism for its refusal to understand the science of signs, the ways in which the human individual is constructed and constrained by structures of thought. The existential emphasis on the thinker as public figure, as speaking to a human condition, struck intellectuals like Foucault as hubristic. Local, rather than universal, pronouncements became the preferred method of exposition.[10]

With the arrival on the scene of Derrida's deconstruction, dripping with irony and comic effects, the high seriousness of existential angst began to seem like an old-fashioned affectation. Yet Heidegger, who like Sartre had imbibed his phenomenology from Edmund Husserl, gained in popularity. Where Sartre was concrete and earnest in his philosophy and concerns, Heidegger was poetic and arch. The ultimate irony, however, was that the distance between Sartre and postmodernists such as Derrida and Foucault was not as great as their denigrations of him suggested. Derrida and the later Foucault agreed that identity is malleable, that the self is a process, something that is made.[11] If Sartre and company stressed the unity of the self more than Derrida and the postmodernists, existentialism should then be viewed as a *via media* between absolutist concepts of a unified self and those of a totally fictive self.[12]

3 EVEN IN THE dark days of the 1980s and early 1990s, existentialism never absented itself from American culture. Given its emphasis on the human condition, on dread and despair, existentialism would of necessity appeal to some intellectuals and artists. Consider, in this regard, the case of Woody Allen. At first glance Allen seems an unlikely candidate to carry the torch of existentialism in America. According to a recent biographer, Allen is neither an intellectual nor a serious reader, even if he kept in his dressing room a copy of *Selections from Kierkegaard*.[13] Yet Allen has constructed a career based on the existential language of angst and confrontation with the problems of God and death. Perhaps the character Sandy Bates in the film *Stardust Memories* best captured the Allen take on existential philosophy. When asked if he studied philosophy in college, Bates responds, "Yes. I got one hundred on the existential philosophy exam by not answering any of the questions."[14] Allen may not in his writing and films have definitively answered all or any of the questions of existential philosophy, but he has certainly examined them as fully as any figure in contemporary American culture.

Throughout his career Allen has employed existential issues as comedic fodder and in knowing asides. But it is humor with larger implications. He turns to existentialism because it deals with his own dread and despair. Comedy is his way of fighting off the demons. In an early essay, "My Philosophy," Allen's character begins reading "Kierkegaard and Sartre," among other thinkers. He remarks, "I remember my reaction to a typically luminous observation of Kierkegaard's: 'Such a relation which relates itself to its own self (that is to say, a self) must either have constituted itself or have been constituted by another.' The concept brought tears to my eyes." The character then resolves to pursue his own metaphysical investigations, beginning with the composition of a "Critique of Pure Dread."[15]

More serious musings—about the meaning of life, the logic of suicide, and the place of responsibility in a world without God and with absolute freedom—exploded across the screen in Allen's film *Crimes and Misdemeanors* (1989). In response to an interviewer's comment that "*Crimes and Misdemeanors* could be defined as an existential film . . . as it takes up some . . . universal existential themes in life and in the world," Allen agreed: "Right, that's the only interesting theme to me . . . [;] existential themes emerged with Kierkegaard and Dostoyevsky and those themes were the natural material of the dramatist."[16] They constitute the drama of the existential question at the heart of *Crimes and Misdemeanors*: If I am free, then how should I act? One of the characters, Judah Rosenthal, is a successful ophthalmologist, and despite hints of financial impropriety at one time, he is a pillar of the community. However, he has been having an affair with a flight attendant that threatens to destroy his life. With anguish, he decides that this woman can be killed, her life erased. Through the intercession of his shady brother, the act is done for him. Judah gets away with murder. His life goes on. Initially he carries the pain of his guilt with him. The words of his religious teachers that "the eyes of God are on us always" torment him. But his horror at his act abates with time, and his sense of responsibility for it seems to vanish in a world without inherent values or meaning.

Another character, a Jewish philosopher, joyfully engages the paradoxes of life and affirms life in the face of suffering. For Allen, this character reflects the search for value and meaning that can be found in the work of someone like existentialist psychologist Victor Frankl or Holocaust survivor Primo Levi. Yet for reasons that remain unknown, as the secrets of the heart must remain unfathomable, he defies the essentials of his own philosophy of survival by committing suicide.

Finally, in yet another of the film's paradoxical situations, an ethically pure rabbi goes blind, a development that suggests that God is blind to human suffering and heroism. In an interview about the film Allen said of his own world view, "I think that at best the universe is indifferent. At best! Hannah Arendt spoke of the banality of evil. The universe is banal as well. And because it's banal, it's evil. . . . Its indifference is evil. If you walk down the street and you see homeless people, starving, and you're indifferent to them, you're in a way being evil. Indifference to me equals evil."[17] To soften the horror of this indifference in the face of despair, of the murderer getting guiltlessly away with murder, Allen ended *Crimes and Misdemeanors* with a voice-over to the effect that we give meaning to an indifferent universe through our own capacity to love. And he also holds out hope that future generations will perhaps come to understand more. Chastened understanding and the joy of simple things become the fate of the ethical figure.

4   AT PRESENT, existentialism is receiving renewed attention in American culture because it speaks to everyone's frustrations in life: to dissatisfaction with ideals of success and to the unavoidably tragic nature of existence. Existentialism is especially relevant to members of the aging babyboom generation, who embrace it less out of nostalgia for a cultural style than in response to the increasingly loud knocks of death on their own doors. In its worst expressions, this return of existentialism confirms Marx's comment that ideas eventually return as farce. But in more serious books recently appearing on the market, such as David S. Awbrey's *Finding Hope in the Age of Melancholy* (1999), one finds a sincere willingness to use existential modes of thinking to examine one's life choices and reach a sober recognition that one must take responsibility for such decisions.[18] While

some baby-boomers desperately cling to their faith in the power of medicine and exercise to ward off death, the existential keeps intruding, becoming apparent each time aging boomers confront themselves in the mirror. The downward gravitational pull of the body compels one to contemplate life within the boundary situation of death. This formulation, existential to the core, demands of the old, as much as of the young, an accounting with the world and the self. The language and ideas of existentialism compel us now, as they did thirty years ago. We are always in a situation, and the death and anguish of daily living are never absent. But death and anguish, dread and despair, must not translate into nihilism, the dead-end turn of existentialism.

Existential questions about the meaning of life, the emptiness of existence, and the absence of compelling values continue to resonate for a new generation of Americans caught up in the procurement of wealth and career, in the dull and dangerous promises of a global information economy. Think here of Ryan Bingham, the main character of Walter Kirn's novel *Up in the Air*. Bingham is a modern counterpart to Dostoevsky's Underground Man. However, he spends his life above ground, flying around in airplanes, living an empty existence divorced from any notion of self. He has no home other than airplane cabins, hotel rooms, and the hospitality lounges of airports. His corporate position is ill defined but well paying. He seemingly exists only to pile up frequent-flyer miles. Bingham's airborne alienation gets him nowhere; he is modern man flying around in circles.[19]

Or consider two recent critically acclaimed films, *Fight Club* (1999) and *American Beauty* (1999). *Fight Club* evokes Richard Wright's *The Outsider* in that it begins with the existential questions: What would you do if you knew you were going to die today? What if you had a chance to create yourself anew? *Fight Club* flaunts a negative existentialism taken to the point of nihilism. The film's bleak corporate landscape reeks of unremitting despair and boredom. When the issue of freedom presents itself, it is dealt with in Nietzschean terms, as a power struggle, a testing of the limits of the human body and human trespass. All of this is set in a world devoid of meaning for young white males. Escape through intense experience presents itself as a solution to the malaise that afflicts them. But it is a dead end, leading only to mysteries of identity and an orgy of destruction. It offers us existential critique without the depth and dauntlessness that are necessary in order to persevere. *American Beauty,* which won an Academy Award, is an existential rhapsody on male midlife crisis. The main character, played by Kevin Spacey, drifts in search of meaning. He cannot find sustenance in his family, in his work, or in the wonders of the mundane. The film recounts the twists and turns of his futile search for transcendence, perhaps even for forgiveness. At the moment of his absurd death, after he has finally accepted his freedom and acted responsibly, he experiences transcendence, a Camusian exultation in the rhythms of life, in the everyday pleasures of the senses. The issue here is not whether these films are coherent in their philosophies or story lines but rather how they attest to a hunger in American culture for meaning and transcendence. The themes of these films are dread and despair, anguish and dauntlessness, viewed through the prism of an existential sensibility.

These contemporary films recognize that the new world order is absurd and contingent. We reside in a culture saturated with the consolation of easy salvation. We seem barely able to recognize sin and responsibility in our own lives, thus negating the logic of salvation: What have we to be saved from? In this new world, it seems, expectations are immense, part and parcel of a giddy optimism and sense of possibility; the world exists for our needs. *Wired*, the magazine of record for the digital-age entrepreneur, captures this ideal: thanks to the power of technology, "no ambition, however extravagant, no fantasy, however outlandish, can any longer be dismissed as crazy or impossible."[20] Hardly the language of existentialism. Indeed, this statement expresses why now, as much as ever, we need existentialism. Our heady confidence will in the end be crushed by the woes of the world and the finitude of existence. At the moment when this shock of recognition hits home, existentialism will once again claim its place.[21]

Existentialism makes a special claim on the attention of Americans at the opening of the twenty-first century. Until (and, alas, even after) September 11, 2001, many Americans wrapped themselves in a sense of invincibility, convinced that material gain would extend indefinitely and American power and global reach protect them from all threats. More recently, such pretensions shattered, we might well judge existence to be quite precarious, threatened by forces that we can neither understand fully nor combat easily. In this frightening world, existentialism invites us to confront the tragic nature of existence and to place simplistic dichotomies and naive optimism behind us. It is an invitation that we turn down only at great risk.

The return of existentialism, and the recognition of an American existential tradition along with a long-term grappling by American thinkers with Kierkegaard, Sartre, Camus, and Beauvoir, may in some manner allow us to join Herman Melville's Ahab in the quest to punch through the "pasteboard masks" of reality. Existential awareness helps the individual to endure, to climb with Sisyphus up the mountain. "No matter, Try Again," writes Samuel Beckett; "Fail Again, Fail Better."[22] Recognition of the despair of the human condition beckons forth new possibilities of existence. To write, to act, to create, and to rebel after a century of totalitarianism and mass destruction, and in the face of new challenges, is to engage in existential transcendence, to erect a sculpture of human possibility, albeit out of the ashes of despair. As William James understood, we pass through despair to, if not salvation, then to a depth of understanding that is at once humbling and enabling.

Notes

One Introduction

1. Quoted in Katherine Ramsland, *Prism of the Night: A Biography of Anne Rice* (New York: Plume/Penguin Books, 1992), 69. Ramsland finds Rice's early fascination with existentialist themes reflected in her vampire novels, especially *Interview with a Vampire* (1976).
2. Marge Piercy, "Contribution," in *Daughters of de Beauvoir*, ed. Penny Foster and Imogen Sutton (London: Women's Press, 1989), 112. Of course, not all were as serious in their adoption of existential style. Writer Barry Hannah recalled that as a young man he "wanted badly once to be an existentialist, but mainly for the beret, turtleneck, cigarettes, and wan chick across the table listening." Hannah, "Mr. Brain, He Want a Song," in *The Eleventh Draft*, ed. Frank Conroy (New York: HarperCollins, 1999), 70.
3. Moses quoted in Robert Penn Warren, "Two for SNCC," *Commentary* 39 (Apr. 1965): 41.
4. Rob Mustard to author, e-mail communication, 20 Nov. 1996.
5. Alice Kaplan, *French Lessons: A Memoir* (Chicago: University of Chicago Press, 1993), 138.
6. Roxanne Dunbar-Ortiz, *Red Dirt: Growing up Okie* (London: Verso, 1997), 206. On Cell 16, see Alice Echols, *Daring to Be Bad: Radical Feminism in America, 1967–1975* (Minneapolis: University of Minnesota Press, 1989), 158–66.
7. Jean-Paul Sartre, "A European Declaration of Independence," *Commentary*, Jan. 1950, 411; Simone de Beauvoir, "An Existentialist Looks at Americans," *New York Times Magazine*, 25 May 1947, 52; Camus quoted in Herbert Lottman, *Albert Camus: A Biography* (Garden City, N.Y.: Doubleday, 1979), 391. For similar perceptions of American optimism from another French visitor, see Alexis de Tocqueville, *Democracy in America*, trans. George Lawrence (New York: Anchor Books, 1969), 453.
8. Michael Lesy, *Wisconsin Death Trip* (New York: Pantheon Books, 1973). For a powerful novelistic rendering of this death-drenched culture, see Stewart O'Nan, *A Prayer for the Dying* (New York: Picador USA, 2000). Hawthorne quoted in Harry Levin, *The Power of Blackness: Hawthorne, Poe, Melville* (New York: Alfred A. Knopf, 1967).
9. Lewis R. Gordon, *Existentia: Understanding Africana Existential Thought* (New York: Routledge, 2000), 7.
10. Jean-Paul Sartre, *Existentialism*, trans. Bernard Frechtman (New York: Philosophical Library, 1947), 27.

11. Carson McCullers, *Clock without Hands* (New York: Bantam, 1961), 1.
12. Jean-Paul Sartre, *Search for a Method,* trans. Hazel E. Barnes (New York: Vintage Books, 1968), xxxiii.
13. Sartre, *Existentialism,* 21.
14. Paul Tillich, *Systematic Theology: Existence and the Christ* (Chicago: University of Chicago Press, 1957), 2:26.
15. Walter Kaufmann, *Existentialism: From Dostoevsky to Sartre* (Cleveland: Meridian Books, 1964), 11.
16. Ibid., 11, 21.
17. Walter Kaufmann, *Critique of Religion and Philosophy* (Princeton: Princeton University Press, 1958), 26.
18. Anthony Mansard, "Existentialism," in *Dictionary of the History of Ideas: Studies of Selected Pivotal Ideas,* ed. in chief Philip P. Wiener (New York: Charles Scribner's Sons, 1973), 2:191.
19. Maurice Natanson, "Jean-Paul Sartre's Philosophy of Freedom," in *Literature, Philosophy, and the Social Sciences* (The Hague: Martinus Nijhoff, 1962), 64.
20. Hazel E. Barnes, *The Literature of Possibility* (Lincoln: University of Nebraska Press, 1959).
21. Quoted in Geoffrey Wheatcroft, "Horrors beyond Tragedy," *Times Literary Supplement,* no. 5071 (9 June 2000): 10.
22. Alan Geller, "An Interview with Ralph Ellison," in *The Black American Writer: Fiction,* ed. C. W. E. Bigsby (DeLand, Fla.: Everett/Edwards, 1969), 1:167.
23. Cal Bedient, "Robert Pinsky's Antlered Brow: An Essay Review," *Salmagundi* no. 116–17 (Fall/Winter 1997): 252.
24. Herman Melville, *Moby-Dick, or The Whale* (New York: Library of America, 1983), 966–67.
25. Ralph Ellison, *Invisible Man* (New York: Modern Library, 1992), 572.
26. The influence of Sartre on American professional philosophers is well discussed in Ann Fulton, *Apostles of Sartre: Existentialism in America, 1945–1963* (Evanston: Northwestern University Press, 1999).
27. Wright quoted in Paul Gilroy, *The Black Atlantic: Modernity and the Double Consciousness* (Cambridge: Harvard University Press, 1993), 159. Wright was showing off his collection to the historian C. L. R. James.
28. William James, *Pragmatism* (Cambridge: Harvard University Press, 1975), 106.

Two The "Drizzly November" of the American Soul

1. Andrew Delbanco, *The Death of Satan: How Americans Have Lost the Sense of Evil* (New York: Farrar, Straus, and Giroux, 1995), 34–35.
2. Robert D. Richardson, Jr., *Emerson: The Mind on Fire* (Berkeley: University of California Press, 1995), 3–5, 23.
3. Herman Melville, *Moby-Dick, or The Whale* (New York: Library of America, 1983), 795.
4. Lewis O. Saum, *The Popular Mood of Pre–Civil War America* (Westport, Conn.: Greenwood Press, 1980); Saum, *The Popular Mood of America, 1860–1890* (Lincoln: University of Nebraska Press, 1990); Michael Lesy, *Wisconsin Death Trip* (New York: Pantheon Books, 1973).

5. Abraham Lincoln, "Second Inaugural Address," 4 Mar. 1865, in *Lincoln: Speeches and Writings, 1859–1865,* ed. Don E. Fehrenbacher (New York: Library of America, 1989), 687. For a compelling analysis of this speech, see Garry Wills, "Lincoln's Greatest Speech?" *Atlantic Monthly* 284 (Sept. 1999), 60–70.

6. On Holmes and the Civil War, see George Cotkin, *William James, Public Philosopher* (Baltimore: Johns Hopkins University Press, 1990), 29; Albert W. Alschuler, *Law without Values: The Life, Work, and Legacy of Justice Holmes* (Chicago: University of Chicago Press, 2000).

7. Quoted in George Cotkin, *Reluctant Modernism: American Thought and Culture, 1880–1900* (New York: Twayne, 1992), 34.

8. Quoted in Alschuler, *Law,* 214, n. 171. There are, of course, affinities here with Henry Adams's sense of the role of power and struggle in human existence. Both were influenced by their unsentimental reading of Darwin. But Adams, unlike Holmes and William James, never gave up the ghost of meaning; he searched for scientific theories that would grant a logic (even one of decline) to the chaos of the world. For this reason I have decided not to include Adams in the roster of American existentials. On Adams, see my *Reluctant Modernism,* 132–34.

9. Walter Kaufmann, *Critique of Religion and Philosophy* (Princeton: Princeton University Press, 1958), 26.

10. Perry Miller, *Jonathan Edwards* (New York: William Sloane, 1949), 159. At the time when Miller was composing his book on Edwards, he was also teaching a course at Harvard on "Masterpieces of the Christian Tradition," which included material on Kierkegaard. Miller to Walter Lowrie, 23 Jan. 1948, Lowrie Papers, Princeton University.

11. George Santayana, "The Genteel Tradition in American Philosophy" (1913), in *The American Intellectual Tradition,* ed. David A. Hollinger and Charles Capper (New York: Oxford University Press, 2001), 2:95.

12. John Patrick Diggins, *The Lost Soul of American Politics: Virtue, Self-Interest, and the Foundations of Liberalism* (Chicago: University of Chicago Press, 1984), 7.

13. Jonathan Edwards, *Freedom of the Will* (1754), excerpt in *Jonathan Edwards: Basic Writings,* ed. Ola Elizabeth Winslow (New York: New American Library, 1966), 200.

14. Miller, *Jonathan Edwards,* 45.

15. Charles L. Cohen, *God's Caress: The Psychology of Puritan Religious Experience* (New York: Oxford University Press, 1986).

16. Jonathan Edwards, *Sinners in the Hands of an Angry God* (1741), excerpt in *Basic Writings,* 160.

17. Jonathan Edwards, "Farewell Sermon" (1750), excerpt in ibid., 179.

18. Hawthorne quoted in James Wood, "The All and the If: God and Metaphor in Melville," in *The Broken Estate: Essays on Literature and Belief* (New York: Random House, 1999), 29.

19. Walker Percy, "Herman Melville" (1983), in *Signposts in a Strange Land,* ed. Patrick Samway (New York: Noonday Press, 1991), 200.

20. Albert Camus, "Three Interviews," in *Lyrical and Critical Essays,* trans. Ellen Conroy Kennedy (New York: Vintage Books, 1970), 355. In the same volume Camus attests to Melville's supreme powers as a maker of myths. See "Herman Melville," 288–94.

21. Herman Melville, *Bartleby* (1853; New York: Dover, 1990), 17.

22. Ibid., 18.

23. Richard Brodhead, ed., *New Essays on Melville's Moby Dick* (Cambridge: Cambridge University Press, 1986), 4.

24. Melville, *Moby-Dick,* 1338. Hereafter, page citations appear in the text.

25. Here I focus on James's philosophy within its cultural context. Affinities might also be drawn, on a purely philosophical level, between the Jamesian notion of consciousness, as consciousness of something, and the work of phenomenology as in Husserl.

26. William James, *Pragmatism* (Cambridge: Harvard University Press, 1975), 133.

27. William James, "Is Life Worth Living?" (1895), in *The Will to Believe* (1897; Cambridge: Harvard University Press, 1979), 39–40.

28. William James, "On Some Hegelianisms" (1882), in ibid., 196–221; James, *A Pluralistic Universe* (Cambridge: Harvard University Press, 1977), 43–62.

29. William James, *The Varieties of Religious Experience* (1902; Cambridge: Harvard University Press, 1985), 73.

30. Ibid., 136.

31. Quoted in Cynthia Griffin Wolff, *Emily Dickinson* (New York: Alfred A. Knopf, 1987), 101.

32. Quoted in Wendy Martin, *An American Triptych: Anne Bradstreet, Emily Dickinson, Adrienne Rich* (Chapel Hill: University of North Carolina Press, 1984), 85.

33. Emily Dickinson, "Death sets a Thing significant" (1862), in *The Complete Poems of Emily Dickinson,* ed. Thomas H. Johnson (Boston: Little, Brown, 1961), 170–71.

34. Emily Dickinson, "Endow the Living" (1862), in ibid., 255.

35. Stephen Crane, *Prose and Poetry* (New York: Library of America, n.d.), 205.

36. Material on Crane comes from Cotkin, *Reluctant Modernism,* 148–49.

37. Alvin Kernan, *In Plato's Cave* (New Haven: Yale University Press, 1999), 99. Kernan misses, however, the sense of tragedy in American literature before the 1950s.

38. Eugene O'Neill, *Long Day's Journey into Night* (New Haven: Yale University Press, 1956), 153.

39. Deborah Lyons and Adam D. Weinberg, eds., *Edward Hopper and the American Imagination* (New York: W. W. Norton and Whitney Museum of American Art, 1995); Gail Levin, *Edward Hopper: An Intimate Biography* (New York: Alfred A. Knopf, 1995).

40. F. Scott Fitzgerald, *This Side of Paradise* (1920; New York: Penguin Books, 1996), 260.

41. Ernest Hemingway, *The Sun Also Rises* (1926; New York: Scribner's Sons, 1970), 97.

42. Reinhold Niebuhr, review of *The Modern Temper* in *Christian Century* 46 (1 May 1929): 587; Peter Gregg Slater, "The Negative Secularism of *The Modern Temper:* Joseph Wood Krutch," *American Quarterly* 33 (Summer 1981): 185–205.

43. Joseph Wood Krutch, *The Modern Temper: A Study and a Confession* (New York: Harcourt, Brace, 1929), xvi. Hereafter, page citations appear in the text.

44. Slater, "Negative Secularism," 190.

45. Walter Lippmann, *A Preface to Morals* (New York: Macmillan, 1929), 59. Hereafter, page citations appear in the text.

46. T. J. Jackson Lears, *No Place of Grace: Antimodernism and the Transformation of American Culture, 1880–1920* (New York: Pantheon Books, 1981), 262–97.

47. Dashiell Hammett, *The Maltese Falcon* (New York: Vintage Books, 1984), 69. Hereafter, page citations appear in the text.
48. This episode is excised from the most famous screen adaptation, produced in 1941, starring Humphrey Bogart.
49. Robert Warshow, "The Gangster as Tragic Hero," in *The Immediate Experience: Movies, Theatre, and Other Aspects of Popular Culture* (Garden City, N.J.: Doubleday, 1962), 131.
50. Geoffrey O'Brien, *Hardboiled America: Lurid Paperbacks and the Masters of Noir* (New York: Da Capo Press, 1997); Nicholas Christopher, *Somewhere in the Night: Film Noir and the American City* (New York: Free Press, 1997); Robert G. Porfirio, "No Way Out: Existential Motifs in the Film Noir," *Sight and Sound* 45 (Autumn 1976): 212–17.
51. William S. Graebner, *The Age of Doubt: American Thought and Culture in the 1940s* (Boston: Twayne, 1991), 38; also Richard Dorfman, "D.O.A. and the Notion of Noir," *Movietone News*, 29 Feb. 1976, 11–16.

Three Kierkegaard Comes to America

1. Frances Perkins, *The Roosevelt I Knew* (New York: Viking Press, 1946), 147–49.
2. Lowrie to Professor Stace, 17 June 1951, in Walter Lowrie Papers, Manuscripts Division of the Department of Rare Books and Special Collections, Princeton University Library.
3. Biographical data may be found in a letter of Lowrie to Dr. Riedel, 20 Nov. 1948, with an attached "Sketch" of his life. Lowrie Papers, Princeton University.
4. Alexander C. Zabriskie, "What Is Christianity," in *Dr. Lowrie of Princeton: Nine Essays in Acknowledgment of a Debt,* ed. Alexander C. Zabriskie (Greenwich, Conn.: Seabury Press, 1957), 209.
5. Walter Lowrie, *Jesus According to St. Mark: An Interpretation of St. Mark's Gospel* (London: Longman's Green, 1929), 13. Hereafter, page citations appear in the text.
6. William R. Hutchinson, *The Modernist Impulse in American Protestantism* (Oxford: Oxford University Press, 1982), 185–225.
7. Lowrie to Albert Schweitzer, 18 Oct. 1931, Lowrie Papers, Princeton University.
8. Religious studies scholars tend to separate the passionate religion of the "lived experience" from the religion of theology and its systems. This negates the passionate embrace of religious issues and faith in the life and work of theologians and religious thinkers such as Lowrie. See David D. Hall, ed., *Lived Religion in America: Toward a History of Practice* (Princeton: Princeton University Press, 1997).
9. Walter Lowrie, introduction to Albert Schweitzer, *The Mystery of the Kingdom of God: The Secret of Jesus' Messiahship and Passion,* trans. Lowrie (New York: Dodd, Mead, 1914), 45. Hereafter, page citations appear in the text.
10. Walter Lowrie, "About 'Justification by Faith Alone,'" *The Journal of Religion* 32 (Oct. 1952): 238; Lowrie, *Jesus,* 44.
11. Walter Lowrie, *Our Concern with the Theology of Crisis* (Boston: Meador, 1932), 53. Hereafter, page citations appear in the text.
12. On the context for the introduction of Barth and the crisis of liberal theology, see William R. Hutchinson, *The Modernist Impulse in American Protestantism* (Oxford: Oxford University Press, 1982), 288–302.

13. Reinhold Niebuhr, *Beyond Tragedy: Essays on the Christian Interpretation of History* (1937; New York: Scribner's, 1965), 12.

14. Reinhold Niebuhr, "Barth—Apostle of the Absolute," *Christian Century* 45 (13 Dec. 1928): 1523.

15. Wilhelm Pauck, "Barth's Religious Criticism of Religion," *Journal of Religion* 8 (July 1928): 463.

16. Niebuhr, "Barth," 1524.

17. Walter Lowrie, *Kierkegaard* (Gloucester, Mass.: Peter Smith, 1970), 1:9.

18. Søren Kierkegaard, *Papers and Journals: A Selection,* trans. Alastair Hannay (London: Penguin Books, 1996), 490.

19. For an overview of the state of Kierkegaard literature and Lowrie's role in popularizing Kierkegaard in America, see Walter Lowrie, "Translators and Interpreters of S.K.," *Theology Today* 12 (Oct. 1955): 312–27. One recent commentator finds Lowrie's translations problematic because they are narrowly concerned with theological issues and miss Kierkegaard's poetic irony. To be sure, Lowrie did have a theological agenda in mind, and he did have many faults as a translator. But he was not absolutely deaf to the ironic qualities of Kierkegaard's prose. Roger Poole, "The Unknown Kierkegaard: Twentieth-Century Receptions," in *The Cambridge Companion to Kierkegaard,* ed. Alastair Hannay and Gerald D. Marino (New York: Cambridge University Press, 1997), 58–60.

20. Søren Kierkegaard, *Either/Or,* trans. Howard V. Hong and Edna H. Hong (Princeton: Princeton University Press, 1987), 1:26.

21. Ibid., 2:157.

22. Lowrie to Alexander Dru, 23 Nov. 1934, Lowrie Papers, Princeton University.

23. Lowrie to David Swenson, 11 June 1935, Lowrie-Swenson Correspondence, University Archives, University of Minnesota; also James O'Flaherty to Donald Fox, 30 Apr. 1978, Lowrie Papers, Princeton University.

24. Lowrie to Dru, 23 Nov. 1934.

25. David F. Swenson, *Something about Kierkegaard,* ed. Lillian Marvin Swenson (1945; Macon, Ga.: Mercer University Press, 1983), vii.

26. Ibid., 139.

27. Lowrie to Swenson, 22 Oct. 1936, Lowrie-Swenson Correspondence, University of Minnesota.

28. Ibid. Swenson considered himself "more a reader of Kierkegaard than . . . a scholar in the field, and I have read him chiefly for my own sake, with very little thought of publication." Swenson to Lowrie, 4 Dec. 1936, Lowrie-Swenson Correspondence, University of Minnesota.

29. Lowrie to Dru, 9 Oct. 1936, Lowrie Papers, Princeton University.

30. Lowrie to Swenson, 2 Jan. 1936, Lowrie-Swenson Correspondence, University of Minnesota.

31. Swenson to Lowrie, 19 May 1938, Lowrie-Swenson Correspondence, University of Minnesota.

32. Walter Lowrie, *A Short Life of Kierkegaard* (Princeton: Princeton University Press, 1942), viii.

33. Henry Miller, "The Prince of Denmark," *New Republic* 108 (10 May 1943): 642–43. Lowrie was pleased with Miller's review and invited him to come for a visit.

Miller, when he learned that Lowrie was a minister, replied, "Naturally I loathe preachers. But there are always exceptions, and I feel you must be one of them. I have the greatest respect and admiration for your work." Miller to Lowrie, 21 July 1943, Lowrie Papers, Princeton University.

34. Kierkegaard, *Papers and Journals,* 71.

35. Ibid., 160.

36. Søren Kierkegaard, *Concluding Unscientific Postscript,* trans. David Swenson, with an introduction by Walter Lowrie (Princeton: Princeton University Press, 1941), 30.

37. Lowrie, *Kierkegaard,* 2:315.

38. Søren Kierkegaard, *Fear and Trembling,* trans. Alastair Hannay (London: Penguin Books, 1985), 65.

39. Ibid., 82.

40. Lowrie, *Kierkegaard,* 2:326.

41. Ibid., 428.

42. Walter Lowrie, introduction to *Kierkegaard's Attack upon "Christendom": 1854–1855,* trans. Walter Lowrie (Princeton: Princeton University Press, 1944), xv.

43. Lowrie, *Kierkegaard,* 2:428.

44. Joseph Haroutunian, *Wisdom and Folly in Religion: A Study in Chastened Protestantism* (New York: Charles Scribner's Sons, 1940), 8.

45. Ibid., vii.

46. "Autobiographical Papers," Lowrie Papers, Princeton University, 3:84.

47. Reinhold Niebuhr, "Intellectual Autobiography," in *Reinhold Niebuhr: His Religious, Social, and Political Thought,* ed. Charles W. Kegley and Robert W. Bretall (New York: Macmillan, 1956), 10. Perhaps Niebuhr's move away from an emphasis on original sin came from his reading of Kierkegaard. See, in this same volume, Richard Kroner, "The Historical Roots of Niebuhr's Thought," 182–85. In the late 1940s Niebuhr suggested that despair too often led to apathy rather than to repentance. Niebuhr, "We Are Men and Not God," *Christian Century* 65 (27 Oct. 1948): 1138.

48. Søren Kierkegaard, *The Point of View,* trans. Walter Lowrie (London: Oxford University Press, 1939), 160.

49. Richard Wightman Fox, *Reinhold Niebuhr: A Biography* (New York: Harper and Row, 1987), 147.

50. Walter Lowrie, *What Is Christianity?* (New York: Pantheon, 1953), 149.

51. Walter Lowrie, "Political Perplexities of Walter Lowrie" (25 Nov. 1940), Lowrie Papers, Princeton University.

52. Walter Lowrie, "No Title" (1939), Lowrie Papers, Princeton University.

53. Walter Lowrie, "Antisemitism of the Jews" (ca. 1940–41), Lowrie Papers, Princeton University.

54. Walter Lowrie, "At War" (2 Feb. 1942), typescript, Lowrie Papers, Princeton University.

55. H. A. Reinhold to Lowrie, 22 Jan. and 2 Feb. 1942, Lowrie Papers, Princeton University.

56. Howard A. Johnson, "Kierkegaard and Sartre," *American-Scandinavian Review,* Autumn 1947, 225.

57. Howard A. Johnson to Walter Lowrie, 14 Dec. 1946, Lowrie Papers, Princeton University.

58. Lowrie, *Kierkegaard*, 1:13–14.

59. Lowrie to Howard A. Johnson, 6 Dec. 1949, Lowrie Papers, Princeton University.

60. Walter Lowrie, "Existentialism" (15 Apr. 1950), unpublished manuscript, Lowrie Papers, Princeton University.

61. Walter Lowrie, "'Existence' as Understood by Kierkegaard and/or Sartre," *Sewanee Review* 63 (July–Sept. 1950): 379–401, quotation at 398. Hereafter, page citations appear in the text.

Four A Kierkegaardian Age of Anxiety

1. Lt. E. MacFerguson to Walter Lowrie, 21 Nov. 1945, Walter Lowrie Papers, Manuscripts Division of the Department of Rare Books and Special Collections, Princeton University Library.

2. Carl R. Pritchett to Walter Lowrie, 12 Sept. 1945, Lowrie Papers, Princeton University.

3. Otto Kraushaar, "Kierkegaard in English," *Journal of Philosophy* 39 (8 Oct. 1942): 563.

4. W. H. Auden, ed., *The Living Thoughts of Kierkegaard* (1952; Bloomington: Indiana University Press, 1963), 18.

5. W. H. Auden, "A Knight of Doleful Countenance," in *Forewords and Afterwords* (New York: Vintage Books, 1974), 197.

6. W. H. Auden, "A Preface to Kierkegaard," *New Republic* 110 (15 May 1944): 683; Richard Davenport-Hines, *Auden* (New York: Vintage Books, 1999), 202–3.

7. W. H. Auden, *The Age of Anxiety* (New York: Random House, 1946), 97. Hereafter, page citations appear in the text.

8. Auden undoubtedly echoes Heidegger's concept of "thrownness," of the contingent nature of existence. In all probability he would have learned of this concept through discussions with Hannah Arendt.

9. Leonard Bernstein, liner notes for "The Age of Anxiety" (Symphony No. 2), Sony Music CD, 7.

10. Robert Bretall, ed., *A Kierkegaard Anthology* (Princeton: Princeton University Press, 1946), xvii. This volume remains in print.

11. Rollo May, *The Meaning of Anxiety* (New York: Ronald Press, 1950).

12. William March, *The Bad Seed* (1954; Hopewell, N.J.: Ecco Press, 1997), 30.

13. On the expansiveness of America during this era, see James T. Patterson, *Grand Expectations: The United States, 1945–1974* (New York: Oxford University Press, 1994). For the other side of the equation, see William S. Graebner, *The Age of Doubt: American Thought and Culture in the 1940s* (Boston: Twayne, 1991).

14. The responses, which originally appeared in *Partisan Review*, were published as a book, *Religion and the Intellectuals* (New York: Partisan Review Press, 1950), 5.

15. Whittaker Chambers, *Witness* (New York: Random House, 1952), 85.

16. Abbott Gleason, *Totalitarianism: The Inner History of the Cold War* (New York: Oxford University Press, 1995), 3. Gleason does not mention Kierkegaard in his work, although he does note an early essay by Paul Tillich condemning totalitarianism in both Germany and the Soviet Union.

17. Of course, agreement on what constituted responsibility did not occur. Nonetheless, in their discussions these intellectuals followed the Niebuhrian course of development from thinking in terms of "personality" to a view that stressed "responsibility." While on some levels an indication of increased social action, it also had conservative effects as well. See Richard Wightman Fox, "Tragedy, Responsibility, and the American Intellectual, 1925–1950," in *Lewis Mumford: Public Intellectual*, ed. Thomas P. Hughes and Agatha C. Hughes (New York: Oxford University Press, 1990), 328–29.

18. Søren Kierkegaard, *Attack upon "Christendom,"* trans. Walter Lowrie (Princeton: Princeton University Press, 1991), 81–82.

19. Archibald MacLeish, "The Alternative," *Yale Review* 44 (June 1955): 481.

20. C. Wright Mills, "The Powerless People: The Role of the Intellectual in Society," *politics* (Apr. 1944): 68, 69, 71.

21. Irving Howe, "Intellectuals' Flight from Politics: A Discussion of Contemporary Trends," *New International* 13 (Oct. 1947): 241–42, 245. Marxist critics were even more dismissive of Kierkegaard and existentialism. One critic referred to "Auden's mummified existentialist man" as indicative of the dangers of existentialism, in contrast to the socialist power of Maxim Gorky's vision of man. See Samuel Greenberg, "Auden: Poet of Anxiety," *Masses and Mainstream,* June 1948, 50; also V. J. Jerome, *Culture in a Changing World* (New York: New Century, 1947), in which existentialists are labeled "Ideologists for a Dying System" (12–29).

22. Norbert Guterman, "Neither-Nor," *Partisan Review* 10 (Mar. Apr. 1943): 134–42, quotation at 138. Hereafter, page citations appear in the text. "A dreadful article . . . hostile, not entirely devoid of insight," in the estimation of Walter Lowrie's disciple, the Reverend Howard A. Johnson. Johnson to Walter Lowrie, 30 Jan. 1945, Lowrie Papers, Princeton University.

23. Otto Kraushaar, "Kierkegaard in English," *Journal of Philosophy* 39 (8 and 22 Oct. 1942): 561–82, 589–607. Hereafter, page citations appear in the text.

24. Kraushaar to Walter Lowrie, 21 Dec. 1942, Lowrie Papers, Princeton University.

25. While existentialism was valuable in the critique of totalitarianism, the case of Heidegger's Nazism clouds the picture considerably.

26. Søren Kierkegaard, *The Present Age,* trans. Alexander Dru (London: Oxford University Press, 1940), 3. Hereafter, page citations appear in the text.

27. Julius Seelye Bixler, "The Contribution of *Existenz-Philosophie,*" *Harvard Theological Review* 33 (Jan. 1948): 47–48. Other philosophers of the late 1940s began to pay attention to Kierkegaard, although they did not focus on the political aspects of his thought. Instead they attempted to incorporate his work into the philosophical canon. Especially important attempts at this are John Wild, "Kierkegaard and Classical Philosophy," *Philosophical Review* 49 (1940): 536–51; Richard McKeon, "The Philosophy of Kierkegaard," *New York Times Book Review* 14 (Nov. 1945): 29–30; James Collins, *The Mind of Kierkegaard* (Chicago: Henry Regnery, 1953); also Hannah Arendt, "Tradition and the Modern Age," *Partisan Review* 21 (Jan. 1954): 65.

28. Peter F. Drucker, "The Unfashionable Kierkegaard," *Sewanee Review* 57 (Oct. 1949): 587. Hereafter, page citations appear in the text.

29. Richard Wightman Fox, *Reinhold Niebuhr: A Biography* (New York: Harper and Row, 1985), 203.

30. Richard Kroner, "The Historical Roots of Niebuhr's Thought," in *Reinhold Niebuhr: His Religious, Social, and Political Thought*, ed. Charles W. Kegley and Robert W. Bretall (New York: Macmillan, 1956), 182–85.

31. Niebuhr's hesitant reformism after the war is criticized strongly in Eugene McCarraher, *Christian Critics: Religion and the Impasse in Modern American Social Thought* (Ithaca: Cornell University Press, 2000), 106–11. Also, for Niebuhr's failings on racial issues, see Carol Polsgrove, *Divided Minds: Intellectuals and the Civil Rights Movement* (New York: Norton, 2001), 42–47.

32. Arthur M. Schlesinger, Jr., *A Life in the Twentieth Century: Innocent Beginnings, 1917–1950* (Boston: Houghton Mifflin, 2000), 250.

33. The spread of such concepts is evident in a collection of essays entitled *The Tragic Vision and Christian Faith*. The volume's editor, Nathan A. Scott, Jr., and others championed Niebuhr's new "moral realism," his passionate pessimism against obdurate optimism. Writers discovered an earlier tragic sensibility, in Hawthorne and Melville, in the religious tragedy of Dostoevsky, and in Kierkegaard's "faith in the tragic world." These writers sought to combine religious faith with Niebuhrian depth. *The Tragic Vision and Christian Faith*, ed. Nathan A. Scott, Jr. (New York: Association Press, 1957).

34. Reinhold Niebuhr, "Intellectual Autobiography," in *Niebuhr: His Religious, Social, and Political Thought*, 10.

35. Reinhold Niebuhr, *The Nature and Destiny of Man* (New York: Charles Scribner's Sons, 1941), 1:182. Hereafter, page citations from vol. 1 appear in the text.

36. Søren Kierkegaard, *The Concept of Dread*, trans. Walter Lowrie (Princeton: Princeton University Press, 1944), 69.

37. Reinhold Niebuhr, "Ten Years That Shook My World," *Christian Century* 56 (Apr. 1939): 545.

38. Reinhold Niebuhr, "Coherence, Incoherence, and Christian Faith," in *Christian Realism and Political Problems* (New York: Charles Scribner's Sons, 1953), 193. The essay originally appeared in the *Journal of Religion* in July 1951.

39. Ibid. Reinhold Niebuhr's brother, Yale theologian H. Richard Niebuhr, was drawn to Kierkegaard as well. Richard had always been fascinated by Karl Barth's theology but never fully embraced it. Richard appreciated Kierkegaard's subjective individualism, his notion that "faith is not something" to be possessed but "a constant struggle, a faith renewed and repeated in the face of repeated doubt," and that Christianity exists as "an affair of living in the constant pain of repentance or in the repetition of repentance day by day." H. Richard Niebuhr, "Sören Kierkegaard," in *Christianity and the Existentialists*, ed. Carl Michalson (New York: Charles Scribner's Sons, 1956), 26, 41. On the theology of Richard Niebuhr, see Richard N. Fox, "H. Richard Niebuhr's Divided Kingdom," *American Quarterly* 42 (Mar. 1990): 93–101; and Fox, "The Niebuhr Brothers and the Liberal Protestant Heritage," in *Religion and Twentieth Century American Intellectual Life*, ed. Michael J. Lacey (Cambridge: Cambridge University Press, 1989), 94–115. Fox convincingly argues that despite their pessimism and chastened spirit, the Niebuhr brothers never rejected the essential tenets of liberal theology.

40. See Lowrie to May, 3 Sept. 1949; Johnson to May, 29 Sept. 1949. The quotation is from Johnson to Lowrie, 12 Sept. 1949, Lowrie Papers, Princeton University.

41. Trained as a psychoanalyst, Fromm was early interested in combining Marxist social analysis with Freudian psychoanalytic theory. Fromm was also steeped in the German existential tradition of philosophy, being concerned with the lived experience and with the condition or Being of man. Erich Fromm, *Escape from Freedom* (New York: Rinehart, 1941), 210.

42. Martin Heidegger, *Being and Time*, trans. John Macquarrie and Edward Robinson (New York: Harper and Row, 1962), 232.

43. May was familiar with an address that Camus had delivered in New York in 1946 and that was reprinted in the journal *Twice a Year*. Albert Camus, "The Human Crisis," in *Civil Liberties and the Arts: Selections from "Twice a Year," 1938–1948*, ed. William Wasserstrom (Syracuse: Syracuse University Press, 1964), 243. May insistently failed to separate fear from anxiety. For instance, while May used Camus to support his characterization of the age, the article from which he quoted made it clear that Camus was referring to fear as the defining characteristic of the time. J. Donald Adams, "Speaking of Books," *New York Times Book Review*, 21 Dec. 1947, 2.

44. May, *Meaning of Anxiety*, 171. Hereafter, page citations appear in the text.

45. Kierkegaard, *Concept of Dread*, 39–41.

46. Ibid., 37.

47. May studied with Tillich at Union Theological Seminary. McCarraher, *Christian Critics*, 120–46.

48. Philip Rieff, *Freud: The Mind of the Moralist* (Chicago: University of Chicago Press, 1979).

49. Herberg to Herschel Matt, 21 Dec. 1947, Herberg Papers, Drew University Archives, Madison, N.J.

50. Rosenzweig was a particularly important figure for Herberg because he had discovered a "third way" between orthodox and modernist Judaism. The political resonance of the notion of a third way, given Herberg's politics in the 1950s, is obvious. Will Herberg, "Rosenzweig's 'Judaism of Personal Existence': A Third Way between Orthodoxy and Modernism," *Commentary* 7 (Dec. 1950): 541–49.

51. John Patrick Diggins speaks, using the terminology of Cardinal Newman and William James, of Herberg as a "twice born soul." Diggins, *Up from Communism: Conservative Odysseys in American Intellectual History* (New York: Harper and Row, 1975), 287.

52. Will Herberg, *Judaism and Modern Man: An Interpretation of Jewish Religion* (New York: Farrar, Straus, and Young, 1951), 3. Hereafter, page citations appear in the text.

53. Will Herberg, *Protestant-Catholic-Jew: An Essay in American Religious Sociology* (Garden City, N.Y.: Doubleday, 1956).

54. Will Herberg, "From Marxism to Judaism: Jewish Belief as a Dynamic of Social Action," *Commentary* 3 (Jan. 1947): 25. Hereafter, page citations appear in the text.

55. Will Herberg, "Personalism against Totalitarianism," *politics* 2 (Dec. 1945): 370.

56. Richard Wightman Fox, "Tragedy, Responsibility, and the American Intellectual, 1925–1950," in *Lewis Mumford: Public Intellectual*, ed. Thomas P. Hughes and Agatha C. Hughes (New York: Oxford University Press, 1990), 323–37.

57. Will Herberg, ed., *Four Existentialist Theologians* (Garden City, N.Y.: Doubleday

Anchor Books, 1958), 3. This volume includes selections from Berdyaev, Buber, Tillich, and Maritain.

58. Lecture notes on Kierkegaard, Herberg Papers, Drew University; also Will Herberg, "The Integrity of the Person," *New Leader* 35 (14 July 1952): 18.

59. Not all Jewish theologians agreed with Herberg on the value of Kierkegaard for contemporary Judaism. See, for example, Milton Steinberg, "Kierkegaard and Judaism," *Menorah Journal* 37 (Spring 1949): 163–80. Nonetheless, Steinberg was supportive of Herberg's overall project. See Herberg, *Judaism and Modern Man*, x.

60. Herberg to Hershey and Gustine [Matt], 30 Apr. 1948, Herberg Papers, Drew University.

61. Will Herberg, "Has Judaism Still Power to Speak? A Religion for an Age of Crisis," *Commentary* 7 (May 1949): 447–57.

62. Milton Steinberg to Dr. Solomon Grayzel, 18 Oct. 1949, Herberg Papers, Drew University. Art critic and New York intellectual Harold Rosenberg was unconvinced by Herberg's belief that Judaism would be of much help to democratic values or rationality. Rosenberg, "Pledged to the Marvelous: An Open Letter to Will Herberg," *Commentary*, Feb. 1947. Herberg's marginalia to this essay accused Rosenberg of "a weird misunderstanding of the Jewish tradition enveloped in clouds of obscurantism—it completely misses what I was trying to say." Herberg Papers, Drew University.

63. Herberg, *Protestant-Catholic-Jew*, 52. Hereafter, page citations appear in the text.

64. His confidence was not always keen. He worried that "direct democracy" threatened stability. See Will Herberg, "Government by Rabble-Rousing," *New Leader* 37 (18 Jan. 1954): 13–16.

65. See Will Herberg, "Riesman's Lonely Man," *Commonweal* 60 (3 Sept. 1954): 538–40.

66. Herberg to Hershey and Gustine [Matt], 7 Dec. 1947, Herberg Papers, Drew University.

67. Indeed, the same claim could be made for Herberg. The allure of existential angst remained real to him, but its danger—how to translate its individuality and passion into something more than relative—remained. Thus, Herberg came to find himself drawn toward natural law doctrine. Burke now replaced Buber as the guide for the perplexed Herberg. On this change of heart and mind, see Will Herberg, "Historicism as Touchstone," *Christian Century* 77 (16 Mar. 1960): 311–13.

68. Will Herberg, "The Religious Stirring on the Campus: A Student Generation 'Accessible to Good,'" *Commentary* 13 (Mar. 1952): 248.

69. On Herberg's animus toward the New Left, see Diggins, *Up from Communism*, 362–65.

70. Harold Bloom, *The American Religion: The Emergence of the Post-Christian Nation* (New York: Simon and Schuster, 1992), 33.

71. Schlesinger acknowledged the power of Chambers's work as autobiography in the American grain and agreed with much of its analysis. But he parted company with Chambers over whether the communists in the government were influential and over whether one needed religion in order to oppose communism. Arthur M. Schlesinger, Jr., "Whittaker Chambers and His 'Witness,'" *Saturday Review of Literature* 35 (24 May 1952): 8–10, 39–41.

72. Arthur M. Schlesinger, Jr., to author, 30 Sept. 1997.

73. Arthur M. Schlesinger, Jr., *The Vital Center: The Politics of Freedom* (New York: Da Capo Press, 1988), 3. Hereafter, page citations appear in the text.

74. Chambers, *Witness*, 6. Hereafter, page citations appear in the text. See also Sam Tanenhaus, *Whittaker Chambers: A Biography* (New York: Random House, 1997).

75. See the unsigned essay by Chambers on Niebuhr, *Time* 51 (8 Mar. 1948): 70–72, 74, 76, 79. Here Chambers reveals his grounding in Niebuhr, Barth, Kierkegaard, and existential, tragic religion. For an earlier piece on the rediscovery of sin among intellectuals, focusing on Niebuhr, see Chambers's essay in *Time* 37 (24 Mar. 1941): 38, 40.

76. I have been unable to locate this particular quotation in Kierkegaard's works, though similar passages on the distance between man and God abound. See, in particular, "But as between God and a human being . . . there is an absolute difference," or "Between God and man, however, there exists an absolute difference, and hence this direct equality is a presumptuous and dizzy thought." Both quotations are from Søren Kierkegaard, *Concluding Unscientific Postscript*, trans. David F. Swenson and Walter Lowrie (Princeton: Princeton University Press, 1941), 369, 439. The passage appears in Chambers on pp. 85, 507, 509, 769. Chambers used part of the same passage in his essay on religion in *Time* 51 (8 Mar. 1948): 71.

77. The tragic sensibility of the New York intellectuals is well captured in Lionel Trilling's fictional rendition of his old friend Whittaker Chambers as Gifford Maxim in *The Middle of the Journey* (1947; New York: Charles Scribner's Sons, 1975). Trilling captured this tragic sensibility when he spoke of the need for liberalism to form an "awareness of complexity and difficulty." Trilling, preface to *The Liberal Imagination* (New York: Viking Press, 1950), xii.

78. In a letter to William F. Buckley, written after publication of *Witness*, Chambers states that he has "sure knowledge" about what God intends for him and certitude about "what God has said to me." In this revealing letter he also states that he has only a single biblical allusion in *Witness*, a reference to "Jonah's words in the belly of the whale, 'Take me up and cast me into the sea, because it is for my sake that this trouble is come upon you.'" The context of this passage is Chambers's despair and decision to commit suicide. Chambers to Buckley, 6 Apr. 1954, in *Odyssey of a Friend: Whittaker Chambers' Letters to William F. Buckley, Jr., 1954–1961*, ed. William F. Buckley, Jr. (New York: G. P. Putnam's Sons, 1969), 61.

79. Schlesinger, "Whittaker Chambers and His 'Witness,'" 41.

80. On the review by Schlesinger, see the discussion in Tanenhaus, *Chambers*, 463–65.

81. Søren Kierkegaard, *Fear and Trembling: A Dialectical Lyric*, trans. Walter Lowrie (Princeton: Princeton University Press, 1941), 118.

82. Of course, for Kierkegaard's Abraham there can only be silence. Communication of the incommensurable is absurd.

83. I do not mean to suggest that the road Chambers traveled was necessary or simply a function of the logic of ideas. As Tanenhaus demonstrates in his biography of Chambers, Chambers was increasingly isolated from and frustrated by McCarthy's tactics. Although he appreciated McCarthy's dedication, he found his tactics to be counterproductive to the cause of anticommunism. In addition, by the early 1950s Chambers was much weakened by the heart problems that would eventually kill him. Tanenhaus, *Chambers*, 443–514.

84. Chambers to Buckley, 5 Aug. 1954, *Odyssey*, 68.

85. Thornton Wilder, "Notes on *The Alcestiad*," in *The Collected Short Plays of Thornton Wilder*, ed. A. Tappan Wilder (New York: Theatre Communications Group, 1998), 2:168.

86. In these concerns Wilder shares a surface similarity with Beckett. But Beckett's landscape is bleaker, less didactic. On Wilder's admiration of Beckett, see David Castronovo, *Thornton Wilder* (New York: Ungar, 1986), 158, n. 7.

87. "The Art of Fiction XVI: Thornton Wilder," interview with Richard H. Goldstone (1957), in *Conversations with Thornton Wilder*, ed. Jackson R. Bryer (Jackson: University Press of Mississippi, 1992), 76.

88. Thornton Wilder, *The Bridge of San Luis Rey* (New York: Harper and Row, 1986), 4. Hereafter, page citations appear in the text.

89. Wilder, "Notes toward *The Emporium*," in *Collected Shorter Plays*, 123. In 1953 he writes of the play, "It was going on a road all too moralizing and didactic."

90. "A 'European in the New World': A Conversation with Thornton Wilder," by Georg Wagner, in *Conversations*, 59. Moreover, he was something of a Neoplatonist as well: "One can only belong to that which is not threatened with extinction." Wilder, "Notes toward *The Emporium*, 126.

91. Wilder, preface to *Three Plays* (New York: Harper and Row, 1957), xii. The texts to his plays *Our Town* and *The Skin of Our Teeth* are contained in this volume. Hereafter, page citations appear in the text.

92. They are less anguished than, for instance, the characters in Sartre's play *No Exit*.

93. Wilder believed the interpretation of his plays and novels to be open. "Many thank me for the 'comfort' they found in the last act of *Our Town;* others tell me that it is a desolating picture of our limitation to 'realize' life—almost too sad to endure." The same distribution of opinion, he argued, applied to *The Bridge*. While both elements exist in the novels and plays, the endlessly hearty optimism of Wilder pushes aside the agony, leaving it on a surface level of engagement. "The Art of Fiction," in *Conversations*, 73.

94. *The Journals of Thornton Wilder, 1939–1961*, ed. Donald Gallup (New Haven: Yale University Press, 1985), 1, 51, 65.

95. Ibid., 3 Mar. 1950, 65.

96. Wilder self-consciously attempted to instill existential, specifically Kierkegaardian content into a host of later novels and plays. His *Ides of March* (1948) presents Julius Caesar as an existential hero grappling with the reality of God and the meaning of life and death. Caesar comes to the conclusion, just before his death, that "where there is an unknowable there is promise." Wilder, *The Ides of March* (New York: Harper and Row, 1948), 239. Existential themes are predominant in other plays as well, such as *The Alcestiad*. Perhaps the play that was intended to be most existential, to bring together Kafka's sense of the unknowable with Kierkegaardian notions of repetition and of the stages of life, was *The Emporium*. Despite working and reworking this play for years, Wilder was unable to complete it. Both it and *The Alcestiad* are found in *The Collected Short Plays of Thornton Wilder*.

97. Wilder, *Collected Short Plays*, 177.

98. Harrington's reading of Kierkegaard helped return him to the fold of the Catholic church, albeit for only a short time. Yet he retained both his politics and his

enthusiasm for Kierkegaard. On Harrington and Kierkegaard, see the excellent biography by Maurice Isserman, *The Other American: The Life of Michael Harrington* (New York: Public Affairs, 2000), 66, 69. Harrington was drawn to Kierkegaard's rejection of systems and to his passionate emphasis on paradox. Michael Harrington, "An Examination of Greatness," *Commonweal* 59 (18 Dec. 1953): 289–90.

99. April Kingsley, *The Turning Point: The Abstract Expressionists and the Transformation of American Art* (New York: Simon and Schuster, 1992), 76.

100. *Barnett Newman: Selected Writings and Interviews*, ed. John P. O'Neill (New York: Alfred A. Knopf, 1990), 159. Hereafter, page citations appear in the text.

101. On Rothko and Nietzsche, see James B. Breslin, *Mark Rothko: A Biography* (Chicago: University of Chicago Press, 1993), 357.

102. Morton Feldman, "After Modernism," *Art in America* 59 (Nov.–Dec. 1971): 72.

103. Dore Ashton, *About Rothko* (New York: Da Capo Press, 1996), 144–45.

104. Quoted in Breslin, *Rothko*, 392.

105. Ibid., 393.

106. Paul Tillich, *On the Boundary: An Autobiographical Sketch* (New York: Charles Scribner's Sons, 1966), 56.

107. Paul Tillich, *The Shaking of the Foundations* (London: SCM Press, 1949), 181.

108. Paul Tillich, *The Courage to Be* (New Haven: Yale University Press, 1952), 150–51, 154. Hereafter, page citations appear in the text.

109. Martin E. Marty, *Modern American Religion: Under God, Indivisible, 1941–1960* (Chicago: University of Chicago Press, 1996), 3:351.

110. Fox, *Niebuhr*, 258.

111. John Updike is another novelist of this period who engaged Kierkegaard. His work, especially his tetralogy of novels about Rabbit Angstrom (angst), emphasizes the journey of a Knight of Faith, but without registering the despair in Kierkegaardian tones. On Updike's Kierkegaardian fiction, see Marshall Boswell, *John Updike's Rabbit Tetralogy: Mastered Irony in Motion* (Columbia: University of Missouri Press, 2001).

112. Walker Percy, "The Man on the Train" (1956), in *The Message in the Bottle* (New York: Farrar, Straus, and Giroux, 1980), 85.

113. Walker Percy, *The Moviegoer* (New York: Alfred A. Knopf, 1961).

114. Out of the abyss—out of his tuberculosis confinement, frustration with his chosen career of physician, and general existential malaise—Percy opted for the order and commitment of Catholicism. His friend Shelby Foote, upon hearing of Percy's desire to convert, exclaimed, "Ours is a mind in full intellectual retreat." Quoted in Jay Tolson, *Pilgrim in Ruins: A Life of Walker Percy* (New York: Simon and Schuster, 1992), 190–91.

Five The Vogue of French Existentialism

Portions of this chapter, now revised, first appeared as "French Existentialism and American Popular Culture, 1945–1948," *The Historian* 61 (Winter 1999): 327–40.

1. René König, *A La Mode: On the Social Psychology of Fashion*, trans. F. Bradley, introduction by Tom Wolfe (1971; New York: Seabury Press, 1973), 47.

2. Gilles Lipovetsky, *The Empire of Fashion: Dressing Modern Democracy*, trans. Catherine Porter (Princeton: Princeton University Press, 1994), 15.

3. Typical of such remarks is Richard McKeon, "The Philosophy of Kierkegaard," *New York Times Book Review*, 25 Nov. 1945, 1.

4. Popularizer of existentialism Walter Kaufmann posited the progression of existentialism from fashion to academy to general audience. He did not, however, believe that existentialism would progress to the point of influencing serious American fiction and thought. Kaufmann, "The Reception of Existentialism in the United States," *Salmagundi*, no. 10–11 (Fall 1969–Winter 1970): 92–93.

5. Pierre Bourdieu, *Distinction: A Social Critique of the Judgement of Taste*, trans. Richard Nice (Cambridge: Harvard University Press, 1984).

6. Hans Robert Jauss, *Toward an Aesthetic of Reception*, trans. Timothy Bahti (Minneapolis: University of Minnesota Press, 1985), 24.

7. On the middle-class politics of the *New Yorker*, see Mary F. Corey, *The World through a Monocle: The "New Yorker" at Midcentury* (Cambridge: Harvard University Press, 1999).

8. Alice Kaplan, *French Lessons: A Memoir* (Chicago: University of Chicago Press, 1993), 138.

9. James T. Patterson, *Grand Expectations: The United States, 1945–1974* (New York: Oxford University Press, 1996).

10. Anna Boschetti, *The Intellectual Enterprise: Sartre and "Les Temps Modernes,"* trans. Richard C. McCleary (Evanston: Northwestern University Press, 1988).

11. Even among philosophers, an accounting with Sartrean existentialism was slow to come, in part because of the paucity of translations of his work prior to 1956, but also because of Sartre's blending of philosophical and literary concerns. On the reception of Sartre among American philosophers, see Ann Fulton, *Apostles of Sartre: Existentialism in America, 1945–1963* (Evanston: Northwestern University Press, 1999).

12. Jean-Paul Sartre, "Paris Alive: The Republic of Silence," *Atlantic Monthly* 174 (Dec. 1944): 39–40. Hereafter, page citations appear in the text.

13. Jean-Paul Sartre, "The New Writing in France: The Resistance 'Taught That Literature Is No Fancy Activity Independent of Politics,'" *Vogue* 105 (July 1945): 85. Hereafter, page citations appear in the text.

14. "Portraits of Paris," *Vogue* 107 (June 1946): 156–62, 222–24. Hereafter, page citations appear in the text.

15. Simone de Beauvoir, "Strictly Personal," trans. Malcolm Cowley, *Harper's Bazaar* 80 (Jan. 1946): 113, 158, 160. Hereafter, page citations appear in the text.

16. Beauvoir's essay was widely disseminated. A piece in *Time* magazine opened by announcing that Sartre "the literary lion of Paris bounced into Manhattan last week" and then proceeded, borrowing material from Beauvoir's essay, to tell American readers about his eating and other personal habits. "Existentialism," *Time* 48 (28 Jan. 1946): 28–29.

17. Janet Flanner, "Paris Journal" for 5 Dec. 1945, in Janet Flanner, *Paris Journal, 1944–1965*, ed. William Shawn (New York: Atheneum, 1965), 49.

18. "Existentialism," *Time*, 29.

19. "Man in a Vacuum," *Time* 47 (20 May 1946): 93.

20. Clement Greenberg, "Jean Dubuffet and French Existentialism," *Nation*, 13 July

1946, reprinted in *The Collected Essays and Criticism of Clement Greenberg: Arrogant Purpose, 1945–1949*, ed. John O'Brien (Chicago: University of Chicago Press, 1986), 91–92.

21. J. Alvarez del Vayo, "Politics and the Intellectual," *Nation* 163 (28 Sept. 1946): 346.

22. Arthur M. Schlesinger, Jr., *The Vital Center: The Politics of Freedom* (New York: Da Capo Press, 1988), 52.

23. Jean-Paul Sartre, "Forgers of Myth," *Theatre Arts* 30 (June 1946): 324–34; Sartre, "American Novelists in French Eyes," *Atlantic* 178 (Aug. 1946): 114–18; Simone de Beauvoir, "Eye for Eye," *politics* 4 (July–Aug. 1947): 134–40. At the conclusion of this essay, translated by Mary McCarthy, readers interested in a fuller interpretation of existentialism were referred in an advertisement to William Barrett's pamphlet "What Is Existentialism?" available from the *Partisan Review Pamphlet Series* for fifty cents a copy.

24. Bernard Frechtman, introduction to *Existentialism* (New York: Philosophical Library, 1947), 1–2.

25. Andrew Ross, *No Respect: Intellectuals and Popular Culture* (New York: Routledge, 1989).

26. Louis Bromfield, "The Triumph of the Egghead," *Freeman* 3 (1 Dec. 1952): 158.

27. George Cotkin, "'The Tragic Predicament': Postwar American Intellectuals, Acceptance, and Mass Culture," in *Intellectuals in Politics: From the Dreyfus Affair to Salman Rushdie*, ed. Jeremy Jennings and Anthony Kemp-Welch (London: Routledge, 1997), 263; "What Is the American Character?" *Time* 64 (22 Sept. 1954): 24–25.

28. On the *Playboy* ideal in the 1950s, see Barbara Ehrenreich, *The Hearts of Men: American Dreams and the Flight from Commitment* (New York: Doubleday, 1983), 42–51.

29. "Existentialism," *Time*, 28–29.

30. Bernard Frizell, "Existentialism," *Life* 20 (17 June 1946): 60.

31. John L. Brown, "Chief Prophet of the Existentialists: Sartre of the Left Bank Has a Philosophy That Provokes Both Sermons and Fistfights," *New York Times Magazine*, 2 Feb. 1947, 20.

32. Ibid., 21, 52.

33. Flanner, "Paris Journal" for 5 Dec. 1945, 49.

34. "No Exit," *Theatre Arts* 31 (Jan. 1947): 16.

35. "Existentialism," *Time*, 29.

36. "Man in a Vacuum," *Time* 47 (20 May 1946): 92–93. A very negative review of Camus, critical of his bleak rendition of the human condition, appeared as "The Eternal Rock Pusher," *Newsweek* 27 (15 Apr. 1946): 97–99.

37. "*Absurdiste*," *New Yorker* 22 (20 Apr. 1946): 22–23.

38. Frizell, "Existentialism," *Life*, 60, 62.

39. Ibid., 59.

40. "Existentialism," *Time*, 29.

41. "Pursuit of Wisdom," *Time* 18 (2 Dec. 1946): 31.

42. Paul F. Jennings, "Thingness of Things," *New York Times Magazine*, 13 June 1948, 19–20.

43. Norman Sak, "Letter to the Editor," *New York Times Magazine,* 27 June 1948, 4.

44. Delmore Schwartz, "Does Existentialism Still Exist?" *Partisan Review* 12 (Dec. 1948): 1361.

Six New York Intellectuals and French Existentialists

1. McCarthy quoted in Carol Brightman, *Writing Dangerously: Mary McCarthy and Her World* (New York: Clarkson Potter, 1992), 329.

2. Clement Greenberg, "Jean Dubuffet and French Existentialism" (13 July 1946), in *Clement Greenberg: The Collected Essays and Criticism,* vol. 2, *Arrogant Purpose, 1945–1949* (Chicago: University of Chicago Press, 1988), 92.

3. On the "refiguration" of intellectual life in the city, see Thomas Bender, *New York Intellect* (New York: Alfred A. Knopf, 1987), 328f.

4. Anatole Broyard, *Kafka Was the Rage: A Greenwich Village Memoir* (New York: Carol Southern Books, 1993), vii.

5. Dan Wakefield, *New York in the 50s* (Boston: Houghton Mifflin, 1992), 116–17.

6. Barnett Newman, "The Plasmic Image," in *Barnett Newman: Selected Writings and Interviews,* ed. John P. O'Neill (New York: Alfred A. Knopf, 1990), 150.

7. Arthur M. Schlesinger, Jr., *The Vital Center: The Politics of Freedom* (1949; New York: Da Capo Press, 1988), xx.

8. Richard Wightman Fox, "Tragedy, Responsibility, and the American Intellectual," in *Lewis Mumford, Public Intellectual,* ed. Thomas P. Hughes and Agatha C. Hughes (New York: Oxford University Press, 1990), 323–37.

9. At the same time, the work of Dostoevsky also became popular with the New York intellectuals and was fitted into an existentialist framework. For example, according to William Phillips, Dostoevsky's system of ideas was "morbid and personal . . . a part of what we can call the modern consciousness." The irrationalism in Dostoevsky, Nietzsche, and Kierkegaard represented an existentialist attempt "to come to grips with man's immediate experience, with his inner writhings and the inescapable presence of death, and to bring man into the orbit of mankind by discovering the more moral or human side of the individual." Phillips, "Dostoevsky's Underground Man," *Partisan Review* 13 (1946): 537.

10. Leslie Fiedler, contribution to the symposium "The State of American Writing," *Partisan Review* 15 (Aug. 1948): 872.

11. James Burnham, "Observations on Kafka," *Partisan Review* 14 (Mar.–Apr. 1947): 192. Such themes would be made available to New York intellectuals in the volume of essays entitled *The Kafka Problem,* ed. Angel Flores (New York: New Directions, 1946).

12. Philip Rahv, "An Introduction to Kafka" (1952), in *Essays on Literature and Politics, 1932–1972,* ed. Arabel J. Porter and Andrew J. Dvosin (Boston: Houghton Mifflin, 1978), 252. Also Rahv, "The Death of Ivan Ilyich and Joseph K.," in *Image and Idea: Fourteen Essays on Literary Themes* (Norfolk, Conn.: New Directions, 1949), 111–27. Not all agreed with the celebration of Kafka. Critic Edmund Wilson stated that Kafka "has left us . . . the half-expressed gasp of a self-doubting soul trampled under. I do not see how one can possibly take him for either a great artist or a moral guide." Wilson, "A Dissenting Opinion on Kafka," in *Classics and Commercials* (1947; New York: Farrar, Straus, 1950), 383, 385, 392.

13. William Barrett, *The Truants: Adventures among the Intellectuals* (Garden City, N.Y.: Anchor Press/Doubleday, 1982), 127.

14. Rahv, "Death of Ivan Ilyich and Joseph K.," 126–27.

15. Daniel Bell, *The End of Ideology: On the Exhaustion of Political Ideas in the Fifties* (New York: Free Press, 1962), 300.

16. Irving Howe, *A Margin of Hope: An Intellectual Autobiography* (New York: Harcourt, Brace, Jovanovich, 1982), 161; Mark Krupnick, "The Two Worlds of Cultural Criticism," in *Criticism in the University,* ed. Gerald Graff and Reginald Gibbons (Evanston: Northwestern University Press, 1985), 160.

17. Ann Fulton, *Apostles of Sartre: Existentialism in America, 1945–1963* (Evanston: Northwestern University Press, 1999).

18. Simone de Beauvoir, *Force of Circumstance,* trans. Richard Howard (New York: G. P. Putnam's Sons, 1964), 17.

19. Jean-Paul Sartre, "Paris Alive: The Republic of Silence," *Atlantic Monthly* 174 (Dec. 1944): 40.

20. "De Gaulle Foes Paid by U.S., Paris Is Told," *New York Times,* 25 Jan. 1945, 3; "M. Sartre Explains Article," *New York Times,* 1 Feb. 1945, 22.

21. Annie Cohen-Solal, *Sartre: A Life,* trans. Anna Cancogni (New York: Pantheon, 1987), 234–44; Ronald Hayman, *Sartre: A Life* (New York: Simon and Schuster, 1987), 227–31.

22. *Time* 48 (28 Jan. 1946): 28.

23. Barrett, *Truants,* 114.

24. Cohen-Solal, *Sartre,* 276–77.

25. William Phillips, *A Partisan View: Five Decades of the Literary Life* (New York: Stein and Day, 1983), 131.

26. Lionel Abel, "Metaphysical Stalinism: A Study of Sartre's 'Critique of Dialectical Reason,'" *Dissent* 8 (Spring 1961): 137–52.

27. J. Alvarez del Vayo, "Politics and the Intellectual," *Nation* 163 (28 Sept. 1946): 348.

28. V. J. Jerome, *Culture in a Changing World: A Marxist Approach* (New York: New Century, 1947), 17, 19. I wish to thank Richard Simon for drawing my attention to this polemic.

29. Marticia Sawin, *Surrealism in Exile and the Beginning of the New York School* (Cambridge: MIT Press, 1995), 376.

30. Quoted in ibid., 375.

31. Jean-Philippe Mathy, *Extrême-Occident: French Intellectuals and America* (Chicago: University of Chicago Press, 1993), 141; Renate Peters, "From Illusion to Disillusion: Sartre's Views of America," *Canadian Review of American Studies* 21 (Fall 1990): 173–82.

32. Jean-Paul Sartre, "A European Declaration of Independence: French Culture Is Doomed, Unless—," *Commentary* 9 (Jan. 1950): 409, 412, 413.

33. "The Talk of the Town: Notes and Comment," *New Yorker* 23 (22 Feb. 1947): 19–20. For her trip to the United States, see Deirdre Bair, *Simone de Beauvoir: A Biography* (New York: Summit Books, 1990), 330–78.

34. On Beauvoir's love for Algren, see *A Transatlantic Love Affair: Letters to Nelson Algren* (New York: New Press, 1998).

35. Phillips, *Partisan View,* 126–27.

36. Barrett, *Truants*, 116.
37. Phillips, *Partisan View*, 128. Mary McCarthy later claimed that Beauvoir was "riding on Sartre's coattails." Quoted in Frances Kiernan, *Seeing Mary Plain: A Life of Mary McCarthy* (New York: W. W. Norton, 2000), 274.
38. Simone de Beauvoir, "An Existentialist Looks at America," *New York Times Magazine*, 25 May 1947, 13, 51, 52.
39. Simone de Beauvoir, *America Day by Day* (New York: Grove Press, 1953), 41, 42, 57.
40. Phillips, *Partisan View*, 115.
41. Quotations from Mary McCarthy, "America the Beautiful" and "Mlle. Gulliver en Amerique," in *On the Contrary* (New York: Farrar, Straus, and Cudahy, 1961), 25–26.
42. Dorothy Norman, *Encounters: A Memoir* (San Diego: Harcourt, Brace, Jovanovich, 1987), 191.
43. Hannah Arendt to Karl Jaspers, 11 Nov. 1946, in *Hannah Arendt, Karl Jaspers Correspondence, 1926–1969*, ed. Lotte Kohler and Hans Saner, trans. Robert and Rita Kimber (New York: Harcourt, Brace, Jovanovich, 1992), 66.
44. Phillips, *Partisan View*, 132.
45. Barrett, *Truants*, 118, 117.
46. Albert Camus, "The Human Crisis," trans. Lionel Abel, *Twice a Year*, no. 14–15 (Fall–Winter 1946–47): 19–33. Hereafter, page citations appear in the text.
47. Beauvoir, *Force*, 107; also Patrick McCarthy, *Camus* (New York: Random House, 1982), 215–16.
48. Dwight Macdonald, "The Root Is Man," appearing in two parts in *politics* 3 (Apr. 1946): 97–115 and (July 1946): 194–216. Hereafter, page citations appear in the text. On this essay's strengths and weaknesses, see Gregory D. Sumner, *Dwight Macdonald and the "politics" Circle* (Ithaca: Cornell University Press, 1996), 150–58.
49. Nicola Chiaromonte, a close friend of Camus's, influenced Macdonald on this point. See Chiaromonte, "Albert Camus and Moderation," *Partisan Review* 15 (Oct. 1948): 1112–45.
50. Sumner, *Dwight Macdonald*, 204–10.
51. Quoted in Michael Wreszin, *A Rebel in Defense of Tradition: The Life and "politics" of Dwight Macdonald* (New York: Basic Books, 1994), 315.
52. Harvey Teres, *Renewing the Left: Politics, Imagination, and the New York Intellectuals* (New York: Oxford University Press, 1996), 148–55.
53. Jean-Paul Sartre, "American Novelists in French Eyes," trans. Evelyn de Solis, *Atlantic* 178 (Aug. 1946): 117–18; also Renate Peters, "From Illusion to Disillusion: Sartre's Views of America," *Canadian Review of American Studies* 21 (Fall 1990): 173–82.
54. Sartre, "American Novelists in French Eyes," 118.
55. Beauvoir, *America Day by Day*, 31.
56. Lionel Trilling, "Reality in America" (1940), in *The Moral Obligation to Be Intelligent*, ed. Leon Wieseltier (New York: Farrar, Straus, and Giroux, 2000), 72–73.
57. Rahv, "Attitudes toward Henry James," in *Image and Idea*, 70.
58. Rahv, "The Cult of Experience in American Writing," in ibid., 6–21; also Rahv, "Paleface and Redskin," in ibid., 1–5.

59. Teres, *Renewing the Left,* 157.

60. Elizabeth Hardwick, "Fiction Chronicle," *Partisan Review* 14 (Sept.–Oct. 1947): 533–35. Hardwick published a similarly unenthusiastic review of Sartre's *The Reprieve* in *Partisan Review* 15 (Jan. 1948): 112–13.

61. James Burnham, "The Extreme and the Plausible," *Partisan Review* 15 (Sept. 1948): 1020–23.

62. Wilson, "Jean-Paul Sartre," in *Classics and Commercials,* 393–403.

63. William Barrett, "Talent and Career of Jean-Paul Sartre," *Partisan Review* 13 (1946): 245.

64. Ibid., 244.

65. Barrett, *Truants,* 116.

66. Barrett, "Talent and Career," 240–41.

67. William Barrett, "The End of Modern Literature," *Partisan Review* 16 (Sept. 1949): 946.

68. Ibid.

69. Ibid., 949–50.

70. Saul Bellow, "Writers, Intellectuals, Politics: Mainly Reminiscence," in *It All Adds Up: From the Dim Past to the Uncertain Future* (New York: Viking, 1994), 106.

71. Ada Aharoni, "Bellow and Existentialism," *Saul Bellow Journal* 2 (Spring–Summer 1983): 42–54. Richard Lehan correctly argues for "an affinity of mind" between Bellow and the French existentialists. See Lehan, *A Dangerous Crossing: French Literary Existentialism and the Modern American Novel* (Carbondale: Southern Illinois University Press, 1973), 80.

72. Philip Rahv, "Saul Bellow's Progress," in *Literature and the Sixth Sense* (New York: Houghton Mifflin, 1969), 395.

73. Aharoni, "Bellow," 44; Bellow, "Writers, Intellectuals, Politics," 106–7.

74. Saul Bellow, *Mr. Sammler's Planet* (New York: Viking Press, 1970), 189.

75. Lionel Trilling, *The Middle of the Journey* (New York: Charles Scribner's Sons, 1947).

76. Quoted in Irving Sandler, *The Triumph of American Painting: A History of Abstract Expressionism* (New York: Harper and Row, 1970), 98.

77. Harold Rosenberg, "Parable of American Painting," in *The Tradition of the New* (Chicago: University of Chicago Press, 1960), 15, 21.

78. Rahv, "Paleface and Redskin," 1–6.

79. Harold Rosenberg, "The Stages: Geography of Action," in *Act and the Actor: Making the Self* (New York: Meridian Books, 1972), 75. The essay was originally published in *Possibilities* (1947).

80. Rosenberg, "Notes and Acknowledgments," in ibid., 206. It is also quite possible, speaking of the anxiety of influence, that Rosenberg's ideas, which Sartre found so intriguing, were actually culled by Rosenberg from critic Kenneth Burke. For Burke on action and actor, see his *A Grammar of Motives* (1945; Berkeley: University of California Press, 1969).

81. Ronald Hayman, *Sartre: A Biography* (New York: Simon and Schuster, 1987), 256.

82. Cohen-Solal, *Sartre,* 317, 338–39.

83. Rosenberg, "Character Change and the Drama" (1932), in *Tradition of the New,* 146–47. Hereafter, page citations appear in the text.

84. Rosenberg, "Stages," 76–77. Hereafter, page citations appear in the text.

85. Jean-Paul Sartre, *Dirty Hands,* in *No Exit and Three Other Plays* (New York: Vintage, 1957), 187. Hereafter, page citations appear in the text.

86. Rosenberg, "The American Action Painters," in *Tradition of the New,* 25. Hereafter, page citations appear in the text.

87. Robert Goodnough, "Pollock Paints a Picture," *Art News* 50 (May 1951): 61.

88. Sandler, *Triumph of American Painting,* 111.

89. On the danger of becoming, see "What Is Art? An Interview by Melvin M. Tumin with Harold Rosenberg," in Harold Rosenberg, *The Case of the Baffled Radical* (Chicago: University of Chicago Press, 1976), 236–37.

90. Harold Rosenberg, "Action Painting: Crisis and Distortion," in *The Anxious Object: Art Today and Its Audience* (New York: Horizon Press, 1964), 38. Hereafter, page citations appear in the text.

91. Susan Sontag, "Notes on 'Camp,'" in *Against Interpretation* (New York: Dell, 1966), 287.

Seven The Canon of Existentialism

1. Especially helpful in this regard, in terms of the role that gender has played in the development of the American literary canon, is Jane Tompkins, *Sensational Designs: The Cultural Work of American Fiction* (New York: Oxford University Press, 1985). Also John Guillory, *Cultural Capital: The Problem of Literary Canon Formation* (Chicago: University of Chicago Press, 1993).

2. On the cultural politics of the existential philosophical and literary scene in France in this period for existentialism, see Anna Boschetti, *The Intellectual Enterprise: Sartre and "Les Temps Modernes,"* trans. Richard C. McCleary (Evanston: Northwestern University Press, 1988).

3. Ann Fulton, *Apostles of Sartre: Existentialism in America, 1945–1963* (Evanston: Northwestern University Press, 1999).

4. Alfred Kazin, *New York Jew* (New York: Alfred A. Knopf, 1978), 195.

5. Irving Howe, *A Margin of Hope: An Intellectual Autobiography* (San Diego: Harcourt, Brace, Jovanovich, 1982), 270.

6. Elisabeth Young-Bruehl, *Hannah Arendt: For Love of the World* (New Haven: Yale University Press, 1984), 220–21.

7. "What Is Existenz Philosophy?" *Partisan Review* 13 (1946): 34–56; "French Existentialism," *Nation* 162 (23 Feb. 1946): 226–28. The two essays have been reprinted, with changes, in Jerome Kohn, ed., *Arendt: Essays in Understanding, 1930–1954* (New York: Harcourt, Brace, 1994), 163–93. The original version will be cited here, with page citations hereafter appearing in the text.

8. Paul Kecskemeti, "Fascination and Philosophy," *Partisan Review* 15 (May 1948): 596.

9. On the role of women in the popularization of existentialism, see Fulton, *Apostles of Sartre,* 78–80. In addition to Arendt, Grene, and Barnes, Catharine Rau and Mary Coolidge played important roles.

10. Marjorie Grene, "In and on Friendship," in *Human Nature and Natural Knowledge: Essays Presented to Marjorie Grene on the Occasion of Her Seventy-fifth Birthday,* ed. Alan Donagan, Anthony Perovich, Jr., and Michael V. Wedin (Dordrecht: D. Reidel, 1986), 360. Hereafter, page citations appear in the text.

11. Marjorie Grene, *A Philosophical Testament* (Chicago: Open Court, 1995), 5.

12. Marjorie Grene, *Dreadful Freedom* (Chicago: University of Chicago Press, 1948), 149.

13. Ibid., 139.

14. Although Kierkegaard's project was devoted to a critique of the rationalism of Hegel, Grene attempted to demonstrate how Kierkegaard in many ways failed to sufficiently jettison the Hegelian mode of philosophy. Ibid., 40. Hereafter, page citations appear in the text.

15. Also in this vein, see Roger L. Shinn, *The Existentialist Posture: A Christian Look at Its Meaning, Impact, Values, Dangers* (New York: Association Press, 1959). This work, although published later than the ones discussed here, was sponsored by the National Board of the Young Men's Christian Association. In this accessible, sometimes witty work, Shinn, a well-known professor of theology at Union Theological Seminary, concluded that existentialism's greatest value consisted in its sense that "there can be no personal living and certainly no Christianity that are not existential." As to specific existential concepts, Shinn accepted some, demurred on others. Shinn, *Existentialist Posture*, 114–22. It is useful to keep in mind that YMCAs, as Doug Rossinow demonstrates, played a major role in the dissemination and discussion of existentialism connected with the birth of a New Left. See Rossinow, *The Politics of Authenticity: Liberalism, Christianity, and the New Left in America* (New York: Columbia University Press, 1998).

16. In an important article on existentialism, Charles Hendel criticized existentialism for its lack of consistency and movement, caught up as it was in the simple dichotomy between essence and existence. He worried that existentialism might be transformed into "part of a psycho-therapeutic process directed by esoteric practitioners." While existentialism had much to offer in terms of art, ethical imperatives, and even self-awareness, it must attempt "the *philosophic* task of justifying its knowledge and truth." Hendel, "The Subjective as a Problem: An Essay in Criticism of Naturalistic and Existential Philosophies," *Philosophical Review* 62 (July 1953): 352–53.

17. James Collins, *The Existentialists: A Critical Study* (Chicago: Henry Regnery, 1952), 188–224.

18. Kurt F. Reinhardt, *The Existentialist Revolt* (1952; rev. ed. New York: Frederick Ungar 1962), 228–43. Hereafter, page citations appear in the text.

19. One Stanford student recalled forty years later how deeply Reinhardt "despised" and "misread" Nietzsche. John Bailiff to author, e-mail communication, 12 Dec. 1996.

20. Helmut Kuhn, *Encounter with Nothingness: An Essay on Existentialism* (Hinsdale, Ill.: Henry Regnery, 1949), x–xi. Hereafter, page citations appear in the text.

21. Collins, *Existentialists*, 21. Hereafter, page citations appear in the text.

22. Ralph Harper, *Existentialism: A Theory of Man* (Cambridge: Harvard University Press, 1948), vii. Hereafter, page citations appear in the text. Harper retained his interest in existentialism. See Harper, *The Seventh Solitude: Metaphysical Homelessness in Kierkegaard, Dostoevsky, and Nietzsche* (Baltimore: Johns Hopkins Press, 1965), and *The Existential Experience* (Baltimore: Johns Hopkins University Press, 1972).

23. Fulton, *Apostles of Sartre,* 48–82.

24. John Wild, *The Challenge of Existentialism* (Bloomington: Indiana University Press, 1955). The book was based on lectures that Wild had delivered in 1953. Hereafter, page citations appear in the text.

25. Not surprisingly, as we shall see, William Barrett shared Wild's animus against the philosophical profession and also worried about the inability of philosophers to respond to the ideological challenge of totalitarian modes of thought. See Barrett's review of Wild, "Wanted: New Philosophers," *Saturday Review of Literature* 39 (18 May 1956): 34; also, in a similar vein, T. V. Smith, "A Lively Philosophy That Recovers Solid Ground," *New York Times Book Review,* 22 July 1956, 7.

26. Roger Soder to author, 18 Nov. 1996, personal communication.

27. William Barrett, *Irrational Man: A Study in Existential Philosophy* (Garden City, N.Y.: Doubleday, 1958), 4. Hereafter, page citations appear in the text. John Wild agreed with this view. See Wild, "Recovery of the Sense of Being," *Saturday Review of Literature* 41 (6 Sept. 1958): 19, 38.

28. William Barrett, *What Is Existentialism?* (New York: Partisan Review Press, 1947); reprinted by Grove Press in 1964 with additional material under the same title.

29. As Virginia P. Held noted in a review, "The question for most of us is not whether man *is* rational, but whether he should try to be." Held, "Underneath the Intellect," *New Republic* 139 (27 Oct. 1958): 20.

30. See the review by Charles Frankel, "Reason and Reality," in *New York Times Book Review,* 7 Sept. 1958, 6.

31. After discussing the history of religion briefly, Barrett segued into a chapter, "The Flight from Laputa," that used the characters in Swift's *Gulliver's Travels* who were chained to "the whore of reason" to illustrate the dangers of abstract intellectualism. He then indicated how, in the literature of Dostoevsky and Tolstoy most famously, a revolt against the faith in reason was encoded in the nineteenth century, figuring as early, proto-existentialist expressions.

32. Walter Kaufmann, *Existentialism: From Dostoevsky to Sartre* (Cleveland: Meridian Books, 1956). Hereafter, page citations appear in the text.

33. Gail Finney to author, 27 Nov. 1996.

34. Biographical data on Kaufmann will be found in his *From Shakespeare to Nietzsche* (Garden City, N.Y.: Doubleday, 1961); also Kaufmann, *Nietzsche: Philosopher, Psychologist, Antichrist* (Princeton: Princeton University Press, 1950).

35. Michael Lind, "Where Have You Gone Louis Sullivan? Will America Recover from Its Fifty-Year Bout of Europhilia," *Harper's* 296 (Feb. 1998): 53–59.

36. Barrett, *Irrational Man,* 9.

37. Ibid., 10.

38. Frederick R. Karl and Leo Hamalian, eds., *The Existential Imagination* (New York: Fawcett World Library, 1963). Hereafter, page citations appear in the text.

39. William Spanos, *A Casebook on Existentialism* (New York: Thomas Y. Crowell, 1966).

40. Spanos was probably thinking here of MacLeish's play *JB* (1958), in which Job's trials and tribulations were presented in a modern setting.

41. Maurice Friedman, *The Worlds of Existentialism* (New York: Random House, 1964).

42. Hazel E. Barnes, *The Story I Tell Myself: A Venture in Existentialist Autobiography* (Chicago: University of Chicago Press, 1997), xii. Hereafter, page citations appear in the text.

43. Some of the themes from that course were captured in an early lecture on existentialism that Barnes delivered in 1951, "Existentialism: Positive Contributions." In this address Barnes defended existentialism against Grene and others, finding it not to be nihilistic, ethically vapid, or solipsistic. Instead, she argued, existentialism has "a very definite ethical view, a morality based on self-discovery, self-integrity, a sense of responsibility toward others, and an insistence on freedom as an absolute value." By and large, Barnes would not deviate from this description over her fifty-year career with existentialism. This essay appeared in *Perspectives in Philosophy* (Columbus: Department of Philosophy at the Ohio State University, 1953), 106.

44. Fulton, *Apostles of Sartre,* 84.

45. On the chapter, see my *William James, Public Philosopher* (Baltimore: Johns Hopkins University Press, 1990), 64–72.

46. Hazel E. Barnes, *The Literature of Possibility: A Study in Humanistic Existentialism* (Lincoln: University of Nebraska Press, 1959), 170–71. Barnes did find that Camus and James parted company on religious issues, with James more given to mystical experiences. But at another point in her analysis she recognized that Camus, especially in his early, lyrical pieces on the Mediterranean, approached a mystical perspective. See *Literature of Possibility,* 172, 189.

47. An earlier expression of the connection of James and Sartre is found in Mary Coolidge, "Some Vicissitudes of the Once-Born and of the Twice-Born Man," *Philosophy and Phenomenological Research* 11 (Sept. 1950): 75–87.

48. Hazel E. Barnes, introduction to Jean-Paul Sartre, *Being and Nothingness,* trans. Barnes (New York: Philosophical Library, 1956), x.

49. Hazel E. Barnes, introduction to Jean-Paul Sartre, *Existential Psychoanalysis,* trans. Barnes (New York: Philosophical Library, 1953), 18. This work was a portion of the translation of *Being and Nothingness,* which would be published three years later.

50. Barnes, *Story,* 144.

51. See, for example, Richard Rorty, "Overcoming the Tradition: Heidegger and Dewey," in *Consequences of Pragmatism: Essays, 1972–1980* (Minneapolis: University of Minnesota Press, 1982), 37–59.

52. For the strongest expressions of this view, see Kate Fulbrook and Edward Fulbrook, *Simone de Beauvoir and Jean-Paul Sartre: The Remaking of a Twentieth-Century Legend* (New York: Basic Books, 1994), and Margaret A. Simons, *Beauvoir and "The Second Sex": Feminism, Race, and the Origins of Existentialism* (Lanham, Md.: Rowman and Littlefield, 1999).

53. Barnes, *Literature of Possibility,* 121–22.

54. Simone de Beauvoir, *The Ethics of Ambiguity,* trans. Bernard Frechtman (New York: Citadel Press, 1996), 156.

55. Hazel E. Barnes, *An Existentialist Ethics* (New York: Alfred A. Knopf, 1967), 38, 39.

56. Jean-Paul Sartre, *Existentialism,* trans. Bernard Frechtman (New York: Philosophical Library, 1947), 21, 27. Hereafter, page citations appear in the text.

57. Barnes, *Literature of Possibility,* 81.

58. Barnes, *Existentialist Ethics,* 140. Hereafter, page citations appear in the text.

Eight "Cold Rage": Richard Wright and Ralph Ellison

Portions of this chapter, now revised, first appeared as "Ralph Ellison, Existentialism, and the Blues," *Letterature d'America* 15 (1995): 33–52.

1. Jean-Paul Sartre, *Nausea,* trans. Hayden Carruth (New York: New Directions, 1959), 131. Hereafter, page citations appear in the text.
2. Ralph Ellison, "The Little Man at Chehaw Station," in *Going to the Territory* (New York: Vintage, 1995), 3–38.
3. Arnold Shaw, *Black Popular Music in America* (New York: Schirmer Books, 1986), 86, 128; Lindsay Patterson, comp., *The Negro in Music and Art* (New York: Publishers Inc., 1969), 126.
4. Paul Gilroy, *The Black Atlantic: Modernity and Modern Consciousness* (Cambridge: Harvard University Press, 1993), 149.
5. Wright, journal entry of 12 Feb. 1945, quoted in Michel Fabre, *The Unfinished Quest of Richard Wright,* 2d ed. (Urbana: University of Illinois Press, 1993), 274.
6. Quoted in ibid., 310. As Paul Gilroy puts it, Wright "was not straining to validate African-American experience in their [existentialist authors'] European terms but rather demonstrating how the everyday experience of blacks in the United States enabled them to see with a special clarity of vision—a dreadful objectivity—the same constellation of problems which these existentialist authors had identified in more exalted settings." Gilroy, *Black Atlantic,* 171.
7. Wright, unpublished journal, 5 Aug. 1947, quoted in Michel Fabre, *Richard Wright: Books and Writers* (Jackson: University Press of Mississippi, 1990), 141.
8. Alan Geller, "An Interview with Ralph Ellison," in *The Black American Writer: Fiction,* ed. C. W. E. Bigsby (DeLand, Fla.: Everett/Edwards, 1969), 1:159–60.
9. Ibid., 167.
10. C. L. R. James, "Black Studies and the Contemporary Student," in *At the Rendezvous of Victory: Selected Writings* (London: Allison and Busby, 1984), 196.
11. Constance Webb, *Richard Wright: A Biography* (New York: G. P. Putnam's Sons, 1968), 279–80.
12. James Baldwin, "Everybody's Protest Novel," in *The Price of the Ticket: Collected Nonfiction, 1948–1985* (New York: St. Martin's/Marek, 1985), 33.
13. Geller, "Interview," 167. Ellison's friend Albert Murray agreed. In his own great style Murray wrote, "It was bad enough that the fiction Wright began to turn out during this time was even worse than that of Jean-Paul Sartre. . . . [Much] more important is the fact that for all the down-home signifying and uptown sassiness he put Sartre and Simone de Beauvoir hip to, or maybe precisely because of it, he was unable to keep the ever square but news prone Mister Sartre, the world's fastest academic hip-shooter, from being sucked in on the politically benevolent racist notions of *negritude.*" Murray, *The Omni-Americans: New Perspectives on Black Experience and American Culture* (New York: Outerbridge and Dienstfrey, 1970), 152–53.
14. For Baldwin's classic critique of Wright, see "Everybody's Protest Novel" (1949). For his account of the dispute, see "Alas, Poor Richard" (1952), in *Price of the Ticket,* 278.
15. Ralph Ellison, *Invisible Man* (New York: Modern Library, 1992), 13.
16. Richard Wright, *Black Boy* (New York: Harper and Brothers, 1945), 277.
17. Ellison, "Little Man at Chehaw Station," 12.

18. For material on the Ellison-Wright friendship, see the indispensable work by Michel Fabre, *Unfinished Quest*, 200.

19. Richard Wright, "The Initiates," in *The God That Failed: Six Studies in Communism* (London: Hamish Hamilton, 1950), 133.

20. Ellison, "Remembering Richard Wright," in *Going to the Territory*, 202.

21. William J. Maxwell, *New Negro, Old Left: African-American Writing and Communism between the Wars* (New York: Columbia University Press, 1999); Jerry Gafio Watts, *Heroism and the Black Intellectual: Ralph Ellison, Politics, and Afro-American Intellectual Life* (Chapel Hill: University of North Carolina Press, 1994).

22. J. Saunders Redding, *On Being Negro in America* (Indianapolis: Bobbs-Merrill, 1951), 72.

23. Wright, "Initiates," 140.

24. Granville Hicks, "The Portrait of a Man Searching," *New York Times Book Review*, 22 Mar. 1953, 1.

25. Lloyd Brown, "The Deep Pit," *Masses and Mainstream* 5 (June 1952): 62–64.

26. Wright, journal entry, 7 Sept. 1947, quoted in Fabre, *Unfinished Quest*, 322.

27. Wright, "Initiates," 154.

28. Fyodor Dostoevsky, *Notes from Underground*, trans. Jessie Coulson (London: Penguin Books, 1972), 43.

29. Ellison, *Invisible Man*, xxiii.

30. Ibid., 572.

31. Albert Murray, *The Hero and the Blues* (1973; New York: Vintage Books, 1995), 16.

32. Margaret Walker, *Richard Wright: Daemonic Genius* (New York: Warner Books, 1988), 235–36. Irving Howe perceptively realized (and the same could be said for Ellison), "Wright was an existentialist long before he heard the name for he was committed to the literature of extreme situations both through the pressures of his rage and the gasping hope of an ultimate catharsis." Howe, "Black Boys and Native Sons," *Dissent* 10 (Autumn 1963): 356.

33. Quoted in Fabre, *Books and Writers*, 40.

34. Ibid.

35. Nathan A. Scott, Jr., "Dostoevski—Tragedian of Excursion into Unbelief," in *The Tragic Vision and the Christian Faith*, ed. Scott (New York: Association Press, 1957), 194, 209.

36. Richard Wright, "The Man Who Lived Underground," in *Eight Men* (New York: Thunder's Mouth Press, 1987), 48. On this story see Yoshinobu Hakutani, "Richard Wright's 'The Man Who Lived Underground,' Nihilism, and Zen," *Mississippi Quarterly* 47 (Spring 1994): 201–14.

37. Wright, "Man Who Lived Underground," 69.

38. Fabre, *Unfinished Quest*, 299.

39. Dorothy Norman, *Encounters: A Memoir* (San Diego: Harcourt, Brace, Jovanovich, 1987), 183, 190–92. Norman wrongly recalls asking Wright to take Sartre and Beauvoir to Harlem, where, she is certain, Wright talked about existentialism with them. Alas, while Wright may have accompanied Sartre and Beauvoir to Harlem, it was on separate occasions. Sartre and Beauvoir were never in New York or even in the United States at the same moment.

40. Fabre, *Unfinished Quest*, 320–21; also Michel Fabre, "Richard Wright and the

French Existentialists," *Melus* 5 (June 1978): 39–51. On Wright and Beauvoir, see Margaret A. Simons, "Richard Wright, Simone de Beauvoir, and *The Second Sex*," in *Beauvoir and "The Second Sex": Feminism, Race, and the Origins of Existentialism* (Lanham, Md.: Rowman and Littlefield, 1999), 167–84. As we shall see in chapter 12, Beauvoir's voluntarism often blamed the victim for her oppression. Wright did not make this mistake.

41. See Simone de Beauvoir, *The Second Sex*, trans. H. M. Parshley (1949; New York: Vintage Books, 1974), 335, 776.

42. Michel-Antoine Burnier, *Choice of Action: The French Existentialists and the Political Front Line*, trans. Bernard Murchland (New York: Random House, 1968).

43. For criticisms of Wright and of the novel, see the comments by Arna Bontemps and Saunders Redding in "Reflections on Richard Wright: A Symposium on an Exiled Native Son," in *Anger and Beyond: The Negro Writer in the United States*, ed. Herbert Hill (New York: Harper and Row, 1966), 203, 205, 208–9.

44. Comments by Bontemps and Redding are in ibid., 207, 209.

45. Hicks, "Portrait," 1.

46. Steven Marcus, "The Outsider," review in *Commentary*, in *Richard Wright: Critical Perspectives Past and Present*, ed. Henry Louis Gates, Jr., and K. A. Appiah (New York: Amistad Press, 1993), 37.

47. Michel Fabre, *The World of Richard Wright* (Jackson: University Press of Mississippi, 1985), 172.

48. Maryemma Graham, introduction to *The Outsider* (New York: HarperCollins, 1993), xx.

49. Walker, *Wright: Daemonic Genius*, 230.

50. Journal entry, in Fabre, *Books and Writers*, 24.

51. Wright, *Outsider*, 308, 442.

52. Fabre, *Unfinished Quest*, 333.

53. Beauvoir to Sartre, 4 Mar. 1947, in Simone de Beauvoir, *Letters to Sartre*, trans. Quintin Hoare (New York: Arcade, 1990), 439.

54. Jean-Paul Sartre, *The Chips Are Down*, trans. Louise Varèse (1948; London: Rider, 1951), 125.

55. Wright, *Outsider*, 585.

56. Walker, *Wright: Daemonic Genius*, 211.

57. Wright, *Outsider*, 17, 21. Hereafter, page citations appear in the text.

58. Søren Kierkegaard, "The Seducer's Diary," in *Either/Or*, trans. Howard V. Hong and Edna H. Hong (Princeton: Princeton University Press, 1987), 1:308.

59. Fabre, *Unfinished Quest*, 368; Mae Henderson, "Drama and Denial in *The Outsider*," in *Wright: Critical Perspectives*, 388–408. Wright imagined "Beyond Freedom" as one possible title for his work.

60. Fabre, *Unfinished Quest*, 456; Richard Wright, *White Man, Listen!* (Garden City, N.Y.: Anchor Books, 1964), xvi–xvii.

61. Albert Murray, *Stomping the Blues* (New York: Vintage, 1982); Ralph Ellison, "Richard Wright's Blues" (1945), in *Shadow and Act* (New York: Vintage, 1995), 78–79.

62. Ellison, *Shadow*, 22.

63. Ellison, *Going to the Territory*, 275.

64. Ellison, *Shadow*, 58.

65. William Lyne, "The Signifying Modernist: Ralph Ellison and the Limits of the Double Consciousness," *PMLA* 107 (Mar. 1992): 319–30.

66. Ellison, *Shadow,* 58.

67. Ralph Waldo Emerson, "The Poet" (1844), in *Essays: First and Second Series* (New York: Library of America, 1990), 232.

68. Ellison, *Going to the Territory,* 243.

69. On Malraux's similar inclination to create identities, see Jean-François Lyotard, *Signed, Malraux* (Minneapolis: University of Minnesota Press, 1999). Ellison, *Going to the Territory,* 43.

70. In Geller, "Interview," 159–60, Ellison identified Malraux and Unamuno, rather than Sartre and Camus, as the existentialist writers with whom he would be most inclined to identify himself. He did not elaborate on these choices of literary ancestors, but they are perhaps a function of those writers he encountered in his most formative years. Ellison and his friend Albert Murray worked hard to avoid being reduced to any single perspective. See *Trading Twelves: The Selected Letters of Ralph Ellison and Albert Murray*, ed. Albert Murray and John F. Callahan (New York: Modern Library Original, 2000), 47–48, 111–12.

71. Murray, *Stomping the Blues,* 42.

72. Watts, *Heroism and The Black Intellectual,* 55, 57.

73. Howe, "Black Boys and Native Sons," 363.

74. Joseph Frank, "Ralph Ellison and a Literary 'Ancestor': Dostoevski," in *Speaking for You: The Vision of Ralph Ellison,* ed. Kimberly W. Benston (Washington, D.C.: Howard University Press, 1987), 231–44.

75. Ellison, *Invisible Man,* 572. Hereafter, page citations appear in the text.

76. For an excellent analysis of this chapter, see John S. Wright, "The Conscious Hero and the Rites of Man: Ellison's War," in *New Essays on Invisible Man,* ed. Robert O'Meally (Cambridge: Cambridge University Press, 1988), 157–86.

77. Houston A. Baker, Jr., *Blues, Ideology, and Afro-American Literature: A Vernacular Theory* (Chicago: University of Chicago Press, 1987), 175.

78. Steven Marx, "Beyond Hibernation: Ralph Ellison's Version of *Invisible Man,*" *Black American Literature Forum* 23 (Winter 1989): 715.

79. Henry Louis Gates, Jr., *The Signifying Monkey: A Theory of African-American Literary Criticism* (New York: Oxford University Press, 1988).

80. Pancho Savery, "'Not Like an Arrow, but a Boomerang': Ellison's Existential Blues," in *Approaches to Teaching Ellison's "Invisible Man"* (New York: Modern Language Association, 1989), 70.

81. Cushing Strout, "'An American Negro Idiom': *Invisible Man* and the Politics of Culture," in ibid., 85.

Nine Norman Mailer's Existential Errand

1. Norman Mailer, "Truth and Being; Nothing and Time" (ca. 1962), in *The Presidential Papers* (New York: G.P. Putnam's Sons, 1963), 273.

2. Interview with Charles Monaghan (1971), in *Conversations with Norman Mailer,* ed. J. Michael Lennon (Jackson: University Press of Mississippi, 1988), 192.

3. Norman Mailer, "First Advertisement for Myself," in *Advertisements for Myself* (1959; Cambridge: Harvard University Press, 1992), 17.

4. "Existential Aesthetics," interview with Laura Adams (1975), in *Conversations with Mailer,* 213.

5. Norman Mailer, "Some Dirt in the Talk: A Candid History of an Existential Movie Called *Wild 90,*" *Esquire* 67 (19 Dec. 1967): 194.

6. Mailer, *Presidential Papers,* 26.

7. Ibid., 9.

8. Mary V. Dearborn, *Mailer: A Biography* (Boston: Houghton Mifflin, 1999), 58–60. Dearborn is quite helpful in establishing a host of common themes in the lives and work of Mailer and Sartre. Indeed, "each would come to define the age in a meaningful way" (58).

9. Mailer to the editor, *New York Times Book Review,* 9 Jan. 2000, 4.

10. Norman Mailer, *Existential Errands* (Boston: Little, Brown, 1972), 210. Why the term "existentialism" would escape this fate is not specified.

11. Thomas H. Schaub, *American Fiction in the Cold War* (Madison: University of Wisconsin Press, 1991), 137–62.

12. Mailer, "Column Seventeen," in *Advertisements for Myself,* 316; Mailer, "A Public Notice on *Waiting for Godot,*" in ibid., 320. Hereafter, page citations to both appear in the text.

13. Mailer's obsessive worries about impotence were an expression of the 1950s discourse of male anxiety. Although in his politics he remained outside the anticommunist consensus, with its emphasis on virility and antihomosexual images, his oppositional discourse adhered to the dominant themes and symbolism of the era: the ideal of the powerful male, the woman as sexual predator sapping the strength of men, an animus against homosexuals, and a propensity toward violence. See K. A. Courdileone, "Politics in an Age of Anxiety: Cold War Political Culture and the Crisis in American Masculinity, 1949–1960," *Journal of American History* 87 (Sept. 2000): 515–45.

14. Norman Mailer, *The Naked and the Dead* (New York: Modern Library, 1948), 660. Hereafter, page citations appear in the text.

15. Mailer, "Third Advertisement for Myself," in *Advertisements for Myself,* 106.

16. Norman Podhoretz, "Norman Mailer: The Embattled Vision," in *Doings and Undoings: The Fifties and after in American Writing* (New York: Farrar, Straus, and Giroux, 1964), 188.

17. Richard Poirier, *Norman Mailer* (New York: Viking Press, 1972), 66; also Stanley T. Gutman, *Mankind in Barbary: The Individual and Society in the Novels of Norman Mailer* (Hanover: University Press of New England, 1975), 32.

18. Howard M. Harper, Jr., finds *Barbary Shore* superior to *The Naked and the Dead.* See his *Desperate Faith: A Study of Bellow, Salinger, Mailer, Baldwin, and Updike* (Chapel Hill: University of North Carolina Press, 1967), 109.

19. Norman Mailer, *Barbary Shore* (New York: Signet Books, 1960), 223.

20. Schaub would reject this view, finding Mailer to be part of the consensus rather than an opponent of it. *American Fiction,* 138–39.

21. Mailer, "The White Negro," in *Advertisements for Myself,* 338. Hereafter, page citations appear in the text.

22. Genet's work was known in New York intellectual circles as early as 1946, with some

of his stories appearing in *Partisan Review*. For Sartre on Genet, see *Saint Genet: Actor and Martyr,* trans. Bernard Frechtman (New York: Pantheon Books, 1983). Of course, Mailer would later champion his own criminal/writer in Jack Henry Abbott. See Dearborn, *Mailer,* 57.

23. James Baldwin, "The Black Boy Looks at the White Boy" (1961), in *The Price of the Ticket* (New York: St. Martin's, 1985), 296–97.

24. Eric Lott, *Love and Theft: Blackface Minstrelsy and the American Working Class* (New York: Oxford University Press, 1993).

25. Albert Murray, *Stomping the Blues* (New York: Vintage, 1982), 250–51.

26. Eric Lott, "Double V, Double-Time: Bebop's Politics of Style," *Callaloo* 11 (1988): 597–605.

27. Henry Louis Gates, Jr., "White Like Me," *New Yorker* 72 (17 June 1996): 66–81; Anatole Broyard, "A Portrait of the Hipster," *Partisan Review* 15 (June 1948): 721–27. Hereafter, page citations appear in the text.

28. Hazel E. Barnes, *An Existentialist Ethics* (Chicago: University of Chicago Press, 1978), 194.

29. Podhoretz, *Doings,* 202.

30. Mailer was at least honest in his presentation when he admitted that this violence could just as easily express itself in fascism as in a liberation process: "The hipster is equally a candidate for the most reactionary and most radical of movements." "White Negro," 355.

31. Nathan A. Scott, Jr., *Three American Moralists: Mailer, Bellow, Trilling* (Notre Dame: University of Notre Dame Press, 1973), 44.

32. "Existential Aesthetics," 214–15.

33. Søren Kierkegaard, *Either/Or,* ed. and trans. Howard V. Hong and Edna H. Hong (Princeton: Princeton University Press, 1987), 1:304.

34. Ibid., 308.

35. Interview with Lyle Stuart (1955), in *Conversations with Norman Mailer,* 32.

36. Norman Mailer, *The Deer Park* (New York: G. P. Putnam's Sons, 1955), 147. Hereafter, page citations appear in the text.

37. This is an updating, perhaps, of the story made famous by Gershom Scholem of Sabbatai Sevi, the leader of a seventeenth-century Jewish messianic movement who led his followers on a rampage of sin so that they might better ready themselves for salvation. Scholem, *Sabbatai Sevi: The Mystical Messiah, 1626–1676,* trans. R. J. Zwi Werblowsky (Princeton: Princeton University Press, 1973).

38. Diana Trilling, "The Moral Radicalism of Norman Mailer," in *Norman Mailer: The Man and His Work,* ed. Robert F. Lucid (Boston: Little, Brown, 1971), 126. The review was originally published in *Encounter* in 1962.

39. On the problematic elements of Faye's nihilism, see Joseph Wenke, *Mailer's America* (Hanover: University Press of New England, 1987), 63f.

40. Kierkegaard, *Either/Or,* 1:426.

41. Mailer, *Existential Errands,* 210–11.

42. Mailer, *Presidential Papers,* 214.

43. Ibid., 213.

44. Mailer's argument here suggests an earlier argument by Josiah Royce on the logic

of evil. See Royce, "The Problem of Job" (1898), in *The American Intellectual Tradition,* ed. David A. Hollinger and Charles Capper (New York: Oxford University Press, 2001), 2:53–64.

45. Interview with Steven Marcus (1964), in *Conversations with Mailer,* 93. An excellent account of Mailer's existential theology may be found in Robert Solotaroff, *Down Mailer's Way* (Urbana: University of Illinois Press, 1974), 82–123.

46. Mailer, *Presidential Papers,* 193.

47. "Hip, Hell, and the Navigator," interview with Richard G. Stern and Robert F. Lucid (1959), in *Conversations with Mailer,* 32–35. Hereafter, page citations appear in the text.

48. "Living Like Heroes," interview with Richard Wollheim (1961), in *Conversations with Mailer,"* 66.

49. "Existential Aesthetics," 212.

50. For an excellent analysis of Mailer's concept of growth, see Solotaroff, *Down Mailer's Way,* 94f.

51. "Existential Aesthetics," 214–15.

52. Solotaroff, *Down Mailer's Way,* 101.

53. Simone de Beauvoir, *The Ethics of Ambiguity,* trans. Bernard Frechtman (New York: Citadel Press, 1996), 83, 144.

54. Mailer, *Presidential Papers,* 214.

55. Tom Wolfe, "Son of Crime and Punishment," in *Norman Mailer,* ed. Lucid, 160. Wolfe's review appeared in *Book Week* in 1965.

56. Richard Lehan, *A Dangerous Crossing: French Literary Existentialism and the Modern American Novel* (Carbondale: Southern Illinois University Press, 1958), 92.

57. Norman Mailer, *An American Dream* (New York: Dial Press, 1965), 17. Hereafter, page citations appear in the text.

58. Wenke, *Mailer's America,* 19.

59. At one point in the novel Mailer actually describes Rojack as addicted to Deborah: "I had a physical need to see her as direct as an addict's panic, waiting for his drug— if too many more minutes must be endured, who knows what intolerable damage can be done?" Mailer, *American Dream,* 19.

60. Richard Slotkin, *Regeneration through Violence: The Mythology of the American Frontier, 1600–1860* (Middletown, Conn.: Wesleyan University Press, 1973).

61. Davis had apparently been a boyfriend of Mailer's wife, Beverly. On the connection, see Dearborn, *Mailer,* 194–95.

62. Søren Kierkegaard, *Fear and Trembling,* trans. Alastair Hannay (London: Penguin Books, 1985), 65–67.

63. Norman Mailer, *The Armies of the Night: History as a Novel, the Novel as History* (New York: New American Library, 1968), 65. Hereafter, page citations appear in the text.

Ten Robert Frank's Existential Vision

Portions of this chapter, now revised, first appeared as "The Photographer in the Beat-Hipster Idiom: Robert Frank's *The Americans,"* *American Studies* 26 (Spring 1985): 19–33.

1. Susan Sontag, *On Photography* (New York: Farrar, Straus, and Giroux, 1977), 48. Interpretations that begin and end with Frank's bleak vision are William Stott, "Walker Evans, Robert Frank, and the Landscape of Dissociation," *Artscanada* 31 (Dec. 1974): 83–89, and Janet Malcolm, *Diana and Nikon: Essays on the Aesthetic of Photography* (Boston: David R. Godine, 1981), 139–62. More balanced interpretations are Tod Papageorge, *Walker Evans and Robert Frank: An Essay on Influence* (New Haven: Yale University Art Gallery, 1981), and Jonathan Green, *American Photography: A Critical History, 1945 to the Present* (New York: Harry N. Abrams, 1984), 31–94.

2. Joyce Johnson, *Minor Characters* (New York: Washington Square Books, 1984), 254. For Frank's discussion of his experiences during the war, see his comments in *The Pictures Are a Necessity: Robert Frank in Rochester, NY, November 1988*, ed. William Johnson (Rochester: George Eastman House, 1999), 26–27; also Dennis Wheeler, "Robert Frank Interviewed," *Criteria* 3 (June 1977): 4–7.

3. Quoted in William Johnson, "Souvenirs," in *Pictures Are a Necessity*, 27. A copy of Camus's *The Plague* could be found on Frank's bookshelf.

4. Not all agree that Frank's political message is clear, or adequate. According to Lili Corbus Bezner, Frank's "viewers face ambiguous and subjectively personal visions in his aestheticized, ironic, and mordant views of the United States." Moreover, "there is no causality or specific blame in the book." To be sure, Frank's vision is personal, but it is not acontextual. If it had been, then it would not have evoked such a storm of criticism. By attacking the assumptions of consensus-era America from his existential perspective, Frank was engaging in an essentially political act— one quite as radical as any work done in the more traditional realm of documentary photography. Bezner, *Photography and Politics in America: From the New Deal into the Cold War* (Baltimore: Johns Hopkins University Press, 1999), 191.

5. Quoted in *Pictures Are a Necessity*, 43.

6. Wheeler, "Robert Frank Interviewed," 6; Robert Frank, "Comments at Wellesley," in *Photography within the Humanities*, ed. Eugenia Parry Janis and Wendy Mac-Neil (Danbury, N.H.: Addison House, 1977), 53; Frank, "A Statement," in *Photographers on Photography*, ed. Nathan Lyons (Englewood Cliffs, N.J.: Prentice-Hall, 1966), 66–67.

7. Frank had seven images in the exhibit. Some of them did capture his emphasis on loneliness, as in the photograph "Peru." Another photograph, "New York," captures the facade of a store, with visual signposts announcing "Hamburgers" and other items for sale prominently displayed. But in this photograph the women captured in the window are smiling for the camera. They do not appear alienated, nor are they mocked. Edward Steichen, *The Family of Man* (New York: Museum of Modern Art and Simon and Schuster, 1955).

8. Eric J. Sandeen, *Picturing an Exhibition: The Family of Man and 1950s America* (Albuquerque: University of New Mexico Press, 1995), 155–80.

9. Quoted in *Pictures Are a Necessity*, 37.

10. Robert Frank, "Application for a Guggenheim Fellowship" (1954), in *Robert Frank: New York to Nova Scotia*, ed. Anne Wilkes Tucker (Houston: Museum of Fine Arts, 1986), 20.

11. Gerald Nicosia, *Memory Babe: A Critical Biography of Jack Kerouac* (New York: Grove Press, 1983), 559–72; Jack Kerouac, introduction to *The Americans* (New York: Aperture, 1969), i.

12. Daniel Belgrad, *The Culture of Spontaneity: Improvisation and the Arts in Postwar America* (Chicago: University of Chicago Press, 1998), 196–221.

13. Robert J. Lifton, "Protean Man," in *The Radical Vision: Essays for the Seventies,* ed. Leo Hamalian and Frederick R. Karl (New York: Crowell, 1970), 58. On the Beats, see John Tytell, *Naked Angels: The Lives and Literature of the Beat Generation* (New York: McGraw-Hill, 1976).

14. Jack Kerouac, *On the Road* (New York: Signet Press, n.d.), 148.

15. Quoted in *Pictures Are a Necessity,* 37.

16. Allen Ginsberg, "Robert Frank to 1985—A Man," in *New York to Nova Scotia,* 74.

17. Quoted in *Pictures Are a Necessity,* 36.

18. Papageorge, *Walker Evans and Robert Frank,* 3–4, is useful on Frank's style; criticism of this style is offered in Stott, "Walker Evans, Robert Frank, and the Landscape of Dissociation," 84. This is not to suggest that Frank did not respect Evans, and vice versa. Evans supported Frank's Guggenheim application, and Frank admitted that Evans "was my teacher. I learned a lot from the way he looked at things; he wanted to look at one thing and look at it very clearly and in a final way. I like this about him because I don't have that . . . and also he wouldn't put up with any shit or give any shit." Quoted in *Pictures Are a Necessity,* 35.

19. Sontag, *On Photography,* 55–56.

20. Roland Barthes, *Camera Lucida: Reflections on Photography,* trans. Richard Howard (New York: Hill and Wang, 1981), 30–32.

21. Jean-Paul Sartre, *The Age of Reason,* trans. Eric Sutton (New York: Bantam Books, 1959).

22. Kerouac, introduction to *The Americans,* vi.

23. Arthur Goldsmith, "An Off-Beat View of the U.S.A.," in *From New York to Nova Scotia,* 37.

24. For a contemporary criticism of Frank's vision, see William Hogan, "Photo Coverage of the Ugly American," *San Francisco Chronicle,* 27 Jan. 1960, 25.

25. Frank, "Comments at Wellesley," 54.

26. Frank has admitted that he found the jukebox to be an American symbol that he could not resist. He stated that its appeal to him was due largely to the element of sound that it gave to his photographs. This may also explain the power and appeal of his well-known photograph "Political Rally—Chicago," in which you can almost hear the words of the politician's speech. Ibid., 55. See the analysis of "Political Rally—Chicago" in Gene Markowski, *The Art of Photography: Image and Illusion* (Englewood Cliffs, N.J.: Prentice-Hall, 1984), 38–39.

27. Interestingly, Frank has said that this is his favorite image in *The Americans,* because "it really expressed a lot of different things, but also it expressed how it feels to be a photographer and suddenly be confronted with that look of, *You bastard, what are you doing!* It's very strong. I like the two people in it, I like the white city in the background." Frank interview, 6 Nov. 1988, in *Pictures Are a Necessity,* 173.

28. Jonathan Green offers a similar interpretation of the black preacher and accompanying photographs in his *American Photography,* 87–88.

29. Frank interview, "Workshop," 5 Nov. 1988, in *Pictures Are a Necessity,* 123.

30. After a long interview session, Frank decided to offer up a toast. He could toast Freedom or Democracy, but instead he announced that it should be Wisdom. Frank interview, "Workshop," 6 Nov. 1988, in ibid., 183.

Eleven Camus's Rebels

1. Germaine Brée, "The Making of a University Professor, USA—1936–84," *PMLA* 109 (Oct. 1994): 937–38. See also James Gilbert, "The Teach-in: Protest or Co-optation?" in *The New Left: A Documentary History,* ed. Massimo Teodori (Indianapolis: Bobbs-Merrill, 1969), 242. Gilbert later recalled that students respected Brée, along with others at Wisconsin such as Harvey Goldberg, George Mosse, and William Appleman Williams, for "moving academics out of the classroom and into the world." Gilbert to author, e-mail communication, 23 May 2000.

2. Serge Doubrovsky, "Camus in America," trans. Ellen Conroy Kennedy, in *Camus: A Collection of Critical Essays,* ed. Germaine Brée (Englewood Cliffs, N.J.: Prentice-Hall, 1962), 16. According to Doubrovsky, Americans appreciated the fact that Camus universalized the ideals of struggle, without making class conflict central. Camus's "atheistic humanism" captured "the secular ethics which is at the heart of this American civilization, where piety is most often merely a pious fraud."

3. Hayden Carruth, *After the Stranger: Imaginary Dialogues with Camus* (New York: Macmillan, 1965), 40.

4. Todd Gitlin, *The Sixties: Years of Hope, Days of Rage* (New York: Bantam Books, 1987), 84, 34.

5. Rev. Ken Sawyer to author, e-mail communication, 8 Apr. 1997.

6. Rob Mustard to author, e-mail communication, 20 Nov. 1996.

7. Quoted in Maurice Isserman, *If I Had a Hammer . . . : The Death of the Old Left and the Birth of the New Left* (New York: Basic Books, 1987), 188.

8. Mark Poster argues that Sartre, in his combining of existentialism and Marxism, developed the theoretical structure for New Left social theory. While this was certainly true in Europe, the theoretical underpinnings of the New Left in America were more varied and rooted in the American soil. Indeed, in their opposition to abstract theory, American radicals were more attuned to Camus than to Sartre. To my mind this was for the good. Poster, *Existential Marxism in Postwar France: From Sartre to Althusser* (Princeton: Princeton University Press, 1975).

9. Jean-Paul Sartre, preface to Frantz Fanon, *The Wretched of the Earth* (1961), trans. Constance Farrington (New York: Grove Press, 1963), 20. In his preface Sartre attacked humanism as an inadequate response to oppression (24–26).

10. Adolph Reed, "Paths to Critical Theory," in *The Sixties without Apology,* ed. Sohnya Sayers et al. (Minneapolis: University of Minnesota Press, 1984), 255.

11. Marcus Raskin, "Sartre: A Life in History," in *First Harvest: The Institute for Policy Studies, 1963–1983,* ed. John S. Friedman (New York: Grove Press, 1983), 313.

12. Jerry Rubin, "Alliance for Liberation," *Liberation* 11 (Apr. 1966): 9, 11.

13. Elisabeth Israels Perry to author, e-mail communication, 27 Mar. 1996.

14. Tom Hayden, *Reunion: A Memoir* (New York: Collier Books, 1988), 42.

15. Staughton Lynd, *Intellectual Origins of American Radicalism* (New York: Vintage Books, 1968); also Lynd, *Nonviolence in America: A Documentary History* (Indi-

anapolis: Bobbs-Merrill, 1966). On Lynd's "enthusiasm" for Camus, see James Miller, *"Democracy in the Streets": From Port Huron to the Siege of Chicago* (New York: Simon and Schuster, 1987), 266.

16. Justin O'Brien, "Albert Camus: Militant," in *Camus: Critical Essays,* 20.

17. Quoted in Lester David and Irene David, *Bobby Kennedy: The Making of a Folk Hero* (New York: Dodd, Mead, 1986), 8. This was a favorite line of Kennedy's; he also uttered it on a David Frost television interview a week before he was assassinated. On Kennedy's turn to Camus, see Evan Thomas, *Robert Kennedy: His Life* (New York: Simon and Schuster, 2000), 22, 319–20; Jack Newfield, *Robert Kennedy: A Memoir* (New York: E. P. Dutton, 1969), 18–19, 58, 256; Arthur M. Schlesinger, Jr., *Robert Kennedy and His Times* (Boston: Houghton Mifflin, 1978), 619. Another favorite line from Camus that appeared in Kennedy's speeches was "I should like to be able to love my country and still love justice." See "The Value of Dissent," speech delivered at Vanderbilt University, Nashville, Tenn., 21 Mar. 1968, in *RFK: Collected Speeches,* ed. Edwin O. Guthman and C. Richard Allen (New York: Viking, 1993), 332. Adam Walinsky, Kennedy's speechwriter, adored Camus. According to Newfield, he had "framed on his desk an old cover of *Motive* magazine" with the preceding quotation on it. Newfield, *Kennedy: A Memoir,* 51.

18. David and David, *Bobby Kennedy,* 222.

19. Philip D. Beidler, *Scriptures for a Generation: What We Were Reading in the Sixties* (Athens: University of Georgia Press, 1994), 6–7, 20, 32.

20. J. Glenn Gray, "Salvation on the Campus: Why Existentialism Is Capturing the Students," *Harper's Magazine* 230 (May 1965): 58–59.

21. Walter Kaufmann, "The Reception of Existentialism in the United States," *Salmagundi,* no. 10–11 (Fall 1969–Winter 1970): 93–94.

22. Hazel E. Barnes, *The Story I Tell Myself: A Venture in Existentialist Autobiography* (Chicago: University of Chicago Press, 1997), 159–61. Stephen Eric Bronner argues convincingly for placing Camus firmly within the mainstream of existentialism. Bronner, *Camus: Portrait of a Moralist* (Minneapolis: University of Minnesota Press, 1999), 39.

23. Moses quoted in Robert Penn Warren, "Two for SNCC," *Commentary* 39 (Apr. 1965): 41.

24. Martin Luther King, Jr., "Selection from a 'Letter from a Birmingham Jail,'" in *The American Intellectual Tradition,* ed. David A. Hollinger and Charles Capper, 4th ed. (New York: Oxford University Press, 2001), 2:377. For King's fullest expression of his existentialist leanings, see "Pilgrimage to Nonviolence," *Christian Century* 77 (13 Apr. 1960): 439–40. While a theology student at Crozer, King wrote papers incorporating material from Karl Barth and Kierkegaard. Unfortunately, many of his insights appear to have been lifted from secondary sources, without attribution. See his 1949 paper with the immense title "What Experiences of Christians Living in the Early Christian Century Led to the Christian Doctrines of the Divine Sonship of Jesus, the Virgin Birth, and the Bodily Resurrection," in *The Papers of Martin Luther King, Jr.: Called to Serve, January 1929–June 1951,* ed. Clayborne Carson (Berkeley: University of California Press, 1992), 232–34.

25. Quoted in Clayborne Carson, *In Struggle: SNCC and the Black Awakening of the 1960s* (Cambridge: Harvard University Press, 1981), 78.

26. Cleveland Sellers, with Robert Terrell, *The River of No Return: The Autobiography of a Black Militant and the Life and Death of SNCC* (New York: William Morrow, 1973), 83.

27. Quoted in Eric R. Burner, *And Gently He Shall Lead Them: Robert Parris Moses and Civil Rights in Mississippi* (New York: New York University Press, 1994), 159.

28. Quoted in Charles Marsh, *God's Long Summer: Stories of Faith and Civil Rights* (Princeton: Princeton University Press, 1997), 48.

29. Bob Cohen, who had been Moses's roommate in 1960 and 1961, recalled that Moses read Camus in French. Quoted in Jack Newfield, *A Prophetic Minority* (New York: New American Library, 1966), 73.

30. Warren, "Two for SNCC," 41.

31. Albert Camus, *The Plague,* trans. Stuart Gilbert (New York: Modern Library, 1948), 270–71.

32. Sally Belfrage, *Freedom Summer* (New York: Viking Press, 1965), 11.

33. Albert Camus, "Letter to Roland Barthes on *The Plague*" (1955), in *Lyrical and Critical Essays,* trans. Ellen Conroy Kennedy (New York: Vintage Books, 1970), 339.

34. Albert Camus, *The Rebel: An Essay on Man in Revolt,* trans. Anthony Bower (1951; New York: Vintage Books, n.d.), 22. Hereafter, page citations appear in the text.

35. Sartre attempted to reconcile his existentialism with Marxism (much to the undermining of the former) in *Search for a Method,* trans. Hazel E. Barnes (1960; New York: Vintage Books, 1968).

36. Jean-Paul Sartre, "Reply to Albert Camus" (1952), in *Situations,* trans. Benita Eisler (Greenwich, Conn.: Fawcett Crest, 1966), 77.

37. Edward W. Said, *Culture and Imperialism* (New York: Alfred A. Knopf, 1994), 169–85. A favorable view of Camus's stance is in Tony Judt, *Burden of Responsibility: Blum, Camus, Aron, and the French Twentieth Century* (Chicago: University of Chicago Press, 1998), 87–136.

38. Townsend Davis, *Weary Feet, Rested Souls: A Guided History of the Civil Rights Movement* (New York: W. W. Norton, 1988), 235.

39. Albert Camus, *Neither Victims nor Executioners,* trans. Dwight Macdonald (New York: Continuum, 1980). Hereafter, page citations appear in the text.

40. Mike to parents, 18 June [1964], in *Letters from Mississippi,* ed. Elizabeth Sutherland (New York: McGraw-Hill, 1965), 10.

41. Warren, "Two for SNCC," 41.

42. Ibid.

43. Robert Parris Moses, "Commentary," in *We Shall Overcome: Martin Luther King, Jr., and the Black Freedom Struggles,* ed. Peter J. Albert and Ronald Hoffman (New York: Pantheon, 1990), 76.

44. Sellers, *River of No Return,* 131.

45. Bruce Payne, "SNCC: An Overview Two Years Later," in *The New Student Left: An Anthology,* ed. Mitchell Cohen and Dennis Hale (Boston: Beacon Press, 1966), 97.

46. Carson, *In Struggle,* 173.

47. Ibid., 4.

48. Albert Camus, "Reflections on the Guillotine," in *Resistance, Rebellion, and Death,* trans. Justin O'Brien (New York: Alfred A. Knopf, 1961), 218.

49. Warren, "Two for SNCC," 41.

50. Bob Moses, "Mississippi: 1961–1962," *Liberation* 14 (Jan. 1970): 12.

51. Unidentified Mississippi freedom worker to parents, 27 June [1964], in *Letters from Mississippi*, 31–32.

52. Quoted in Jeffrey Isaac, *Arendt, Camus, and Modern Rebellion* (New Haven: Yale University Press, 1992), 15. Isaac is particularly insightful on the politics of Camus's moderation.

53. Unidentified Mississippi freedom worker to parents, 27 June [1964], 32.

54. Quoted in Burner, *And Gently,* 219.

55. The announcement of the name change is described in detail in Sellers, *River of No Return,* 138. According to Sellers, Moses began with "a complicated existential exposition" of his decision.

56. On these years in Moses's life, see Burner, *And Gently,* 220–22.

57. On these social radicals, see Casey Nelson Blake, *Beloved Community: The Cultural Criticism of Randolph Bourne, Van Wyck Brooks, Waldo Frank, and Lewis Mumford* (Chapel Hill: University of North Carolina Press, 1990).

58. T. J. Jackson Lears, *No Place of Grace: Antimodernism and the Transformation of American Culture, 1880–1920* (New York: Pantheon, 1981).

59. Wilfred M. McClay, *The Masterless Self and Society in Modern America* (Chapel Hill: University of North Carolina Press, 1994), 233–61 passim.

60. Excellent on the new industrial state, affluence, and alienation is Howard Brick, *Age of Contradiction: American Thought and Culture in the 1960s* (New York: Twayne, 1998).

61. Herbert Marcuse, *One-Dimensional Man: Studies in the Ideology of Advanced Industrial Society* (Boston: Beacon Press, 1969), xii.

62. Peter Clecak, *Radical Paradoxes: Dilemmas of the American Left, 1945–1970* (New York: Harper and Row, 1973), 201–9.

63. Marcuse, *One-Dimensional Man,* xv.

64. Norman O. Brown, *Life against Death: The Psychoanalytic Meaning of History* (1959; New York: Vintage Books, n.d.), 307.

65. Theodore Roszak, new introduction to *The Making of a Counter Culture: Reflections on the Technocratic Society and Its Youthful Opposition* (Berkeley: University of California Press, 1995), xix. Thomas Frank presents a differing interpretation, finding that capitalism and advertising all too easily appropriated images of rebellion in order to sell products and create identities. See Frank, *Conquest of Cool: Business Culture, Counterculture, and the Rise of Hip Consumerism* (Chicago: University of Chicago Press, 1997).

66. Doug Rossinow, *The Politics of Authenticity: Liberalism, Christianity, and the New Left in America* (New York: Columbia University Press, 1998), 53, 59. Hereafter, page citations appear in the text.

67. Nelson N. Lichtenstein to author, e-mail communication, 20 Apr. 1996.

68. The experiences of this first New Left generation at the University of Texas may be atypical. Many New Leftists came to their radicalism without any religious feelings. But nearly all of them traveled along the same road with Camus, as the quotations at the opening of this chapter indicate.

69. Hayden, *Reunion,* 52. Hereafter, page citations appear in the text.

70. On Hayden, see James J. Farrell, *The Spirit of the Sixties: The Making of Postwar Radicalism* (New York: Routledge, 1997), 139–42 passim; Miller, *Democracy;* Paul Westbrook, "A Thematic Analysis of the Advocacy of Thomas Emmet Hayden as a Radical Intellectual Activist in the New Left Social Movement," Ph.D. diss., Department of Speech, Southern Illinois University, 1976.

71. Tom Hayden, "New Student Action in a World of Crisis," *Michigan Daily,* 16 Sept. 1960, 4.

72. Tom Hayden, "Who Are the Student Boat-Rockers?" *Mademoiselle* 53 (Aug. 1961): 335–37.

73. Nicola Chiaromonte, "Albert Camus and Moderation," *Partisan Review* 15 (Oct. 1948): 1142–45. There is no reason to assume that Hayden had read this piece, but it captured aspects of Camus's *Neither Victims nor Executioners,* which was available at this time to him.

74. Tom Hayden, "A Letter to the New (Young) Left," in *New Student Left,* 4, 3. Hereafter, page citations appear in the text.

75. Miller, *Democracy,* 145. On the connection between Dewey and the sentiments of the Port Huron Statement, see the brief comments, which second much of Miller's analysis, in Robert B. Westbrook, *John Dewey and American Democracy* (Ithaca: Cornell University Press, 1991), 549–50.

76. Miller, *Democracy,* 98, 146.

77. Rossinow, *Politics,* 81–84.

78. Tom Hayden, "Manifesto Notes: A Beginning Draft" (19 Mar. 1962) in Students for a Democratic Society Collection, series 1, reel 3, microfilm edition, State Historical Society of Wisconsin.

79. The full text of the Port Huron Statement appears as an appendix to Miller, *Democracy,* 330. Hereafter, page citations appear in the text.

80. Yet as Stanley Aronowitz notes, the Port Huron Statement was typically American in its emphasis on "popular self-government" and its unwillingness to engage with "socialist discourse." See Aronowitz, "When the New Left Was New," in *Sixties without Apology,* 18.

81. Gitlin, *Sixties,* 381, 347. On the hardening of lines in this period, see David Farber, *The Age of Great Dreams: America in the 1960s* (New York: Hill and Wang, 1994), 190–211.

82. Tom Hayden, *Rebellion in Newark: Official Violence and Ghetto Response* (New York: Random House, 1967), 71–72.

83. Tom Hayden, "Two, Three, Many Columbias" (1968), in *New Left: A Documentary History,* 346.

84. Jonathan Weiss, "Tom Hayden's Political Evolution during the New Left Years: Rebel without a Theory," *Michigan Journal of Political Science* 5 (1984), 22.

85. Steven V. Roberts, "Will Tom Hayden Overcome?" *Esquire* 70 (Dec. 1968): 208–9.

86. For a good evaluation of the legacy of the New Left, see Maurice Isserman and Michael Kazin, *America Divided: The Civil War of the 1960s* (Oxford: Oxford University Press, 2000).

87. The difficult question—and perhaps an unanswerable one—is, Can a mass movement be built, or even individual participation sustained, on the basis of a chastened sensibility? How does one manage, day by day, in the face of opposition, to

maintain a sense of balance and belief in the goals to be striven for? Can Camusian distance keep one active, or does it eventually lead one to the sidelines?

88. Roberts, "Will Tom Hayden," 209.

89. Nichols quoted in "CineBooks' Motion Picture Guide Review," www.geocities.com/Hollywood/8200/graduate.html.

Twelve Existential Feminists: Beauvoir and Friedan

1. Rosalind Fraad Baxandall, "Were These Proto Feminist Acts?" in *The Feminist Memoir Project: Voices from Women's Liberation,* ed. Rachel Blau DuPlessis and Ann Snitow (New York: Three Rivers Press, 1998), 210; also Baxandall, "Another Madison Bohemian," in *History and the New Left: Madison, Wisconsin, 1950–1970,* ed. Paul Buhle (Philadelphia: Temple University Press, 1990), 139. Baxandall majored in French and history, later becoming a professor of history at SUNY, Old Westbury.

2. Kate Millett, contribution to *Daughters of de Beauvoir,* ed. Penny Forster and Imogen Sutton (London: Women's Press, 1989), 22.

3. Sheila Tobias, "Betty Friedan and the Feminine Mystique," in *Faces of Feminism: An Activist's Reflections on the Women's Movement* (Boulder: Westview Press, 1997), 58, 59.

4. Susan Brownmiller, *In Our Time: Memoir of a Revolution* (New York: Dial Press, 1999), 3.

5. Judith Hennessee, *Betty Friedan: Her Life* (New York: Random House, 1999), 201–2. The main source for this meeting comes from Friedan's account, "A Dialogue with Simone de Beauvoir," in *It Changed My Life: Writings on the Women's Movement* (New York: Random House, 1976), esp. 304–6.

6. Quoted in Deirdre Bair, *Simone de Beauvoir: A Biography* (New York: Summit Books, 1990), 609.

7. Diane Ravitch, "Mama in Search of Herself," *New Leader* 46 (15 Apr. 1963): 29.

8. Sandra Dijkstra, "Simone de Beauvoir and Betty Friedan: The Politics of Omission," *Feminist Studies* 6 (Summer 1980): 297, 294.

9. Betty Friedan Papers, box 15, folder 568, "Notes on DeBeauvoir," Schlesinger Library, Radcliffe Institute, Harvard University.

10. Bettye Goldstein, "For Defense of Democracy," *Smith College Monthly* 1 (31 Oct. 1940): 11.

11. Friedan, *It Changed My Life,* 191.

12. Most famously in *The Anxiety of Influence: A Theory of Poetry* (Oxford: Oxford University Press, 1973).

13. Friedan, "Dialogue with Beauvoir," 304.

14. Ibid., 306.

15. Friedan's use of the term "existential," in the context of her memoir, is muddled. She writes, "Using Freudian terms (and Jewish theology) to understand my original embrace of Marxism, I think, looking back, it gave first shape to my superego, my Jewish existential conscience, that sense which always seems to drive me, though I dread its appearance, that I have to use my life to make the world better, have to protest, have to step off that sidewalk and march against injustice." While her linking of an existential attitude with activism is unproblematic, just how "ex-

istential" and "superego" are related is unclear. Nonetheless, it is important that Friedan chose to use the term. And, as we shall see, she was not averse to referring to her existentialism in other contexts as well. Friedan's memoir also presents evidence that growing up she felt a sense of being an outsider, an Other, which may have inclined her toward an existential sensibility. Betty Friedan, *Life So Far: A Memoir* (New York: Simon and Schuster, 2000), 71.

16. So opens *The Adventures of Augie March* (1953; New York: Penguin Books, 1966), 3.

17. Friedan, *It Changed My Life,* 191.

18. Kate Fullbrook and Edward Fullbrook, *Simone de Beauvoir and Jean-Paul Sartre: The Remaking of a Twentieth-Century Legend* (New York: Basic Books, 1994).

19. Ruth Rosen, "The Female Generation Gap: Daughters of the Fifties and the Origins of Contemporary American Feminism," in *U.S. History as Women's History: New Feminist Essays,* ed. Linda Kerber et al. (Chapel Hill: University of North Carolina Press, 1995), 331. Rosen finds that Beauvoir was most successful when she pushed aside her existentialism and embraced the women's movement, as if the two were necessarily distinct approaches.

20. Toril Moi, *Feminist Theory and Simone de Beauvoir* (London: Basil Blackwell, 1990), 21–60; Moi, *Simone de Beauvoir: The Making of an Intellectual Woman* (Oxford: Basil Blackwell, 1994).

21. Moreover, Friedan's personal and feminist agenda was so limited that she was antagonistic to the participation of lesbians within the movement, referring to them at one point as "the lavender menace." On Friedan's phobia (later revised, somewhat), see Alice Echols, *Daring to Be Bad: Radical Feminism in America, 1967–1975* (Minneapolis: University of Minnesota Press, 1989), 212f.

22. Susan Brownmiller quoted in Rosalind Rosenberg, *Divided Lives: American Women in the Twentieth Century* (New York: Hill and Wang, 1992), 202.

23. Simone de Beauvoir, *The Ethics of Ambiguity,* trans. Bernard Frechtman (1948; New York: Citadel, 1996), 156.

24. Simone de Beauvoir, *The Second Sex,* trans. and ed. H. M. Parshley (New York: Alfred A. Knopf, 1953), 267. Hereafter, page citations appear in the text.

25. Many radical feminists in the 1970s looked to Beauvoir for guidance and inspiration. Shulamith Firestone, for instance, dedicated her highly influential work *The Dialectic of Sex* to Beauvoir, "who endured." For Firestone, a radical agenda began with a rejection of biological categories, the importance of understanding the depth of sexual oppression throughout society and within the home, and for a woman-centered politics. Firestone, *The Dialectic of Sex: The Case for Feminist Revolution* (New York: William Morrow, 1970).

26. Jean-Paul Sartre, *Existentialism,* trans. Bernard Frechtman (New York: Philosophical Library, 1947), 15. The phrase was first used by Sartre in an influential lecture in Paris in 1945.

27. Margaret A. Simons, "Richard Wright, Simone de Beauvoir, and *The Second Sex,*" in *Beauvoir and "The Second Sex": Feminism, Race, and the Origins of Existentialism* (Lanham, Md.: Rowman and Littlefield, 1999), 167–84. A similar approach to the question of the Other was employed by Sartre in *Anti-Semite and Jew,* trans. George J. Becker (1944; New York: Schocken Books, 1948), 61f.

28. See Millett's contribution to *Daughters of de Beauvoir*, 23.

29. Elaine Tyler May, *Homeward Bound: American Families in the Cold War Era* (New York: Basic Books, 1988).

30. Friedan, *It Changed My Life*, 70.

31. Betty Friedan, *The Feminine Mystique* (1963; New York: W. W. Norton, 1997, with new introduction), 83. Hereafter, page citations appear in the text.

32. The feminine mystique, some argue, was nothing more than a new expression of the "cult of true womanhood," albeit "dressed in fifties garb." This objection is certainly valid, although it does not diminish the force of Friedan's challenge to the mystique. See Leila J. Rupp and Verta Taylor, *Survival in the Doldrums: The American Women's Rights Movement, 1945 to the 1960s* (New York: Oxford University Press, 1987), 14–15.

33. Joanne Meyerowitz, "Beyond the Feminine Mystique: A Reassessment of Postwar Mass Culture, 1946–1958," *Journal of American History* 79 (Mar. 1993): 1455–82; Eva Moskowitz, "'It's Good to Blow Your Top': Women's Magazines and a Discourse of Discontent, 1945–1965," *Journal of Women's History* 8 (Fall 1996): 67.

34. Fascinatingly, Beauvoir managed to find value in Philip Wylie's wildly misogynist work *Generation of Vipers* (1942), in which he lays on the doorstep of Momism, the cult of castrating mother figures, the problems of modern American males: "There is much truth in this aggressive satire," writes Beauvoir. See *Second Sex*, 173, 594.

35. Mary Lowenthal Felstiner, "Seeing *The Second Sex* through the Second Wave," *Feminist Studies* 6 (Summer 1980): 266.

36. Simons argues that Beauvoir's editor excised passages in the English translation that dealt with active, heroic women. But the sum total of such excisions would not offset the essential thrust of her argument. If it did, then Beauvoir's work would be beset with deep contradictions. See "The Silencing of Simone de Beauvoir: Guess What's Missing from *The Second Sex*," in Simons, *Beauvoir*, 101–14.

37. Simone de Beauvoir, *The Blood of Others*, trans. Roger Senhouse and Yvonne Moyse (New York: Pantheon Books, 1948), 286.

38. Mary King, *Freedom Song: A Personal Story of the 1960s Civil Rights Movement* (New York: William Morrow, 1987), 78.

39. William H. Chafe, *The American Woman: Her Changing Social, Economic, and Political Roles, 1920–1970* (New York: Oxford University Press, 1972), 232.

40. Betty Friedan, "The Family as New Feminist Frontier," in *The Second Stage* (New York: Summit Books, 1981), 57–90.

41. Friedan, "Dialogue with Beauvoir," 307. Hereafter, page citations appear in the text.

42. Simone de Beauvoir, *The Coming of Age*, trans. Patrick O'Brian (New York: G. P. Putnam's Sons, 1972), 9. Hereafter, page citations appear in the text. A truer translation of the French title would have been *Old Age*, but Beauvoir's American publishers felt that such a title would be too depressing and would limit sales of the volume. Bair, *Beauvoir*, 529.

43. Jean-Paul Sartre, *Being and Nothingness: An Essay on Phenomenological Ontology*, trans. Hazel E. Barnes (New York: Philosophical Library, 1956), 545–53.

44. See the definition of the term, along with its opposite, "praxis," in Hazel Barnes's introduction to her translation of Sartre, *Search for a Method* (New York: Vintage Books, 1968), xvi–xvii.

45. Quoted in Bair, *Beauvoir,* 540.

46. Quoted in ibid., 529.

47. For Beauvoir's chronicle of Sartre's decline, see *Adieux: A Farewell to Sartre,* trans. Patrick O'Brian (1981; New York: Vintage Books, 1984).

48. Quoted in Bair, *Beauvoir,* 541.

49. For a favorable assessment of Sartre's project, see Hazel E. Barnes, *Sartre and Flaubert* (Chicago: University of Chicago Press, 1981).

50. William James, *Principles of Psychology* (Cambridge: Harvard University Press, 1981), 1:125. Of course, James also acknowledged the value of habit in fitting the individual for life.

51. Not all reviewers disparaged Friedan's accomplishment. See Nancy Mairs, review of *The Fountain of Age, New York Times Book Review,* 3 Oct. 1993, 1, 28.

52. Betty Friedan, *The Fountain of Age* (New York: Simon and Schuster, 1993), 69. Hereafter, page citations appear in the text.

53. Ruth Rosen, *The World Split Open: How the Modern Women's Movement Changed America* (New York: Viking, 2000), 314–15; also Ellen Herman, *The Romance of American Psychology: Political Culture in the Age of Experts* (Berkeley: University of California Press, 1995), 276–303.

54. Albert Murray, *The Blue Devils of Nada: A Contemporary Approach to Aesthetic Statement* (New York: Pantheon, 1996).

55. F. Scott Fitzgerald, *The Great Gatsby* (New York: Scribner Paperback Fiction, 1995), 189.

Thirteen Conclusion: Existentialism Today and Tomorrow

1. Herbert Gold, *Bohemia* (New York: Touchstone Books, 1994), 145, 197.

2. Eric Alterman, "The News from Quinn-Broderville," *Nation* 267 (14 Dec. 1998): 10.

3. Quoted in George F. Will, "A Weird Sincerity," *Newsweek* 126 (13 Nov. 1995): 94.

4. Kenneth Turan, "Seeking the Meaning of (Shelf) Life," *Los Angeles Times,* 19 Nov. 1999, section F, 1.

5. Michael Sragow, "How One Role Made Bogart into an Icon," *New York Times,* 16 Jan. 2000, section 2, 3.

6. William R. Macklin, "Peanuts No Less Than Existential in Pen and Ink," *San Luis Obispo* (Calif.) *Tribune,* 19 Sept. 1999, B8.

7. Allan Bloom, *The Closing of the American Mind* (New York: Simon and Schuster, 1987), 219.

8. To be sure, existentialism remained central in the curriculum. And many philosophers and literary critics worked through its central texts. The Society for Phenomenology and Existential Philosophy, founded in 1962, remains a viable entity to this day. On the origins of this group, see Ann Fulton, *Apostles of Sartre: Existentialism in America, 1945–1963* (Evanston: Northwestern University Press, 1999), 112–13.

9. Claude Lévi-Strauss, *The Savage Mind* (1962; Chicago: University of Chicago Press, 1970), 246; also Howard Gardner, *The Quest for Mind: Piaget, Lévi-Strauss, and the Structuralist Movement* (Chicago: University of Chicago Press, 1981), 222–23.

10. Mark Poster, "Sartre's Concept of the Intellectual," in *Critical Theory and Post-structuralism: In Search of a Context* (Ithaca: Cornell University Press, 1989), 34–52.

11. For Foucault's shift to a new concern with "The Cultivation of the Self," see his *The Care of the Self: The History of Sexuality,* trans. Robert Hurley (1984; New York: Random House, 1986), 39f.

12. Calvin O. Schrag, *The Self after Postmodernity* (New Haven: Yale University Press, 1997); James O. Bennett, "Selves and Personal Existence in the Existentialist Tradition," *Journal of the History of Philosophy* 37 (Jan. 1999): esp. 155–56. Sartre seems poised to make a return to the center of French intellectual life, thanks in part to Bernard-Henri Lévy, *Le siècle de Sartre* (Paris: Bernard Grasset, 2000).

13. Marion Meade, *The Unruly Life of Woody Allen: A Biography* (New York: Scribner, 2000), 86. Interviews with Allen belie the ignorance that Meade imputes to him. See, for instance, his comments on Edward Hopper and Rainer Maria Rilke in *Woody Allen on Woody Allen: In Conversation with Stig Bjorkman* (New York: Grove Press, 1993), 85, 199–200.

14. Quoted in Foster Hirsch, *Love, Sex, Death, and the Meaning of Life: The Films of Woody Allen* (New York: Limelight Editions, 1991), 196.

15. Woody Allen, "My Philosophy," originally published in *Getting Even,* collected in *The Complete Prose of Woody Allen* (New York: Wings Books, 1991), 169–70.

16. Allen interview on *Crimes and Misdemeanors,* in *Woody Allen on Woody Allen,* 209.

17. Ibid., 225.

18. David S. Awbrey, *Finding Hope in the Age of Melancholy* (Boston: Little, Brown, 1999).

19. Walter Kirn, *Up in the Air* (New York: Doubleday, 2001).

20. Jedediah Purdy, *For Common Things: Irony, Trust, and Commitment in America Today* (New York: Alfred A. Knopf, 1999), 25. Quotation appears on 33.

21. The declension of an existentialist sensibility is more than a function of the possibilities of technology or the confidence of the age of American world domination. In academe in the 1980s, as the gospel of deconstruction spread, the universalism in Sartre came under attack. So too did existentialism come to be viewed as part of the failed project of modernism. Yet in its emphasis on the creation of the self, existentialism actually had much in common with deconstruction and poststructuralism. Unfortunately, these successors to existentialism lacked its sense of tragedy, limitation, and responsibility.

22. Samuel Beckett, *Worstward Ho* (London: John Calder, 1983), 7.

Essay on Sources

1 ODD, PERHAPS, to begin an "Essay on Sources" for a book about American existentialism with works by European existentialists, but almost all the ink of scholarship has been spilled on such figures. And rightfully so, since modern existentialism as a cultural and intellectual force has been indelibly marked by the influence of Jean-Paul Sartre, Simone de Beauvoir, Albert Camus, and Søren Kierkegaard.

An elementary, and sometimes misleading, introduction is Jean-Paul Sartre's *Existentialism*, trans. Bernard Frechtman (New York: Philosophical Library, 1947). Two works, both translated by Hazel E. Barnes, chart the evolution of Sartre's thinking: *Being and Nothingness* (New York: Philosophical Library, 1956) and *Search for a Method* (New York: Vintage Books, 1968). The classic statement of the engaged writer is Sartre's *What Is Literature?* trans. Bernard Frechtman (New York: Philosophical Library, 1949). Important early expressions of an existential sense of alienation and despair appear in Sartre's novel *Nausea,* trans. Lloyd Alexander (New York: New Directions, 1964), and in *No Exit and Three Other Plays,* trans. Gilbert Stuart (New York: Alfred A. Knopf, 1949). Helpful compilations of Sartre's philosophical and literary views can be found in Robert Denoon Cumming, ed., *The Philosophy of Jean-Paul Sartre* (New York: Vintage, 1965), and Wade Baskin, ed., *Essays in Existentialism* (New York: Citadel Press, 1995).

Simone de Beauvoir's existential sensibility is starkly evident in *The Ethics of Ambiguity,* trans. Bernard Frechtman (New York: Philosophical Library, 1948). Beauvoir offers an enticing, barely disguised glimpse into the heady days of French existentialism in her novel *The Mandarins,* trans. Leonard M. Friedman (Cleveland: World Publishing, 1956).

Albert Camus's humanity powers all of his work. In fiction, begin with *The Stranger,* trans. Stuart Gilbert (New York: Random House, 1946), then try *The Plague,* trans. Stuart Gilbert (New York: Random House, 1948). For his philosophy and social criticism, see *The Myth of Sisyphus,* trans. Justin O'Brien (New York: Alfred A. Knopf, 1955), and *The Rebel: An Essay on Man in Revolt,* trans. Anthony Bower (New York: Alfred A. Knopf, 1956).

All of Søren Kierkegaard's writings sparkle with passion, but the most scintillating are *Fear and Trembling,* trans. Alastair Hannay (London: Penguin, 1985); *The Concept of Dread,* trans. Walter Lowrie (Princeton: Princeton University Press, 1944); and *Either/Or,* trans. Howard V. Hong and Edna H. Hong (Princeton: Princeton University Press, 1987). Two influential anthologies are W. H. Auden, ed., *The Living Thoughts of Kierkegaard* (Bloomington: Indiana University Press, 1963), and Robert Bretall, ed., *A Kierkegaard Anthology* (Princeton: Princeton University Press, 1946). Helpful material on Kierkegaard's life and philosophy can be found in Josiah Thompson, *Kierkegaard* (New York: Alfred A. Knopf, 1973), and Patrick Gardiner, *Kierkegaard* (Oxford: Oxford University Press, 1988).

The prototype vision of the existential nihilist is Fyodor Dostoevsky, *Notes from Underground,* trans. Jessie Coulson (London: Penguin, 1972).

Forests have been felled to provide paper for the many scholarly analyses and anthologies dealing with existentialism and its leading figures. Helpful sources on Sartre include Annie Cohen-Solal, *Sartre: A Life,* trans. Anna Cancogni (New York: Pantheon, 1987); Ronald Hayman, *Sartre: A Biography* (New York: Simon and Schuster, 1987); John Gerassi, *Jean-Paul Sartre: Hated Conscience of His Century* (Chicago: University of Chicago Press, 1989); and Iris Murdoch, *Sartre: Romantic Rationalist* (London: Penguin, 1989).

On Beauvoir, two books highly recommend themselves: Deirdre Bair, *Simone de Beauvoir: A Biography* (New York: Summit, 1990), and Toril Moi, *Simone de Beauvoir: The Making of an Intellectual Woman* (Oxford: Blackwell, 1994).

For Camus, see Herbert R. Lottman, *Albert Camus: A Biography* (Garden City, N.Y.: Doubleday, 1979); Olivier Todd, *Albert Camus: A Life,* trans. Benjamin Ivry (New York: Alfred A. Knopf, 1997); David Sprintzen, *Camus: A Critical Examination* (Philadelphia: Temple University Press, 1988); Donald Lazere, *The Unique Creation of Albert Camus* (New Haven: Yale University Press, 1973); and Stephen Eric Bronner, *Camus: Portrait of a Moralist* (Minneapolis: University of Minnesota Press, 1999). For an excellent discussion of Camus's relation to the Resistance and the question of postwar executions of collaborators, see James D. Wilkinson, *The Intellectual Resistance in Europe* (Cambridge: Harvard University Press, 1981).

On existential philosophy in general, especially within the context of American explications, see William Barrett, *Irrational Man: A Study in Existential Philosophy* (Garden City, N.Y.: Doubleday Anchor, 1958); John Wild, *The Challenge of Existentialism* (Bloomington: Indiana University Press, 1955); Marjorie Grene, *Dreadful Freedom: A Critique of Existentialism* (Chicago: University of Chicago Press, 1948); Hazel E. Barnes, *An Existentialist Ethics* (Chicago: University of Chicago Press, 1978); Barnes, *The Literature of Possibility: A Study in Humanistic Existentialism* (Lincoln: University of Nebraska Press, 1979); and Ralph Harper, *The Existential Experience* (Baltimore: Johns Hopkins University Press, 1972). Also Ernst Breisach, *Introduction to Modern Existentialism* (New York: Grove Press, 1962); Mary Warnock, *Existentialism* (London: Oxford University Press, 1970); Gabriel Marcel, *The Philosophy of Existentialism,* trans. Manya Harari (New York:

Citadel, 1995); David E. Cooper, *Existentialism* (Oxford: Blackwell, 1990); and Mark Poster, *Existential Marxism in Postwar France: From Sartre to Althusser* (Princeton: Princeton University Press, 1975).

Significant collections of existentialist writings are Walter Kaufmann, ed., *Existentialism: From Dostoevsky to Sartre* (Cleveland: World Publishing, 1956); Maurice Friedman, ed., *The Worlds of Existentialism* (New York: Random House, 1964); and Robert C. Solomon, ed., *Existentialism* (New York: Modern Library, 1974).

Invaluable sources on the European context of postwar French existentialism are H. Stuart Hughes, *The Obstructed Path: French Social Thought in the Years of Desperation, 1930–1960* (New York: Harper and Row, 1968), and Anna Boschetti, *The Intellectual Enterprise: Sartre and "Les Temps Modernes,"* trans. Richard C. McCleary (Evanston: Northwestern University Press, 1988). Strongly antagonistic to Sartre is Tony Judt, *Past Imperfect: French Intellectuals, 1944–1956* (Berkeley: University of California Press, 1992). See also Judt, *The Burden of Responsibility: Blum, Camus, Aron, and the French Twentieth Century* (Chicago: University of Chicago Press, 1998), and Sunil Khilnani, *Arguing Revolution: The Intellectual Left in Postwar France* (New Haven: Yale University Press, 1993).

2   SCHOLARLY LITERATURE on American existentialism before the twentieth-century introduction of Kierkegaard and Sartre is nonexistent. One must therefore seek out hints of this attitude in the work of particular thinkers. On a tragic sensibility among American writers, begin with Harry Levin, *The Power of Blackness: Hawthorne, Poe, Melville* (New York: Alfred A. Knopf, 1967). On the terror at the center of the American literary imagination, see Leslie A. Fiedler, *Love and Death in the American Novel,* rev. ed. (New York: Scarborough, 1982). A valuable rumination on the decline of thinking seriously about evil is Andrew Delbanco, *The Death of Satan: How Americans Have Lost the Sense of Evil* (New York: Farrar, Straus, and Giroux, 1995).

The following works will be helpful to readers wishing to examine the life, thought, and existential aspects of figures discussed here as American precursors of existentialism. Although he never quite calls Jonathan Edwards a Kierke-gaardian, that is surely the crucial subtext in Perry Miller's *Jonathan Edwards* (New York: William Sloane, 1949). On Lincoln, Melville, and other thinkers, see John P. Diggins, *The Lost Soul of American Politics: Virtue, Self-Interest, and the Foundations of Liberalism* (Chicago: University of Chicago Press, 1984). The best work on Melville's anguished conscience is Lawrence R. Thompson, *Melville's Quarrel with God* (Princeton: Princeton University Press, 1952). For Melville and the tragic sense of life, see Lewis Mumford, *Herman Melville* (New York: Harcourt, Brace, 1929). Impressively detailed on Melville is Hershel Parker, *Herman Melville: A Biography, 1819–1851* (Baltimore: Johns Hopkins University Press, 1996).

Albert W. Alschuler calls Oliver Wendell Holmes an existentialist, albeit without approval, in *Law without Values: The Life, Work, and Legacy of Justice Holmes*

(Chicago: University of Chicago Press, 2000). More favorable to Holmes are Louis Menand, *The Metaphysical Club* (New York: Farrar, Straus, Giroux, 2001), and Richard A. Posner, *The Problems of Jurisprudence* (Cambridge: Harvard University Press, 1990). See also David A. Hollinger, "The 'Tough-Minded' Justice Holmes, Jewish Intellectuals, and the Making of an American Hero," in *The Legacy of Oliver Wendell Holmes, Jr.*, ed. Robert W. Gordon (Stanford: Stanford University Press, 1992), 216–28.

On James, see George Cotkin, *William James, Public Philosopher* (Baltimore: Johns Hopkins University Press, 1990). James's connections with phenomenology are pursued in John Wild, *The Radical Empiricism of William James* (New York: Anchor Books, 1970), and Bruce Wilshire, *William James and Phenomenology: A Study of "The Principles of Psychology"* (Bloomington: Indiana University Press, 1979).

On Crane and other thinkers in this period, see George Cotkin, *Reluctant Modernism: American Thought and Culture, 1880–1900* (New York: Twayne, 1992), and T. J. Jackson Lears, *No Place of Grace: Antimodernism and the Transformation of American Culture, 1880–1920* (New York: Pantheon, 1981). Excellent sources on Edward Hopper are Deborah Lyons and Adam D. Weinberg, eds., *Edward Hopper and the American Imagination* (New York: W. W. Norton and Whitney Museum of American Art, 1995), and Gail Levin, *Edward Hopper: An Intimate Biography* (New York: Alfred A. Knopf, 1995). The writers of the "Lost Generation" are examined in explicitly existential terms in Roderick Nash, *The Nervous Generation: American Thought, 1917–1930* (Chicago: Rand McNally, 1971), and John Killinger, *Hemingway and the Dead Gods: A Study in Existentialism* (Lexington: University of Kentucky Press, 1960). Ann Douglas's emphasis on the generation of the 1920s as beset by a "terrible honesty" ties nicely into the existential imperative to rebel against illusions and inauthenticity. See Douglas, *Terrible Honesty: Mongrel Manhattan in the 1920s* (New York: Farrar, Straus, and Giroux, 1995). Also Lynn Dumenil, *The Modern Temper: American Culture and Society in the 1920s* (New York: Hill and Wang, 1995). For an excellent discussion of Krutch, see Peter Gregg Slater, "The Negative Secularism of *The Modern Temper:* Joseph Wood Krutch," *American Quarterly* 33 (Summer 1981): 185–205. On Lippmann, see Ronald Steel, *Walter Lippmann and the American Century* (Boston: Little, Brown, 1980).

For light on the dark screen of noir, see Geoffrey O'Brien, *Hardboiled America: Lurid Paperbacks and the Masters of Noir* (New York: Da Capo Press, 1997); Foster Hirsch, *Film Noir: The Dark Side of the Screen* (New York: Da Capo Press, 1991); Nicholas Christopher, *Somewhere in the Night: Film Noir and the American City* (New York: Free Press, 1997); Joan Copjec, ed., *Shades of Noir* (London: Verso, 1993); Robert G. Porfirio, "No Way Out: Existential Motifs in the Film Noir," *Sight and Sound* 45 (Autumn 1976): 212–17. On the context of anxiety and doubt for film noir and *D.O.A.*, see William S. Graebner, *The Age of Doubt: American Thought and Culture in the 1940s* (Boston: Twayne, 1991).

3 ON THE RELIGIOUS context of Neo-Orthodoxy and the reception of Kierkegaard and Barth, see William R. Hutchinson, *The Modernist Impulse in American Protestantism* (Oxford: Oxford University Press, 1982). Sidney Ahlstrom argues that the First World War barely affected theology in America. Ahlstrom, "Continental Influence on American Christian Thought since World War I," *Church History* 27 (Sept. 1958): 256–72. For material on the introduction of Karl Barth's theology in America, see Dennis N. Voskuil, "America Encounters Karl Barth, 1919–1939," *Fides et Historia* 12 (Spring 1980): 61–74, and Douglas Horton, "God Lets Loose Karl Barth," *Christian Century* 45 (16 Feb. 1928): 204–7. On the reception of Kierkegaard, mostly in Europe, see Habib C. Malik's impressive *Receiving Søren Kierkegaard: The Early Impact and Transmission of His Thought* (Washington: Catholic University Press of America, 1997).

For information on Lowrie, consult the rich collection of his papers at the Manuscripts Division of the Department of Rare Books and Special Collections, Princeton University Library. For understanding Reinhold Niebuhr, the best place to start is Richard Wightman Fox, *Reinhold Niebuhr: A Biography* (New York: Harper and Row, 1987). See also Fox, "The Niebuhr Brothers and the Liberal Protestant Persuasion," in *Religion and Twentieth-Century Intellectual Life,* ed. Michael J. Lacey (Cambridge: Cambridge University Press, 1989), 94–115, and Fox, "Tragedy, Responsibility, and the American Intellectual, 1925–1950," in *Lewis Mumford: Public Intellectual,* ed. Thomas P. Hughes and Agatha C. Hughes (New York: Oxford University Press, 1990), 323–37.

While there is a considerable literature on American intellectuals in the postwar years, none of it deals with existential elements. The best works on this period are Richard H. Pells, *The Liberal Mind in a Conservative Age: American Intellectuals in the 1940s and 1950s* (New York: Harper and Row, 1985); Russell Jacoby, *The Last Intellectuals: American Culture in the Age of Academe* (New York: Basic Books, 1987); Douglas Tallack, *Twentieth-Century America and the Intellectual and Cultural Context* (London: Longman, 1991); and Howard Brick, *Daniel Bell and the Decline of Intellectual Radicalism: Social Theory and Political Reconciliation in the 1940s* (Madison: University of Wisconsin Press, 1986).

On the anxiety generated for postwar intellectuals, see George Cotkin, "'The Tragic Predicament': Postwar American Intellectuals, Success, and Mass Culture," in *Intellectuals in Politics: From the Dreyfus Affair to Salman Rushdie,* ed. Jeremy Jennings and Anthony Kemp-Welch (London: Routledge, 1997), 248–70. Auden's Kierkegaardianism is discussed in Richard Davenport-Hines, *Auden* (New York: Vintage, 1999), and Herbert Greenberg, *Quest for the Necessary: W. H. Auden and the Dilemma of Divided Consciousness* (Cambridge: Harvard University Press, 1968). The influence of Erich Fromm's *Escape from Freedom* (New York: Rinehart, 1941) must not be underestimated. On Fromm, see Daniel Burston, *The Legacy of Erich Fromm* (Cambridge: Harvard University Press, 1991). For Fromm's connection with the Frankfurt School and the attempt to synthesize

Marxism and psychoanalysis, see Martin Jay, *The Dialectical Imagination: A History of the Frankfurt School and the Institute of Social Research, 1923–1950* (Boston: Little, Brown, 1973), 113–72.

A good work establishing the context for the therapeutic Christianity of May and Tillich is Eugene McCarraher, *Christian Critics: Religion and the Impasse in Modern American Social Thought* (Ithaca: Cornell University Press, 2000). Excellent for fitting Will Herberg into the movement of intellectuals away from Marxism to conservatism is John P. Diggins, *Up from Communism: Conservative Odysseys in American Intellectual History* (New York: Harper and Row, 1975). See also Harry J. Ausmus, *Will Herberg: From Right to Right* (Chapel Hill: University of North Carolina Press, 1987). On Herberg's *Protestant-Catholic-Jew*, see Martin E. Marty, *Modern American Religion: Under God, Indivisible, 1941–1960* (Chicago: University of Chicago Press, 1996).

For material on Schlesinger and Chambers, two excellent works are Stephen P. Depoe, *Arthur M. Schlesinger, Jr., and the Ideological History of American Liberalism* (Tuscaloosa: University of Alabama Press, 1994), and Sam Tanenhaus, *Whittaker Chambers: A Biography* (New York: Random House, 1997). Tanenhaus, while excellent on Chambers's life overall, is silent on the Chambers-Kierkegaard connection. Also helpful for understanding Chambers is Terry Teachout, ed., *Ghosts on the Roof: Selected Journalism of Whittaker Chambers, 1931–1959* (Washington, D.C.: Regnery Gateway, 1989).

A good overview of Thornton Wilder, whose great intellectual curiosity about other writers led him into a quagmire, is David Castronovo, *Thornton Wilder* (New York: Ungar, 1986). Two fine biographies of Wilder are Gilbert A. Harrison, *The Enthusiast: A Life of Thornton Wilder* (New York: Fromm International, 1987), and Linda Simon, *Thornton Wilder, His World* (Garden City, N.Y.: Doubleday, 1979). On Wilder's existentialism, see Paul Lifton, *Vast Encyclopedia: The Theatre of Thornton Wilder* (Westport, Conn.: Greenwood Press, 1995). Walker Percy's existentialism is intelligently discussed in Martin Luschei, *The Sovereign Wayfarer: Walker Percy's Diagnosis of the Malaise* (Baton Rouge: Louisiana State University Press, 1972), and Robert Coles, *Walker Percy: An American Search* (Boston: Little, Brown, 1978). For the importance of existentialism to another writer, not discussed in this book, see Marshall Boswell, *John Updike's Rabbit Tetralogy: Mastered Irony in Motion* (Columbia: University of Missouri Press, 2001).

Useful for comprehending Paul Tillich's theology are Mark Kline Taylor, introduction to *Paul Tillich: Theologian of the Boundaries* (London: Collins Liturgical Publications, 1987); L. Gordon Tait, *The Promise of Paul Tillich* (Philadelphia: J. B. Lippincott, 1971); James R. Lyon, ed., *The Intellectual Legacy of Paul Tillich* (Detroit: Wayne State University Press, 1969); Arne Unhjem, *Dynamics of Doubt: A Preface to Tillich* (Philadelphia: Fortress Press, 1966); and Guy B. Hammond, "Tillich, Adorno, and the Debate about Existentialism," *Laval théologique et philosophique* 47 (Oct. 1991): 343–55. Eugene McCarraher's *Chris-*

tian Critics condemns aspects of Tillich's therapeutic theology while also finding within them a radical critique of containment culture.

4   THE FASCINATION of New York artists with Kierkegaard and existentialism is touched on in Dore Ashton, *The New York School: A Cultural Reckoning* (New York: Viking Press, 1973). An excellent source on Newman is April Kingsley, *The Turning Point: The Abstract Expressionists and the Transformation of American Art* (New York: Simon and Schuster, 1992). The best sources on Rothko are James B. Breslin, *Mark Rothko: A Biography* (Chicago: University of Chicago Press, 1993), and Dore Ashton, *About Rothko* (New York: Da Capo Press, 1996). For material on the New York artists working during this period, see Nancy Jachec, *The Philosophy and Politics of Abstract Expressionism, 1940–1960* (New York: Cambridge University Press, 2000); Stephen Polcari, *Abstract Expressionism and the Modern Experience* (Cambridge: Cambridge University Press, 1991); Michael Leja, *Reframing Abstract Expressionism: Subjectivity and Painting in the 1940s* (New Haven: Yale University Press, 1993); and Serge Guilbaut, *How New York Stole the Idea of Modern Art: Abstract Expressionism, Freedom, and the Cold War,* trans. Arthur Goldhammer (Chicago: University of Chicago Press, 1983). There is nearly a consensus that abstract expressionism was part and parcel of a corporate liberal Cold War culture. A good analysis, more sympathetic to the possibilities that creativity and primitivism opened up for postwar artists and intellectuals, is Daniel Belgrad, *The Culture of Spontaneity: Improvisation and the Arts in Postwar America* (Chicago: University of Chicago Press, 1988). Less favorable is Frances Stonor Saunders, *The Cultural Cold War: The CIA and the World of Arts and Letters* (New York: New Press, 1999). I disagree with the view of hegemonic American corporate liberalism's ability to co-opt all forms of protest. See my essay "No Exit?" *Intellectual History Newsletter* 21 (1999): 70–75.

On the New York intellectuals, see William Barrett, *The Truants: Adventures among the Intellectuals* (Garden City, N.Y.: Anchor Press/Doubleday, 1982), and Irving Howe, "The New York Intellectuals," in *The Decline of the New* (New York: Harcourt, Brace, and World, 1970), 211–65. For the early years, consult James Burkhart Gilbert, *Writers and Partisans: A History of Literary Radicalism in America* (New York: John Wiley and Sons, 1968), and Terry A. Cooney, *The Rise of the New York Intellectuals: "Partisan Review" and Its Circle, 1934–1945* (Madison: University of Wisconsin Press, 1986). For analyses of the New York intellectuals from beginning to end, see Alexander Bloom, *Prodigal Sons: The New York Intellectuals and Their World* (New York: Oxford University Press, 1986), and Alan M. Wald, *The New York Intellectuals: The Rise and Decline of the Anti-Stalinist Left from the 1930s to the 1980s* (Chapel Hill: University of North Carolina Press, 1987).

For an argument that the New York intellectuals were anything but open to radical innovations, at least after 1940, see Ann Douglas, "The Failure of the New York Intellectuals," *Raritan* 17 (1998): 1–23. For an opposing argument, see Harvey Teres's sharp and balanced *Renewing the Left: Politics, Imagination, and the New York Intellectuals* (New York: Oxford University Press, 1996). An excellent source on the political context of the New York intellectuals' anticommunism is Neil Jumonville, *Critical Crossings: The New York Intellectuals in Postwar America* (Berkeley: University of California Press, 1991).

On French exiles in New York City, see Jeffrey Mehlman, *Emigré New York: French Intellectuals in Wartime Manhattan, 1940–1944* (Baltimore: Johns Hopkins University Press, 2000), and, more generally, Stephanie Barron, with Sabina Ekmann, *Exiles+Emigrés: The Flight of European Artists from Hitler* (Los Angeles: Los Angeles County Museum of Art and Harry N. Abrams, 1997). For literary expressions of existentialism among postwar American authors, especially Bellow, see Howard M. Harper, Jr., *Desperate Faith: A Study of Bellow, Salinger, Mailer, Baldwin, and Updike* (Chapel Hill: University of North Carolina Press, 1967), and Richard Lehan, *A Dangerous Crossing: French Literary Existentialism and the Modern American Novel* (Carbondale: Southern Illinois University Press, 1973). Surprisingly little has been done on Harold Rosenberg. See Annette Cox, *Art as Politics: The Abstract Expressionist Avant-Garde and Society* (Ann Arbor: UMI Research Press, 1982); Jerome Klinkowitz, *Rosenberg/Barthes/Hassan: The Postmodern Habit of Thought* (Athens: University of Georgia Press, 1988); and Amy Goldin, "Harold Rosenberg's Magic Circle," *Arts Magazine* 40 (Nov. 1965): 37–39.

5 HELPFUL FOR understanding the formation of literary canons, albeit without reference to existentialism, are Jane Tompkins, *Sensational Designs: The Cultural Work of American Fiction* (New York: Oxford University Press, 1985), and John Guillory, *Cultural Capital: The Problem of Literary Canon Formation* (Chicago: University of Chicago Press, 1993). On the introduction of Sartrean existentialism within the American philosophical profession, begin with the excellent work by Ann Fulton, *Apostles of Sartre: Existentialism in America, 1945–1963* (Evanston: Northwestern University Press, 1999). Fulton views American philosophers as moving from a position of initial skepticism to one of increasing attention and then to one of integration of existentialism into their own philosophical perspectives. Her work is excellent on the reception of Sartrean existentialism among professional philosophers, but she does not venture beyond this scope.

The literature on Hannah Arendt expands exponentially with each year. Still the best on her relation to existentialism is Martin Jay, "The Political Existentialism of Hannah Arendt," in *Permanent Exiles: Essays on the Intellectual Migration from Germany to America* (New York: Columbia University Press, 1985), 237–56. See also Elisabeth Young-Bruehl, *Hannah Arendt: For Love of the World* (New Haven: Yale University Press, 1984), 220–21. Young-Bruehl effectively notes some of David Riesman's hesitations about Arendt's thesis. On the metaphysical aspects of Arendt's analysis, I am very impressed with Jeffrey C. Isaac, *Arendt, Camus, and Modern Rebellion* (New Haven: Yale University Press, 1992). For some background on the strange relationship, philosophical and personal, between Arendt and Heidegger, see Elzbieta Ettinger, *Hannah Arendt–Martin Heidegger* (New Haven: Yale University Press, 1995).

Hazel E. Barnes played an enormous role in the popularization and explication of French existentialism in America. See her memoir, *The Story I Tell Myself: A Venture in Existentialist Autobiography* (Chicago: University of Chicago Press, 1997). See also Eleanore Holveck, "The Birth of American Existentialism: Hazel E. Barnes, a Singular Universal," *Philosophy Today*, supplement, 1998, 7–16; William M. Calder III, Ulrich K. Goldsmith, and Phyllis B. Kenevan, eds., *Hypatia: Essays in Classics, Comparative Literature, and Philosophy Presented to Hazel E. Barnes on Her Seventieth Birthday* (Boulder: Colorado Associated University Press, 1985); and Ann Fulton, "Apostles of Sartre: Advocates of Early Sartreanism in American Philosophy," *Journal of the History of Ideas* 55 (Jan. 1994): 113–27. On the trials and tribulations of another early popularizer of existentialism in America, see Marjorie Grene, *A Philosophical Testament* (Chicago: Open Court, 1995).

6 AN EXCELLENT secondary literature exists on Richard Wright, Ralph Ellison, and other African-American writers. For a view of Ellison as a pragmatic pluralist, in language not so distant from my designation of Ellison as an existentialist, see Ross Posnock, *Color and Culture: Black Writers and the Making of the Modern Intellectual* (Cambridge: Harvard University Press, 1998). Helpful in establishing connections between African-American and European thought, sometimes existential, is Paul Gilroy, *The Black Atlantic: Modernity and Modern Consciousness* (Cambridge: Harvard University Press, 1993). On the existential tenor of Africana thought, see Lewis Gordon, *Existentia: Understanding Africana Existential Thought* (New York: Routledge, 2000). A smart analysis of the various shadings of the pathology thesis for African Americans can be found in Daryl Michael Scott, *Contempt and Pity: Social Policy and the Image of the Damaged Black Psyche, 1880–1996* (Chapel Hill: University of North Carolina Press, 1997). Favorable assessments of the influence of the Communist Party on African-American life are William J. Maxwell, *New Negro, Old Left: African-American Writing and Communism between the Wars* (New York: Columbia University Press, 1999), and Mark Naison, *Communists in Harlem during the Great Depression* (Urbana: University of Illinois Press, 1983). A polemic against the role of the Communist Party in Harlem is Harold Cruse, *The Crisis of the Negro Intellectual: From Its Origins to the Present* (New York: William Morrow, 1967).

A critique of Ellison's heroic individualism can be found in Jerry Gafio Watts, *Heroism and the Black Intellectual: Ralph Ellison, Politics, and Afro-American Intellectual Life* (Chapel Hill: University of North Carolina Press, 1994). On Dostoevskian themes in both Wright and Ellison, see Michael F. Lynch, *Creative Revolt: A Study of Wright, Ellison, and Dostoevsky* (New York: Peter Lang, 1990). The centrality of Emerson in Ellison's individualism is discussed in James M. Albrecht,

"Saying Yes and Saying No: Individualist Ethics in Ellison, Burke, and Emerson," *PMLA* 114 (Jan. 1999): 43–63; Kun Jong Lee, "Ellison's *Invisible Man:* Emersonianism Revisited," *PMLA* 107 (Mar. 1992): 331–44; Eleanor Lyons, "Ellison's Narrator as Emersonian Scholar," in *Approaches to Teaching Ellison's Invisible Man*, ed. Susan Resneck Parr and Pancho Savery (New York: Modern Language Association, 1989), 75–78; and Leonard J. Deutsch, "Ralph Waldo Ellison and Ralph Waldo Emerson: A Shared Moral Vision," *CLA Journal* 16 (Dec. 1972): 159–78.

In a well-known formulation, critic Roger Rosenblatt proclaims that while black heroes in literature are confronted with an existential universe of despair and dread, they are not existentialists because they remain hopeful. Such a reading is mistaken, since it presumes that an existentialist hero must be without hope. When existentialism is limited to a literature of hopeless despair, then such a definition works, but only by limiting the existential tradition—by breaking it into distinct pieces. And as Samuel Beckett well recognized, there is a type of hope in the recognition of one's despair. Out of such recognition comes, if nothing else, art. See Rosenblatt, *Black Fiction* (Cambridge: Harvard University Press, 1974), 163. Also Robert A. Coles, "Richard Wright's *The Outsider:* A Novel in Transition," *Modern Language Studies* 13 (Summer 1983): 53–61. On existential themes in Wright's first novel, see James R. Jaye, "Richard Wright's Freedom: The Existentialism of *Uncle Tom's Children*," *Midwest Quarterly* 35 (Summer 1994): 420–35. Anyone seeking to understand Wright is indebted to the work of Michel Fabre. See his *The Unfinished Quest of Richard Wright*, 2d ed. (Urbana: University of Illinois Press, 1993), and *Richard Wright: Books and Writers* (Jackson: University Press of Mississippi, 1990). A good source of personal information on Wright is Margaret Walker, *Richard Wright: Daemonic Genius* (New York: Warner Books, 1988). For a first-rate analysis of Kierkegaardian categories in Wright's novel, see Claudia C. Tate, "Christian Existentialism in *The Outsider*," in *Richard Wright: Critical Perspectives Past and Present*, ed. Henry Louis Gates, Jr., and K. A. Appiah (New York: Amistad Press, 1993), 369–87. Also, on the Kierkegaard-Wright connection, see Sandra Adell, "Richard Wright's *The Outsider* and the Kierkegaardian Concept of Dread," *Comparative Literature Studies* 28, no. 4 (1991): 379–94, and Lewis A. Lawson, "Cross Damon: Kierkegaardian Man of Dread," *CLA* 14 (1971): 298–316.

To understand Ellison, it is imperative to dance to a blues song. Excellent on the blues is Albert Murray, *Stomping the Blues* (New York: Vintage, 1976). Also Houston A. Baker, Jr., *Blues, Ideology, and Afro-American Literature: A Vernacular Theory* (Chicago: University of Chicago Press, 1984), and Paul Oliver, *Blues Fell This Morning: Meaning in the Blues* (1960; Cambridge: Cambridge University Press, 1990). A reading of the blues as autonomous black music is offered in LeRoi Jones, *Blues People* (New York: William Morrow, 1963). On the distinctions between Jones's take on the blues and Ellison's, see Kimberly W. Benston, "Ellison, Baraka, and the Faces of Tradition," *Boundary 2* 6 (Winter 1978): 333–54. On jazz as the exemplar of modernism, see the intriguing essay by Berndt Ostendorf, "Anthropology, Modernism, and Jazz," in *Ralph Ellison: Modern Critical Views,* ed. Harold Bloom (New York: Chelsea House, 1986), 145–72. Also Alfred Appel, Jr., "Pops Art: Louis Armstrong, Race, and the Power of Song," *New Republic* 213 (21 and 28 Aug. 1995): 31–38. On the relationship between jazz and freedom, see Peter J. Steinberger, "Culture and Freedom in the Fifties: The Case of Jazz," *Virginia Quarterly Review* 74 (Winter 1998): 118–33. Alas, as of this writing no biography of Ellison exists. Helpful for getting a sense of him are his essays, *The Collected Essays of Ralph Ellison,* ed. John F. Callahan (New York: Modern Library, 1995). For his jazz sensibility and views on many topics, see *Trading Twelves: The Selected Letters of Ralph Ellison and Albert Murray,* ed. Albert Murray and John F. Callahan (New York: Modern Library, 2000).

7 FOR THE DETAILS, sometimes sordid, of Mailer's life and times, see Mary V. Dearborn, *Mailer: A Biography* (Boston: Houghton Mifflin, 1999). Existential themes are readily apparent in Mailer's writings, and critics have discussed them. Laura Adams finds Darwinian elements in Mailer's *The Naked and the Dead.* See Adams, *Existential Battles: The Growth of Norman Mailer* (Athens: Ohio University Press, 1976). Michael Cowan compares that novel with Melville's *Moby-Dick* in "The Quest for Empowering Roots: Mailer and the American Literary Tradition," in *Critical Essays on Norman Mailer,* ed. J. Michael Lennon (Boston: G. K. Hall, 1986), 159–64. An excellent discussion of Mailer's existential theology can be found in Robert Solotaroff, *Down Mailer's Way* (Urbana: University of Illinois Press, 1974). See also Samuel Holland Hux, "American Myth and Existential Vision: The Indigenous Existentialism of Mailer, Bellow, Styron, and Ellison" (Ph.D. diss., University of Connecticut, 1965); Richard Poirier, *Norman Mailer* (New York: Viking, 1972); Stanley T. Gutman, *Mankind in Barbary: The Individual and Society in the Novels of Norman Mailer* (Hanover: University Press of New England, 1975); Nathan A. Scott, Jr., *Three American Novelists: Mailer, Bellow, Trilling* (Notre Dame: University of Notre Dame Press, 1973); and Joseph Wenke, *Mailer's America* (Hanover: University Press of New England, 1987).

Thomas H. Schaub argues, interestingly but unconvincingly, that for all of Mailer's criticisms, his work played into the dominant ideological assumptions of the postwar years. See Schaub, *American Fiction in the Cold War* (Madison: University of Wisconsin Press, 1991). See also, in this connection, J. D. Connor, "The Language of Men: Identity and Existentialism in the American Postwar" (Ph.D. diss., Johns Hopkins University, 1999). On masculinist and homophobic hegemony in this era, see K. A. Courdileone, "Politics in an Age of Anxiety: Cold War Political Culture and the Crisis in American Masculinity, 1949–1960," *Journal of American History* 87 (Sept. 2000): 515–45, and David Savran, *Taking It Like a Man: White Masculinity, Masochism, and Contemporary American Culture* (Princeton: Princeton University Press, 1988).

The most interesting commentary on Mailer's novels is usually his own. See the classic collections *Advertisements for Myself* (Cambridge: Harvard University Press, 1992) and *Existential Errands* (Boston: Little, Brown, 1972). A fine collection of interviews with Mailer is J. Michael Lennon, ed., *Conversations with Norman Mailer* (Jackson: University Press of Mississippi, 1988).

On the Beat and the hipster during the time of Mailer's "White Negro" essay, see the humorous piece by Herbert Gold, "How to Tell the Beatniks from the Hipsters," *Noble Savage* (New York: Meridian, 1960), 1:132–39. Also Anatole Broyard, *Kafka Was the Rage: A Greenwich Village Memoir* (New York: Carol Southern Books, 1993). On how the Beat image could be appropriated by women, see Wini Breines, "The 'Other Fifties': Beats and Beat Girls," in *Not June Cleaver: Women and Gender in Postwar America, 1945–1960,* ed. Joanne Meyerowitz (Philadelphia: Temple University Press, 1994), 382–408. On the history of minstrelsy, see Eric Lott, *Love and Theft: Blackface Minstrelsy and the American Working Class* (New York: Oxford University Press, 1993).

8 BIOGRAPHICAL INFORMATION on Robert Frank can be found in Martin Gasser, "Zurich to New York," and Philip Brookman, "Windows on Another Time: Issues of Autobiography," both in *Robert Frank: Moving Out,* ed. Sarah Greenough and Philip Brookman (Washington, D.C.: National Gallery of Art/Scalo Press, 1994), 40–50 and 142–65. On Frank's bleak vision, see William Stott, "Walker Evans, Robert Frank, and the Landscape of Dissociation," *Artscanada* 31 (Dec. 1974): 83–89, and Janet Malcolm, *Diana and Nikon: Essays on the Aesthetic of Photography* (Boston: David R. Godine, 1981). More balanced interpretations appear in Tod Papageorge, *Walker Evans and Robert Frank: An Essay on Influence* (New Haven: Yale University Art Gallery, 1981), and Jonathan Green, *American Photography: A Critical History, 1945 to the Present* (New York: Harry N. Abrams, 1984). Critical of Frank's aesthetic of irony is Lili Corbus Bezner, *Photography and Politics in America: From the New Deal into the Cold War* (Baltimore: Johns Hopkins University Press, 1999). A good evaluation of the Steichen *Family of Man* show can be found in Eric J. Sandeen, *Picturing an Exhibition: The Family of Man and 1950s America* (Albuquerque: University of New Mexico Press, 1995).

Frank was connected with many of the Beats. Helpful for understanding a Beat perspective is John Tytell, *Naked Angels: The Lives and Literature of the Beat Generation* (New York: McGraw-Hill, 1976). The best book on Frank's admirer Kerouac is Gerald Nicosia, *Memory Babe: A Critical Biography of Jack Kerouac* (New York: Grove Press, 1983).

On some of the philosophical issues concerning death in photographic images, see Susan Sontag's classic *On Photography* (New York: Farrar, Straus, and Giroux, 1977). Also Roland Barthes, *Camera Lucida: Reflections on Photography,* trans. Richard Howard (New York: Hill and Wang, 1981). Invaluable to understanding Frank are his answers to questions posed at a photography workshop, collected in *The Pictures Are a Necessity: Robert Frank in Rochester, NY, November 1988*, ed. William Johnson (Rochester: George Eastman House, 1999).

9 THE STUDENT MOVEMENT, especially at the grass-roots level, is well covered in Terry H. Anderson, *The Movement and the Sixties: Protest in America from Greensboro to Wounded Knee* (Oxford: Oxford University Press, 1995). Balanced coverage is presented in Maurice Isserman and Michael Kazin, *America Divided: The Civil War of the 1960s* (Oxford: Oxford University Press, 2000). See also Allen J. Matusow, *The Unraveling of America: A History of Liberalism in the 1960s* (New York: Harper and Row, 1986); James J. Farrell, *The Spirit of the Sixties: The Making of Postwar Radicalism* (New York: Routledge, 1997); James Tracy, *Direct Action: Radical Pacifism from the Union Eight to the Chicago Seven* (Chicago: University of Chicago Press, 1996); David Burner, *Making Peace with the 60s* (Princeton: Princeton University Press, 1996); David Farber, *The Age of Great Dreams: America in the Sixties* (New York: Hill and Wang, 1994); and Farber, *Chicago '68* (Chicago: University of Chicago Press, 1988). The best work on the period, connecting ideas and social problems, is Howard Brick, *Age of Contradiction: American Thought and Culture in the 1960s* (New York: Twayne, 1998). See also Peter Clecak, *Radical Paradoxes: Dilemmas of the American Left, 1945–1970* (New York: Harper and Row, 1973). On the intellectual debates that informed social theory during this period, see Job Leonard Dittberner, *The End of Ideology and American Social Thought, 1930–1960* (Ann Arbor: UMI Research Press, 1979). On David Riesman and the importance of his social theory, the place to begin is Wilfred M. McClay, *The Masterless Self and Society in Modern America* (Chapel Hill: University of North Carolina Press, 1994).

I have profited greatly from Doug Rossinow's rich study of the convergence of religion and existentialism among a cohort of students at the University of Texas, *The Politics of Authenticity: Liberalism, Christianity, and the New Left in America* (New York: Columbia University Press, 1998). The reading habits of the generation of the 1960s are discussed in Philip D. Beidler, *Scriptures for a Generation: What We Were Reading in the Sixties* (Athens: University of Georgia Press, 1994). Although Beidler notes the influence of existentialist writers, he does not include their works in his synopses of key texts. A good overview of the writers and social theorists that influenced the New Left is Andrew Jamison and Ron Eyerman, *Seeds of the Sixties* (Berkeley: University of California Press, 1995).

For Students for a Democratic Society, I have relied upon the general surveys of the period and the firsthand accounts by Todd Gitlin, *The Sixties: Years of Hope, Days of Rage* (New York: Bantam, 1987), and Tom Hayden, *Reunion: A Memoir* (New York: Collier, 1989). Surprisingly, Hayden has yet to be fully analyzed. For some help, try Paul Westbrook, "A Thematic Analysis of the Advocacy of Thomas Emmet Hayden as a Radical Intellectual Activist in the New Left Social Movement" (Ph.D. diss., Southern Illinois University, 1976). On the Port Huron Statement, Hayden, and the SDS, consider James Miller, *"Democracy Is in the Streets":* *From Port Huron to the Siege of Chicago* (New York: Simon and Schuster, 1987). On the Port Huron Statement's connection with John Dewey's ideas on democracy, see Robert B. Westbrook, *John Dewey and American Democracy* (Ithaca: Cornell University Press, 1991). Stanley Aronowitz argues that the Port Huron Statement was in the American grain of democratic thinking and, hence, unwilling to engage with socialist thought. Aronowitz, "When the New Left Was New," in *The Sixties without Apology,* ed. Sohnya Sayers et al. (Minneapolis: University of Minnesota Press, 1983). Useful for its analysis of the consumerism of the student generation, even if a bit overinsistent on connecting it with a certain style of advertising, is Thomas Frank, *The Conquest of Cool: Business Culture, Counterculture, and the Rise of Hip Consumerism* (Chicago: University of Chicago Press, 1997).

Many of the debates among radicals in the United States mirrored divisions in France. On Camus and his debate with Sartre, see Germaine Brée, *Camus and Sartre: Crisis and Commitment* (New York: Delta, 1972). On Sartre's political activities in this period, see Simone de Beauvoir, *Adieux: A Farewell to Sartre,* trans. Patrick O'Brian (New York: Pantheon, 1984), and Michel-Antoine Burnier, *Choice of Action: The French Existentialists on the Political Front,* trans. Bernard Murchland (New York: Random House, 1968).

Robert Moses has not received sufficient attention. The best place to turn for information on Moses is Eric R. Burner, *And Gently He Shall Lead Them: Robert Parris Moses and Civil Rights in Mississippi* (New York: New York University Press, 1994). Other valuable sources on Moses and the Student Nonviolent Coordinating Committee in the early years are Clayborne Carson, *In Struggle: SNCC and the Black Awakening of the 1960s* (Cambridge: Harvard University Press, 1981); Doug McAdam, *Freedom Summer* (New York: Oxford University Press, 1988); Howard Zinn, *SNCC: The New Abolitionists* (Boston: Beacon Press, 1964); John Dittmar, *Local People: The Struggle for Civil Rights in Mississippi* (Urbana: University of Illinois Press, 1994); Charles M. Payne, *I've Got the Light of Freedom: The Organizing Tradition and the Mississippi Freedom Struggle* (Berkeley: University of California Press, 1995); Nicolaus Mills, *Like a Holy Crusade: Mississippi 1964—The Turning of the Civil Rights Movement in America* (Chicago: Ivan R. Dee, 1992); Emily Stoper, *The Student Nonviolent Coordinating Committee: The Growth of Radicalism in a Civil Rights Organization* (Brooklyn: Carlson, 1989); Charles Marsh, *God's Long Summer: Stories of Faith and Civil Rights* (Princeton: Princeton University Press, 1997); and Sally Belfrage, *Freedom Summer* (New York: Viking Press, 1965).

10 ONLY A SINGLE article examines the thought of Betty Friedan in relation to that of Simone de Beauvoir. It argues that Friedan does not stand up to Beauvoir intellectually, and that her feminism is insufficiently radical. See Sandra Dijkstra, "Simone de Beauvoir and Betty Friedan: The Politics of Omis-

sion," *Feminist Studies* 6 (Summer 1980): 290–303. See also Shira Tarrant, "Constrained Yet Not Forgotten: Continuities in Feminist Intellectual History, 1945–1972," *UCLA Historical Journal* 16 (1996): 81–102.

Many works analyze the ideas that Beauvoir explores in *The Second Sex.* Particularly helpful are Margaret A. Simons, *Beauvoir and "The Second Sex": Feminism, Race, and the Origins of Existentialism* (London: Rowman and Littlefield, 1999); Karen Vintges, *Philosophy as Passion: The Thinking of Simone de Beauvoir* (Bloomington: Indiana University Press, 1996); and Toril Moi, *Feminist Theory and Simone de Beauvoir* (London: Blackwell, 1990). An excellent source on Beauvoir and existentialism is Josephine Donovan, *Feminist Theory: The Intellectual Traditions of American Feminism* (New York: Continuum, 1996). A critique of the existential strain in Beauvoir's feminism can be found in Michele Le Doeuff, "Simone de Beauvoir and Existentialism," *Feminist Studies* 6 (Summer 1980): 277–89, and Naomi Greene, "Sartre, Sexuality, and *The Second Sex,*" *Philosophy and Literature* 4 (1980): 199–211. A more balanced view is Mary Lowenthal Felstiner, "Seeing *The Second Sex* through the Second Wave," *Feminist Studies* 6 (Summer 1980): 247–76. Attacks on sexism in Sartre's philosophical images, such as his equating the feminine with inertia and slime, appear in Margery L. Collins and Christine Pierce, "Holes and Slime: Sexism in Sartre's Psychoanalysis," *Philosophical Forum* 5 (Fall–Winter 1973–74): 112–27, and Peggy Holland, "Jean-Paul Sartre as a NO to Women," *Sinister Wisdom*, no. 6 (Summer 1978): 72–79. A spirited defense of Sartre appears in Hazel E. Barnes, "Sartre and Sexism," *Philosophy and Literature* 14 (1990): 340–47, and Barnes, "Sartre and Feminism: Aside from *The Second Sex* and All That," in *Feminist Interpretations of Jean-Paul Sartre,* ed. Julien S. Murphy (University Park: Penn State University Press, 1999), 22–44. Also examine the essays, especially those by Eleanore Holveck and Karen Vintges, in *The Philosophy of Simone de Beauvoir,* a special issue of *Hypatia* 14 (Fall 1999). For an analysis of Beauvoir, rather than Sartre, as the originator of existentialism, see Kate Fullbrook and Edward Fullbrook, *Simone de Beauvoir and Jean-Paul Sartre: The Remaking of a Twentieth-Century Legend* (New York: Basic Books, 1994).

Beauvoir's influence on American and British feminism has been great. Accounts of it can be found in the essays in Penny Forster and Imogen Sutton, eds., *Daughters of de Beauvoir* (London: Women's Press, 1989). Two works that show Beauvoir's mark in America are Kate Millett, *Sexual Politics* (Garden City, N.Y.: Doubleday, 1970), and Shulamith Firestone, *The Dialectics of Sex: The Case for Feminist Revolution* (New York: William Morrow, 1970). Although Millett mentions Beauvoir only a couple of times in the work, her reading of D. H. Lawrence was beholden to Beauvoir. An excellent discussion of radical feminism in the United States in the 1970s is Alice Echols, *Daring to Be Bad: Radical Feminism in America, 1967–1975* (Minneapolis: University of Minnesota Press, 1989). For the connections between the New Left and feminism, with some references to

Beauvoir's help in raising feminist consciousness, see Sara Evans, *Personal Politics: The Roots of Women's Liberation in the Civil Rights Movement and the New Left* (New York: Vintage, 1980). Also Mary King, *Freedom Song: A Personal Story of the 1960s Civil Rights Movement* (New York: William Morrow, 1987).

To understand Friedan, one must begin with the context of American women's attempts at self-realization in the face of constraints. Especially helpful are Leila J. Rupp and Verta Taylor, *Survival in the Doldrums: The American Women's Rights Movement, 1945–1960s* (New York: Oxford University Press, 1987); William H. Chafe, *The American Woman: Her Changing Social, Economic, and Political Roles, 1920–1970* (New York: Oxford University Press, 1972); Rosalind Rosenberg, *Divided Lives: American Women in the Twentieth Century* (New York: Hill and Wang, 1992); Elaine Tyler May, *Homeward Bound: American Families in the Cold War Era* (New York: Basic Books, 1988); and Ruth Rosen, *The World Split Open: How the Modern Women's Movement Changed America* (New York: Viking, 2000). Rosen is especially critical of therapeutic feminism, although she realizes that the dichotomy between self-realization and feminist politics is not absolute. Ellen Herman argues that a focus on questions of identity and self-realization could help women undermine patriarchal assumptions. She does not, however, deny that this mode of thinking was largely based on a context of an economy of abundance, an assumption that Betty Friedan accepted. Herman, *The Romance of American Psychology: Political Culture in the Age of Experts* (Berkeley: University of California Press, 1995). Friedan famously argued in *The Feminine Mystique* that women in the postwar years were bombarded with messages that they belonged in the home. Two studies indicate that the messages directed toward women by American popular magazines of the period were more complex. See Joanne Meyerowitz, "Beyond the Feminine Mystique: A Reassessment of Postwar Mass Culture, 1946–1958," *Journal of American History* 79 (Mar. 1993): 1455–82, and Eva Moskowitz, "'It's Good to Blow Your Top': Women's Magazines and a Discourse of Discontent," *Journal of Women's History* 8 (Fall 1996): 66–98.

The literature on Friedan is surprisingly thin. The best analysis, which focuses on Friedan's radical past and her role as a journalist, is Daniel Horowitz, *Betty Friedan and the Making of the Feminine Mystique: The American Left, the Cold War, and Modern Feminism* (Amherst: University of Massachusetts Press, 1998). The most helpful biography is Judith Hennessee, *Betty Friedan: Her Life* (New York: Random House, 1999). Of course, the main source for the details of Friedan's life are her various volumes of memoirs, especially *It Changed My Life: Writings on the Women's Movement* (New York: Random House, 1976) and *Life So Far* (New York: Simon and Schuster, 2000). The Betty Friedan Papers at the Schlesinger Library, Radcliffe Institute, Harvard University, contain her reading notes and drafts of *The Feminine Mystique*. Unfortunately, her correspondence and journals are closed to researchers at present.

11   EXISTENTIALISM REMAINS a force in American culture, especially in psychoanalysis. While some of those pushing existential analysis promoted a benign vision of becoming and adjustment, others worked within a psychology of despair and possibility. Especially important is the work of Irvin D. Yalom, *Existential Psychotherapy* (New York: Basic Books, 1980). Yalom pursued ideas presented in the important volume edited by Rollo May, Ernest Angel, and Henri F. Ellenberger, *Existence: A New Dimension in Psychiatry and Psychology* (New York: Basic Books, 1958). Also in this mode, see Peter Koestenbaum, *The Vitality of Death: Essays in Existential Psychology and Philosophy* (Westport, Conn.: Greenwood, 1971).

The strongest presentation—albeit one with a comic patina—of existential themes in American culture today may be found in the films and short stories of Woody Allen. Helpful interpretations of Allen's views are Graham McCann, *Woody Allen* (New York: Polity Press, 1990); Foster Hirsch, *Love, Sex, Death, and the Meaning of Life: The Films of Woody Allen* (New York: Limelight, 1991); and Maurice Yacowar, *Loser Take All: The Comic Art of Woody Allen* (New York: Continuum, 1991). Allen's own views may be found in *Woody Allen on Woody Allen: In Conversation with Stig Bjorkman* (New York: Grove Press, 1993).

Existential themes may also be found in the films of Martin Scorsese and in the work of Wallace Shawn, such as the film *My Dinner with André*. For Scorsese, see Lawrence S. Friedman, *The Cinema of Martin Scorsese* (New York: Continuum, 1997), and Lee Keyser, *Martin Scorsese* (New York: Twayne, 1992). For Shawn, see W. D. King, *Writing Wrongs: The Work of Wallace Shawn* (Philadelphia: Temple University Press, 1997).

Index